Probability

The School Mathematics Project

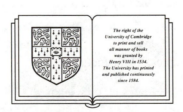

The right of the
University of Cambridge
to print and sell
all manner of books
was granted by
Henry VIII in 1534.
The University has printed
and published continuously
since 1584.

Cambridge University Press

Cambridge   New York   Port Chester   Melbourne   Sydney

Main authors	Chris Belsom
	Stan Dolan
	Leslie Glickman
	Ron Haydock
Project director	Stan Dolan

The authors would like to give special thanks to Ann White for her help in preparing this book for publication.

The publishers would like to thank the following for supplying photographs:

page 91 - Ashbourne News Telegraph

Cartoons on pages 33 and 52 by Gordon Hendry

Other cartoons by Margaret Ackroyd and Paul Holland

Published by the Press Syndicate of the University of Cambridge
The Pitt Building, Trumpington Street, Cambridge CB2 1RP
40 West 20th Street, New York, NY 10011-4211, USA
10 Stamford Road, Oakleigh, Melbourne 3166, Australia

First published 1991

Produced by 16-19 Mathematics, Southampton

Printed in Great Britain by Scotprint Ltd., Musselburgh.

ISBN 0 521 42645 6

Contents

FOR

The late Leslie Glickman

whose ideas have greatly

enhanced this book

1 First ideas

1.1 Introduction

Though everyone must learn to live with uncertainty, an existence in which you could **never** predict the behaviour of the objects in your environment would be intolerable. One aspect of maturing is learning to estimate the likelihood of outcomes in various situations. In the mathematical treatment of probability, numbers in the range from 0 to 1 are allocated to correspond to such likelihoods.

likelihood	impossible	———————————	certain
probability	0	———————————	1

For example, the probability that the sun will rise tomorrow is 1; the probability of a hole in one in golf may be about 10^{-6}; the probability of a baby being a girl is about 0.5, and so on.

Sometimes probabilities are based on experience. A Greek olive grower spreads his cloths on the ground before shaking an olive tree; he expects olives to fall downwards rather than upwards because this is what has happened in the past.

Any probability based upon relative frequencies is subject to revision and change in the light of experiment. For example, if you have thrown a die 100 times and on 10 occasions a six has turned up, then your best estimate of throwing a six is $\frac{1}{10}$. However, this estimate is bound to change (to $\frac{10}{101}$ or $\frac{11}{101}$) if you make another throw. **Observed probabilities** can only ever be approximate and should be based on a very large number of experiments.

1

Some probabilities are theoretically very easy to assign by **symmetry.** For instance, in throwing a fair die - a perfect unloaded cube - you would expect the numbers from 1 to 6 to occur with similar frequency.

> **Is the probability determined by symmetry or by experience in the following cases:**
>
> **(a)   throwing a six with a die;**
> **(b)   a baby being a boy;**
> **(c)   living to the age of 100?**

The need for a mathematical study of probability arises when a particular event involves the combination of simpler events.

The theory has its roots in problems concerning gambling, apparently starting with one posed in the seventeenth century by the Chevalier de Méré. Pascal and Fermat took up his challenge and it was in correspondence between these two great French mathematicians that probability theory was developed.

The problems they first considered concerned unfinished competitions involving games of chance played with dice, coins or cards as in the following example.

La problème des points

In a competition between A and B, each contributes equally to the stake. The competition consists of games in which A and B have an equal chance of winning (by the toss of a coin, say). The first player to win three games wins the stake. Unfortunately, A is killed in a duel before the end of the competition, when he has won two games and B has won one. How should the stake be divided between A's estate and B?

> **(a)   List the ways in which the competition could have finished.**
>
> **(b)   How should the stake be divided?**
>
> **(c)   In a similar incomplete competition, how should the stake be divided when**
>
> **(i) A needs one more win and B needs three;**
> **(ii) A needs two more wins and B needs three?**

2

Exercise 1

1. In throwing a pair of fair dice:

   (a) what are the possible outcomes;

   (b) what is the most likely total score;

   (c) what is the probability of obtaining that score?

2. By listing all possible families of four children, disregarding multiple births, find the probability that in such a family there would be

   (a) no girls;

   (b) two boys and two girls;

   (c) children of alternate sexes in the age sequences.

3. In English prose, which consists of letters, spaces and punctuation signs, it is found that among the letters of the alphabet and the space the relative frequency of the space is approximately 20%.

   (a) How would you express this statement in terms of probability?

   (b) In a passage of 1000 characters, disregarding punctuation, approximately how many spaces would you expect?

   (c) What is the average length of a word?

4. Make a tally of 100 tosses of a die (or dice) and record in a table the relative frequencies of the scores 1-6. By arranging for a group of ten people to do this, or otherwise, find the results of 1000 tosses and again draw up a table of relative frequencies. Comment on your results.

1.2   Equally likely outcomes

The next example leads to a definition of probability in cases determined by symmetry.

Example 1

Two ordinary dice are thrown. What is the probability that the total score is prime?

Solution

There are 36 possible **outcomes**, each outcome being as likely as any other. The set of all possible outcomes is called the **sample space**. It may be represented thus:

(1, 1)   (1, 2)   (1, 3)   (1, 4)   (1, 5)   (1, 6)

(2, 1)   (2, 2)   (2, 3)   (2, 4)   (2, 5)   (2, 6)

. . .

(6, 1)   (6, 2)   (6, 3)   (6, 4)   (6, 5)   (6, 6)

> **Explain the difference between, say, (1, 2) and (2, 1).**

Of these 36 outcomes, the outcomes where the sum of the numbers in the brackets is prime are:

(1, 1)   (1, 2)   (2, 1)   (1, 4)   (4, 1)   (1, 6)   (6, 1)   (2, 3)   (3, 2)

(2, 5)   (5, 2)   (3, 4)   (4, 3)   (5, 6)   (6, 5)

There are 15 favourable outcomes in all.

So the probability of a favourable outcome is $\frac{15}{36} = \frac{5}{12}$.

> **Explain in terms of relative frequencies what this result means.**

In a general **trial** (experiment) where all outcomes are equally likely,

$$\text{The probability of an event} = \frac{\text{number of favourable outcomes}}{\text{total number of possible outcomes}}$$

4

Exercise 2

1. You draw a single card from an ordinary pack of playing cards. What is the probability that it is

    (a) black   (b) a club   (c) a king?

2. Consider an experiment in which you ask pairs of people at random to name their months of birth.

    (a) What is the sample space of outcomes?

    (b) What is the probability of their having being born in the same month? Comment on this method of finding that probability.

3. Three dice are thrown simultaneously.

    (a) How many members are there in the sample space of outcomes?

    (b) Find the probability that

        (i)   the sum of the scores is 12;

        (ii) the product of the scores is 12.

4. The letters A, B, C and D are written on identical cards and the cards are shuffled. The top three cards are then turned over, one after the other, and laid down in line. What is the probability that they form the word CAB?

1.3 Events as sets

Example 2

If three fair coins are tossed, find the probability of there being at least two heads.

Solution

The sample space is a set and this may be stressed by writing its members in braces { } thus:

$$S = \{HHH, HHT, HTH, THH, HTT, THT, TTH, TTT\}$$

The favourable event of at least two heads is a **subset** of S.

$$E = \{HHH, HHT, HTH, THH\}$$

So the required probability is $\dfrac{\text{no. of favourable outcomes}}{\text{total no. of outcomes}} = \dfrac{4}{8} = 0.5$

The number of elements in a set A is written $n(A)$; so in the example above $n(S) = 8$, $n(E) = 4$ and the probability of E is

$$P(E) = \frac{n(E)}{n(S)} = \frac{4}{8}$$

> **In a trial with equally likely outcomes, with sample space S, for any event E,**
> $$P(E) = \frac{n(E)}{n(S)}$$

Exercise 3

In the following cases give the sample space and the subset representing the favourable event. Find also the probability of that event:

1. The month of birth of a person chosen at random begins with the letter *J*.

2. A woman's three children are all girls.

Since you will use sets in your work on probability, some knowledge of the algebra of sets is needed.

 TASKSHEET 1S - *The algebra of sets*

1.4   The addition law

If, for a single die, A and B are the events

    A :   a six is thrown,
    B: a number less than 4 is thrown

then A and B cannot both occur. They are said to be **mutually exclusive.**

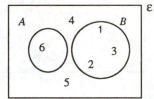

In set theoretic terms

$$A \cap B = \phi,$$

where ϕ represents the **empty set**, which has no members.

(a)   Explain why, if A and B are mutually exclusive events,
$$P(A \cup B) = P(A) + P(B)$$

(b)   Illustrate using a Venn diagram the general addition law:
if A and B are *any* events in the same sample space,
$$P(A \cup B) = P(A) + P(B) - P(A \cap B)$$

(c)   Explain why the first result is a particular case of the second.

Example 3

If you are dealt a card at random from an ordinary pack, what is the probability that it is

(a)   a heart or a spade   (b)   a heart or a queen.

Solution

(a)   The events are mutually exclusive.
$$P(\text{heart or spade}) = P(\text{heart}) + P(\text{spade}) = \frac{1}{4} + \frac{1}{4} = \frac{1}{2}.$$

(b)   Here the events are not mutually exclusive and the more general formula is needed.
$$P(H \cup Q) = P(H) + P(Q) - P(H \cap Q) = \frac{1}{4} + \frac{1}{13} - \frac{1}{52} = \frac{4}{13}.$$

[Note that $P(H \cap Q)$ translates as 'the probability of the queen of hearts'.]

For any two events A and B,
$$P(A \cup B) = P(A) + P(B) - P(A \cap B)$$

7

1.5   Independent events

Suppose that you are about to toss a coin and then cut a pack of cards.

H is the event: the coin lands head uppermost
Q is the event: a queen is cut

The probabilities are as shown

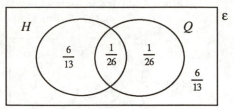

(a)   Noting that P(H) = $\frac{1}{2}$ and P(Q) = $\frac{1}{13}$, what simple rule gives the probability of head and queen?

(b)   Explain how the other probabilities on the Venn diagram can be found.

(c)   What is the probability of head or queen?

Whether or not you obtain a head does not affect your chance of cutting a queen. The events are said to be **statistically independent**. The probabilities of independent events satisfy the following multiplication law.

When events A and B are independent,
$$P(A \cap B) = P(A) \times P(B)$$

Example 4

In a certain town, 80% of households have a telephone and 20% have a dog. What are the chances of a household chosen at random having both a telephone and a dog?

Solution

The question cannot be answered with any certainty. Common sense suggests that the events are likely to be reasonably independent.

Assuming independence,

$$P(T \cap D) = P(T) \times P(D) = 0.8 \times 0.2 = 0.16$$

Example 5

At a children's party a lucky dip contains two teddies and three dolls in identical boxes. Richard and Susan each pull out a box at random. Find the probability that they both receive teddies.

Solution

In this example, the events of Richard and Susan receiving a teddy are **dependent** on each other. The probability of Richard receiving a teddy is $\frac{2}{5}$. If this does occur, Susan then has a probability of only $\frac{1}{4}$ of receiving a teddy. The probability of their both receiving teddies is then $\frac{2}{5} \times \frac{1}{4} = \frac{1}{10}$.

Exercise 4

1. On a skiing holiday the probability of breaking a leg is 0.1 and the probability of catching a cold is 0.2. Find the probability of

    (a) breaking a leg and catching a cold,
    (b) breaking a leg or catching a cold.

2. If events A and B are such that
$$P(A) = 0.4, \quad P(B) = 0.6, \quad P(A \cup B) = 0.9,$$

    show that A and B are neither mutually exclusive nor independent.

3. 80% of candidates pass the language test from a bank of aptitude tests. 70% pass the mathematics test and 10% fail both. Find the probability of a candidate

    (a) passing both,   (b) passing mathematics but failing language.

4. (a) Generalise the multiplication law for independent events to n independent events E_1, E_2, ..., E_n.

    (b) A bag contains 6 red balls, 4 blue balls and 2 yellow balls.

      (i) A trial consists of withdrawing a ball at random **and replacing it.** Find the probability of withdrawing three red balls in three successive trials.

      (ii) If the trial is changed so that a ball is withdrawn at random and **not** replaced, find the probability of withdrawing three red balls in three successive trials.

5. In three trials of the type described in 4(b), find the probability of drawing three balls of the same colour

    (a) when the ball is replaced after each trial,
    (b) when the ball is not replaced.

1.6　System, counting and ordering

You will already have seen that sample spaces may be large and it is sometimes difficult to keep track of outcomes and events, making sure that none has been overlooked. It helps to be systematic in listing; for example you might list the sample space for four tosses of a coin as follows:

no tails	HHHH
one tail	HHHT, HHTH, HTHH, THHH
two tails	HHTT, HTHT, THHT, THTH, HTTH, TTHH
three tails	HTTT, THTT, TTHT, TTTH
four tails	TTTT

However, just being systematic is sometimes not enough. A result which may help is called the **r, s principle**. It can be developed in the following way.

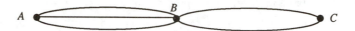

There are three routes from *A* to *B* and two from *B* to *C*.

> **How many routes are there from *A* to *C* via *B*?**

More generally, if there are three outcomes of trial 1 and two outcomes of trial 2 , there are 3 x 2 = 6 possible outcomes of the sequence of trials.

To generalise further, if there are *r* outcomes of trial 1 and *s* outcomes of trial 2, then there are *rs* possible outcomes of the sequence of two trials. This is called **the r, s principle** and it can be extended:

> **In a sequence of *n* independent trials, if there are r_1 possible outcomes for the first trial, r_2 for the second, ..., r_n for the *n*th, then the total number of outcomes for the sequence is $r_1 r_2 ... r_n$.**

Example 6

A fair die is cast and a card is drawn at random from an ordinary pack. What is the probability of throwing a six and choosing the ace of spades?

Solution

In the notation above, $r = 6$ and $s = 52$, so the number of outcomes is $6 \times 52 = 312$. These are equally likely and only one is favourable, so the required probability is $\frac{1}{312}$.

Example 7

Find the probability of throwing exactly one head in five tosses of a fair coin.

Solution

On each toss there are two possible outcomes and the outcome of any toss is independent of that for any other, so $n(S) = 2^5 = 32$.
The subset of favourable events is

$$E = \{\text{HTTTT, THTTT, TTHTT, TTTHT, TTTTH}\}$$

$$n(E) = 5; \quad P(E) = \frac{5}{32}$$

Exercise 5

1. A girl packing a suitcase for the holidays includes clothes which 'mix and match'. She puts in 6 tops, 2 skirts, 2 pairs of jeans and 4 pairs of shoes. How many different outfits can she wear?

2. A window is to be fitted with three identical rectangular panes of glass. The glazier arrives with them, already cut to size. In how many different ways can the panes be fitted into the frames?

3. At the reception desk of a hotel letters are placed in three boxes, according to their destination (London area, provinces and abroad). In the long run the boxes are used with equal frequency. On a certain evening four letters are posted. What is the probability that they will all be in the 'provinces' box?

   What assumption did you make in arriving at your answer?

1.7   Permutations and combinations

Example 8

A delegation of three is to be chosen by lot from eight volunteers. How many possible delegations are there?

Solution

For the first name drawn from the hat there are 8 possibilities. Then only seven are left, so for the next name there are 7 possibilities. Finally, on the third draw there are 6 possibilities. The selections are made independently, so the total number of outcomes is

$$8 \times 7 \times 6 = 336$$

However, unless the team of delegates is to have a 'batting order' you will not differentiate between, say, {Armand, Brian, Cheryl} and {Cheryl, Armand, Brian}. In fact, for each triple of delegates there are 3 x 2 x 1 possible orderings as may be shown using the extended r, s, principle. So the answer in this case is $336 \div 6 = 56$ teams of delegates.

   TASKSHEET 2 - *Hands of cards*

Given n distinct objects, you can choose r of the objects in

$$\frac{n!}{(n-r)!}$$ possible arrangements (**permutations**)

or, if the ordering is unimportant, in

$$\frac{n!}{(n-r)!\,r!}$$ possible selections (**combinations**)

The notations used for permutations and combinations are shown in the following definitions.

$$_n\mathrm{P}_r = \frac{n!}{(n-r)!}$$

$$\binom{n}{r} = \frac{n!}{(n-r)!\,r!}$$

[Note: The word 'combination', though standard, is not well chosen. The combination of a safe or bicycle lock is really a permutation. Similarly, a 'perm' on the football pools is really a mathematical combination.]

Example 9

What is the probability that the first three cards dealt from a well shuffled pack are

(a) all hearts;
(b) the ace, king and queen of hearts;
(c) the ace, king and queen of hearts dealt in that order?

Solution

(a) The sample space is all combinations of three cards from a pack of 52.

$$n\,(S) \;=\; \binom{52}{3} \;=\; \frac{52 \cdot 51 \cdot 50}{1 \cdot 2 \cdot 3} \;=\; 22100$$

The event is a triple of hearts. Since there are 13 hearts in all,

$$n\,(E) \;=\; \binom{13}{3} \;=\; \frac{13 \cdot 12 \cdot 11}{1 \cdot 2 \cdot 3} \;=\; 286$$

The required probability is $\dfrac{n\,(E)}{n\,(S)} = \dfrac{286}{22100} \approx 0.013$

(b) The required probability is $\dfrac{1}{22100} \approx 0.00005$.

(c) In this case the sample space is the set of **ordered** triples of cards.

$$n\,(S) \;=\; {}_{52}P_3 \;=\; 52 \times 51 \times 50 \;=\; 132600$$

The required probability is $\dfrac{1}{132600} \approx 0.000008$

Example 10

How many different four-letter arrangements can be formed using the five letters of the word EVENT?

Solution

For any given arrangement there are two possibilities; it may include two E's or only one E.

If both E's are present then the other two letters may be selected in $\binom{3}{2} = 3$ ways. This gives a set of four letters, E_1, E_2 and two others. Such a set can be arranged in $4! = 24$ ways. However, if you now remove the subscripts from the E's, the 24 arrangements fall into 12 indistinguishable pairs; for instance, what were previously E_1VE_2N and E_2VE_1N now both become simply EVEN. So each of the 3 ways of selecting the two non-E's gives 12 arrangements and hence there are 36 arrangements with two E's.

If only one E is present, the four letters can be arranged in $4! = 24$ ways.

The total number of arrangements is $36 + 24 = 60$.

> How many different *selections* of four letters can be made from the five letters of the word EVENT?

Exercise 6

1. Show that the definitions of $_nP_r$ and $\binom{n}{r}$ hold if and only if $0! = 1$. (0! has this value whenever it is encountered.)

2. You will have met $\binom{n}{r}$ previously as the $(r + 1)$th element in the nth row of Pascal's triangle:

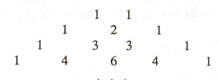

$$
\begin{array}{ccccccccc}
 & & & 1 & & 1 & & & \\
 & & 1 & & 2 & & 1 & & \\
 & 1 & & 3 & & 3 & & 1 & \\
1 & & 4 & & 6 & & 4 & & 1
\end{array}
$$

. . .

   (a) Prove algebraically from the definition of $\binom{n}{r}$ the results:

   (i) $\binom{n}{r} = \binom{n}{n-r}$ (ii) $\binom{n+1}{r} = \binom{n}{r} + \binom{n}{r-1}$.

   (b) How do these results enable you to extend Pascal's triangle?

3. How many different arrangements can be made of all the letters of the words

   (a) PRISM,   (b) SPASM,   (c) PASSES?

4. The nine digits 1, 2, 3, 4, 5, 6, 7, 8 and 9 are written on cards which are then shuffled. A four digit number is formed by laying down the top four cards. Find the probability that the number

   (a) starts with 9,   (b) is even,   (c) starts with 9 and is even.

5. (a) (i) How many different committees of four can be selected from a group of eight people?

      (ii) How many different committees of four can be selected from a group of nine people?

      (iii) How many different committees of four can be selected from a group of nine people if one of the members must be last year's chairperson (who is one of the nine people)?

   (b) Use a method suggested by part (a) to show that

   $$\binom{n+1}{r} = \binom{n}{r} + \binom{n}{r-1}.$$

After working through this chapter you should:

1. understand the term 'observed probability' (or relative frequency);

2. be able to judge when probabilities may be found theoretically, using symmetry, and find such probabilities;

3. be familiar with the language and notation of sets – in particular, sample space, event, complement, union, intersection and representation using Venn diagrams;

4. be able to apply the formula

$$P(E) = \frac{n(E)}{n(S)}$$

for a trial with equally likely outcomes;

5. understand and use the formula

$$P(A \cup B) = P(A) + P(B) - P(A \cap B);$$

6. know that when A and B are mutually exclusive events,

$$A \cap B = \varnothing, \text{ so } P(A \cap B) = 0;$$

7. know that when A and B are independent events,

$$P(A \cap B) = P(A)P(B);$$

8. understand and apply to problems in probability the formulas:

for permutations $\quad {}_n P_r = \dfrac{n!}{(n-r)!}$

for combinations $\quad \dbinom{n}{r} = \dfrac{n!}{(n-r)!\,r!}$

The algebra of sets

The basic operations of the algebra of sets may be shown by examples. In the following cases the result of the operation is shown by shading on a Venn diagram (named after John Venn, an English logician 1834 - 1923).

The set of all elements under consideration is called the 'universal set' and is often denoted by the symbol 'ε'.

In the illustrations below,

$$\varepsilon = \{1, 2, 3, 4, 5, 6\}, \quad A = \{2, 4, 6\} \text{ and } B = \{1, 2, 3\}$$

1. The **complement** of A is the set of members of ε which are **not** members of A. It is denoted by A'.

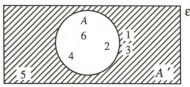

$A' = \{1, 3, 5\}$ is shaded.

2. The **union** of A and B is the set of members of ε which are in A or B or both. It is denoted by $A \cup B$.

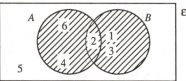

$A \cup B = \{1, 2, 3, 4, 6\}$ is shaded.

3. The **intersection** of A and B is the set of members of ε which are in **both** A **and** B. It is denoted by $A \cap B$.

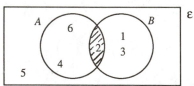

$A \cap B = \{2\}$ is shaded.

In the definitions of set operations you will have noticed the following correspondence:

English word	Set operation
not	′ (complement)
and/both	∩ (intersection)
either/or	∪ (union)

(continued)

16

Example 1

Let the sample space $\varepsilon = \{1, 2, 3, 4, 5, 6, 7, 8, 9, 10\}$.

If $A = \{2, 4, 6, 8, 10\}$ and $B = \{1, 2, 3, 4\}$ show that

$$(A \cup B)' = A' \cap B'$$

(a)   in this case,   (b)   in general, for any chosen sample space and events.

Solution

(a) $A \cup B \quad = \{1, 2, 3, 4, 6, 8, 10\}$

$\quad (A \cup B)' = \{5, 7, 9\}$

$\qquad\quad A' = \{1, 3, 5, 7, 9\}, \; B' = \{5, 6, 7, 8, 9, 10\}$

$A' \cap B' = \{5, 7, 9\}$

Hence $(A \cup B)' = A' \cap B' = \{5, 7, 9\}$.

(b)   A demonstration using Venn diagrams is possible.

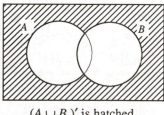
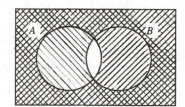

$(A \cup B)'$ is hatched A' is hatched ⁄⁄ B' is hatched ＼＼
                                 $A' \cap B'$ is cross-hatched

1.   (a)   If $\varepsilon = \{1, 2, 3, 4, 5, 6, 7, 8, 9, 10\}$, $A = \{2, 4, 6, 8, 10\}$ and $B = \{1, 2, 3, 4\}$,
            show that $(A \cap B)' = A' \cup B'$.

      (b)   Use Venn diagrams to show that this result holds generally.

2.   (a)   If a member of set ε in Example 1 is chosen at random, find the probability that it
            is an element of B. (This probability is written as P(B)).

      (b)   Find P(B'). What connection is there between P(B) and P(B')?

      (c)   Find P($A \cup B$) + P($A \cap B$) and also find P(A) + P(B). Comment on your
            answers.

Hands of cards

A pack of playing cards has
four suits : spades, hearts,
diamonds and clubs. There
are 13 cards in each suit.

In each suit there are:

picture cards

1. (a) A pack is shuffled and the top card is
        dealt. How many possibilities are there?

    (b) The next card is dealt and turned over to the
        right of the first. How many possibilities
        are there for that card?

    (c) Use the r, s principle to determine how many possible ordered pairs can be dealt
        from a pack.

    (d)   How many ordered sets of four cards
        can be dealt from a pack?

2. Now suppose that you are not interested in the order in which cards are dealt, only in
    the cards in the hand. How many possible hands are there consisting of

    (a) 2 cards,

    (b) 3 cards,

    (c) 4 cards ?

(continued)

18

In the following questions, the use of the word 'hand' indicates that the order of the cards does not matter.

3.   Let H_n be the number of possible hands of n cards.

      (a)   Write down an expression for the value of H_5 .

      (b)   Show that $H_5 = \dfrac{48}{5} \times H_4$.

      (c)   Complete these statements:

$$H_6 = \quad \times H_5 ,$$

$$H_{n+1} = \quad \times H_n .$$

      (d)   Make a table of values of H_n for $n = 1, 2, 3, \ldots, 13$.

      (e)   What is the probability of your being dealt a hand consisting of all 13 hearts, from a well-shuffled pack? What is the probability of any other given hand?

4.   (a)   Verify that the number of **ordered sets** of r cards which can be dealt from the pack is

$$52 \times 51 \times 50 \times \ldots \times (52 - r + 1) = \frac{52!}{(52 - r)!} .$$

      (b)   Write down an expression for the number of **hands** of r cards.

      (c)   Generalise the formulas in (a) and (b) to the case when the pack contains n cards.

Tutorial sheet

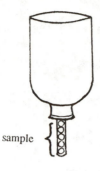

sample

sampling bottle

The experimental work described may be speeded up by using a sampling bottle, which can be obtained commercially or improvised.

1. A bottle contains beads, all of the same shape and size. 10 of them are red, 6 blue and 4 yellow.

    Samples of three beads are taken at random. Find the theoretical probability that they should consist of:

    (a)   a red, a blue and a yellow, in any order;

    (b)   red, blue and yellow, in that order.

    Compare with the observed probabilities, first using a small number of trials (say 50) and then a much larger number.

2. Using the same set of beads, what is the theoretical probability of a sample of 4 consisting of:

    (a)   two reds, a blue and a yellow, in any order;

    (b)   red, blue, red, yellow, in that order.

3. A pack of 12 cards consists of three identical aces of each of the four suits: spades, hearts, diamonds and clubs.

    (a)   How many distinct hands of three cards can be dealt from the pack?

    (b)   Consider in a similar way the possible hands of four, five, six cards. What is the most likely type of hand in each case?

4. If a hand of 13 cards is dealt from a standard pack of 52, what is the most likely distribution among the four suits?

2 *n-stage experiments*

2.1   Tree diagrams

Some calculations require the use of both the addition and multiplication rules for probabilities of two events.

> **Quote the two rules and the conditions under which they apply.**

To help keep track of a range of possible outcomes a tree diagram is often used.

Example 1

There is a probability of $\frac{2}{3}$ that my alarm clock will wake me. If it does then there is a probability of $\frac{9}{10}$ that I will catch the bus to work. Otherwise the probability of my catching the bus is only $\frac{3}{5}$. What is the probability of my catching the bus on one particular morning?

Solution

Using A to represent the event of being woken by the alarm and B to represent the event of catching the bus, the following tree diagram is obtained.

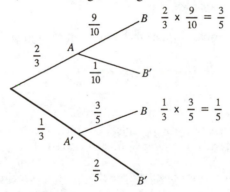

The required probability is $\frac{3}{5} + \frac{1}{5} = \frac{4}{5}$.

> **(a)   Explain why the probabilities along branches are multiplied.**
>
> **(b)   Explain why the probabilities at the two tips are added.**

   TASKSHEET 1E - *The Hardy-Weinberg law*

Exercise 1

1. Draw a tree diagram to show the possible outcomes of three tosses of a fair coin, with their probabilites. Use the tree to find the probabilities of

    (a)   exactly two heads,   (b)   alternate heads and tails.

2. A possible model for answering multiple-choice examination questions where there are five options is shown below in the form of a tree. For one question out of ten the student simply guesses the answer.

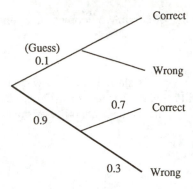

    (a)   Assign the missing probabilities, assuming that when the student guesses she has no idea which option is correct.

    (b)   Find the probability that the correct option is given.

    (c)   From your experience, assign different values to the probabilities and find the probability of a correct answer in this case.

3. A darts player has to score 57, finishing with a double, using no more than three darts. Her preferred method is to finish in two darts with 19 followed by double 19. Assume that if she misses 19 on her first throw she is sure to hit 3, in which case she tries for 18 followed by double 18. If the probability of hitting any single she aims for is 0.9 and the probability of hitting any double she aims for is 0.4, find the probability that she will finish the game by scoring

    (a)   19 and double 19 in just two darts;

    (b)   3, 18 and double 18.

2.2   Bernoulli trials

Example 2

A die is thrown four times. Find the probability of at least one six.

Solution

On each throw,

$$P\text{ (six)} = \frac{1}{6}, \quad P\text{ (not six)} = \frac{5}{6}$$

and the results of the throws are independent. The only **unfavourable** outcome is the one in which not-sixes are thrown every time.

$$P\text{ (unfavourable outcome)} = \left(\frac{5}{6}\right)^4 = \frac{625}{1296} \approx 0.48$$

$$P\text{ (favourable outcome)} \approx 1 - 0.48 = 0.52$$

The type of experiment described in Example 2 is named after Jacob Bernoulli (1654 - 1705), a member of a gifted Swiss family.

In a sequence of Bernoulli trials,

1. **the outcome of each trial is** *independent* **of the outcome of any other;**

2. **the probabilities of the possible outcomes are** *the same in every trial.*

Which of these do you think give Bernoulli sequences?

(a) **Repeated cuts of a pack of cards.**

(b) **Dealing a pack of cards.**

(c) **Repeated throws of a biased die.**

(d) **A snooker match between two players.**

One interesting class of questions about Bernoulli sequences concerns the lengths of runs of a particular outcome.

Example 3

In tossing a fair coin, what is the probability of a run of (a) exactly three heads, (b) at least three heads? Generalise your answers.

Solution

(a) The sequence must run HHHT. In each trial $P(H) = P(T) = \frac{1}{2}$ and the trials are independent. The required probability is

$$\left(\frac{1}{2}\right)^4 = \frac{1}{16}.$$

(b) The sequence starts HHH and this is the only requirement. The required probability is

$$\left(\frac{1}{2}\right)^3 = \frac{1}{8}.$$

Generalisation: $P(\text{run of exactly } r \text{ heads}) = \left(\frac{1}{2}\right)^{r+1}$

$P(\text{run of at least } r \text{ heads}) = \left(\frac{1}{2}\right)^r$

Note that when you toss a coin you get a tail, with probability $\frac{1}{2}$, or you start a run of heads of length 1, 2, 3, ...

run length	0	1	2	3	...
probability	$\frac{1}{2}$	$\left(\frac{1}{2}\right)^2$	$\left(\frac{1}{2}\right)^3$	$\left(\frac{1}{2}\right)^4$	...

These events are mutually exclusive and so the probability of one of these outcomes occurring is $\frac{1}{2} + \frac{1}{4} + \frac{1}{8} + \frac{1}{16} + ...$

an infinite geometric series whose sum is 1, as expected.

Why should you expect a sum of 1?

Exercise 2

1.   An archer hits the bull's-eye with probability 0.8. Find the probability that

(a)   her first four arrows hit the bull's-eye;
(b)   her first four arrows score bull's-eyes, but the fifth arrow does **not**.

2.   For the situation in question 1, draw a graph illustrating the probability of an initial run of 0, 1, 2, 3, 4, ... bull's-eyes.

2.3   The binomial distribution

In Bernoulli trials there may be more than two outcomes with fixed probabilities. Series of trials with many outcomes can lead to lengthy analysis, so far the sake of simplicity, introductory books on probability concentrate on trials with only two outcomes. A typical problem is of the type:

> In a series of *n* independent trials, in each of which there is a probability *p* of success, what is the probability of a total of *r* successes?

In Example 2 of the last section, (throwing a die), there were in fact six possible outcomes to each trial but five of them were lumped together as 'not–six'. In this way, many multiple-outcome trials can be treated as having only two relevant outcomes, often called 'success' and 'failure'. The possible outcomes when a die is thrown four times are shown in this tree diagram.

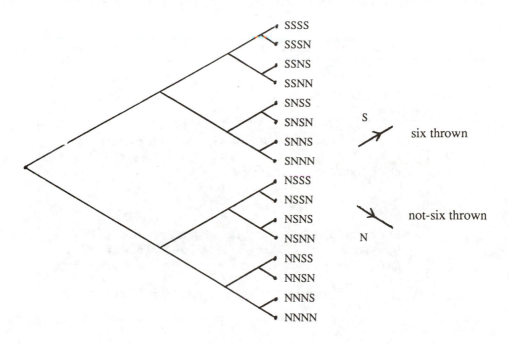

In how many cases are there two N's? Three N's? Four N's?

Because the events are independent, the probability of, for example, SSNS is $\frac{1}{6} \times \frac{1}{6} \times \frac{5}{6} \times \frac{1}{6}$.

Because the cases SSSN, SSNS, SNSS, NSSS are mutually exclusive,

$$P(3\text{ S's, }1\text{ N}) = \left(\frac{1}{6}\right)^3 \left(\frac{5}{6}\right) + \left(\frac{1}{6}\right)^3 \left(\frac{5}{6}\right) + \left(\frac{1}{6}\right)^3 \left(\frac{5}{6}\right) + \left(\frac{1}{6}\right)^3 \left(\frac{5}{6}\right) = 4 \times \left(\frac{1}{6}\right)^3 \left(\frac{5}{6}\right)$$

Letting $p = \frac{1}{6}$, $q = \frac{5}{6}$, this is the value of the term $4p^3q$ in the expansion of $(p + q)^4$.

(a) Write out the complete expansion of $(p + q)^4$.

(b) Verify that the probabilities P(2 S's, 2 N's), P(1 S, 3 N's) are given by the next two terms in this expansion.

You will note that

•   the coefficients in the expansion are $\binom{4}{0}$, $\binom{4}{1}$, $\binom{4}{2}$, $\binom{4}{3}$ and $\binom{4}{4}$, the elements of the fourth row of Pascal's triangle;

•   since $p + q = 1$, the sum of all the terms is 1 as expected, since one or other of the outcomes is inevitable.

These results may be generalised:

> In a sequence of Bernoulli trials in which the probability of a favourable outcome in each trial is p, the probability of r favourable outcomes in n trials is
>
> $$\binom{n}{r} p^r (1 - p)^{n-r}.$$
>
> For given values of n and p, the set of probabilities of this form for $r = 0, 1, 2, ..., n$ is called a *binomial probability distribution*.

Example 4

In five throws of a pair of dice, what is the probability of throwing two 7's?

Solution

The probability of a favourable outcome is $p = \frac{1}{6}$. Substituting $p = \frac{1}{6}$, $n = 5$, $r = 2$ in the formula above, the required probability is

$$\binom{5}{2}\left(\frac{1}{6}\right)^2 \left(\frac{5}{6}\right)^3 = \frac{5 \times 4}{1 \times 2} \times \frac{1}{36} \times \frac{125}{216} \approx 0.16.$$

Example 5

A marksman has a probability of 0.8 of scoring a bull's-eye with any shot. If he misses the bull's-eye he invariably scores an inner. If 10 marks are awarded for a bull and 8 for an inner, find the probability of a total greater than 95 in 10 shots.

Solution

He must score more than seven bull's-eyes.

$$P(8 \text{ or } 9 \text{ or } 10) = P(8) + P(9) + P(10)$$

$$= \binom{10}{8}(0.8)^8 (0.2)^2 + \binom{10}{9}(0.8)^9 (0.2) + \binom{10}{10}(0.8)^{10}$$

$$\approx \quad 0.3020 \quad + \quad 0.2684 \quad + \quad 0.1074$$

$$= \quad 0.678 \text{ (to 3 s.f.)}$$

> **Explain why P(8 or 9 or 10) = P(8) + P(9) + P(10).**
> **Check the details of the calculation.**

A binomial probability distribution is assumed in solving many practical problems.

Example 6

Microchips are supplied to a computer company with the guarantee that 80% of them will be satisfactory. A sample batch of ten is taken at random and it is found that five of them are defective. Does this invalidate the supplier's guarantee?

Solution

The probability that six or more are satisfactory should be

$$\binom{10}{6}(0.8)^6 (0.2)^4 + \binom{10}{7}(0.8)^7 (0.2)^3 + \dots + \binom{10}{10}(0.8)^{10}$$

$$= 0.0881 + 0.2013 + 0.3020 + 0.2684 + 0.1074$$

$$= 0.967 \text{ (to 3 s.f.)}$$

This probability is higher than the 95% level often taken as indicating virtual certainty in such cases, so the company would probably not accept the supplier's guarantee.

Other probability models are possible and they may be applied to continuous as well as to discrete data.

 TASKSHEET 2 - *A continuous probability model*

Exercise 3

1. A commuter notes that her train is late on 20% of occasions. What is the probability that it is late on

   (a) exactly three days of the working week (Monday - Friday),

   (b) at least three days of the working week?

2. In ten throws of a die, which is the more likely, exactly one six or exactly two sixes?

3. An army gunner is training to shoot at moving targets. Hits are scored on 60% of occasions. What is the most likely number of hits in 10 trials?

4. Caitlin cuts a pack of cards four times, showing the card cut each time. Find the probability that the cards are all

   (a) clubs,   (b) of the same suit.

5. Leroy is dealt a hand of four cards from a well-shuffled pack. Find the probability that the cards are all

   (a) clubs,   (b) of the same suit.

6. A and B are to play five games of table tennis. The probability of A winning any one game is 0.6. Find the probability that A wins the set, i.e. at least three games out of the five.

7. Five people taken at random are each asked to taste a sample of Brand A and a sample of Brand B margarine. Four of them prefer Brand A. Do you feel this provides conclusive evidence that 'people prefer Brand A to Brand B'? Give your reason.   [SMP]

2.4   Conditional probability

Colour blindness is a defect of vision reducing the ability to distinguish between colours. In the principal type there is an inability to distinguish between colours in the red/yellow/green range, for example, between red and yellow or between yellow and green.

Because males are more likely to be colour blind than females the probability of colour blindness is **conditional** on a person's sex.

 TASKSHEET 3 - *Colour blindness*

> The conditional probability $P(B \mid A)$ is the probability that event B will happen given that event A happens.
>
> $$P(B \mid A) = \frac{P(A \cap B)}{P(A)}$$

Note that the branches of a two-stage tree diagram may be labelled as shown.

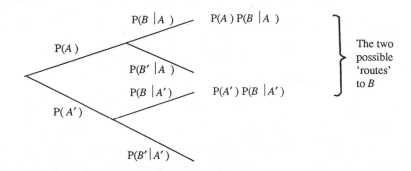

From the diagram you can see that

$$P(B) = P(A)\ P(B \mid A) + P(A')\ P(B \mid A').$$

> **Write down a similar expression for $P(B')$.**

If you consider only the topmost branch you find

$$P(A \cap B) = P(A)\ P(B \mid A).$$

> **Write down similar expressions for**
>
> (a) $P(A \cap B')$,   (b) $P(A' \cap B)$,   (c) $P(A' \cap B')$.

Example 7

The events A and B are such that $P(A) = \frac{1}{2}$, $P(A' \mid B) = \frac{1}{3}$ and $P(A \cup B') = \frac{3}{5}$.
Find $P(B)$.

Solution

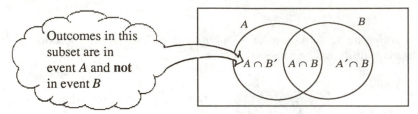

You will see from the Venn diagram that

$$P(A \cup B) = P(A \cap B) + P(A \cap B') + P(A' \cap B)$$

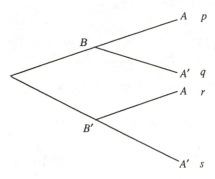

The tree diagram has tips labelled
p, q, r and s. From the result
above,

$$P(A \cup B) = p + q + r.$$

From the information given,

$$p + q + r = \frac{3}{5},$$

$$p \quad + r = \frac{1}{2},$$

$$q \quad = \frac{3}{5} - \frac{1}{2} = \frac{1}{10}.$$

So $P(B) \times \frac{1}{3} = \frac{1}{10}$ and hence $P(B) = \frac{3}{10}$.

The idea of a conditional probability helps to redefine independence of events. A and B are independent if the probability of B occurring does not depend on whether A occurs.

> **The events A and B are independent if**
> $$P(B \mid A) = P(B).$$

> **Show that when A and B are independent, $P(A \cap B) = P(A)\ P(B)$.**

Example 8

In a certain sample space the events A and B are independent and $P(A \cup B) = \frac{5}{8}$, $P(A \cap B') = \frac{7}{24}$.

Calculate   (a) $P(B)$ (b) $P(A)$ (c) $P(A \cap B)$ (d) $P(A' \cup B')$

Solution

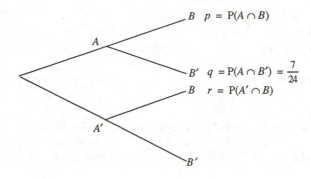

(a) $P(A \cup B) = \frac{5}{8}$

$p + \frac{7}{24} + r = \frac{5}{8}$

$P(B) = p + r = \frac{5}{8} - \frac{7}{24} = \frac{1}{3}$.

Because of the independence of A and B, $P(B \mid A) = P(B \mid A') = P(B)$. The branches of the tree may be labelled as shown:

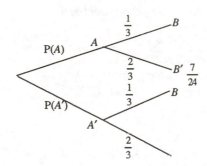

(b) $P(A) \times \frac{2}{3} = \frac{7}{24}$

$P(A) = \frac{7}{16}$

(c) $P(A \cap B) = P(A) \times P(B) = \frac{7}{16} \times \frac{1}{3} = \frac{7}{48}$

(d) $P(A' \cup B') = P[(A \cap B)'] = 1 - P(A \cap B) = \frac{41}{48}$

31

Exercise 4

1. State conditions on probabilities associated with the events A and B such that A and B

   (a) are independent
   (b) are mutually exclusive
   (c) exhaust the sample space.

2. Simplify the expressions

   (a) $P(A) + P(A')$ (b) $P(A \mid B) + P(A' \mid B)$

   (c) $P(A' \mid B)\ P(B)$ (d) $P(A \cup B) + P(B') \times P(A' \mid B')$

3. The probability that a blue-eyed person is left-handed is $\frac{1}{7}$. The probability that a left-handed person is blue-eyed is $\frac{1}{3}$. The probability that a person has neither of these characteristics is $\frac{4}{5}$. What is the probability that a person has both?

   [SMP]

4. Two events A and B are such that

$$P(A) = \tfrac{1}{2}, \qquad P(B) = \tfrac{1}{3}, \qquad P(A \mid B) = \tfrac{1}{4}.$$

   Evaluate

   (a) $P(A \cap B)$ (b) $P(A \cup B)$ (c) $P(A' \cap B')$

   Another event C is such that A and C are independent and

$$P(A \cap C) = \tfrac{1}{12}, \qquad P(B \cup C) = \tfrac{1}{2}.$$

   Show that B and C are mutually exclusive.

2.5   Bayes' theorem

Some of the most interesting work in probability theory has been in the resolution of paradoxes - problems having two apparently contradictory solutions. A famous one is sometimes called the 'Three Prisoners' paradox.

A paradox

The president of Vinovia has decreed that of three political prisoners, A, B and C, two will be executed as an example to others. The jailer is to choose two at random, not revealing which until the morning of the execution.

Some time before this the prisoners are all in solitary confinement and A asks the jailer to name one of the others to be executed. The jailer reasons that since A cannot communicate with the other prisoners and since he knows that at least one of B and C is to be executed there can be no harm in this. He tells A, 'B is to be executed'.

Before the jailer spoke, A knew that his survival was one of three equally likely events and therefore had probability $\frac{1}{3}$. Now, however, A reasons that the survivor will be either C or himself and so his chances have improved to $\frac{1}{2}$. Is A correct, or was the jailer right in assuming that the information he gave was of no use to A?

The paradox can be resolved by methods already met in this book, and it would be a pity not to give you the opportunity to try. A neat solution uses a theorem named after the eighteenth-century mathematician Thomas Bayes, and will be given later. The theorem is introduced by an example.

Example 9

An automated blood pressure machine is being tested. Members of the public, about 20% of whom have high blood pressure (hypertension), try it out and are then seen by a doctor. She finds that 80% of those with hypertension and 10% of those with normal blood pressure have been diagnosed as hypertensive by the machine. How useful is the machine?

Solution

The probabilities of the various compound events may be illustrated using a tree.

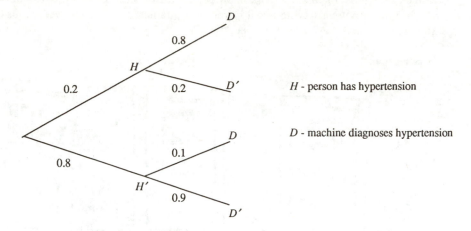

H - person has hypertension

D - machine diagnoses hypertension

One probability the doctor wants to find is that of correct positive diagnosis, i.e. $P(H \mid D)$. She calculates this as follows:

$$P(H \cap D) = P(H) \times P(D \mid H) = 0.2 \times 0.8 = 0.16$$

$$P(D) = P(H \cap D) + P(H' \cap D) = 0.16 + 0.08 = 0.24$$

So $P(H \mid D) = \dfrac{P(H \cap D)}{P(D)} = \dfrac{0.16}{0.24} \approx 0.67$

The doctor also calculates the probability of a correct negative diagnosis, i.e. $P(H' \mid D')$.

$$P(H' \cap D') = P(H') \times P(D' \mid H') = 0.8 \times 0.9 = 0.72$$

$$P(D') = P(H \cap D') + P(H' \cap D') = 0.04 + 0.72 = 0.76$$

So $P(H' \mid D') = \dfrac{P(H' \cap D')}{P(D')} = \dfrac{0.72}{0.76} \approx 0.95$

The machine is a good tool for initial screening. If it does not find you hypertensive then you can be reasonably confident that your blood pressure is normal. If it diagnoses hypertension, then you should consult your doctor for further tests.

In the solution above, $P(H \cap D)$ was expressed both as

$$P(H) \times P(D \mid H) \text{ and as } P(D) \times P(H \mid D)$$

The equality of these two expressions is one statement of Bayes' theorem. It is more often used in the form:

$$P(D \mid H) = \dfrac{P(D) \times P(H \mid D)}{P(H)}$$

The denominator is often calculated with the help of a tree diagram. Sometimes the whole calculation can be managed without a diagram, using conditional probabilities, in which case the statement would take the form

$$P(A \mid B) = \frac{P(A) \times P(B \mid A)}{P(A) \times P(B \mid A) + P(A') \times P(B \mid A')}$$

Bayes' theorem:

You are now in a position to tackle the 'Three Prisoners' paradox using Bayes' theorem.

Let A denote the event that A is to be executed and similarly for B and C. Then initially

$$P(A) = P(B) = P(C) = \frac{2}{3}$$

After the jailer's information, A calculated the probability

$$P(A \mid B) = \frac{P(A \cap B)}{P(B)} = \frac{\frac{1}{3}}{\frac{2}{3}} = \frac{1}{2}$$

However, he should have calculated $P(A \mid S_B)$, where S_B is the event that the jailer says that B is to be executed. S_B is not the same as B. Since the jailer knows which two prisoners are to be executed, $P(S_B) = P(S_C) = \frac{1}{2}$ by symmetry.

Then

$$P(A \mid S_B) = \frac{P(A) \times P(S_B \mid A)}{P(S_B)} = \frac{\frac{2}{3} \times \frac{1}{2}}{\frac{1}{2}} = \frac{2}{3}.$$

The jailer was correct. The probability of A's being executed has not been changed.

(a) Explain why $P(S_B \mid A) = \frac{1}{2}$.

(b) Calculate $P(S_B)$ as $P(A) \times P(S_B \mid A) + P(A') \times P(S_B \mid A')$.

Example 10

A mail-order firm recruits all its agents through newspaper advertisements. The firm receives three times as many applications through the tabloid press as through the quality press. Furthermore, applicants reached through the tabloid press are three times as likely to become active as those reached through the quality press.

Find the probability that a randomly selected active agent takes a tabloid newspaper.

Solution

Using the notation

T - reached through a tabloid,

A - active,

$$P(T|A) = \frac{P(T)\,P(A|T)}{P(T)\,P(A|T) + P(T')\,P(A|T')}$$

$$= \frac{0.75 \times 0.75}{0.75 \times 0.75 + 0.25 \times 0.25}$$

$$= 0.9.$$

Exercise 5

1. Of a library of 100 books, 60 are non-fiction and 40 are fiction. Of the non-fiction books, 40 are hardbacks. Of the fiction books, 10 are hardbacks. A book selected at random from the library is found to be hardback. What is the probability that it is a work of fiction?

2. It is estimated that one quarter of the drivers on the road between 11 p.m. and midnight have been drinking during the evening. If a driver has not been drinking, the probability that he will have an accident at that time of night is 0.004%; if he has been drinking, the probability of an accident goes up to 0.2%. What is the probability that a car selected at random at that time of night will have an accident?

   A policeman on the beat at 11.30 p.m. sees a car run into a lamp-post and jumps to the conclusion that the driver has been drinking. What is the probability that he is right? [SMP]

3E. If $\{A_i \mid i = 1, 2, ..., n \}$ is a partition* of the sample space then

$$P(B) = \sum_{i=1}^{n} P(B \mid A_i) \times P(A_i).$$

Use this result to generalise the form of Bayes' theorem expressed using conditional probabilities.

4. [This calculation uses the generalised form of Bayes' theorem from question 3E].

A friend sets off to visit you. You know from past experience that he will come on foot, by bus, by bike or by car with probabilities 0.3, 0.2, 0.1, 0.4, respectively. The probabilities that he will be late are

on foot $\frac{1}{4}$, by bus $\frac{1}{3}$, by bike $\frac{1}{12}$, by car 0.

He arrives late. What is the probability that he came on foot?

* **Partition:** the subsets $A_1, A_2, ..., A_n$ partition the sample space S if

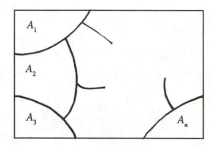

(1) the union of $A_1, A_2, ..., A_n$ is S;

(2) the intersection of any pair of the A_i is empty.

2.6   Further applications of Bayes' theorem.

The words prior and posterior (or the latin phrases 'a priori' and 'a posteriori') are often used in probability theory to describe the probability of an event before and after another event upon which it is conditional. In the formula

$$P(A|B) = \frac{P(A) \times P(B|A)}{P(B)},$$

the prior probability of A is $P(A)$ and the posterior probability (after the event B has occurred) is $P(A|B)$.

Another illustration of the use of these words is given in the following example, which shows a typical 'real-life' application of Bayes' theorem as part of a decision-making process.

Example 11

A broker is offered a consignment of fruit from South America at a favourable price. To import it into the EEC and make a good profit he needs a licence. Unfortunately the granting of a licence takes a long time and is by no means certain. If he delays, the deal may fall through. To help him make a decision he could seek the services of a consultant. The consultant is not infallible but usually makes a correct assessment. Her track record on similar assessments is shown in the table.

Assessment	licence granted	licence denied	decision referred
Favourable	80	10	5
Unfavourable	20	40	20

(In 80 out of 100 cases when a licence has been granted, the consultant's decision has been favourable and so on.)

Based on previous experience, the prior probabilities are:

licence granted, 0.6;   denied, 0.3;   referred, 0.1.

What would be the posterior probabilities following a favourable decision by the consultant?

Solution

The abbreviations used are:

G - granted, D - denied, R - referred, F - favourable.

Care must be taken in interpreting the table. The probabilities needed are such as $P(F|D)$, i.e. the probability of a favourable decision having been given when a licence is denied.

38

$P(F \mid D) = \dfrac{0.1}{0.1 + 0.4} = 0.2$. Similarly, $P(F \mid G) = 0.8$ and $P(F \mid R) = 0.2$

$$P(G \mid F) = \frac{P(G)\,P(F \mid G)}{P(G)\,P(F \mid G) + P(D)\,P(F \mid D) + P(R)\,P(F \mid R)}$$

$$= \frac{0.6 \times 0.8}{(0.6 \times 0.8) + (0.3 \times 0.2) + (0.1 \times 0.2)}$$

$$= \frac{6}{7} \approx 0.86$$

> **Find the other two posterior probabilities and check that the sum of all three probabilities is 1.**

Exercise 6

1. The marketing director of the Sudso corporation thinks that the probability that New Sudso is better than Kleenrite is 0.9. Because he lacks confidence in his intuition he arranges a hasty survey. The market research company can only manage a small sample over a short period and will only allow 80% reliability - i.e. there is a probability of 0.2 that their conclusion will be incorrect.

    Find the probability that New Sudso will prove better than Kleenrite if their survey predicts this.

2. An electronics company has bought a batch of resistors from a manufacturer. The company knows that all the resistors are produced on one of two machines, A and B. 10% of the output of A and 20% of the output of B are defective. The manufacturer has guaranteed that 70% of the batches come from A and 30% from B. Three resistors chosen randomly from the batch are all satisfactory.

    (a) If the batch came from A, find the probability that three randomly chosen resistors will be satisfactory.

    (b) Find the probability that the batch came from A.

3. A mining company assesses the chances of finding minerals in a certain area as follows:

low grade spar (*L*) – 0.5, high grade spar (*H*) – 0.25,
high grade spar with viable metallic ore   (*M*) – 0.25.

If a detailed geological survey is made, the findings will be good (*G*) or poor (*G′*) with probabilities as shown in this table.

Mineral	Survey result	
	G	G′
L	0.2	0.8
H	0.5	0.5
M	0.9	0.1

To decide whether to commission a survey the company needs the six posterior probabilities conditional on the survey. Calculate these probabilities.

4. You assess the probability of an event *E* as being in the range given by $0.5 < P(E) < 0.7$.

If *E* happens, then *F* is 90% certain to happen. Otherwise the probability of *F* is only 0.2.

Given that *F* happens, what is the chance of *E* ?

Comment on your answer

(a)   in strictly mathematical terms;

(b)   in terms of a possible application.

After working through this chapter you should:

1. be able to use tree diagrams as an aid and illustration in situations involving several probabilities and stages;

2. know the definition of a Bernoulli sequence;

3. be able to use the binomial probability distribution in problems, including simple decision-making;

4. know the definition of a conditional probability;

5. be able to construct and use formulas such as

$$P(B) = P(A) P(B \mid A) + P(A') P(B \mid A'),$$

$$P(A \cap B) = P(A) P(B \mid A);$$

6. given prior probabilities and relevant conditional probabilities, be able to find posterior probabilities, using the generalised form of Bayes' theorem.

The Hardy-Weinberg law

Children take after their parents. Such passing on of characteristics, determined by genes, is called genetic inheritance. The characteristics of the parents may be opposite in kind, for example:

> having six toes - *S*
> having the normal number of toes - *N*.

Offspring inherit an allele (gene - type) from each parent, the various possibilities being as shown in this table:

		Mother	
		S	*N*
Father	*S*	*SS*	*SN*
	N	*NS*	*NN*

The pairs *SN* and *NS* are indistinguishable. Which parent contributes which allele is immaterial.

Suppose that at a particular time for a particular population the probability of inheriting *S* from either parent is p. Then the probabilities of the various allele pairs in offspring are shown in this tree diagram.

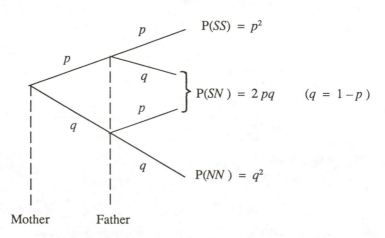

(continued)

You will see that the second generation has a population in which

the event SS occurs with probability p^2
the event NN occurs with probability q^2
the event SN occurs with probability $2pq$

Individuals with allele-pair SS or NN are called **homozygotes** (homo - the same) and those with allele-pair SN are called **heterozygotes** (hetero - different).

1.   Show that the probabilities given in the tree diagram for the offspring total 1.

2.   Suppose that the distribution of the genotypes in the population is given by

$$P(SS) = p^2 \ , \ \ P(SN) = 2pq \ , \ \ P(NN) = q^2$$

Assume also that a heterozygote (SN) has an equal chance of passing either characteristic (S or N) forward to the next generation.

Consider the probabilities of the various allele-pairs in the following generation.

(a)   Explain the entries in this table

Event	P (Event)	Assuming the event		
		$P(SS)$	$P(SN)$	$P(NN)$
both parents SS	p^4	1	0	0
one SS, other SN	$4p^3q$	$\frac{1}{2}$	$\frac{1}{2}$	0
one SS, other NN				
both SN	$4p^2q^2$	$\frac{1}{4}$	$\frac{1}{2}$	$\frac{1}{4}$
one SN, other NN				
both NN				

(b)   Complete the table.

(c)   Find the probabilities of the various allele pairs.

3.   Explain why the model results in a stable distribution of genotypes in the population. [This is the Hardy-Weinberg law.]

4.   Suppose that six-toedness is a dominant characteristic, that is that any individual with either one or two S alleles will have six toes.   If at any time in a stable population 20% have six toes, what percentage would be SS genotypes?

You may be interested to discover how the incidence of other characteristics change from one generation to another. Haemophilia and sickle-cell anaemia would be worth investigating.

A continuous probability model

Uranium rods are supplied with a nominal length of 25 cm ± 0.2 cm, with a triangular probability distribution, as shown by the graph. The shaded area represents the probability that the length of a rod chosen at random lies between 24.8 cm and x cm.

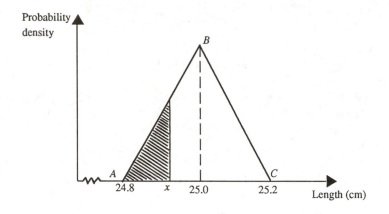

1.   What is the area of triangle ABC ?

2.   (a)   If $24.8 < x < 25.0$, use similar triangles to explain why

$$\text{P(length between 24.8 and } x) \;=\; \frac{1}{2} \times \left(\frac{x - 24.8}{25.0 - 24.8} \right)^2.$$

(b)   Find the following probabilities.

P(length between 24.8 and 25.0)
P(length between 24.8 and 24.9)
P(length between 24.9 and 25.0)
P(length between 24.9 and 25.1)

3.   If $x > 25.0$ find P(length between 24.8 and x).

4.   Draw the cumulative probability graph, i.e. the graph of

P(length between 24.8 and x) against x

for $24.8 < x < 25.2$

5.   If the rods have lengths in the range $25 \pm t$ cm with 95% certainty, find t.

Colour blindness

The probability of colour blindness in the adult population is 0.03 but males are more prone to the condition than females and the probability among males is 0.05.

1.   Out of a population of 1000 'typical' adults, how many would you expect in each of these categories?

        (a)   male and colour blind
        (b)   male and not colour blind
        (c)   female and colour blind
        (d)   female and not colour blind

2.   Let $P(C \mid M)$ stand for the **conditional** probability of colour blindness given that the subject is male. What is the value of $P(C \mid M)$?

3.   Interpret and find the value of $P(C' \mid F)$.

4.

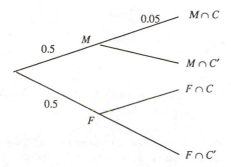

Copy and complete the tree diagram, giving the probabilities at each tip.

5.   Verify that

$$P(C \mid M) = \frac{P(M \cap C)}{P(M)}$$

6.   Write similar formulas for

        (a) $P(C' \mid M)$ (b) $P(C \mid F)$ (c) $P(C' \mid F)$.

7.   Find a formula for $P(C)$ in terms of conditional probabilities.

Tutorial sheet

1. A tennis player has the psychological quirk that the probability of her winning a given set in a match is

    $$\left(\frac{1}{2}\right)^{k+1}$$

    where k is the number of sets she has won so far. What is the probability of her winning a three-set match? [To win a three-set match in tennis you must win two sets.]

2. A large company employs men and women in the ratio 1 : 3. The company's records show that a male employee is ten times as likely to become a supervisor as is a female employee.

    (a) Insert probabilities on the tree diagram.

    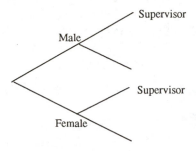

    (b) What is the probability that a randomly chosen supervisor is female? What assumptions have you made in answering this question?

3. In a certain athletics meeting, competitors are allowed to enter for only one event. A particular athlete is able to compete in the 100 m sprint, long jump or 80 m hurdles. A fortnight before the meeting he talks over his prospects with a friend, who gains the impression that the probabilities of his entering for each of them are 0.5, 0.3 and 0.2 respectively. In the conversation, the athlete assesses his chances of winning each event to be 0.2, 0.3 and 0.9 respectively. Some time after the athletics competition the friend hears that the athlete won one of the events, but not which one. How should she now revise her impressions of the probabilities of the athlete entering for the three events?

4. A mathematics teacher has two children.

    (a) She tells her class that at least one of her children is a boy. What is the probability that both her children are boys?

    (b) The class later discovers that her youngest child is a boy. Does this affect the probability of both her children being boys?

3 Occupancy and random walks

3.1 Counting problems

You have seen that you should use permutations when answering a counting question of the form 'in how many ways can you choose a number of objects from a wider collection taking order into account?' You should use combinations when the question is something like: 'in how many ways can you choose a number of objects from a wider collection disregarding order?'

This section introduces another, very useful, way of thinking about some types of counting problems.

From a group of four students, Armand, Brian, Cheryl and Diane, you are to choose a committee.

In how many ways can you do this if:

(a)   a committee of two is to be chosen, both members having equal status;

(b)   a chairperson and a treasurer are to be chosen, the jobs being given to different students;

(c)   a chairperson and a treasurer are to be chosen, and the same student can assume both tasks?

Suppose you have four boxes, one for each of the four students. Take two tokens, one for each committee task. How can the above counting experiments be modelled by allocating the tokens to the boxes?

Consider the allocation of r tokens to n boxes. The discussion point illustrated three basic **occupancy models**.

Model 1

> The tokens are not distinguishable and no box may contain more than one token.
>
> The number of possible allocations is
>
> $$\binom{n}{r} = \frac{n!}{r!\,(n-r)!}$$

Model 2

> The tokens are distinguishable and no box may contain more than one token.
>
> The number of possible allocations is
>
> $$_n P_r = \frac{n!}{(n-r)!}$$

Model 3

> The tokens are distinguishable and each box may contain any number (including zero) of tokens.
>
> The number of possible allocations is
>
> $$n^r$$

> In models 1, 2 and 3, show that the numbers of allocations are
>
> $$\binom{n}{r}, \quad _n P_r \text{ and } n^r,$$
>
> respectively.

3.2 Choosing a model

The following two examples illustrate that care needs to be exercised in deciding **which** model is appropriate for a particular allocation problem.

Example 1

On a television quiz show, 3 prizes are placed at random in 5 boxes numbered 1 to 5. If the prizes are identical and if a box may contain at most one prize, then what is the probability that each of the boxes 1, 2 and 3 contains a prize?

Solution

The first step is to determine the total number of possible outcomes of the probability experiment. The tokens (prizes) are not distinguishable and there is at most one token to a box, so occupancy model 1 with $n = 5$ and $r = 3$ is applicable. The total number is

$$\binom{5}{3} = 10 .$$

Of the 10 possible allocations only one is favourable and the probability is therefore $\frac{1}{10}$.

Example 2

On another quiz show, 4 prizes are placed at random in 6 boxes numbered 1 to 6. Each box may contain at most one prize, but now the prizes are distinguishable and have different monetary values. Find the probability that box 1 contains the most expensive prize and box 6 contains the least expensive one.

Solution

In this case the tokens (prizes) are distinguishable and there is at most one token to a box. So occupancy model 2 is applicable with $n = 6$ and $r = 4$. The total number of possible allocations is

$$_6P_4 = 360$$

For the required event, two prizes have their locations fixed and the remaining 2 prizes are allocated at random to the remaining 4 boxes. This can be done in

$$_4P_2 = 12 \text{ ways.}$$

The required probability is therefore $\frac{12}{360} = \frac{1}{30}$.

> **What is the probability of a prize in box 1 and a prize in box 6 if all four prizes are indistinguishable?**

The decision as to what are 'tokens' and what are 'boxes' is not always as straightforward as in Examples 1 and 2.

Example 3

In a digital computer a **bit** is one of the digits 0 or 1. Typically, a **word** is defined to be any string of 32 bits. How many possible words can the computer store? What are the boxes and what are the tokens that will provide a model for this problem?

Solution

Regarding the digits as boxes labelled 0 and 1 respectively and the tokens as numbered according to the position of the bit in the word, model 3 applies with $n = 2$ and $r = 32$. The first token (bit) can be allocated either 0 or 1, that is, two possibilities; the second token can also be allocated either 0 or 1 and so on. The total number of possible words is therefore 2^{32}, a very large number indeed!

   TASKSHEET 1 - *Birthdays and birthmates*

Exercise 1

In each of these questions use an occupancy model to describe the experiment before attempting to find the solution.

1.   There are three different routes connecting the foot of a mountain with the summit. In how many ways can a round trip be made from foot to summit and back.

2.   A computer centre has three processors, each one being able to support essentially an unlimited number of jobs. It receives n different jobs which are assigned to processors purely at random so that all possible assignments are equally likely. How many possible assignments are there? What is the probability that one particular processor receives no jobs?

3.   Four cyclists in a timed race wear numbers 1, 2, 3, 4 on their backs. They are started one after another in random order. Find the probabilities of the following events.

   (a)   Cyclist 1 is started first, then cyclist 2, then cyclist 3, and lastly, 4.

   (b)   Cyclist 1 is started first.

   (c)   The starting positions of at least two cyclists correspond with the numbers on their backs.

   (d)   The starting positions of exactly two cyclists agree with the numbers on their backs.

3.3   The matching problem

The following cards exhibit the Zener symbols which are widely used in experiments where subjects are tested for ESP (extra-sensory perception).

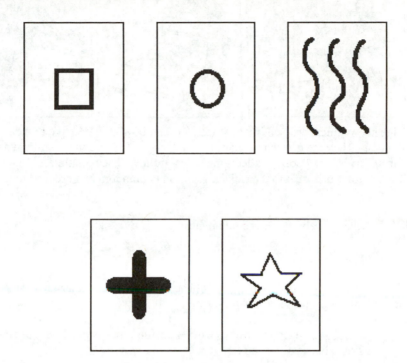

A typical experiment involves shuffling these five cards well and laying them face down in a row. The subject takes a long hard look at the cards, and records next to each the symbol thought to be on that card. The original cards are turned over and the subject's record is compared with the revealed cards. If there are matches, that is, agreements between the subject's record and the cards, then the obvious question to ask is: what is the probability of getting such a number of matches if it is assumed that the subject is only guessing?

> (a)   **Show how the matching experiment described above can be represented by an occupancy model.**
>
> (b)   **What is the probability that a person would obtain a perfect match by guessing?**

The ESP experiment is just one of many and varied occurrences of a long-established **matching problem.** This type of problem was first put forward in 1708 by Pierre Remond de Montmort (1678-1719) in his analysis of a gambling game called Treize.

Example 4

Three commuters dressed in pin-stripe suits and bowler hats arrive at their railway destination. They are greeted by gusts of wind which disperse their hats and a customer-caring British Rail porter collects them on a trolley. The commuters, who by this time are late for work, rush to the trolley, grab a hat at random and proceed to the wrath of their employers.

What is the probability that no commuter gets his own hat?

Solution

Call the commuters a, b, and c. Possible outcomes of the experiment of grabbing a hat at random can be presented as follows:

   (a, b, c) with each letter in its natural position means that a obtained
   his own hat as did b and c;

   (a, c, b) means that a chose his own hat, but b took c's hat and c
   took b's.

> **What does (c, a, b) mean?**

There are $3! = 6$ possibilities:

   $\{ (a, b, c), (a, c, b), (b, a, c), (b, c, a), (c, a, b), (c, b, a) \}$

No letter is in its 'correct' rank order position in 2 out of the 6 permutations, namely :

   (b, c, a) and (c, a, b).

The probability of no one getting his own hat is $\frac{2}{6} = \frac{1}{3}$.

> **A permutation which leaves no letter in its original position is referred to as a *derangement*.**

> **(a)** If four commuters choose their hats at random, find the probability of a derangement.
>
> **(b)** What is the probability that at least one commuter gets his own hat?

Some probabilities associated with the matching problem are relatively easy to find.

Example 5

Each of n people at a table in a fast-food restaurant orders a different sandwich but the orders are delivered at random.

(a) What is the probability that each person gets the correct sandwich?

(b) What is the probability that exactly $n - 1$ people are served their correct sandwiches?

Solution

(a) Since only one out of the $n!$ possible permutations agrees with the original order, the probability that each person gets the correct sandwich is

$$\frac{1}{n!}.$$

(b) The probability that **exactly** $n - 1$ people are served their correct sandwiches is 0. If $n - 1$ people get their correct orders, then the remaining person must receive the correct order as well.

Exercise 2

1. A magazine prints the photographs of four film stars and a picture of each star when he/she was a baby. Readers are asked to match the baby with the star. What is the probability that a reader, by purely random matching of the pictures, gets at least three right?

2. An encyclopaedia consisting of 6 volumes is kept on a library shelf with the volumes in correct numerical order, that is, with volume 1 on the left, volume 2 next, and so on. The volumes are all taken down for cleaning and are replaced on the shelf in random order. Calculate the respective probabilities for finding exactly 6, 5 and 4 volumes in their correct positions.

3. Generalise question 2 to the case of n volumes and determine the respective probabilities for finding exactly n, $n - 1$ and $n - 2$ volumes in their correct positions.

3.4 Recurrence relations

Tossing coins, rolling dice, drawing tokens from urns and allocating tokens to boxes are not simply intellectual games; they have 'real world' relevance in that they provide devices for modelling realistic phenomena. However, some problems are not amenable to elementary counting methods as you will see for yourself if you attempt to find the probability of a derangement of a large number of hats in the matching example discussed earlier. The remaining sections of this chapter consider some further methods for tackling such problems.

Example 6

You repeatedly toss a coin and score 1 point for each 'head' that appears and 2 for each 'tail'. What is the probability that at some stage your total score is precisely n ?

Solution

Let p_n = P(total becomes n). It is quite easy to write down the values of p_n for small n. You can attain a total of 1 only if the first toss results in a head. So $p_1 = \frac{1}{2}$.

Similarly, a total of 2 will occur only if the first toss results in a tail, or if the first is a head and the second toss is also a head. So $p_2 = \frac{1}{2} + \frac{1}{2} \times \frac{1}{2} = \frac{3}{4}$.

For large values of n such reasoning becomes extremely laborious. However, you can make progress by using the following argument:

If a score of n is achieved, then precisely one of the following has occurred:

- a total of $n - 1$ is reached and then a H is thrown;
- a total of $n - 2$ is reached and then a T is thrown;

So $p_n = p_{n-1} \times \frac{1}{2} + p_{n-2} \times \frac{1}{2}$

> **Explain how the above equation is obtained.**

A relationship such as

$$p_n = \frac{1}{2}(p_{n-1} + p_{n-2})$$

where the nth term is linked to previous terms is known as a **recurrence relation**.

The first two probabilities in the sequence,

$$p_1 = \frac{1}{2} \quad \text{and} \quad p_2 = \frac{3}{4},$$

are needed to set the recurrence process in motion and are called the **initial conditions**.

The recurrence relation together with the initial conditions can be used to generate the other probabilities $p_3, p_4, \ldots$ For example,

$$p_3 = \frac{1}{2}(p_2 + p_1) = \frac{5}{8}$$

> **Check the above value for p_3 and find p_4 and p_5.**
>
> **Write a program for a calculator or computer to generate the probabilities p_n.**

The use of recurrence relations can be extended to a variety of other problems.

Example 7

If p_n is the probability that an odd number of sixes is obtained when n dice are thrown, obtain a recurrence relation for p_n.

Solution

A similar approach to that of Example 6 is used:

- the event is expressed as the union of two disjoint events;

- the laws of probability are then applied.

For an odd number of sixes to be thrown with n dice, then either:

- $n-1$ dice yield an odd number of sixes and then a non-six is thrown;

- $n-1$ dice yield an even number of sixes and then a six is thrown.

So $p_n = p_{n-1} \times \frac{5}{6} + (1 - p_{n-1}) \times \frac{1}{6}$

$$\Rightarrow p_n = \frac{1}{6} + \frac{2}{3}p_{n-1}$$

> (a) **Carefully explain how the recurrence relation is obtained.**
>
> (b) **Calculate p_1 and p_2 from first principles. Check that you obtain the same answers when applying the recurrence relation with the initial condition $p_0 = 0$.**

You will recall that the derangement probabilities associated with the matching problem are rather difficult to calculate by direct counting. However, recurrence relations can be used to lead neatly to the required results.

TASKSHEET 2E - *Derangement probabilities*

Exercise 3

1. A coin is tossed until heads appears for the first time. If p_k is the probability that heads appears for the first time at toss k, find a recurrence relation for p_k and a suitable initial condition. Derive an explicit expression for p_k.

2. Let p_k be the probability that an even number of heads is obtained when a coin is tossed k times.

   Find a recurrence relation for p_k, $k \geq 1$. Hence find an explicit expression for p_k.

3. Recurrence relations can be derived for counts as well as probabilities. Let C_n denote the number of ways of tossing a coin n times without the appearance of any successive heads. The C_n arrangements can be divided into two mutually exclusive groups

   • those in which the first $n - 1$ tosses contain no successive heads and the nth toss is tails;

   • those arrangements in which the first $n - 2$ tosses contain no successive heads, the $(n - 1)$th toss is tails and the nth toss is heads.

   (a) Write down a recurrence relation and initial conditions for C_n. What well-known sequence of numbers does this recurrence relation generate?

   (b) What is the probability that there are no successive heads in the n tosses of the coin?

   (c) What is the probability of obtaining at least two successive heads in n tosses of the coin?

4E. A biased coin with probability of heads equal to p, $0 < p < 1$, is tossed n times. Let p_n be the probability that there are no successive heads in the n tosses. Derive a recurrence relation for p_n together with suitable initial conditions.

3.5 Reasoning by renewal

If an experiment involves an infinite sequence of trials, it is sometimes useful to examine what happens at the first trial and then to view the experiment as a whole from that point onwards and see if it **renews** itself. Recurrence relations and 'reasoning by renewal' are powerful tools for solving realistic and quite complex probability problems in a few easy stages. The following example initially looks difficult and intractable, but viewing it as a renewal problem leads to a solution involving only a few lines of mathematics.

Example 8

A coin is tossed successively. What is the probability that a **run** of two heads (HH) occurs before a run of three tails (TTT)?

Let p_H = P(run of HH precedes a run of TTT when the first toss is a H)
and p_T = P(run of HH precedes a run of TTT when the first toss is a T)

The following diagram depicts the crucial role of the first toss in the experiment.

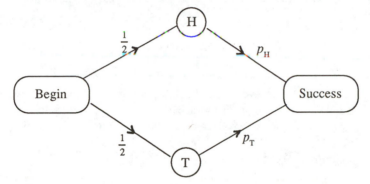

The probability p of success is given by

$$p = \frac{1}{2} p_H + \frac{1}{2} p_T \quad ①$$

To investigate the 'p_H' branch of the above diagram, assume the outcome of the first toss is a head. Taking this as your starting point, you can then 'reason by renewal' as follows: if the next toss is a head then the process stops as you have a run of HH before TTT; if the next toss is a tail, you renew the process from this point and ask what is the probability of success the first toss is a tail. The diagram below clarifies this reasoning

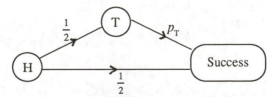

and yields the equation:

$$p_H = \frac{1}{2} + \frac{1}{2} p_T \quad ②$$

Use a similar method to investigate the p_T branch and show that

$$p_T = \frac{1}{2}p_H + \frac{1}{4}p_H = \frac{3}{4}p_H \quad \text{\textcircled{3}}$$

The equations ①, ② and ③ can be solved easily to obtain

$$p_H = \frac{4}{5}, \quad p_T = \frac{3}{5} \quad \text{and} \quad p = \frac{7}{10}.$$

Exercise 4

1. (a) Cheryl and Diane repeatedly throw a fair die in succession. The winner is the player who first throws a six. Use a 'renewal' type diagram and equation to find their respective probabilities of winning.

   (b) Solve the problem of part (a) by the alternative method of calculating the probabilities that Cheryl wins on the first throw, on the third throw, on the fifth throw, etc. and then summing all these probabilities.

2. The game of squash consists of a sequence of rallies. Whoever wins a rally serves in the next rally. To win a point you must win a rally for which you were the server.

   Assume that you have probability p of winning any particular rally. Let p_n be the probability that you reach a score of $n - 0$ against your opponent if you serve first. Use 'reasoning by renewal' to obtain the relations

   $$p_n = p_{n-1}p_1$$

   $$p_1 = p + p(1-p)p_1$$

   Hence find the probability of winning a game $9 - 0$ against an evenly matched opponent given that you serve first.

3. In a game, a counter is moved forward repeatedly a number of squares along a track according to the throws of a fair die. p_n is the probability that the counter occupies the nth square at some stage of the game.

   (a) Show by means of reasoning from the result of the first throw and a suitable 'renewal' diagram, that

   $$p_n = \frac{1}{6}(p_{n-1} + p_{n-2} + p_{n-3} + p_{n-4} + p_{n-5} + p_{n-6})$$

   for all $n > 0$.

   (b) What are the values of p_0 and p_n, $n < 0$?

   (c) Use a calculator or a computer program to find the numerical values of p_n for $n = 1, 2, 3, ..., 20$. What can you say about the behaviour of p_n for large n?

58

3.6 Random walks

In 1657 Christianus Huygens published a treatise on probability which contained the following exercise:

> *A and B take each twelve counters and play with three dice*
> *on this condition, that if 11 is thrown A gives a counter to B,*
> *and if 14 is thrown B gives a counter to A; and he wins the*
> *game who first obtains all the counters. Show that A's*
> *chance is to B's as 244140625 is to 282429536481.*

If *A* and *B* play with monetary units instead of counters, then the winner is the player who 'ruins' his opponent. This is the first reference to what is now known as the **gambler's ruin** problem.

James Bernoulli in his *Ars Conjectandi* (1713) solved this problem and generalised the result.

 TASKSHEET 3 - *Gamblers's ruin*

The gambler's ruin problem can be represented as a **random walk** problem.

Consider the interval [0, *a*] on the real line where *a* is an integer. A particle is placed at position *n* (also an integer) on the line where $0 < n < a$.

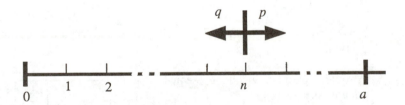

With probability *p*, $0 < p < 1$, the particle moves one unit to the right; with probability $q = 1 - p$, it moves one unit to the left. This experiment is repeated until the particle hits a boundary point (0 or *a*) in which case it remains there forever. This is an example of a **one-dimensional walk with two absorbing barriers.**

Example 9

A particle is placed at position *n* (a positive integer) on the real line. A biased coin is tossed. The probability of heads is *p*, $0 < p < 1$, and the probability of tails is $q = 1 - p$. If heads is obtained the particle moves two units to the right; if tails then it moves one unit to the left. This experiment is repeated until the particle hits the boundary point 0 in which case it remains there forever. What type of random walk is this? Find a recurrence relation for p_n, the probability that the particle eventually reaches 0 when starting from position *n*.

Solution

The following diagram highlights the fact that this is a **one-dimensional random walk with one absorbing barrier** at 0.

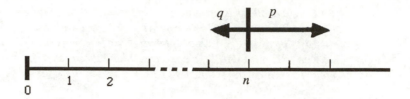

Using straightforward 'reasoning by renewal' leads to the following formulation of the recurrence relation for p_n: if tails occurs (with probability q) the particle will go to position $n-1$ and the process will renew itself from that point; if heads occurs (with probability p) the particle will go to position $n+2$ and the process will repeat itself from there. So

$$p_n = qp_{n-1} + pp_{n+2}, \text{ for } n \geq 1.$$

Exercise 5

1. Explain how the gambler's ruin problem can be represented by a random walk with two absorption barriers.

2. A fair die is repeatedly thrown. Find the probability that a six is obtained before three 'non-sixes'. Explain how this problem could be formulated as a random walk problem.

3. Solve Huygens' original gambler's ruin problem given at the beginning of this section.

4. A square board is divided into 9 equal squares as shown

1	2	3
4	5	6
7	8	9

A counter is placed on one of the squares. It is repeatedly moved randomly by one square in one of the four possible horizontal and vertical directions until it moves off the board. Let p_n be the probability that a counter starting on square n moves off the board in a horizontal direction.

(a) Explain why $p_1 = p_3 = p_5 = p_7 = p_9 = \frac{1}{2}$.

(b) Explain why $p_2 = p_8$, $p_4 = p_6$ and $p_2 = 1 - p_4$.

(c) Find p_2.

3.7   Solving recurrence relations

You have seen how useful recurrence relations can be in solving probability problems. General methods have been developed for solving some types of recurrence relations and, in particular, there is a simple method for solving equations such as

$$q_n = \frac{1}{6}(q_{n-1} + q_{n-2} + q_{n-5})$$

which only involve constant multiples of terms of the sequence.

> **Which of the following recurrence relations involve only constant multiples of terms of the sequence?**
>
> (a) $p_{n+1} - 2p_n = 0$
>
> (b) $q_n = q_{n-1}^2$
>
> (c) $r_n = nr_{n-1}$
>
> (d) $f_{n+2} = f_{n+1} + f_n$

The simplest form of recurrence relation of this type involves just two successive terms of the sequence and can be solved by inspection.

Consider the relation $u_{n+1} - \frac{1}{2}u_n = 0$.   Then $u_2 = \frac{1}{2}u_1$, $u_3 = \frac{1}{2}u_2 = \left(\frac{1}{2}\right)^2 u_1$, $u_4 = \frac{1}{2}u_3 = \left(\frac{1}{2}\right)^3 u_1$ and so on. The general solution is given by

$$u_n = A\left(\frac{1}{2}\right)^n.$$

The value of A can be found using any initial condition(s). For example, if $u_1 = 3$ then substituting $n = 1$ in the equation for the general solution,

$$3 = A\left(\frac{1}{2}\right) \Rightarrow A = 6$$

So $u_n = 6\left(\frac{1}{2}\right)^n$.

The method can be extended to recurrence relations which also have a constant term, such as

$$u_{n+1} - \frac{1}{2}u_n = 2, \quad u_1 = 3$$

A simple solution in which all the terms are the same can be found by putting each term equal to a constant c.

$$c - \frac{1}{2}c = 2 \Rightarrow c = 4.$$

The general solution can be found by adding this particular solution to the general solution of $u_{n+1} - \frac{1}{2}u_n = 0$.

(a)   Check that $u_n = A \left(\frac{1}{2}\right)^n + 4$ satisfies

$$u_{n+1} - \frac{1}{2} u_n = 2.$$

(b)   Given that $u_1 = 3$, find A.

In general, recurrence relations of the form $au_n + bu_{n+1} + cu_{n+2} + \ldots = 0$, $(a, b, c \ldots$ constant), are called **linear recurrence relations.** Such recurrence relations have solutions of the form

$$A \lambda_1^n + B \lambda_2^n + \ldots$$

The method of solution is illustrated by Examples 10 and 11.

Example 10

Solve $f_{n+2} = f_{n+1} + f_n$, where $f_0 = 0, f_1 = 1$.

Solution

Let $f_n = \lambda^n$, then $\lambda^{n+2} = \lambda^{n+1} + \lambda^n$

$\Rightarrow \lambda^2 - \lambda - 1 = 0$ (assuming $\lambda \neq 0$)

$\Rightarrow \lambda = \frac{1 \pm \sqrt{5}}{2}$

The general solution is $f_n = A \left(\frac{1+\sqrt{5}}{2}\right)^n + B \left(\frac{1-\sqrt{5}}{2}\right)^n$

The initial conditions are used to find A and B:

$n = 0:\ 0 = A + B$

$n = 1:\ 1 = A \left(\frac{1+\sqrt{5}}{2}\right) + B \left(\frac{1-\sqrt{5}}{2}\right) = (A - B) \frac{\sqrt{5}}{2}$

From these two equations, $A = \frac{1}{\sqrt{5}}$ and $B = -\frac{1}{\sqrt{5}}$.

$$f_n = \frac{1}{\sqrt{5}} \left(\frac{1+\sqrt{5}}{2}\right)^n - \frac{1}{\sqrt{5}} \left(\frac{1-\sqrt{5}}{2}\right)^n.$$

Use a similar method to find the general solution of the relation

$$u_{n+2} - 3u_{n+1} - 2u_n = 0.$$

Example 11

Solve $u_{n+1} - \frac{1}{2} u_n = \frac{1}{8}$, $u_1 = \frac{1}{2}$

Solution

The equation $u_{n+1} - \frac{1}{2} u_n = 0$ has solution $u_n = A \left(\frac{1}{2}\right)^n$.

A particular solution of $u_{n+1} - \frac{1}{2} n_n = \frac{1}{8}$ can be found by putting each term u_i equal to a constant c. Then

$$c - \frac{1}{2} c = \frac{1}{8} \Rightarrow c = \frac{1}{4}.$$

The general solution is then found by adding c to $A \left(\frac{1}{2}\right)^n$

$$u_n = A \left(\frac{1}{2}\right)^n + \frac{1}{4}$$

$$n = 1 : \frac{1}{2} = A \times \frac{1}{2} + \frac{1}{4} \Rightarrow A = \frac{1}{2}$$

$$u_n = \frac{1}{2} \left(\frac{1}{2}\right)^n + \frac{1}{4} = \left(\frac{1}{2}\right)^{n+1} + \frac{1}{4}$$

> **Use the same method to solve**
>
> $$u_{n+1} - \frac{1}{3} u_n = 1, \; u_1 = 2$$

The general method of solution of linear recurrence relations is

- find a general solution of the equation omitting any constant term;
- if necessary, find a particular solution by, for example, taking each member of the sequence to be a constant c;
- add the above solutions;
- use the initial condition(s) to find any constant(s).

Exercise 6

1. Suppose that each day is classified as being either wet or dry. Suppose further that the probability the weather changes from one day to the next is $\frac{1}{4}$. Let p_n be the probability that the nth day is dry.

    (a) Prove that $p_n - \frac{1}{2} p_{n-1} - \frac{1}{4} = 0$.

    (b) Find p_n if the first day is dry.

    (c) Find p_n if the first day is wet.

    (d) Comment on what happens to your answers to (b) and (c) as n becomes very large.

2.   A die is placed on a flat table with the number 6 uppermost. Successive moves of the die involve rotating it through $90°$ about a randomly chosen edge in contact with the table. Let p_n denote the probability that a 1 or 6 is uppermost after n moves.

(a)   Explain why $p_0 = 1$ and $p_1 = 0$.

(b)   Prove that $p_{n+1} = \frac{1}{2}(1 - p_n)$. Hence find p_n.

(c)   What is the probability that the 6 is uppermost after n moves?

3E.   The gambler's ruin recurrence relation is

$$pr_{n+1} - r_n + qr_{n-1} = 0, \quad r_0 = 1, \quad r_a = 0,$$

where $p + q = 1$. Find the general solution of this recurrence relation. Hence, assuming $p \neq \frac{1}{2}$, obtain the solution

$$r_n = \frac{\left(\frac{q}{p}\right)^a - \left(\frac{q}{p}\right)^n}{\left(\frac{q}{p}\right)^a - 1}.$$

After working through this chapter you should:

1.   be able to solve a variety of counting questions by modelling them as occupancy problems;

2.   understand what is meant by a derangement and be able to calculate the probability of a given derangement;

3.   understand how to use recurrence relations and renewal in simplifying probability questions;

4.   understand what is meant by gambler's ruin and random walk problems;

5.   know how to solve simple recurrence relations.

Birthdays and birthmates

The birthday problem

1. Consider a group of three students. Each student's name is written on a separate ticket. There are five boxes numbered 1 to 5 respectively and you allocate the three tickets at random to the boxes so that there is no restriction on the number of tickets each box may contain.

    (a) How many possible allocations are there of student names to boxes?

    (b) How many possible allocations are there such that each box contains no more than one ticket?

    (c) What is the probability that at least two tickets appear in the same box?

2. Assume that a year consists of 365 days. A class contains r students where $r \leq 365$.

    (a) What is the probability that at least two students have the same birthday? Formulate the problem as an occupancy model before answering the question.

    (b) What do you intuitively feel the smallest value of r should be so that the probability in part (a) is at least 0.5?

    (c) For students in your own class, discover whether there is a birthday match. Note the size of your class.

3. If $Q_j = \dfrac{365 \times 364 \times (365 - j + 1)}{365^j}$ for $j = 1, 2, ..., r$, show that

    $$Q_j = Q_{j-1} \times \frac{(365 - j + 1)}{365}$$

    Use this result and a calculator or a computer program to generate the probability calculated in question 2(a) for various values of r. For what value of r does the probability of at least two matching birthdays just exceed 0.5? Compare this answer with your intuitive estimate in question 2(b).

(continued)

The birthmate problem

4.   Consider a group of three students. Each student's name is written on a separate ticket. There are five boxes numbered 1 to 5 respectively and you allocate the three tickets at random to the boxes so that there is no restriction on the number of tickets each box may contain. What is the probability that box number 1 contains at least one token?

5.   Repeat question 4 for 365 boxes and r students. Show that the required probability is

$$1 - \frac{364^r}{365^r}$$

6.   (a)   Assume that a year consists of 365 days and that your class contains r students. What is the probability that at least one other student has the same birthday as yours, i.e. is your **birthmate**? Formulate the problem as an occupancy model before answering the question.

        (b)   What do you intuitively feel the smallest value of r should be so that the probability in part (a) is at least 0.5?

        (c)   Determine whether you have at least one birthmate in your own class. Note the size of your class.

7.   If

$$Q_j = \frac{364^j}{365^j}$$

        for $j = 1, 2, ..., r$, show that

$$Q_j = Q_{j-1} \times \frac{364}{365}.$$

        Use this result and a calculator or computer program to generate the probability calculated in question 6(a) for various values of r. For what value of r does the probability of at least one birthmate just exceed 0.5? Compare this answer with your intuitive estimate.

8.   Describe how occupancy models allow you to distinguish the essential differences between the birthday and birthmate problems.

Derangement probabilities

At a party n people check their hats. On leaving (in a befuddled state) each person takes a hat at random.

1.   Complete the following table for small values of n.

n	1	2	3	4
Number of derangements, d_n	0	1		
Total number of arrangements	1	2!	3!	4!
Probability of a derangement, p_n				

The direct approach to finding the probability of a derangement is to count all permutations of hats which leave no person with their own hat and then to consider this number as a proportion of the total number of possible permutations. Even for $n = 5$ the counting processes looks formidable.

To determine d_5, assume that the party-goers are Armand, Brian, Cheryl, Diane and Elaine. A recurrence relation can be used to solve this problem providing a good method of splitting up the derangements can be found.

The trick is to split the derangements into

•   those where A swaps hats with another person;

•   those where A has another person's hat but that person does **not** have A's.

2.   (a)   Explain why there are d_3 derangements involving A and B swapping hats. Hence show that there are $4 \times d_3$ derangements where A swaps hats with another person.

        (b)   Explain why there are $4 \times d_4$ derangements such that A does not swap hats with another person.

3.   Use your answers to question 2 to determine d_5.

4.   Try to extend the above argument to $d_6, d_7 \ldots$ Can you find a general recurrence relation for d_n?

(continued)

67

A general recurrence relation for derangements is given by $d_n = (n-1) \times d_{n-1} + (n-1) \times d_{n-2}$.

5.   (a)   Explain the general recurrence relation.

       (b)   Use this relation to show that

$$p_n - p_{n-1} = -\frac{1}{n}\,(p_{n-1} - p_{n-2})$$

       (c)   Write down the value of $p_2 - p_1$. Hence find $p_3 - p_2, p_4 - p_3, p_5 - p_4, \ldots$

6.   By writing p_n as

$$p_1 + (p_2 - p_1) + (p_3 - p_2) + \ldots + (p_{n-1} - p_{n-2}) + (p_n - p_{n-1})$$

show that the general form of the probability of a derangement of n hats is

$$p_n = \frac{1}{0!} - \frac{1}{1!} + \frac{1}{2!} - \ldots + (-1)^n \frac{1}{n!}$$

7.   Do you recognise the series expansion for p_n?

Investigate the sum of the series using a calculator or computer program. What can you deduce about the probability of a derangement for moderately large values of n?

Gambler's ruin

The general problem can be stated as a game:

> 'Armand starts with capital n units and his opponent Cheryl starts with capital $a - n$, the total 'stake' being a units. At each play of the game Armand wins one unit from Cheryl with probability p or loses one unit to Cheryl with probability q where $p + q = 1$. The game continues until one of the players is 'ruined'. What is the probability that Armand is eventually ruined?'

The answer to the question is clearly going to depend on n. If r_n is the probability that Armand is ruined starting with a capital of n units, then the following diagram highlights the role that 'reasoning by renewal' and recurrence relations are going to play in the solution of the problem.

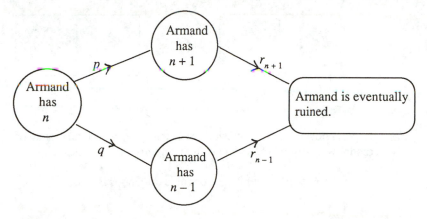

After the first play Armand will either have increased his capital to $n + 1$ with probability p or decreased it to $n - 1$ with probability $1 - p = q$. In each of these cases you can view the problem anew and ask what is the probability that he is ultimately ruined.

1. Show that the recurrence relation for r_n is $r_n = pr_{n+1} + qr_{n-1}$, for $1 \le n \le a - 1$.

2. Explain the 'boundary' conditions: $r_0 = 1$, $r_a = 0$.

3. In the case $p = q = \frac{1}{2}$, show that $r_n = \frac{a-n}{a}$ satisfies the recurrence relation and initial conditions. Can you give an intuitive interpretation of this solution?

4. If $p \ne q$, show that
$$r_n = \frac{\left(\frac{q}{p}\right)^a - \left(\frac{q}{p}\right)^n}{\left(\frac{q}{p}\right)^a - 1}$$
satisfies the recurrence relation.

1. Find the probability that in six throws with a fair die all six faces occur. Describe this problem with an occupancy model.

2. In a dentist's waiting room 6 chairs are arranged in a row. If there are 4 patients in the waiting room, in how many ways can they be distributed among the chairs? What is the probability that all occupied chairs are adjacent?

3. A domino is a rectangular wooden block with two sections. Each section of a domino displays 1, 2, 3, 4, 5 or 6 spots or is blank. Since the sections of a domino are indistinguishable, the dominoes

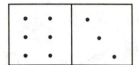 and

are the same.

(a) Explain how each domino can be represented by a particular state of an occupancy model with seven boxes and two indistinguishable tokens.

(b) Hence show that the number of possible dominoes is

$$\binom{7}{2} + 7 = 28.$$

(c) 28 is also equal to $\binom{8}{2}$. Can you find an occupancy model of type 1 with 8 boxes and two tokens which could be used to represent all the possible dominoes?

4. The game of Treize examined by Montmort is played with a deck of thirteen cards consisting of an ace (1), nine numerals (2 to 10), jack (11), queen (12) and king (13). The banker shuffles the cards and turns up the thirteen cards one after the other. As he turns up the cards he calls out 1, 2, ... , 13. If in this sequence there is a coincidence in the turning up of the thirteen cards, for example, if an ace is the first card to be turned up or a two turns up when the banker has called two, the banker wins. Otherwise the player wins.

Montmort proposed the problem of determining the probability that the banker wins, that is, the probability of at least one coincidence. Find this probability.

(continued)

5. Three children of equal chess playing ability take it in turns to play chess in pairs according to the rule that the loser always sits out the next game.

(a) Given that Clare wins the first game let p be the probability that she is the first child to win two successive games.

Prove that $p = \dfrac{1}{2} + \dfrac{1}{8}p$.

(b) Given that Clare does not play in the first game, show that the probability that Ahmed is the first to win two successive games is

$$\frac{1}{2}p + \frac{1}{8}p$$

and find this probability.

6. A tetrahedron with faces numbered 1, 2, 3, 4 is placed on a table. Each move of the tetrahedron consists of rotating it about a randomly chosen edge on the table until a new face is in contact with the table. Let p_n denote the probability that face 1 is in contact with the table after n moves.

(a) Show that $p_{n+1} = \dfrac{1}{3} - \dfrac{1}{3}p_n$.

(b) Find p_n if face 1 is initially in contact with the table.

(c) What happens to p_n when n becomes very large? Comment on your answer.

7. A square board is divided into 9 smaller squares. A counter is placed at random on one of the squares and is then moved n times remaining on the board throughout. Each move is by one square horizontally or vertically, all possible moves being equally likely.

Let c_n, e_n, m_n respectively be the probabilities of the counter being on a **particular** corner, edge or middle square after n moves.

Probabilities
after 3 moves:

c_3	e_3	c_3
e_3	m_3	e_3
c_3	e_3	c_3

(a) Explain why $4c_n + 4e_n + m_n = 1$ for all n.

(b) Show that $c_n = \dfrac{2}{3}e_{n-1}$. Find two similar expressions for e_n and m_n.

(c) Find a recurrence relation for e_n. State the values of c_0, e_0 and m_0 and solve the recurrence relation for e_n.

4 Sequences of random events

4.1 Will it rain tomorrow?

In January - April 1990 in Matlock, Derbyshire the days followed this pattern (*W* - wet, *D* - Dry).

WWDDW   WWDDW   DDWDW   WDDWD   DWWWW   WWWWW
WWWWD   DDWWD   WWWWW   WWDWD   WWWDD   WWWWW
WDDDD   DDDWD   DWWDD   DDDWD   WDWWD   DDDDD
DDWWD   DDDDD   DDDDD   DWWWW   WDDDD   DWDDD

A first analysis reveals that there were 57 wet days and 63 dry days, the sort of roughly equal numbers you might expect in the Midlands at this time of year.

> **Would you expect a similar pattern (of *H*'s and *T*'s) for 120 tosses of a coin? Explain your answer.**

The analysis may be taken further by asking questions of the type:

> How often is a wet day followed by another wet day?

As you can check, this table is formed.

		Yesterday		
		W	*D*	
Today	*W*	37	19	Total 56
	D	20	43	Total 63
	Totals	57	62	

> **Relate the row and column totals to the numbers of wet and dry days.**

72

37 out of 57 wet days are followed by a wet day and so $P(W \mid W) = \frac{37}{57} \approx 0.65$

Find $P(D \mid D)$.

A table of conditional probabilites can be obtained.

		Yesterday	
		W	D
Today	W	0.65	0.31
	D	0.35	0.69

Assume (quite unjustifiably!) that the table defines conditional probabilities for the weather at this time of year. The probability of passing from W to D is 0.35, which may be represented:

Continuing in this way you can build up a **transition diagram:**

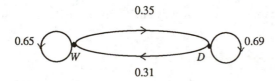

Example 1

Given that 1 March is wet, find the probability that 4 March will be wet

Solution

The possibilities can be represented by the following diagram:

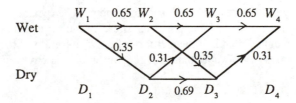

73

The possible 'routes' from W_1 (wet on 1 March) to W_4 (wet on 4 March) are

$$
\begin{aligned}
W_1 &- W_2 - W_3 - W_4 , \\
W_1 &- W_2 - D_3 - W_4 , \\
W_1 &- D_2 - W_3 - W_4 , \\
W_1 &- D_2 - D_3 - W_4 .
\end{aligned}
$$

So the required probability is

$$(0.65)^3 + (0.65)(0.31)(0.35) \times 2 + (0.35)(0.69)(0.31) = 0.49$$

A random sequence of trials in which

- **probabilities are conditional only on the outcome in the trial immediately preceding,**

- **conditional probabilities of each possible outcome are fixed**

is called a Markov sequence or Markov chain

Such sequences are named after the Russian mathematician Andrei Markov (1856 - 1922).

Bernoulli and Markov sequences are both examples of **stochastic processes** (Greek: **stochos** - a guess), in which the outcome of each trial is uncertain but randomly determined by fixed probabilities. Whether the workings of Nature are stochastic is an open philosophical question. Einstein, for example, inclined to the determinist view and delivered the famous opinion 'God does not play dice'when confronted by Heisenberg's Uncertainty Principle. Whether chance plays a part in natural occurrences or not, calculations based upon probabilities are used in modelling all kinds of natural phenomena, ranging from subatomic to meteorological and astronomical.

You might say that a Bernoulli trial is a 'zero memory' experiment – the outcome is independent of the results of any previous trials. In the same kind of language a Markov trial would depend on the memory of one generation. Stochastic processes involving the memory of more than one generation can be envisaged.

Exercise 1

1. Invent a story to explain this transition diagram.

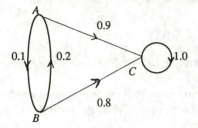

2. You will recall the transition diagram for Matlock weather.

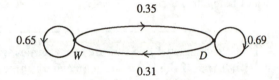

   Given that 1 March is wet calculate the probability that 4 March will be dry.

   How can you check your answer simply?

3. A ferret is able to move between three interconnected chambers.

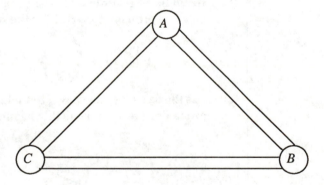

   The ferret starts in chamber A and is twice as likely to change chambers in a clockwise direction as in an anti-clockwise direction. Show that after four changes of chamber the ferret is most likely to be in chamber C.

4.2　Stochastic matrices

For a Markov process, it can be useful to consider the table of conditional probabilities as a matrix. For the weather in Matlock you would have the matrix

$$\begin{pmatrix} P(W \mid W) & P(W \mid D) \\ P(D \mid W) & P(D \mid D) \end{pmatrix} = \begin{pmatrix} 0.65 & 0.31 \\ 0.35 & 0.69 \end{pmatrix}$$

Such a matrix of probabilities is called a **stochastic matrix.**

The probabilities of different outcomes at a particular stage can also be written in matrix form as an **outcome probability vector.** For the weather in Matlock, the vector

$$\begin{pmatrix} P(W) \\ P(D) \end{pmatrix} = \begin{pmatrix} 0.4 \\ 0.6 \end{pmatrix}$$

would indicate that the weather on a particular day had probability 0.4 of being wet. and probability 0.6 of being dry.

In a sequence of five-minute chess games with Alan, Beryl finds that if she has won the previous game she wins on three-quarters of occasions, whereas if she has lost previously there is only an even chance of her winning. The chance of a draw is negligible.

(a)　Write down the stochastic matrix for Beryl's chess games.

(b)　Given that Beryl wins the first game, show that the outcome probability vector for the second game is

$$\begin{pmatrix} P(W) \\ P(L) \end{pmatrix} = \begin{pmatrix} \frac{3}{4} \\ \frac{1}{4} \end{pmatrix}$$

(c)　Use the tree diagram shown to find the outcome probability vector for the third game.

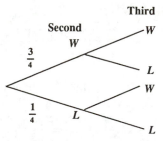

(d)　By considering your answer to (c), describe how the elements of the stochastic matrix and the outcome probability vector for one game can be used to find the outcome probability vector for the next game.

(e)　Hence find the outcome probability vector for the fourth game.

The process of using the stochastic matrix and the outcome probability vector for one stage to find the outcome probability vector for the next stage is a particular example of a general process called matrix multiplication. Straightforward practice of this process can be found on Tasksheet 1S.

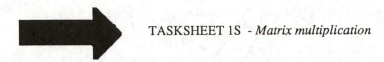

TASKSHEET 1S - *Matrix multiplication*

For the example of the weather in Matlock, the calculation is as follows:

$$\begin{array}{cc} \text{Next day} & \qquad\qquad \text{One day} \end{array}$$

$$\begin{pmatrix} P(W) \\ P(D) \end{pmatrix} = \begin{pmatrix} 0.65 & 0.31 \\ 0.35 & 0.69 \end{pmatrix} \begin{pmatrix} 0.4 \\ 0.6 \end{pmatrix}$$

$$= \begin{pmatrix} 0.65 \times 0.4 + 0.31 \times 0.6 \\ 0.35 \times 0.4 + 0.69 \times 0.6 \end{pmatrix}$$

$$\approx \begin{pmatrix} 0.45 \\ 0.55 \end{pmatrix}$$

So, if the probability that a day is wet is 0.4 then the probability that the next day will be wet is 0.45.

You should note that the elements in the columns of any stochastic matrix always add up to 1 (as do the elements of an outcome vector).

$$\begin{pmatrix} 0.65 & 0.31 \\ 0.35 & 0.69 \end{pmatrix}$$

A stochastic matrix is a square matrix with non-negative entries such that the sum of the entries in any column is 1.

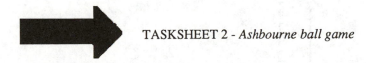

TASKSHEET 2 - *Ashbourne ball game*

Example 2

A family estimates that the transition diagram for the main annual holiday looks like this.

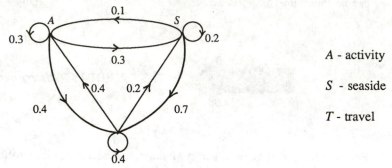

A - activity

S - seaside

T - travel

In 1992 the family have a seaside holiday. Find the probabilities of the three types of holiday in 1994.

Solution

The transition matrix is

$$
\begin{array}{c}
 \\
\text{next} \\
\text{year}
\end{array}
\begin{array}{cc}
 & \begin{array}{ccc} & \text{this year} & \\ A & S & T \end{array} \\
\begin{array}{c} A \\ S \\ T \end{array} &
\left[\begin{array}{ccc}
0.3 & 0.1 & 0.4 \\
0.3 & 0.2 & 0.2 \\
0.4 & 0.7 & 0.4
\end{array} \right] = \mathbf{M}
\end{array}
$$

and the initial outcome probability vector is $\begin{bmatrix} 0 \\ 1 \\ 0 \end{bmatrix} = \mathbf{V}_0$

The required probability vector is $\mathbf{V}_2 = \mathbf{M}^2 \mathbf{V}_0$

$$
\mathbf{M}^2 = \begin{bmatrix}
0.09 + 0.03 + 0.16 & 0.03 + 0.02 + 0.28 & 0.12 + 0.02 + 0.16 \\
0.09 + 0.06 + 0.08 & 0.03 + 0.04 + 0.14 & 0.12 + 0.04 + 0.08 \\
0.12 + 0.21 + 0.16 & 0.04 + 0.14 + 0.28 & 0.16 + 0.14 + 0.16
\end{bmatrix}
$$

$$
= \begin{bmatrix}
0.28 & 0.33 & 0.30 \\
0.23 & 0.21 & 0.24 \\
0.49 & 0.46 & 0.46
\end{bmatrix}
$$

$$
\mathbf{M}^2 \mathbf{V}_0 = \begin{bmatrix} 0.33 \\ 0.21 \\ 0.46 \end{bmatrix}
$$

So the probabilities are: activity 0.33, seaside 0.21, travel 0.46.

(a)   **Work Example 2 using the alternative method of calculating $V_1 = MV_0$, then $V_2 = MV_1$.**

(b)   **Note that the columns of M^2 are almost alike. What do you deduce?**

Exercise 2

1.   The transition diagram for probabilities of wins in the Oxford - Cambridge boat race is approximately

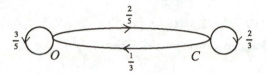

(a)   Write down the probability $P(C_{k+1} \mid 0_k)$.

(b)   Write down the transition matrix.

(c)   If Oxford win in year k find the probabilities of wins for each university in years $(k + 1)$ and $(k + 2)$.

2.

		Previous result		
		A	D	E
New result	A	5	4	2
	D	4	3	4
	E	2	4	3

A - win for Australia
D - draw
E - win for England

The frequency table is based on England v Australia Test Matches, 1980 - 1989. A betting shop manager decides to calculate the probabilities of future results on the assumption that outcomes form a Markov chain.

The Australians won the first match of the 1990-91 series. Find the manager's predicted probabilities for the results of the next two matches of the series.

3E.   If $\begin{bmatrix} a & b \\ c & d \end{bmatrix} \begin{bmatrix} p \\ q \end{bmatrix} = \begin{bmatrix} x \\ y \end{bmatrix}$

and $a + c = b + d = p + q = 1$, show that $x + y = 1$

How does this result relate to the theory of stochastic matrices?

79

4.3 Gambler's ruin revisited

Consider a simple example of the type of problem met in Chapter 3.

Example 2

A gambler G and his opponent O start a gambling game with £1 and £2 respectively. The game consists of wagers of £1 each on the toss of a coin, to be repeated until one of the contestants has nothing left. What is G's chance of winning?

Solution

The possible states at any time in the game, shown in the form
(G's cash in £, O's cash in £) are

$$S_1: (0, 3), \quad S_2: (1, 2), \quad S_3: (2, 1), \quad S_4: (3, 0)$$

and the diagram showing probabilities of transitions between these states is

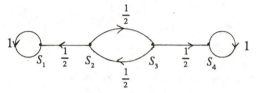

S_1 and S_4 are **absorbing states,** representing the two ways in which the game can end.

So the transition matrix is $\mathbf{T} = \begin{bmatrix} 1 & \frac{1}{2} & 0 & 0 \\ 0 & 0 & \frac{1}{2} & 0 \\ 0 & \frac{1}{2} & 0 & 0 \\ 0 & 0 & \frac{1}{2} & 1 \end{bmatrix}$

> **What feature of T shows the existence of absorbing states?**

The initial state in the game is S_2 and hence $\mathbf{V}_0 = \begin{bmatrix} 0 \\ 1 \\ 0 \\ 0 \end{bmatrix}$

The probability outcome vector after one toss is $\mathbf{V}_1 = \mathbf{TV}_0 = \begin{bmatrix} \frac{1}{2} \\ 0 \\ \frac{1}{2} \\ 0 \end{bmatrix}$

> **Find the outcome vector after two tosses, $\mathbf{V}_2 = \mathbf{TV}_1$.**
> **How is $\mathbf{V}_2$ related to $\mathbf{V}_0$?**
> **What is the probability that G wins after two tosses?**

Exercise 3

1. (a) For the game described in Example 2, evaluate the matrices $\mathbf{T}^2$, $\mathbf{T}^3$, $\mathbf{T}^4$. What features common to $\mathbf{T}$ and its powers simplify the calculation?

   (b) What is the probability that G wins

      (i) on the third throw ;

      (ii) on the fourth throw?

   (c) What are G's chances of winning the game at some stage?

2. What would be the transition matrix if at the outset

   (a) G had £2 and O had £3,

   (b) G had £k and O had £$(n - k)$?

3. Suppose that G and O start with £1 and £2 respectively and that the game is played by casting a die, G wagering £1 on the throw and losing his wager unless a 5 or 6 is thrown, in which case he receives £2 from O. What would be the transition matrix in this game?

4E.

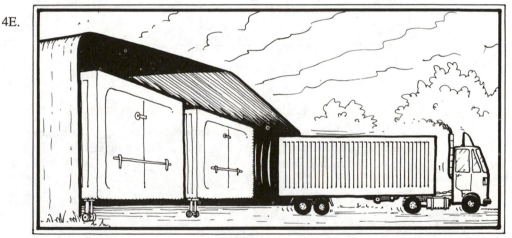

A storage compound can take up to three goods containers. Each day a single container may be taken out, with probability $\frac{1}{4}$, or a container may arrive, with probability $\frac{1}{2}$. Only one departure or arrival occurs in any one day.

   (a) Draw the transition diagram between possible states of the compound. In what ways does this differ from such a diagram in a gambler's ruin problem?

   (b) Form the transition matrix and hence find the steady state outcome probability vector. Interpret the vector.

4.4   Run lengths

One way of distinguishing between some Bernoulli and Markov sequences is to look at the lengths of runs of the various outcomes.

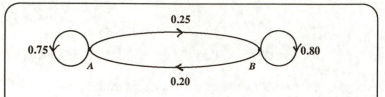

What sort of runs would you expect in a Markov chain with this transition diagram? What sort of frequencies for *A* and *B* would you expect in the long run?

Example 3

For a Bernoulli sequence with P(success) = *p*, what is the probability of a run of *k* successes followed by a failure?

Solution

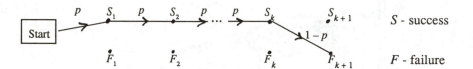

The diagram shows what must happen for a run of precisely *k* successes.
Note that it does not matter whether the start is the beginning of the whole sequence or follows a previous failure.

The probability is $p^k (1 - p)$

Example 4

A Markov chain of wet and dry days has transition diagram as below.

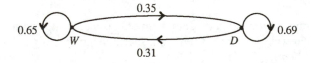

Given that one day is wet, find the probability that there is then a run of five dry days followed by a wet day.

Solution

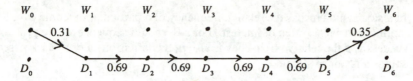

The day before the start of the run is wet, so the diagram looks like this. The probability is $0.31 \times (0.69)^4 \times 0.35 = 0.025$

Exercise 4

1. Let a Bernoulli sequence be throws of a fair die, with a throw of 6 being called a success. Find the probability of

    (a) a run of three successes followed by a failure,
    (b) precisely three successes in five trials,
    (c) precisely three successes in five trials, the third success occurring in the fifth trial,
    (d) a run of at least three successes in five trials.

2. In a Bernoulli sequence with probability of success p, find the probability of the kth success occurring in the nth trial.

3.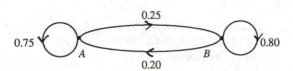

    In a Markov sequence given by this transition diagram, the previous outcome was A. Find the probability of

    (a) a run of at least three B's in the next four outcomes,
    (b) the next four outcomes to include precisely three B's.

4.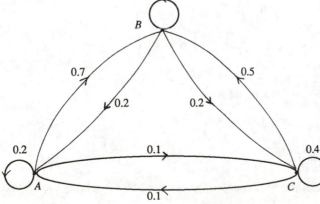

    In a Markov sequence given by this transition diagram, the previous outcome was A. Find the probability of a run of at least three B's in the next four outcomes.

4.5   In the long run

In a stochastic process the relative frequency of a particular outcome over a large number of trials is often of interest. For a Bernoulli sequence where probability of success is p the relative frequency is also p, by definition! For a Markov sequence the solution is not so simple.

Example 5

If John goes to the Youth Club on any evening there is a probability of 0.7 that he will also go there on the next. If he does not then the probability that he will not go on the following evening is 0.6. Discuss his behaviour in the long run.

Solution

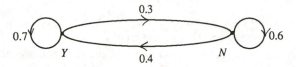

The transition matrix is $\mathbf{T} = \begin{bmatrix} 0.7 & 0.4 \\ 0.3 & 0.6 \end{bmatrix}$

First, suppose that on day 0 he does not go to the club. Then $\mathbf{V}_0 = \begin{bmatrix} 0 \\ 1 \end{bmatrix}$

$$\mathbf{T}\mathbf{V}_0 = \begin{bmatrix} 0.4 \\ 0.6 \end{bmatrix}, \qquad \mathbf{T}^2 \mathbf{V}_0 = \begin{bmatrix} 0.52 \\ 0.48 \end{bmatrix}, \qquad \dots$$

> **Verify these results and calculate the next few values of the sequence $\mathbf{T}^n \mathbf{V}_0$.**

The sequence converges fairly rapidly to $\begin{bmatrix} 0.571 \\ 0.429 \end{bmatrix}$ (3-figure accuracy).

To find this **steady state vector** exactly, you could reason as follows.
Suppose that the steady state vector is $\mathbf{V}$. Then if $\mathbf{V}$ is multiplied by $\mathbf{T}$ it will remain unchanged; that is, $\mathbf{V}$ satisfies the equation

$$\mathbf{T}\mathbf{V} = \mathbf{V}$$

So, if $\mathbf{V} = \begin{bmatrix} p \\ 1-p \end{bmatrix}$ then $\begin{bmatrix} 0.7 & 0.4 \\ 0.3 & 0.6 \end{bmatrix}\begin{bmatrix} p \\ 1-p \end{bmatrix} = \begin{bmatrix} p \\ 1-p \end{bmatrix}$

Comparing first rows on the left and right,

$$0.7p + 0.4(1-p) = p$$
$$\Rightarrow p = \tfrac{4}{7} \approx 0.57143$$

You can easily check that the same result is obtained by comparing the second rows.

(a) Suppose now that John goes to the club on day 0. Calculate the first few members of the sequence $T^n V_0$ with a new V_0.

(b) Explain why, in the long run, John goes to the Youth Club on average on four evenings a week.

For a Markov chain with transition matrix T, if a steady state vector exists then it is the vector V found by solving the equation

$$TV = V.$$

The steady state vector contains the probabilites of the various outcomes in the long run.

Example 6

Find the steady state vector for the Markov chain with transition matrix

$$\begin{bmatrix} 0.3 & 0.1 & 0.4 \\ 0.3 & 0.2 & 0.2 \\ 0.4 & 0.7 & 0.4 \end{bmatrix}.$$

Solution

Let the steady state vector be $\begin{bmatrix} a \\ b \\ 1-a-b \end{bmatrix}$

Then $\begin{bmatrix} 0.3 & 0.1 & 0.4 \\ 0.3 & 0.2 & 0.2 \\ 0.4 & 0.7 & 0.4 \end{bmatrix} \begin{bmatrix} a \\ b \\ 1-a-b \end{bmatrix} = \begin{bmatrix} a \\ b \\ 1-a-b \end{bmatrix}$

So, comparing the first and second components on left and right,

$$0.3a + 0.1b + 0.4\,(1 - a - b) = a$$
$$0.3a + 0.2b + 0.2\,(1 - a - b) = b$$

Simplifying, $1.1a + 0.3b = 0.4$
$$0.1a - 1.0b = -0.2,$$

with solution $a = 0.30$, $b = 0.23$;   so the steady state vector is $\begin{bmatrix} 0.30 \\ 0.23 \\ 0.47 \end{bmatrix}$.

TASKSHEET 3E – *Eigenvectors*

85

Exercise 5

1. Find the steady state vector, if it exists, for a Markov chain with transition diagram

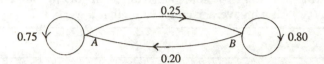

2. The probability of a team winning a match is 0.6 and of drawing 0.3 if the previous match was won. If the previous match was drawn the corresponding probabilities are 0.2 and 0.6, and if it was lost 0.2 and 0.4. Find the transition matrix, and hence the probabilities of winning or drawing any particular match in the distant future if the probabilities remain the same. [SMP]

3. The central office of a large organisation periodically reclassifies the data received from its branches into three categories I, I and III. New and unprocessed data is placed in category I, currently available data is placed in category II and obsolete data is placed in category III. Obsolete data is replaced by new data as this becomes available. The category transition matrix is

	I	II	III
I	0.3	0	0.8
II	0.6	0.7	0
III	0.1	0.3	0.2

(a) Explain briefly what happens to obsolete data.

(b) Find the limiting probabilities of each category in the long run.

4.

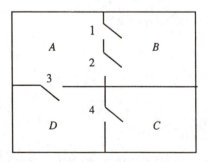

A mouse is placed in a box with four compartments, A, B, C, D connected by doors 1, 2, 3, and 4, as shown. When in any compartment the mouse is equally likely to use any of the available doors and it changes compartments at a constant rate.

How much of the time does the mouse spend in compartment A?

5. Repeat question 4, assuming that door 1 is one-way, so that the mouse can use it to pass from B to A only.

After working through this chapter you should be able to:

1. carry out matrix multiplications;

2. construct a transition diagram showing probabilities of changes between states in a sequence;

3. use the transition matrix or diagram in calculating the probability of a given state after a number of changes;

4. define a **Markov sequence**, a **stochastic matrix** and an **outcome probability vector**;

5. calculate the probability of a run of given length in a Bernoulli or Markov sequence;

6. calculate the steady state outcome probability vector in the case of a convergent Markov chain.

Matrix multiplication

Here is the transition diagram for Beryl's chess results.

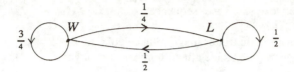

W - Beryl wins

L - Beryl loses

The transition matrix is

$$\mathbf{T} = \begin{bmatrix} P(W \mid W) & P(W \mid L) \\ P(L \mid W) & P(L \mid L) \end{bmatrix} = \begin{bmatrix} \frac{3}{4} & \frac{1}{2} \\ \frac{1}{4} & \frac{1}{2} \end{bmatrix}$$

Assume that Beryl wins the first game so that $\mathbf{V}_1 = \begin{bmatrix} 1 \\ 0 \end{bmatrix}$

In both the matrix $\mathbf{T}$ and the outcome probability vector $\mathbf{V}_1$ the first row is associated with a win for Beryl, the second with a loss.

The outcome probability vector for the second game is $\mathbf{V}_2 = \begin{bmatrix} \frac{3}{4} \\ \frac{1}{4} \end{bmatrix}$

This may be expressed by the equation $\mathbf{TV}_1 = \mathbf{V}_2$: in full,

$$\begin{bmatrix} \frac{3}{4} & \frac{1}{2} \\ \frac{1}{4} & \frac{1}{2} \end{bmatrix} \begin{bmatrix} 1 \\ 0 \end{bmatrix} = \begin{bmatrix} \frac{3}{4} \\ \frac{1}{4} \end{bmatrix}$$

You have here a special case of **matrix multiplication**. The procedure for this operation follows the rule:

> **If M and N are matrices then the term in the rth row and sth column of the product matrix MN is found by multiplying the elements of the rth *row* of M by corresponding elements of the sth *column* of N and adding the results.**

Another illustration of matrix multiplication is given in the following example.

(continued)

Example 1

(a)   In the product $\begin{bmatrix} 1 & 3 & 2 \\ 4 & 1 & 5 \\ 3 & 8 & 4 \end{bmatrix} \begin{bmatrix} 2 & 4 & 6 \\ 1 & 3 & 5 \\ 2 & 3 & 5 \end{bmatrix}$

How is the element in the second row and third column calculated?

(b)   What is the complete product?

Solution

(a)

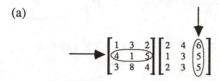

Corresponding elements in the second row and third column are multiplied together. The results are then added. The entry is

$$(4 \times 6) + (1 \times 5) + (5 \times 5) = 54.$$

(b)
$$\begin{bmatrix} (1 \times 2) + (3 \times 1) + (2 \times 2) & (1 \times 4) + (3 \times 3) + (2 \times 3) & (1 \times 6) + (3 \times 5) + (2 \times 5) \\ (4 \times 2) + (1 \times 1) + (5 \times 2) & (4 \times 4) + (1 \times 3) + (5 \times 3) & (4 \times 6) + (1 \times 5) + (5 \times 5) \\ (3 \times 2) + (8 \times 1) + (4 \times 2) & (3 \times 4) + (8 \times 3) + (4 \times 3) & (3 \times 6) + (8 \times 5) + (4 \times 5) \end{bmatrix}$$

$$= \begin{bmatrix} 9 & 19 & 31 \\ 19 & 34 & 54 \\ 22 & 48 & 78 \end{bmatrix}$$

Example 2

Which values of r and s give the element $\frac{1}{4}$ in the outcome probability vector V_2 ?

Solution

You may not have thought of vectors as matrices, but they are; V_1 and V_2 are matrices having only one column. In the matrix product TV_1, $\frac{1}{4}$ occurs as $(\frac{1}{4} \times 1) + (\frac{1}{2} \times 0)$, the combination of the second row of T and the first and only column of V_1.
$r = 2$, $s = 1$.

Example 3

If $A = \begin{bmatrix} 4 & 2 & 8 \\ 3 & 3 & 7 \end{bmatrix}$, $B = \begin{bmatrix} 1 & 4 \\ 6 & 1 \\ 5 & 9 \end{bmatrix}$,   find AB.

Solution

$$AB = \begin{bmatrix} (4 \times 1) + (2 \times 6) + (8 \times 5) & (4 \times 4) + (2 \times 1) + (8 \times 9) \\ (3 \times 1) + (3 \times 6) + (7 \times 5) & (3 \times 4) + (3 \times 1) + (7 \times 9) \end{bmatrix} = \begin{bmatrix} 56 & 90 \\ 56 & 78 \end{bmatrix}$$

(continued)

1.   In Example 3, find **BA** .

2.   If $C = \begin{bmatrix} 2 & 1 \\ 3 & 4 \end{bmatrix}$ find **ABC**, as **(AB)C** and as **A(BC)**.
Comment on some differences between the multiplication of matrices and numbers.
Explain why you cannot find **BAC**.

3.   Calculate the products

(a) $\begin{bmatrix} 3 & -1 \\ 2 & 4 \end{bmatrix} \begin{bmatrix} 4 & 1 \\ -2 & 3 \end{bmatrix}$

(b) $\begin{bmatrix} 3 & -1 \\ 2 & 4 \end{bmatrix} \begin{bmatrix} 4 \\ 3 \end{bmatrix}$

(c) $\begin{bmatrix} 0.6 & 0 & 0.4 \\ 0.1 & 1 & 0.4 \\ 0.3 & 0 & 0.2 \end{bmatrix} \begin{bmatrix} 0.5 \\ 0.5 \\ 0 \end{bmatrix}$

4.   For Beryl:

(a)   find T^2 ,   (b)   find TV_2 ,   (c)   find T^2V_1 .

Explain your findings.

5.   Still with Beryl:

Find the vector V_5 giving outcome probabilities for the fifth game, in two distinct ways using matrix multiplication.

Ashbourne ball game

Every year, on Shrove Tuesday and Ash Wednesday, ancient rivalries resurface in Ashbourne, Derbyshire, as the Up'ards and Down'ards do battle with a highly decorated oblate spheroid. The object of the game is to play this ball to your goal and knock it three times on the goal board. The teams are indeterminate in number and the goals are three miles apart, at Sturston and Clifton.

See if you can calculate whether the results of the Ashbourne ball game can be modelled with any accuracy by a Markov chain. You are warned that this will involve a great deal of counting; the use of tally marks is advised.

The last hundred results are as follows (C, S - goaled at Clifton, Sturston, respectively). (Read across the lines.)

SSSSS	CSSSC	SSSSC	SCSSS	CSCSC	CSSSC	CCSCS
CSCSS	CSCSC	CCCSC	SSCSC	CSSCS	SSCCC	CSCSC
SCCCC	SCSSC	SCCSC	CCCCS	CSCSC	CSSCC	

(continued)

1. Check that this table starts as shown and fill in the remainder.

| | Last goal | |
	C	S
This goal C	20	
S		

2. Find the transition matrix of probabilities, **T**.

3. Find $\mathbf{T}^2$.

One way to check whether a table of results forms a Markov chain is to compare the theoretical probabilities in $\mathbf{T}^2$ with the actual probabilities, based on relative frequencies, found in the table:

| | Last goal but one | |
	C	S
This goal C		
S		

4. Explain why the probabilities should agree.

5. Calculate the actual probabilities in the 'last but one' table.

6. What do you conclude?

Eigenvectors

The transition diagram for John's Youth Club visits is as follows:

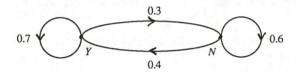

The transition matrix is $\mathbf{T} = \begin{bmatrix} 0.7 & 0.4 \\ 0.3 & 0.6 \end{bmatrix}$

If on day 0 he does not go to the club then $\mathbf{V}_0 = \begin{bmatrix} 0 \\ 1 \end{bmatrix}$

1. (a) Find $\mathbf{V}_1 = \mathbf{T}\mathbf{V}_0$ and $\mathbf{V}_2 = \mathbf{T}\mathbf{V}_1 = \mathbf{T}^2\mathbf{V}_0$.

    (b) Show that $\mathbf{V} = \begin{bmatrix} 4/7 \\ 3/7 \end{bmatrix}$ is the steady state vector for $\mathbf{T}$.

2. Consider the vectors $\mathbf{V}_0$, $\mathbf{V}_1$, $\mathbf{V}_2$ and $\mathbf{V}$ to be position vectors. Plot the corresponding points on a cartesian grid. Show that the points all lie on the same straight line l. Find the equation of this line.

3. Repeat question 2 for $\mathbf{V}_0 = \begin{bmatrix} 1 \\ 0 \end{bmatrix}$. What do you notice?

4. (a) For any point $\begin{bmatrix} x \\ y \end{bmatrix}$ on l, find $\mathbf{T}\begin{bmatrix} x \\ y \end{bmatrix}$. Hence show that the line l is mapped onto itself by $\mathbf{T}$.

    (b) Is the result in (a) true for any stochastic matrix? Explain the significance of your answer.

> If $\mathbf{T}$ is a transition matrix and $\mathbf{V}$ is a vector such that
>
> $$\mathbf{T}\mathbf{V} = \lambda\mathbf{V},$$
>
> where λ is a number, then λ is called an eigenvalue and $\mathbf{V}$ the corresponding eigenvector of the matrix $\mathbf{T}$.

(continued)

5. (a) Show that **T** maps $\begin{bmatrix} 1 \\ -1 \end{bmatrix}$ onto a multiple of itself.

    (b) Explain why **any** 2 x 2 stochastic matrix maps $\begin{bmatrix} 1 \\ -1 \end{bmatrix}$ onto a multiple of itself.

6. (a) In question 5, you saw that $\begin{bmatrix} 1 \\ -1 \end{bmatrix}$ is an eigenvector of **T** with eigenvalue 0.3.

    Find another eigenvector **V** and the corresponding eigenvalue for **T**, commenting on what you find.

    (b) Any two dimensional vector **v** can be expressed in the form

    $$\mathbf{v} = a \begin{bmatrix} 4 \\ 3 \end{bmatrix} + b \begin{bmatrix} 1 \\ -1 \end{bmatrix}.$$

    Show that $\mathbf{Tv} = a \begin{bmatrix} 4 \\ 3 \end{bmatrix} + 0.3b \begin{bmatrix} 1 \\ -1 \end{bmatrix}.$

    Hence find $\mathbf{T}^n \mathbf{v}$, for any n.

    (c) Given that **v** is an outcome probability vector find the value of a. Find also the value of $\mathbf{T}^n \mathbf{v}$ for large values of n.

7. (a) Suppose that **T** is a 3 x 3 stochastic matrix. What geometrical result analogous to that of question 4 would you expect?

    (b) Verify your conjecture for

    $$\mathbf{T} = \begin{bmatrix} 0.3 & 0.1 & 0.4 \\ 0.3 & 0.2 & 0.2 \\ 0.4 & 0.7 & 0.4 \end{bmatrix}$$

1. Find the steady state vectors for the stochastic matrices

    (a) $\begin{bmatrix} 0.2 & 0.4 \\ 0.8 & 0.6 \end{bmatrix}$

    (b) $\begin{bmatrix} \frac{1}{2} & 0 & \frac{1}{3} \\ \frac{1}{2} & \frac{1}{2} & \frac{1}{3} \\ 0 & \frac{1}{2} & \frac{1}{3} \end{bmatrix}$

2. Each day, a particular student either brings a packed lunch to school or has a school meal. When she has a packed lunch there is a 1 in 5 chance that she will do the same the next day. When she has a school meal the chances are 3 in 5 that she will do the same the next day. On the first day of term she brings a packed lunch.

    (a) Find the probabilities that she has a packed lunch and a school meal on the third day of term.

    (b) Find the corresponding probabilities for the last day of term.

3. (a) Show that the matrix $\begin{bmatrix} \frac{1}{2} & \frac{1}{2} & 0 \\ 0 & \frac{1}{3} & \frac{2}{3} \\ \frac{1}{2} & \frac{1}{6} & \frac{1}{3} \end{bmatrix}$ has steady state vector $\begin{bmatrix} \frac{1}{3} \\ \frac{1}{3} \\ \frac{1}{3} \end{bmatrix}$

    (b) Prove that any 3 x 3 stochastic matrix with each row sum equal to 1 has the same steady state vector

95

5 *Simulation*

5.1   Introduction

Practical problems often involve probabilistic considerations which are more difficult to analyse than those encountered so far in this unit. In such cases you can often gain some insight into the problem by performing a **simulation**.

> **Three fair coins are tossed. After each toss those coins that come up heads are removed and the remaining coins are tossed again. This is repeated until no coins are left.**
>
> **(a)**   **Perform this experiment a number of times to obtain an estimate of the average number of tosses needed to remove all the coins.**
>
> **(b)**   **Use a computer or programmable calculator to simulate the experiment a large number of times. Hence obtain an improved estimate of the average number of tosses.**
>
> **(c)**   **Use the probability theory you have learnt in this unit to analyse the procedure.**

You have seen that the analysis of even an extremely small probability experiment can be very complicated.

The coin tossing experiment has practical applications in analysing the performance of systems which can still function even when some parts of the system have failed. In science and engineering such systems are called **redundant systems**. They occur in areas as diverse as neurophysiology (if a small area of the human brain is damaged then other areas can take over its functions) and aerodynamics (redundant systems are used to improve the reliability of aircraft).

In a practical application, it may be essential to determine the probability that the system will still be functioning under various circumstances. Simulations can enable you to do this rapidly and with a reasonable degree of confidence even when the system is too complicated for you to analyse precisely.

5.2 Pseudo-random numbers

To simulate a random process a computer or calculator uses random numbers. It is possible to store a table of random numbers in the computer's memory. Usually, however, computers use special recipes or **algorithms** to generate random numbers.

> **Give two properties that random numbers generated by a computer should exhibit.**

One particular algorithm commonly employed in calculators and computers uses modular arithmetic. For previously chosen integers c and N, the computer generates the sequence

$$x_0, x_1, x_2 \ldots$$

where

$$x_{n+1} \equiv cx_n \pmod{N}.$$

The initial number x_0 is called the seed.

Example 1

Use the relationship $x_{n+1} \equiv cx_n \pmod{N}$ with $x_0 = 13$, $c = 7$ and $N = 29$ to generate a sequence of 5 random numbers.

Solution

$$x_{n+1} \equiv 7x_n \pmod{29}$$

$$x_1 \equiv 7 \times 13 \equiv 91 \pmod{29}$$

$$\Rightarrow x_1 = 4.$$

Then $x_2 \equiv 7 \times 4 \pmod{29}$

$$\Rightarrow x_2 = 28.$$

This process is repeated, obtaining the sequence 13, 4, 28, 22, 9.

> **What would happen if one number in the sequence was the same as an earlier number?**

Ideally, computer generated random numbers should behave like numbers obtained from a 'pure' random device such as a coin, die or box and tokens. However, it is clear that if you and a friend each use the same generator and the same seed, you will both produce the same sequence of random numbers. You should now realise that the numbers manufactured by such algorithms are not 'pure' random numbers but exhibit a behaviour pattern which eventually is predictable (in fact, once the seed of a particular generator is chosen, all the subsequent random numbers are determined). The numbers provided by computers are more accurately called **pseudo-random numbers**.

When carrying out a simulation it is important to ensure that the generated sequence of random numbers is 'long' enough to cover the lifetime of the simulation and does not become predictable (degenerate) before the end of the experiment.

> **How can you use your calculator to simulate the throw of a fair coin?**

Exercise 1

1. Use the following generator:

    $$x_{n+1} \equiv 9x_n + 13 \pmod{32}, \ x_0 = 0$$

    to produce a sequence of numbers. List at least 20 of these numbers. What conclusions can you draw about the 'randomness' of this sequence?

2. Consider the generator

    $$x_{n+1} \equiv 8x_n \pmod{11}$$

    How might you use the output of this generator to produce random numbers in the interval $(0, 1)$?

3. Use your calculator or computer to generate a random sequence of days of the week.

Random streams of digits can be produced by physical processes (hardware) as well as by software. In fact, any natural phenomenon that is considered random can be regarded as a candidate for generating random numbers. The computer ERNIE (employed to select winning premium bond numbers) uses the electronic 'noise' (random fluctuations) of neon tubes to generate the numbers. Such hardware suffers from 'wear and tear' over a period of time and, consequently, there must be regular checks to ensure the randomness of the device.

5.3   Empirical probability distributions

Past behaviour can be used to predict future patterns. From past records and experience you can obtain the proportional frequencies of various outcomes and you can then use these to set up an **empirical probability distribution**. This distribution enables you to check how the process is likely to behave in the future.

In the following illustration, imagine you are the plant manager in an industrial complex and you have been given the task of assessing the feasibility of introducing a new version of a plant unit which comprises two basic components. From past records you have obtained a picture of the separate failure patterns of the two components as follows:

For component A:

Hours between failures	Class midpoint	Frequency	Percentage frequency
0 and under 10	5	80	40
10 and under 20	15	30	15
20 and under 30	25	20	10
30 and under 40	35	20	10
40 and under 50	45	40	20
50 and more	55	10	5
		200	100

For component B:

Hours between failures	Class midpoint	Frequency	Percentage frequency
0 and under 10	5	10	7
10 and under 20	15	30	20
20 and under 30	25	50	33
30 and under 40	35	40	27
40 and more	45	20	13
		150	100

The whole unit will fail when one of the components fails. You need to know the failure pattern of the new combined unit in order to establish maintenance intervals and servicing requirements.

A simulation can be used to obtain this information and, in particular, to estimate the average time interval between failures.

The new unit will contain one A component and one B component. The whole unit will fail when one of the components fails. To simulate the running time of a unit the following tables can be used:

Component A

Hours between failures	Random numbers
5	00-39
15	40-54
25	55-64
35	65-74
45	75-94
55	95-99

Component B

Hours between failures	Random numbers
5	00-06
15	07-26
25	27-59
35	60-86
45	87-99

> **Explain the choice of the random numbers 00-39 in the table for component A.**

The simulation procedure can be implemented by obtaining two-digit random numbers by any convenient means. One number will correspond to a running time for component A according to the table above. The second random number can similarly be used to determine the time before unit B will cease to function.

For example:

• a random number of 53 for A suggests A will fail after 15 hours.

• a random number of 72 for B suggests B will fail after 35 hours.

The unit therefore runs for 15 hours.

> **Perform the above simulation a sufficient number of times to enable you to estimate the average time between failures of the unit. Calculate the average run time of the unit.**

A simple example of decision-making is considered on the next tasksheet.

TASKSHEET 1 - *Profiting from simulation*

5.4 The Monte Carlo method

The discussion so far has concentrated on the simulation of discrete random variables. However, many random variables are continuous and special methods have been developed to enable you to simulate their behaviour.

Suppose that a time and motion study in a particular office has gathered data on the times between successive incoming telephone calls.

The times could be grouped and the data then plotted as below.

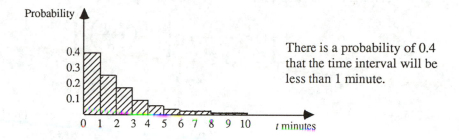

There is a probability of 0.4 that the time interval will be less than 1 minute.

Since the telephone can ring at any time, it is more appropriate to model the data with a continuous function. Suppose in this case that the probabilities can be modelled by the area under the function $0.5e^{-0.5t}$.

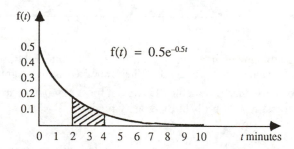

The shaded area therefore represents the probability that the time between successive calls lies between 2 and 4 minutes.

What would you expect to be the value of $\displaystyle\int_{0}^{\infty} f(t)\, dt$ **?**

101

Probabilities for a continuous distribution can be found from areas under the graph of an appropriate function. This function is called the *probability density function* of the random variable.

A probability density function must be such that
- it is non-negative;
- the total area under its graph is 1.

The functions used for probability density functions are often complicated and difficult to work with. For example, for a Normal distribution with mean μ and standard deviation σ, the probability density function is ϕ, where

$$\phi(z) = \frac{1}{\sigma\sqrt{2\pi}} \exp\left[-\frac{1}{2}\left(\frac{z-\mu}{\sigma}\right)^2 \right]$$

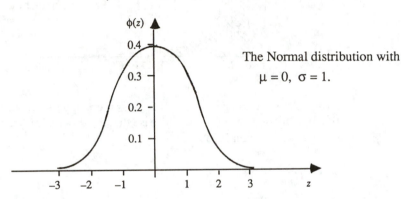

The Normal distribution with $\mu = 0,\ \sigma = 1$.

It is not possible to obtain an analytical form for the integral of $\phi(z)$ and so numerical tables of areas have been produced. When functions are as complicated as this, simulations can be particularly valuable. However, most computers are only pre-programmed for the simplest type of probability density function.

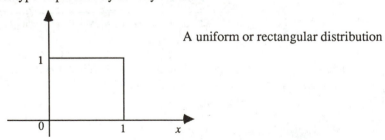

A uniform or rectangular distribution

Most computers will give you a stream of random numbers uniformly distributed on the interval [0, 1].

How can you adjust this stream of numbers to be

(a)   uniform on the interval [0, 2] ;
(b)   uniform on the interval [–3, 3] ?

The Monte Carlo method for simulating a non-uniform distribution involves

- boxing the distribution in a rectangle;

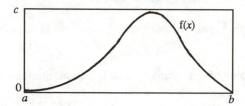

- choosing a value x of a variable X uniformly distributed on $[a, b]$.

- deciding whether to keep or discard x according to whether a value of a variable Y uniformly distributed on $[0, c]$ is less than or greater than $f(x)$.

Deciding whether to keep or discard x in this way ensures that the stream of values of X has the required distribution.

For example, the following BBC BASIC routine generates a value of a variable which is Normally distributed with mean 0 and standard deviation 1.

```
10      X = 6*RND(1) – 3
20      Y = 0.4*RND(1)
30      IF Y>EXP(–0.5*X^2/SQR(2*PI) THEN 10
40      PRINT X
```

(a)   In the above program, explain why X is taken to be 6*RND(1) –3.

(b)   Use a calculator or computer to generate the times between successive incoming telephone calls for the office considered earlier.

Hence estimate the mean time between calls.

After working through this chapter you should:

1. be aware of the type of problems for which simulation might be useful;

2. appreciate some of the means by which random numbers are generated;

3. be able to conduct a simple probabilistic simulation based on original data;

4. know how to generate values for a random variable whose probability density function is known;

5. be able to use the Monte Carlo method within a simulation experiment.

Profiting from simulation

A scientific funding council is evaluating a project submitted by a university research institute. From previous experience of similar projects the council estimates the required expenditure to be as in the following table:

Expenditure £	Estimated probabilities
60 000	0.3
40 000	0.3
30 000	0.3
20 000	0.1

The project is of an applied nature and its benefits will be felt in industry. From information given by the research team, the council estimates the income (from its use in industry) to be as follows:

Income £	Estimated probabilities
120 000	0.1
80 000	0.4
60 000	0.4
20 000	0.1

1. Explain in detail how to perform a simulation to obtain estimates of the net profits that can accrue from the above project.

2. Carry out the simulation described in question 1. Tabulate your results in such a way as to demonstrate the progress of the simulation.

3. Construct graphs of the simulated expenditures and incomes and compare the results visually with the empirical probability distributions given above.

4. Draw a graph of the simulated net profits and comment on what you see. This will provide a 'risk profile' of the project being investigated.

5. If you were a member of the funding council, would you decide to allocate funds to the research team?

6. Is it possible to estimate the expected profit from the project **without** performing a simulation?

Tutorial sheet

1.   A sequence such as

        H H H T H T T H ...

produced by repeatedly tossing a coin can be analysed according to the frequencies of runs of various lengths of each of the outcomes H and T.

The given sequence would have frequency table as shown

Run length	1	2	3
Frequency	2	1	1

$$\overline{\overline{\text{H H H}} \; \overline{\text{T}} \; \overline{\text{H}} \; \underline{\text{T T}}}$$

Write a program to simulate the repeated tossing of a coin. Produce a table of frequencies and discuss any pattern(s) you notice.

2.   The lifetimes (t hours) of the batteries produced by a factory can be modelled by the probability density function f(t), where f(t) = $0.01\mathrm{e}^{-0.01t}$ ($t \geq 0$).

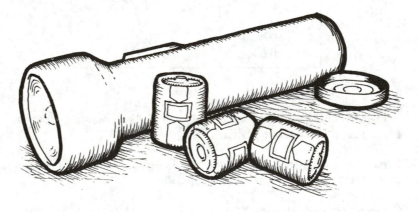

Three batteries are used in a torch. Simulate the lifetime of at least 20 torches. Hence, estimate the expected time before at least one battery will need replacing.

SOLUTIONS

1   First ideas

1.1   Introduction

> **Is the probability determined by symmetry or by experience in the following cases:**
>
> (a)   throwing a six with a die;
> (b)   a baby being a boy;
> (c)   living to the age of 100?

(a)   For an unbiased die, the probability is determined by symmetry.

(b)   You might think that symmetry applies in this case also. However, this is based upon the assumption that an ovum is as likely to be fertilised by a sperm carrying the male (X) chromosome as by one carrying the female (Y) chromosome, and that the resulting male and female embryos are equally likely to survive. In fact, female births are slightly more frequent than male.

(c)   The chance of living to 100 is an observed probability which has increased steadily for many years. Insurance company actuaries base their calculations on tables of mortality, compiled from death registers.

Exercise 1

1.   (a)   Selecting one of the dice as the 'first' die, the other as the 'second' (it would help if they had different colours), the possible outcomes are

$(1, 1)$ $(1, 2)$ $(1, 3)$ $(1, 4)$ $(1, 5)$ $(1, 6)$

$(2, 1)$ $(2, 2)$ $(2, 3)$ $(2, 4)$ $(2, 5)$ $(2, 6)$

$(3, 1)$ $(3, 2)$ $(3, 3)$ $(3, 4)$ $(3, 5)$ $(3, 6)$

$(4, 1)$ $(4, 2)$ $(4, 3)$ $(4, 4)$ $(4, 5)$ $(4, 6)$

$(5, 1)$ $(5, 2)$ $(5, 3)$ $(5, 4)$ $(5, 5)$ $(5, 6)$

$(6, 1)$ $(6, 2)$ $(6, 3)$ $(6, 4)$ $(6, 5)$ $(6, 6)$

(b)   Taking all these outcomes as equally likely, by symmetry, the most likely score is 7, since this can be thrown in the greatest number of different ways, namely 6.

(c)   Since a score of 7 occurs in 6 out of 36 equally likely outcomes, the probability is $\frac{6}{36} = \frac{1}{6}$.

2.   Taking the 16 outcomes

GGGG		BGGG	GBGG	GGBG	GGGB
GGBB	GBGB	GBBG	BGBG	BGGB	BBGG
GBBB	BGBB	BBGB	BBBG		BBBB

as equally likely, the answers are

(a) $\frac{1}{16}$,   (b) $\frac{6}{16} = \frac{3}{8}$,   (c) $\frac{2}{16} = \frac{1}{8}$.

3.   (a) If a member of the set were chosen at random from a randomly chosen piece of English prose the probability of its being a space is 20% or $\frac{1}{5}$.

(b) 20% of the 1000 characters should be spaces, i.e. 200.

(c) Since approximately 1 in every 5 characters is a space the average word length is about 4 letters.

4.   The observed probability should tend to that expected by symmetry as the number of trials becomes very large, otherwise you would suspect bias in the die or in the way it is thrown.

1.2   Equally likely outcomes

> **Explain the difference between, say, (1, 2) and (2, 1).**

Outcomes for a pair of dice are combinations of the simpler outcomes for each member of the pair, which are identified as the 'first' die and the 'second' die. (1, 2) means that the first die shows 1 and the second 2; (2, 1) that the first shows 2 and the second 1.

In setting up a sample space it is important that the members should be equally likely. If the number pairs here were not ordered then {1, 2}, for example, would be twice as likely as {2, 2}.

> **Explain in terms of relative frequencies what this result means.**

If the trial is repeated a very large number of times then a prime sum will occur in about $\frac{5}{12}$ of cases.

Exercise 2

1. (a) $\frac{26}{52} = \frac{1}{2}$ (b) $\frac{13}{52} = \frac{1}{4}$ (c) $\frac{4}{52} = \frac{1}{13}$

2. (a) The sample space has $12^2 = 144$ members, namely

   (Jan, Jan) (Jan, Feb) ... (Jan, Dec) (Feb, Jan) ... (Dec, Dec)

   Note that the members are not equally probable because lengths of months vary. The slight error this introduces will be ignored.

   (b) 12 members of the sample space are favourable. The required probability is $\frac{12}{144} = \frac{1}{12}$.

   This answer could have been obtained much more easily by observing that, having asked one person's month of birth there is a 1 in 12 chance that the second person will have the same month of birth.

3. (a) The outcomes are ordered triplets (1, 1, 1), (1, 1, 2) etc. The sample space has $6 \times 6 \times 6 = 216$ members.

   (b) (i) There are 25 favourable cases:

   (6, 1, 5) (6, 5, 1) (6, 2, 4) (6, 4, 2) (6, 3, 3)
   (5, 1, 6) (5, 6, 1) (5, 2, 5) (5, 5, 2) (5, 3, 4) (5, 4, 3)
   (4, 2, 6) (4, 6, 2) (4, 3, 5) (4, 5, 3) (4, 4, 4)
   (3, 3, 6) (3, 6, 3) (3, 4, 5) (3, 5, 4)
   (2, 4, 6) (2, 6, 4) (2, 5, 5)
   (1, 5, 6) (1, 6, 5)

   The probability is $\frac{25}{216}$

   (ii) There are 15 favourable cases:

   (6, 1, 2) (6, 2, 1) (4, 1, 3) (4, 3, 1) (3, 1, 4) (3, 4, 1) (3, 2, 2)
   (2, 1, 6) (2, 6, 1) (2, 2, 3) (2, 3, 2) (1, 2, 6) (1, 6, 2) (1, 3, 4)
   (1, 4, 3)

   The probability is $\frac{15}{216}$

4. The sample space has 24 members.

   ABCD   ABDC   ACBD   ACDB   ADBC   ADCB
   BACD   BADC   BCAD   BCDA   BDAC   BDCA
   (CABD)   CADB   CBAD   CBDA   CDAB   CDBA
   DABC   DACB   DBAC   DBCA   DCAB   DCBA

   The only favourable case is ringed. Its probability is $\frac{1}{24}$.

1.3   Events as sets

Exercise 3

1.   The sample space is the set of all months. The 12 members are not quite equally likely as months of birth but the slight error introduced will be ignored.   The favourable subset is E = {Jan, Jun, Jul}.

The required probability is $\dfrac{n(E)}{n(S)}$ = $\dfrac{3}{12}$ = $\dfrac{1}{4}$

2.   The sample space showing all possible families is

GGG   GGB   GBG   BGG   GBB   BGB   BBG   BBB

with 8 members: $n(S)$ = 8

The only favourable event is GGG, so $n(E) = 1$.

The required probability is $\dfrac{1}{8}$.

1.4   The addition law

> (a)   **Explain why, if A and B are mutually exclusive events,**
> $$P(A \cup B) = P(A) + P(B)$$
>
> (b)   **Illustrate using a Venn diagram the general addition law: if A and B are *any* events in the same sample space,**
> $$P(A \cup B) = P(A) + P(B) - P(A \cap B)$$
>
> (c)   **Explain why the first result is a particular case of the second.**

(a)   If A and B are mutually exclusive events then the corresponding sets have no members in common. So

$$P(A \cup B) = \frac{n(A \cup B)}{n(\varepsilon)} = \frac{n(A) + n(B)}{n(\varepsilon)} = \frac{n(A)}{n(\varepsilon)} + \frac{n(B)}{n(\varepsilon)} = P(A) + P(B).$$

(b)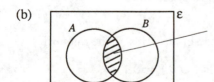

In the sum $n(A) + n(B)$ the elements in the shaded area are counted twice. So

$$n(A \cup B) = n(A) + n(B) - n(A \cap B).$$

The required result is obtained on dividing by $n(\varepsilon)$.

(c)   If A and B are mutually exclusive events then $A \cap B = \varnothing$, so $n(A \cap B) = 0$ and the second result reduces to the first.

1.5   Independent events

(a)   Noting that $P(H) = \frac{1}{2}$ and $P(Q) = \frac{1}{13}$, what simple rule gives the probability of head and queen?

(b)   Explain how the other probabilities on the Venn diagram can be found.

(c)   What is the probability of head or queen?

(a)   Probability of head and queen = $P(H \cap Q) = P(H) \times P(Q) \quad \left[\frac{1}{26} = \frac{1}{2} \times \frac{1}{13} \right]$.

(b)   The sample space has 104 members, since each of the 52 cards may be associated with either head or tail.

H has 52 members and Q has 8, of which 4 are in $H \cap Q$.

Probabilities are found on dividing by 104.

(c) $P(H \cup Q) = P(H) + P(Q) - P(H \cap Q)$

$\quad\quad\quad\quad = \frac{1}{2} + \frac{1}{13} - \frac{1}{26} = \frac{7}{13}$.

Exercise 4

1.   (a)   The events appear to be independent so, in an obvious notation,

$\quad\quad P(B \cap C) = 0.1 \times 0.2 = 0.02$.

(b) $P(B \cup C) = P(B) + P(C) - P(B \cap C) = 0.1 + 0.2 - 0.02 = 0.28$.

[It should be stressed here that the word 'or' is used in an inclusive sense: those with a broken leg and also a cold are included in $B \cup C$.]

2.   If A and B were mutually exclusive then the condition

$\quad\quad P(A \cup B) = P(A) + P(B)$

would be satisfied; but it is not, the sum of the terms on the right being 1.0.

Also, $P(A \cap B) = P(A) + P(B) - P(A \cup B) = 0.1$, so

$\quad\quad P(A \cap B) \neq P(A) \times P(B) = 0.24$

A and B are therefore not independent.

3. Taking ε to be a sample space of 100 'typical' students, in an obvious notation,

$$n(L \cup M) = 100 - 10 = 90$$

$$n(L \cap M) = n(L) + n(M) - n(L \cup M) = 80 + 70 - 90 = 60.$$

Numbers in the various regions of the Venn diagram are as shown.

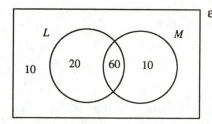

(a) $P(L \cap M) = \dfrac{60}{100} = 0.6$

(b) $P(M \cap L') = \dfrac{10}{100} = 0.1$

4. (a) $P(E_1 \cap E_2 \cap \ldots \cap E_n) = P(E_1) \times P(E_2) \times \ldots \times P(E_n)$

(b) (i) The three trials are independent. In each trial $P(R) = \dfrac{1}{2}$, so

$$P(RRR) = \dfrac{1}{2} \times \dfrac{1}{2} \times \dfrac{1}{2} = \dfrac{1}{8}$$

(ii) In the first trial $P(R) = \dfrac{1}{2}$. In the second there are 5 balls among the remaining 11, so $P(R) = \dfrac{5}{11}$. For the third trial, $P(R) = \dfrac{4}{10}$.

$$P(RRR) = \dfrac{1}{2} \times \dfrac{5}{11} \times \dfrac{4}{10} = \dfrac{1}{11}.$$

5. The possibilities RRR, BBB and YYY are mutually exclusive, so their probabilities must be added, i.e.

$$P(\text{same colour}) = P(RRR) + P(BBB) + P(YYY).$$

(a) $\left(\dfrac{1}{2}\right)^3 + \left(\dfrac{1}{3}\right)^3 + \left(\dfrac{1}{6}\right)^3 = \dfrac{1}{6}.$

(b) $\dfrac{1}{11} + \left(\dfrac{4}{12} \times \dfrac{3}{11} \times \dfrac{2}{10}\right) + 0 = \dfrac{1}{11} + \dfrac{1}{55} = \dfrac{6}{55}$

$P(YYY) = 0$ because there are only 2 yellow balls

1.6   System, counting and ordering

> **How many routes are there from *A* to *C* via *B* ?**

Since each of the three routes from *A* to *B* may be paired with each of the two from *B* to *C* there are 3 x 2 = 6 such routes.

Exercise 5

1. Taking skirts and jeans as equivalent in this case, the number of outfits is

$$6 \times (2 + 2) \times 4 \ = \ 96.$$

2. There are 6 ways of matching up the panes and frames. Each pane can then be fitted into its frame in four ways. There are therefore 6 x 4 = 24 different ways of glazing the window.

3. For each letter there are 3 possible boxes, so the number of ways of posting the letters is 3 x 3 x 3 x 3 = 81. The required probability is $\frac{1}{81}$.

    Although **in the long run** boxes are used with equal frequency this may not apply **on any given evening**. For instance, at certain times of year the hotel's guests may be almost all foreigners. So the assumption of equal likelihood of posting in the four boxes may be incorrect.

1.7   Permutations and combinations

> **How many different *selections* of four letters can be made from the five letters of the word EVENT?**

With 2 E's, $\binom{3}{2} = 3$

With 1E,   1

There are 4 combinations or selections.

Exercise 6

1. nPn is the number of ways of ordering n things, which is $n!$

   (The first thing may be chosen in n ways, second in $(n-1)$ and so on, giving a total of $n \times (n-1) \times (n-2) \times \ldots \times 2 \times 1$.) So

   $$n! = nPn = \frac{n!}{(n-n)!} = \frac{n!}{0!},$$

   which can be true only if $0! = 1$.

   $\binom{n}{n}$ is the number of ways of choosing n things from n, which is 1. So

   $$1 = \binom{n}{n} = \frac{n!}{(n-n)! \, n!} = \frac{1}{0!}$$

   which again is true only if $0! = 1$.

2. (a) (i) $\binom{n}{r} = \frac{n!}{(n-r)! \, r!} = \frac{n!}{[n-(n-r)]! \, (n-r)!} = \binom{n}{n-r}$.

   (ii) In this answer you need to use the results:

   $$r! = r \times (r-1)! \quad \text{and} \quad (n-r+1)! = (n-r+1) \times (n-r)!$$

   $$\binom{n}{r} + \binom{n}{r-1} = \frac{n!}{(n-r)! \, r!} + \frac{n!}{(n-r+1)! \, (r-1)!}$$

   $$= \frac{n!(n-r+1) + n! \, r}{(n-r+1)! \, r!}$$

   $$= \frac{n!(n-r+1+r)}{(n-r+1)! \, r!}$$

   $$= \frac{n!(n+1)}{(n+1-r)! \, r!}$$

   $$= \frac{(n+1)!}{(n+1-r)! \, r!} = \binom{n+1}{r}.$$

   If you find the addition of terms difficult, try a particular numerical case, for example:

   $$\binom{7}{3} + \binom{7}{2} = \frac{7!}{4! \, 3!} + \frac{7!}{5! \, 2!}$$

   $$= \frac{7! \times 5 + 7! \times 3}{5! \times 3!}, \text{ etc.}$$

(b) The results tell you two things about Pascal's triangle.

    (i) The rows are symmetrical about their mid-points; hence you only need to calculate up to the middle of a row.

    (ii) Every element, apart from the 1's, is the sum of the two neighbouring elements in the row above. Thus, given the fourth row, the fifth row is found as shown:

fourth row		1		4		6		4		1	
fifth row	1		5		10		10		5		1

3. (a) $5! = 120$

(b) If you could distinguish between the S's by arranging, say, $S_1 PAS_2 M$ there would be $5! = 120$ ways. However, when the subscripts are removed, these arrangements fall into indistinguishable pairs. ($S_1 PAS_2 M$ and $S_2 PAS_1 M$ would both become SPASM, for example.) So the answer is $120 \div 2 = 60$

(c) Using a similar argument the answer is $\frac{6!}{3!} = 120$

4. In each case the arrangement may be made in $_9P_4 = 9 \times 8 \times 7 \times 6$ ways.

(a) The number of 4-digit numbers starting with 9 is $1 \times 8 \times 7 \times 6$.
(The first digit may be chosen in only one way, then the second in 8, etc.)

The required probability is $\frac{8 \times 7 \times 6}{9 \times 8 \times 7 \times 6} = \frac{1}{9}$

This answer could have been obtained more easily by symmetry; a number is as likely to start with 9 as with any other digit.

(b) It is best to build the number in reverse. The last digit may be chosen in 4 ways (2, 4, 6 or 8). Then the next digits in 8, 7 and 6 ways respectively.

The required probability is $\frac{4 \times 8 \times 7 \times 6}{9 \times 8 \times 7 \times 6} = \frac{4}{9}$

Again, look for a simpler alternative solution by symmetry.

(c) The number of ways of forming the number is $1 \times 4 \times 7 \times 6$.

The required probability is $\frac{4 \times 7 \times 6}{9 \times 8 \times 7 \times 6} = \frac{1}{18}$

Note that the answer to (c) is not the product of the answers to (a) and (b) since starting with 9 and being even are not independent events. Can you see why?

5.　(a)　(i)　　$\binom{8}{4} = \frac{8 \cdot 7 \cdot 6 \cdot 5}{1 \cdot 2 \cdot 3 \cdot 4} = 70$

　　　　(ii)　　$\binom{9}{4} = \frac{9 \cdot 8 \cdot 7 \cdot 6}{1 \cdot 2 \cdot 3 \cdot 4} = 126$

　　　　(iii)　　Since one of the members is fixed, only 8 people are left, from whom 3 must be chosen to join the ex-chairperson.

$$\binom{8}{3} = \frac{8 \cdot 7 \cdot 6}{1 \cdot 2 \cdot 3} = 56$$

Note that $126 = 70 + 56$

　　(b)　Given $(n + 1)$ things, one of them is identified; call it X. Selections of r things from the $(n + 1)$ are of two kinds:

I　those not containing X,

II　those containing X.

In case I there are only n things left to choose from, and selection may be made in $\binom{n}{r}$ ways.

In case II there are again only n things to choose from and only $(r - 1)$ left to choose, so selection may be made in $\binom{n}{r-1}$ ways.

Finally, cases I and II are mutually exclusive and exhaust all the possibilities, so the number of ways of choosing r from $(n + 1)$ is

$$\binom{n+1}{r} = \binom{n}{r} + \binom{n}{r-1}$$

2   *n-stage experiments*

2.1   Tree diagrams

> Quote the two rules and the conditions under which they apply.

Addition :   if A and B are mutually exclusive, $P(A \cup B) = P(A) + P(B)$.
Multiplication: if A and B are independent, $P(A \cap B) = P(A) \times P(B)$.

> **(a)**   **Explain why the probabilities along branches are multiplied.**
>
> **(b)**   **Explain why the probabilities at the two tips are added.**

(a)   The pairs of successive events are independent.

(b)   The events 'being woken by the alarm and catching the bus' and 'not being woken by the alarm and catching the bus' are mutually exclusive.

Exercise 1

1.

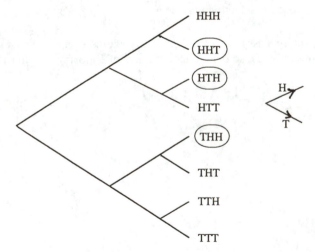

(a)   Exactly two heads occur in 3 cases out of the possible 8 (shown ringed). Required probability is $\frac{3}{8}$

(b)   There are two favourable cases, HTH and THT. Answer is $\frac{2}{8} = \frac{1}{4}$

2.

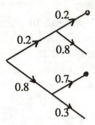

(a)   The probabilities are as shown, since the student has a 1 in 5 chance of guessing the correct option.

(b)   The favourable tips of the tree are indicated. The required probability is
      (0.2 x 0.2) + (0.8 x 0.7) = 0.60

(c)   Assuming that you can routinely eliminate either two or three options as clearly wrong, the missing probabilities might be 0.4 and 0.6 respectively in which case the required probability would be

      (0.2 x 0.4) + (0.8 x 0.7) = 0.64.

      Your answer should be greater than 0.60 but not greater than 0.70.

3.

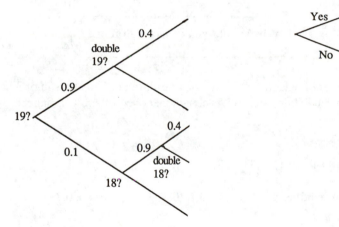

(a)   0.9 x 0.4 = 0.36

(b)   0.1 x 0.9 x 0.4 = 0.036

2.2   Bernoulli trials

> **Which of these do you think give Bernoulli sequences?**
>
> **(a)**   **Repeated cuts of a pack of cards.**
>
> **(b)**   **Dealing a pack of cards.**
>
> **(c)**   **Repeated throws of a biased die.**
>
> **(d)**   **A snooker match between players.**

(a)   A Bernoulli sequence.

(b)   Not a Bernoulli sequence. This is an example of a trial 'without replacement'. For example, before the first card is dealt $P(\text{heart}) = \frac{1}{4}$. For the next card dealt, $P(\text{heart}) = \frac{12}{51}$ or $\frac{13}{51}$, depending on whether the first was or was not a heart. In a Bernoulli sequence the outcomes must have fixed probabilities.

(c)   A Bernoulli sequence. The fact that the probabilities of the various scores are not equal does not mean that they are not individually fixed.

(d)   Not a Bernoulli sequence. The differences in temperament of the players will, in general, lead to a change in the probability of a particular outcome as the match proceeds.

> **Why should you expect a sum of 1?**

The infinite set of outcomes: tail, run of 1 head, run of 2 heads, run of 3 heads …
exhaust all probabilities and so it is certain that one of them will happen.

Exercise 2

1.   (a) $(0.8)^4 \approx 0.41$ (b) $(0.8)^4 \times (0.2) \approx 0.08$

2.   The probabilites are 0.2, 0.8×0.2, $(0.8)^2 \times 0.2$, $(0.8)^3 \times 0.2 \ldots$

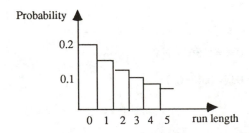

2.3   The binomial distribution

> **In how many cases are there two N's? Three N's? Four N's?**

There are two N's in 6 cases, three in 4 cases and four in one case.

> **Explain why P(8 or 9 or 10) = P(8) + P(9) + P(10).**
> **Check the details of the calculation.**

Scoring 8, 9 and 10 bull's-eyes are mutually exclusive possibilities and so the addition law (extended to three terms) may be used.

In checking the details of the calculation, note that $\binom{10}{8} = \frac{10 \times 9}{1 \times 2}$

In general, $\binom{n}{r} = \dfrac{n(n-1)\ldots(n-r+1)(n-r)\ldots 2.1}{(n-r)!\,r!}$

$\qquad\qquad = \dfrac{n(n-1)\ldots(n-r+1)}{r!}$

Exercise 3

1. Lateness is the 'favourable' event with $p = 0.2$. There are 5 trials (working days), so $n = 5$.

(a) $\binom{n}{r} p^r (1-p)^{n-r}$, with $n = 5$, $r = 3$, $p = 0.2$ becomes

   $\binom{5}{3}(0.2)^3 (1-0.2)^2 = 10 \times 0.008 \times 0.64 = 0.0512$

(b) P(late on 3 or 4 or 5 days) = P(late on 3 days)
$\qquad\qquad\qquad\qquad\qquad\qquad$ + P(late on 4 days) + P(late on 5 days).

   P(late on 4 days) = $\binom{5}{4}(0.2)^4 (1-0.2)^1 = 0.0064$

   P(late on 5 days) = $\binom{5}{5}(0.2)^5 = 0.00032$

   The required probability is $0.0512 + 0.0064 + 0.00032$

$\qquad\qquad\qquad = 0.05792 \approx 0.058$

   If you find this answer surprising you can check it by finding P(late on 0 or 1 or 2 days).

2. Assuming the die to be unbiased

$$P(\text{one six}) = \binom{10}{1}\left(\tfrac{1}{6}\right)\left(\tfrac{5}{6}\right)^5 = \tfrac{25}{3}\left(\tfrac{1}{6}\right)\left(\tfrac{5}{6}\right)^4$$

$$P(\text{two sixes}) = \binom{10}{2}\left(\tfrac{1}{6}\right)^2\left(\tfrac{5}{6}\right)^4 = \tfrac{45}{6}\left(\tfrac{1}{6}\right)\left(\tfrac{5}{6}\right)^4$$

Since $\tfrac{25}{3} > \tfrac{45}{6}$, $\quad$ $P(\text{one six}) > P(\text{two sixes})$.

3. $P(r \text{ hits}) = \binom{10}{r}(0.6)^r(0.4)^{n-r}$

You could calculate this probability for different values of r.
Alternatively, you could use this method:

$$\frac{P(r+1 \text{ hits})}{P(r \text{ hits})} = \frac{0.6}{0.4} \times \frac{10-r}{r+1} = \frac{30-3r}{2r+2}$$

This fraction is greater than 1 if $30 - 3r > 2r + 2$

i.e. $\qquad\qquad\qquad\qquad r < 5.6$

Hence the answer is 5 or 6. Finally $\dfrac{P(6 \text{ hits})}{P(5 \text{ hits})} = \dfrac{15}{12} > 1$,

so the most likely number of hits is 6.

4. (a) The cuts form a Bernoulli sequence with $n = r = 4$, $p = \tfrac{1}{4}$

Probability is $\left(\tfrac{1}{4}\right)^4 = \tfrac{1}{256}$

(b) The required probability is P(all spades) + P(all hearts)

$\qquad\qquad\qquad\qquad$ + P (all diamonds) + P(all clubs)

$\qquad = 4 \times$ P(all clubs), by symmetry

$\qquad = \tfrac{1}{64}$

5. (a) The deal does not form a Bernoulli sequence since the probability of a given event is not fixed. After the first club is dealt with probability $\tfrac{1}{4}$ there are only 12 clubs left among the remaining 51 cards, and so on. The four events of dealing cards are independent so the multiplication law is used.

The required probability is $\tfrac{1}{4} \times \tfrac{12}{51} \times \tfrac{11}{50} \times \tfrac{10}{49} = \tfrac{11}{4165}$

(b) Again, by symmetry, the required probability is $4 \times \tfrac{11}{4165} = \tfrac{44}{4165}$

6. $\binom{5}{3}(0.6)^3(0.4)^2 + \binom{5}{4}(0.6)^4(0.4) + \binom{5}{5}(0.6)^5$

$= 0.3456 + 0.2592 + 0.0778 \approx 0.68$

7. Suppose that people could not distinguish between the brands; then
    P(Brand A preferred) $= \frac{1}{2}$. In this case, the probability of at least 4 out of 5
    preferring Brand A is

$$\binom{5}{4}\left(\tfrac{1}{2}\right)^4\left(\tfrac{1}{2}\right) + \binom{5}{5}\left(\tfrac{1}{2}\right)^5 = \frac{3}{16}, \quad \text{a little less than 20\%}$$

Even if people simply tossed a coin to make a choice, out of a sample of 5 there
would be a chance of nearly 20% that **at least** 4 choose Brand A. This chance is
too high for the event to be surprising, so the statement as given is not significant.

2.4 Conditional probability

> **Write down a similar expression for P(B').**

$$P(B') = P(A) P(B' \mid A) + P(A') P(B' \mid A')$$

> **Write down similar expressions for**
>
> **(a) P($A \cap B'$),   (b) P($A' \cap B$),   (c) P($A' \cap B'$).**

(a) $P(A \cap B') = P(A) P(B' \mid A)$,   (b) $P(A' \cap B) = P(A') P(B \mid A')$,

(c) $P(A' \cap B') = P(A') P(B' \mid A')$.

Note also that since $A \cap B = B \cap A$ ($\cap$ is a **commutative** operation),

$$P(A \cap B) = P(B) P(A \mid B),$$

with similar alternative expressions for the other probabilities.

> **Show that when A and B are independent, P($A \cap B$) = P(A) P(B).**

A and B independent, so $P(B \mid A) = P(B)$

$$\Rightarrow P(A) P(B \mid A) = P(A) P(B)$$

$$\Rightarrow \quad P(A \cap B) = P(A) P(B)$$

Exercise 4

1. (a) $P(A \cap B) = P(A)\,P(B)$ or $P(B \mid A) = P(B)$ or $P(A \mid B) = P(A)$.

   (b) $P(A \cup B) = P(A) + P(B)$

   (c) $P(A \cup B) = 1$. [Note that $P(A') = P(B)$ is a **sufficient condition**, as is the equivalent statement $P(A) + P(B) = 1$, but that this condition is not **necessary**.]

2. (a) $P(A) + P(A') = 1$,   (b) $P(A \mid B) + P(A' \mid B) = 1$

   (c) $P(A' \mid B)\,P(B) = P(A' \cap B)$,

   (d) $P(A \cup B) + P(B') \times P(A' \mid B') = P(A \cup B) + P(A' \cap B')$
$$= P(A \cup B) + P[(A \cup B)']$$
$$= 1$$

3. Abbreviations used are: B - blue-eyed, L - left-handed

   $P(L \mid B) = \frac{1}{7}$ $P(B \mid L) = \frac{1}{3}$ $P(L' \cap B') = \frac{4}{5}$

   You have to find $P(L \cap B)$

$$P(L \mid B) = \frac{P(L \cap B)}{P(B)} \quad \text{and} \quad P(B \mid L) = \frac{P(L \cap B)}{P(L)}$$

   So, putting $P(L \cap B) = x$, $P(B) = 7x$ and $P(L) = 3x$

   Now, $P(L' \cap B') = P[(L \cup B)'] = \frac{4}{5}$ so $P(L \cup B) = \frac{1}{5}$

   But $P(L \cup B) = P(L) + P(B) - P(L \cap B)$, i.e.
$$\frac{1}{5} = 3x + 7x - x = 9x$$

   Hence $P(L \cap B) = x = \frac{1}{45}$

4. (a) $P(A \cap B) = P(B)\,P(A \mid B) = \frac{1}{3} \times \frac{1}{4} = \frac{1}{12}$

   (b) $P(A \cup B) = P(A) + P(B) - P(A \cap B) = \frac{1}{2} + \frac{1}{3} - \frac{1}{12} = \frac{3}{4}$

   (c) $P(A' \cap B') = P[(A \cup B)'] = 1 - P(A \cup B) = \frac{1}{4}$

   Since A and C are independent $P(A \cap C) = P(A)\,P(C)$, hence
$$P(C) = \frac{1}{12} \div \frac{1}{2} = \frac{1}{6}$$

   Then to show that B and C are mutually exclusive verify that

$$P(B \cup C) = P(B) + P(C).$$

2.5　Bayes' theorem

> (a)　Explain why $P(S_B | A) = \frac{1}{2}$
>
> (b)　Calculate $P(S_B)$ as $P(A) \times P(S_B | A) + P(A') \times P(S_B | A')$.

(a)　If A is to be executed, then the other is equally likely to be B or C. If A is not to be executed, then B and C are to be executed and the jailer is equally likely to name either. In both possible cases the probability of the jailer choosing to name B is $\frac{1}{2}$.

(b)　The formula is a symbolic form of the explanation just given. The value of the expression is

$$\frac{2}{3} \times \frac{1}{2} + \frac{1}{3} \times \frac{1}{2} = \frac{1}{2}.$$

Exercise 5

1.　Abbreviations used are: F - fiction, H - hardback.

$$P(F) = 0.4, \quad P(F') = 0.6, \qquad P(F \cap H) = 0.1, \qquad P(H) = 0.5$$

$$P(F | H) = \frac{P(F \cap H)}{P(H)} = 0.2$$

2.　Abbreviations used (for night drivers): D - drinking, A - accident

$$P(D) = \frac{1}{4}, \qquad P(A | D') = 4 \times 10^{-5}, \quad P(A | D) = 2 \times 10^{-3}.$$

First you have to find $P(A)$.

$$\begin{aligned}
P(A) &= P(D)\,P(A | D) + P(D')\,P(A | D') \\[4pt]
&= \frac{1}{4} \times 2 \times 10^{-3} + \frac{3}{4} \times 4 \times 10^{-5} \\[4pt]
&= 5.3 \times 10^{-4}.
\end{aligned}$$

The probability that the policeman's guess is correct is $P(D | A)$.

By Bayes' theorem,

$$P(D | A) = \frac{P(D)\,P(A | D)}{P(A)}$$

$$= \frac{\frac{1}{4} \times 2 \times 10^{-3}}{5.3 \times 10^{-4}} \approx 0.94$$

3E.

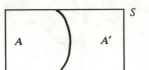

The given result is a generalisation of
$$P(B) = P(B \mid A) P(A) + P(B \mid A') P(A'),$$
since A and A' partition the sample space.

Generalised form of Bayes' theorem : for any event A_j,

$$P(A_j \mid B) = \frac{P(A_j) P(B \mid A_j)}{P(B)}$$

$$= \frac{P(A_j) P(B \mid A_j)}{\displaystyle\sum_{i=1}^{n} P(B \mid A_i) P(A_i)}$$

4.   Using abbreviations:

A_1 - on foot, A_2 - by bus, A_3 - by bike, A_4 - by car, B - late.

Then you wish to find $P(A_1 \mid B)$. By Bayes' theorem,

$$P(A_1 \mid B) = \frac{P(A_1) P(B \mid A_1)}{P(B)}$$

$$P(B) = \sum_{i=1}^{4} P(A_i) P(B \mid A_i)$$

$$= (0.3 \times \tfrac{1}{4}) + (0.2 \times \tfrac{1}{3}) + (0.1 \times \tfrac{1}{12}) + (0.4 \times 0)$$

$$= 0.15$$

So $P(A_1 \mid B) = \dfrac{0.075}{0.15} = 0.5$

2.6   Further applications of Bayes' theorem

> **Find the other two posterior probabilities and check that the sum of all three probabilities is 1.**

$$P(D \mid F) = \frac{P(D)\, P(F \mid D)}{P(F)} = \frac{0.3 \times 0.2}{0.56} = \frac{3}{28}$$

$$P(R \mid F) = \frac{P(R)\, P(F \mid R)}{P(F)} = \frac{0.1 \times 0.2}{0.56} = \frac{1}{28}$$

$$\frac{6}{7} + \frac{3}{28} + \frac{1}{28} = 1$$

Exercise 6

1. Abbreviations used : B - New Sudso is better than Kleenrite
    F - favourable report

    Prior probability $P(B)$ is 0.9 and conditional probabilities $P(F \mid B)$ and $P(F \mid B')$ are 0.8 and 0.2 respectively.

    You have to find $P(B \mid F)$. From Bayes' theorem,

    $$P(B \mid F) = \frac{P(B)\ P(F \mid B)}{P(B)\ P(F \mid B) + P(B')P(F \mid B')}$$

    $$= \frac{0.9 \times 0.8}{(0.9 \times 0.8) + (0.1 \times 0.2)} \approx 0.97$$

    The example shows how a not very reliable survey can be a powerful reinforcement of a hunch.

2. Abbreviations : A, B - resistors come from machines A, B
    E - sample of three are all good

    (a) $P(E \mid A) = (0.9)^3 = 0.729$

    Similarly $P(E \mid B) = (0.8)^3 = 0.512$

    (b) $P(A \mid E) = \dfrac{P(A)\ P(E \mid A)}{P(A)\ P(E \mid A) + P(B)P(E \mid B)}$

    $$= \frac{0.7 \times 0.729}{(0.7 \times 0.729) + (0.3 \times 0.512)} \approx 0.77$$

3. $P(L \mid G) = \dfrac{P(L)\ P(G \mid L)}{P(L)P(G \mid L) + P(H)P(G \mid H) + P(M)\ P(G \mid M)}$

    $$\frac{0.5 \times 0.2}{(0.5 \times 0.2) + (0.25 \times 0.5) + (0.25 \times 0.9)} \approx 0.222$$

    Similarly, $P(L \mid G') = 0.727$, $P(H \mid G) = 0.278$, $P(H \mid G') = 0.227$,

    $P(M \mid G) = 0.500$, $P(M \mid G') = 0.045$, all to 3 decimal places.

4. Taking $P(E) = 0.5$

$$P(E \mid F) = \frac{P(E)\,P(F \mid E)}{P(E)\,P(F \mid E) + P(E')\,P(F \mid E')}$$

$$= \frac{0.5 \times 0.9}{(0.5 \times 0.9) + (0.5 \times 0.2)} \approx 0.82$$

Taking $P(E) = 0.7$

$$P(E \mid F) = \frac{0.7 \times 0.9}{(0.7 \times 0.9) + (0.3 \times 0.2)} \approx 0.91$$

(a) In both cases a conjecture is strongly supported by a contingent event. As the prior probability increases by 0.2 the posterior probability increases by rather less than 0.1; the weaker the conjecture, the greater is the strengthening effect.

(b) Much scientific progress is based on this idea. Theories are tested by experiment and reinforced, weakened or rejected as a result.

Medical diagnosis proceeds according to the same model. Jaundice may make a doctor suspect gallstones. Using knowledge of other symptoms of this complaint the doctor asks questions and performs tests which may lead to reinforcement of the original suspicion. If necessary an X-ray examination will virtually settle the matter.

3 Occupancy and random walks

3.1 Counting problems

> In models 1, 2 and 3, show that the numbers of allocations are
>
> $$\binom{n}{r}, \ _n\mathrm{P}_r \text{ and } n^r,$$
>
> respectively.

Model 1

You must simply choose the boxes which are to contain the tokens i.e. r boxes from n. This can be done in $\binom{n}{r}$ ways.

Model 2

You must choose r boxes **in order** i.e. the box containing token 1, the box containing token 2 ,... This can be done in $_n\mathrm{P}_r$ ways.

Model 3

Token 1 can be allocated to any one of the n boxes. Token 2 can then be allocated to any one of the boxes and similarly for each of the other tokens. The r, s principle then gives a total number of ways of

$$\underbrace{n \times n \times \ \ldots \ \times n}_{r \text{ factors}} = n^r$$

3.2 Choosing a model

> What is the probability of a prize in box 1 and a prize in box 6 if all four prizes are indistinguishable?

Since no box may contain more than 1 prize and the prizes are indistinguishable, occupancy model 1 with $n = 6$ and $r = 4$ is applicable. The total number of possible allocations is $\binom{6}{4} = 15$.

If box 1 and box 6 are each to contain a prize then the remaining 2 prizes must be allocated among the remaining 4 boxes. This can be done in $\binom{4}{2} = 6$ ways.

Applying the rule for equally likely outcomes, the required probability is $\frac{6}{15} = \frac{2}{5}$.

Exercise 1

1. Associate a box with each of the 3 routes and use two tokens, one labelled 'up' and the other 'down'. With $n = 3$, $r = 2$ and with no restriction on the number of tokens to a box (the 'up' route can also be the 'down' route), occupancy model 3 applies. The number of possible trips is $3^2 = 9$.

2. Associate a box with each of the 3 processors and a distinguishable token with each of the n different jobs. Since a processor may be allocated any number of jobs, occupancy model 3 is relevant and the total number of possible assignments is 3^n.

   If the first processor receives no jobs then the n jobs must be allocated among the 2 remaining processors which can be achieved in 2^n ways. The probability is therefore $\left(\frac{2}{3}\right)^n$.

3. Consider the 4 starting positions as boxes and the 4 number tags as tokens. There can be only one tag in any one starting position and the tags are clearly distinguishable by their number. So occupancy model 2 applies with $n = 4$ and $r = 4$ and there are $_4P_4 = 24$ possible allocations.

   (a) There is only 1 such allocation which can be represented by $(1, 2, 3, 4)$. Its probability is therefore $\frac{1}{24}$.

   (b) If tag 1 is in position 1, then the other 3 tags must be allocated among the remaining 3 positions. This can be done in $_3P_3 = 6$ ways. The probability is $\frac{6}{24} = \frac{1}{4}$.

   (c) It is easy to list the favourable events:

   $(1, 2, 3, 4)$, $(1, 2, 4, 3)$, $(1, 4, 3, 2)$, $(1, 3, 2, 4)$, $(4, 2, 3, 1)$, $(3, 2, 1, 4)$ and $(2, 1, 3, 4)$. The probability is $\frac{7}{24}$.

   (d) The favourable events are as in (c) but excluding $(1, 2, 3, 4)$. The probability is $\frac{6}{24} = \frac{1}{4}$.

3.3 The matching problem

> (a) Show how the matching experiment described above can be represented by an occupancy model.
>
> (b) What is the probability that a person would obtain a perfect match by guessing?

(a) Associate each Zener card with a box. The subject (presumably) records a different Zener symbol on each token, so the tokens are distinguishable and only one token is allocated to each box. The appropriate occupancy model is 2 with $n = 5$ and $r = 5$. The total number of possible allocations is $_5P_5 = 120$.

(b) $\frac{1}{120}$.

130

> **What does (c, a, b) mean?**

(c, a, b) means that c takes a's hat, a takes b's hat and b takes c's hat. In this case no one ends up with his own hat.

> **(a)** If four commuters choose their hats at random, find the probability of a derangement.
>
> **(b)** What is the probability that at least one commuter gets his own hat?

(a)   The total number of possible allocations of hats to commuters is $_4P_4 = \dfrac{4!}{(4-4)!} = 24$

The following allocations are derangements:

(b, a, d, c) (b, c, d, a) (b, d, a, c)
(c, a, d, b) (c, d, a, b) (c, d, b, a)
(d, a, b, c) (d, c, a, b) (d, c, b, a)

The probability of a derangement is $\dfrac{9}{24} = \dfrac{3}{8}$.

(b) $1 - \text{P(derangement)} = \dfrac{5}{8}$.

Exercise 2

1. $\text{P(exactly 3 right)} + \text{P(exactly 4 right)} = 0 + \dfrac{1}{24} = \dfrac{1}{24}$.

2.   This is the matching problem with $n = 6$ and $r = 6$. There are $_6P_6 = 720$ possible arrangements of the 6 volumes.

$$\text{P(6 correct)} = \frac{1}{720}.$$

Exactly 5 volumes cannot be in their correct positions without the sixth also being correctly placed. $\text{P(5 correct)} = 0$.

Choose 4 out of the 6 volumes to put in their correct positions. There are $\binom{6}{4} = 15$ such combinations of volumes. One example is $(\bullet, 2, 3, 4, 5, \bullet)$; the remaining 2 volumes can be 'deranged' in only one way to give $(6, 2, 3, 4, 5, 1)$. In total there are $15 \times 1 = 15$ possible allocations with 4 volumes in their correct positions. The probability of this event is $\dfrac{15}{720} = \dfrac{1}{48}$.

3. There are $n!$ possible arrangements of the volumes on the shelf.

Only one arrangement has all the volumes in their correct positions with corresponding probability $\frac{1}{n!}$.

As before, the probability of exactly $n - 1$ volumes in their correct positions is zero.

Choose $n - 2$ volumes to go in their correct positions. There are $\binom{n}{n-2}$ possible combinations of such volumes. The remaining 2 can be 'deranged' in only one way. The required probability is therefore

$$\frac{\binom{n}{n-2}}{n!} = \frac{n!}{(n-2)! \, 2!} \times \frac{1}{n!} = \frac{1}{2(n-2)!}$$

3.4   Recurrence relations

> **Explain how the above equation is obtained.**

'A total of $(n - 1)$ followed by H' and 'a total of $(n - 2)$ followed by T' are mutually exclusive possibilities and so their probabilities are added. Since $P(H) = P(T) = \frac{1}{2}$ the required result follows, using the multiplication rule for independent events.

> **Check the above value for p_3 and find p_4 and p_5.**
>
> **Write a program for a calculator or computer to generate the probabilities p_n.**

$$p_3 = \frac{1}{2}(p_2 + p_1) = \frac{1}{2}\left(\frac{3}{4} + \frac{1}{2}\right) = \frac{1}{2} \times \frac{5}{4} = \frac{5}{8}$$

$$p_4 = \frac{1}{2}\left(\frac{5}{8} + \frac{3}{4}\right) = \frac{11}{16}$$

$$p_5 = \frac{1}{2}\left(\frac{11}{16} + \frac{5}{8}\right) = \frac{21}{32}$$

A BBC BASIC program:

```
10   LET N = 10
20   DIM P(N)
30   LET P(1) = 0.5
40   LET P(2) = 0.75
50   FOR C = 3 TO N
60   P(C) = (P(C − 1) +  P(C − 2)) * 0.5
70   PRINT  P(C)
80   NEXT C
```

> **(a)** Carefully explain how the recurrence relation is obtained.
>
> **(b)** Calculate p_1 and p_2 from first principles. Check that you obtain the same answers when applying the recurrence relation with the initial condition $p_0 = 0$.

(a) Since there must be an odd or an even number of sixes,

$$P(\text{even number of sixes}) = 1 - P(\text{odd number of sixes})$$
$$= 1 - p_{n-1}$$

The events

'odd number of sixes from $(n-1)$ dice' and 'non-six thrown on the nth throw' are independent and so the probability of the compound event formed by those two events in sequence is found by the multiplication law, and is $p_{n-1} \times \frac{5}{6}$.

Similarly, the compound event

'even number of sixes from $(n-1)$ dice followed by six' has probability $(1 - p_{n-1}) \times \frac{1}{6}$.

Since the two compound events are mutually exclusive their probabilities are added to give p_n.

$$p_n = p_{n-1} \times \frac{5}{6} + (1 - p_{n-1}) \times \frac{1}{6}$$
$$= \frac{5}{6} p_n + \frac{1}{6} - \frac{1}{6} p_{n-1}$$
$$= \frac{1}{6} + \frac{2}{3} p_{n-1}$$

(b) $P(\text{six thrown}) = \frac{1}{6}$ so $p_1 = \frac{1}{6}$.

For an odd number of sixes in two throws the possibilities are

(six, non-six) and (non-six, six),

with total probability $\left(\frac{1}{6} \times \frac{5}{6} \right) + \left(\frac{5}{6} \times \frac{1}{6} \right) = \frac{5}{18}$. So $p_2 = \frac{5}{18}$.

Clearly the probability of throwing an odd number of sixes when no dice are thrown is zero, i.e. $p_0 = 0$. Using the recurrence relation,

$$p_1 = \frac{1}{6} + \left(\frac{1}{3} \times 0 \right) = \frac{1}{6},$$

$$p_2 = \frac{1}{6} + \left(\frac{2}{3} \times \frac{1}{6} \right) = \frac{5}{18}.$$

Exercise 3

1. For a head to appear for the first time on the kth toss there must be no head in the first $(k-1)$ tosses and the kth toss must be a head. So

    $$p_k = (1 - p_{k-1}) \times \frac{1}{2}.$$

    The sequence is:

    $$p_0 = 0, \quad p_1 = \frac{1}{2}, \quad p_2 = \frac{1}{4}, \quad p_3 = \frac{1}{8}, \quad \dots, \quad p_k = \left(\frac{1}{2}\right)^k.$$

    A simpler way to obtain this result will probably occur to you!

2. An even number of heads in k tosses results from

    - an even number of H's in $(k-1)$ tosses followed by a T, or

    - an odd number of H's in $(k-1)$ tosses followed by a H.

    So

    $$p_k = p_{k-1} \times \frac{1}{2} + (1 - p_{k-1}) \times \frac{1}{2} = \frac{1}{2}.$$
    $$\Rightarrow p_k = \frac{1}{2} \text{ for all } k \geq 1. \quad \text{(The recurrence relation is \textbf{degenerate}.)}$$

3. (a) $C_n = C_{n-1} + C_{n-2}, \quad C_0 = 1, C_1 = 2.$

    This relation generates the Fibonacci sequence 1, 2, 3, 5, 8, ...

    (b) For n tosses there are 2^n possible outcomes, of which C_n are favourable.

    The required probability is $\dfrac{C_n}{2^n}$.

    (c) P(at least two successive heads) $= 1 - \dfrac{C_n}{2^n}$.

4E. Using the mutually exclusive groups described in question 3,

    $$p_n = p_{n-1} \times (1 - p) + p_{n-2} \times p\,(1 - p)$$

    with $p_0 = p_1 = 1$.

3.5   Reasoning by renewal

> Use a similar method to investigate the p_T branch and show that
>
> $$p_T = \frac{1}{2}p_H + \frac{1}{4}p_H = \frac{3}{4}p_H \qquad ③$$

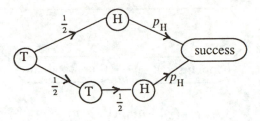

$$p_T = \frac{1}{2} \times p_H + \frac{1}{2} \times \frac{1}{2} \times p_H = \frac{3}{4}p_H$$

Exercise 4

1. (a) Assume that Cheryl has first throw. Let p be the probability that she wins. If Cheryl throws a non-six on her first throw then she becomes the second player and has a probability $(1-p)$ of success.

$$p = \frac{1}{6} + \frac{5}{6}(1-p)$$
$$\Rightarrow p = \frac{6}{11}.$$

The probabilities that Cheryl and Diane win are $\frac{6}{11}$ and $\frac{5}{11}$, respectively.

(b) The probability is $\dfrac{1}{6} + \dfrac{5}{6} \times \dfrac{5}{6} \times \dfrac{1}{6} + \dfrac{5}{6} \times \dfrac{5}{6} \times \dfrac{5}{6} \times \dfrac{5}{6} \times \dfrac{1}{6} + \ldots$

$$= \frac{1}{6}\left[1 + \left(\frac{5}{6}\right)^2 + \left(\frac{5}{6}\right)^4 + \ldots\right], \quad \text{an infinite G.P.}$$

$$= \frac{\frac{1}{6}}{1 - \left(\frac{5}{6}\right)^2}$$

$$= \frac{6}{11}.$$

2.

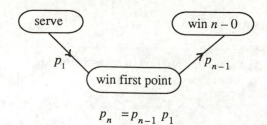

$$P_n = P_{n-1} P_1$$

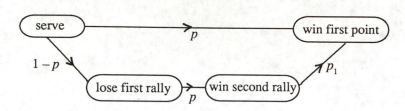

$$p_1 = p + p(1-p)p_1$$

From the second relation, $p_1 = \frac{1}{2} + \frac{1}{2} \times \frac{1}{2} \times p_1 \Rightarrow p_1 = \frac{2}{3}$

From the first relation, $p_2 = p_1 p_1 = p_1{}^2$, $p_3 = p_1{}^3$, ...

So the probability of winning $9 - 0$ is $\left(\frac{2}{3}\right)^9$

3. (a) On the first throw there is a probability $\frac{1}{6}$ of landing on each of the squares $1 - 6$. The diagrams then show the probabilities of landing on square n

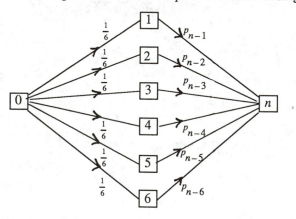

$$P_n = \frac{1}{6}\left(P_{n-1} + P_{n-2} + P_{n-3} + P_{n-4} + P_{n-5} + P_{n-6}\right)$$

(b) $P_0 = 1$ and $p_n = 0$ for $n < 0$.

(c) $p_1 = \frac{1}{6}$, $p_2 = \frac{1}{6}\left(\frac{1}{6}+1\right) = \frac{7}{36}$, $p_3 = \frac{1}{6}\left(\frac{7}{36}+\frac{1}{6}+1\right)$, ...

The values of p_n are given correct to 3 d.p. in the following table:

n	1	2	3	4	5	6	7	8	9	10
p_n	0.167	0.194	0.227	0.265	0.309	0.360	0.254	0.268	0.281	0.289
n	11	12	13	14	15	16	17	18	19	20
p_n	0.294	0.291	0.280	0.284	0.286	0.287	0.287	0.286	0.285	0.286

For large n, p_n has a stable value of about 0.286.

3.6 Random walks

Exercise 5

1. The diagram represents a random walk with two absorption barriers.

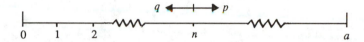

The points on the line represent the first gambler's capital at all possible stages. If her capital reaches 0 then she is ruined and the game ends; if her capital reaches a then her opponent is ruined and again the game ends.

2. P(six before three non-sixes) $= \frac{1}{6} + \frac{5}{6} \times \frac{1}{6} + \left(\frac{5}{6}\right)^2 \times \frac{1}{6} = \frac{91}{216}$.

This can be thought of as a random walk with two absorption barriers.

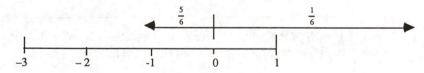

3. In Huygens' problem,

$$p = P(\text{throw of } 14) = \frac{15}{216}$$

$$q = P(\text{throw of } 11) = \frac{27}{216}$$

So $\frac{q}{p} = \frac{27}{15} = 1.8.$

Then $P(A \text{ ruined}) = \dfrac{1.8^{24} - 1.8^{12}}{1.8^{24} - 1} = 0.999136$

So $P(B \text{ ruined}) = 1 - 0.999136 = 0.000864$ and $\dfrac{P(B \text{ ruined})}{P(A \text{ ruined})} \approx 8.65 \times 10^{-4}$.

This is equal to the ratio of the numbers given by Huygens, who must have done all his working without any help from a machine or even tables of logarithms.

4. (a) The squares 1, 3, 5, 7, 9 lie on the diagonals of the board and so a counter on one of these squares is equally likely to move off horizontally or vertically. Hence, by symmetry,

$$p_1 = p_3 = p_5 = p_7 = p_9 = \tfrac{1}{2}$$

(b) By symmetry, $p_2 = p_8$ and $p_4 = p_6$.

Also by symmetry, the probability of moving off horizontally when starting at 2 is the same as the probability of moving off vertically when starting at 4. Therefore $p_2 = 1 - p_4$.

(c)

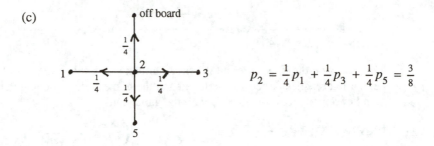

$$p_2 = \tfrac{1}{4}p_1 + \tfrac{1}{4}p_3 + \tfrac{1}{4}p_5 = \tfrac{3}{8}$$

3.7 Solving recurrence relations

> **Which of the following recurrence relations involve only constant multiples of terms of the sequence?**
>
> (a) $p_{n+1} - 2p_n = 0$
>
> (b) $q_n = q_{n-1}^2$
>
> (c) $r_n = nr_{n-1}$
>
> (d) $f_{n+2} = f_{n+1} + f_n$

(a) and (d) involve only constant multiples of terms of the sequences (p_n) and (f_n) respectively.

> **(a)** Check that $u_n = A \left(\frac{1}{2}\right)^n + 4$ satisfies
>
> $$u_{n+1} - \frac{1}{2} u_n = 2.$$
>
> **(b)** Given that $u_1 = 3$, find A.

(a) $\quad u_{n+1} - \frac{1}{2} u_n = A \left(\frac{1}{2}\right)^{n+1} + 4 - \frac{1}{2} \left[A \left(\frac{1}{2}\right)^n + 4 \right]$

$$= A \left(\frac{1}{2}\right)^{n+1} + 4 - A \left(\frac{1}{2}\right)^{n+1} - 2$$

$$= 2$$

(b) Substituting $n = 1$ into the general formula for u_n,

$$3 = A \left(\frac{1}{2}\right)^1 + 4$$

$$\Rightarrow A = -2$$

> **Use a similar method to find the general solution of the relation**
>
> $$u_{n+2} - 3u_{n+1} - 2u_n = 0.$$

Let $u_n = \lambda^n$. Then

$$\lambda^{n+2} - 3\lambda^{n+1} - 2\lambda^n = 0$$

$$\Rightarrow \lambda^2 - 3\lambda - 2 = 0$$

$$\Rightarrow \lambda = \frac{3 \pm \sqrt{17}}{2}$$

The general solution is

$$u_n = A \left(\frac{3 + \sqrt{17}}{2}\right)^n + B \left(\frac{3 - \sqrt{17}}{2}\right)^n$$

where A and B are constants which may be found when the values of any two members of the sequence are known.

> **Use the same method to solve**
>
> $$u_{n+1} - \frac{1}{3}u_n = 1, \quad u_1 = 2$$

A particular (constant) solution of the equation may be found by setting $u_{n+1} = u_n = c$. Then

$$\frac{2}{3}c = 1 \Rightarrow c = \frac{3}{2}.$$

The general solution of

$$u_{n+1} - \frac{1}{3}u_n = 0$$

is $u_n = A\left(\frac{1}{3}\right)^n$.

Hence the general solution of the given equation is

$$u_n = A\left(\frac{1}{3}\right)^n + \frac{3}{2}.$$

Since $u_1 = 2$, $\quad 2 = A\left(\frac{1}{3}\right) + \frac{3}{2} \Rightarrow A = \frac{3}{2}.$

Therefore, $u_n = \frac{3}{2}\left(\frac{1}{3}\right)^n + \frac{3}{2}.$

Exercise 6

1. (a)   On the $n-1$th day:

   - with probability p_{n-1} it is dry and there is then a probability $\frac{3}{4}$ of the nth day being dry;

   - with probability $1 - p_{n-1}$ it is wet and there is then a probability $\frac{1}{4}$ of the nth day being dry.

   $$\text{So } p_n = \frac{3}{4} \times p_{n-1} + \frac{1}{4} \times (1 - p_{n-1})$$
   $$\Rightarrow p_n - \frac{1}{2}p_{n-1} - \frac{1}{4} = 0$$

   (b) $p_n = A\left(\frac{1}{2}\right)^n + \frac{1}{2}$

   Given that $p_1 = 1$, $p_n = \left(\frac{1}{2}\right)^n + \frac{1}{2}$

   (c)   Given that $p_1 = 0$, $p_n = -\left(\frac{1}{2}\right)^n + \frac{1}{2}$

   (d)   As $n \to +\infty$, $p_n \to \frac{1}{2}$ irrespective of the weather on the first day.

2. (a) After 0 moves the 6 is uppermost and after 1 move the 6 cannot be uppermost. Therefore $p_0 = 1$ and $p_1 = 0$.

(b) After n moves:

- with probability p_n the 1 or 6 is uppermost and therefore cannot be uppermost after $n + 1$ moves;

- with probability $1 - p_n$ the 1 or 6 is not uppermost and there is then a probability $\frac{2}{4}$ of 1 or 6 being uppermost after $n + 1$ moves.

So $p_{n+1} = 0 \times p_n + \frac{1}{2} \times (1 - p_n) = \frac{1}{2}(1 - p_n)$

Then $p_{n+1} + \frac{1}{2} p_n = \frac{1}{2} \Rightarrow p_n = A \left(-\frac{1}{2}\right)^n + \frac{1}{3}$

$n = 0: \quad 1 = A + \frac{1}{3} \Rightarrow A = \frac{2}{3}$

$$p_n = \frac{1}{3} + \frac{2}{3} \left(-\frac{1}{2}\right)^n$$

(c) For $n > 0$, the 1 and 6 are equally likely to be uppermost and so the probability is

$$\frac{1}{2} p_n = \frac{1}{6} + \frac{1}{3} \left(-\frac{1}{2}\right)^n$$

3E. Let $r_n = \lambda^n$, then $p\lambda^2 - \lambda + q = 0$.

$$\Rightarrow (\lambda - 1)(p\lambda - q) = 0$$

$$\Rightarrow \lambda = 1 \text{ or } \frac{q}{p}$$

The general solution is $A \times 1^n + B \left(\frac{q}{p}\right)^n = A + B \left(\frac{q}{p}\right)^n$.

$n = 0: \quad A + B = 1$

$n = a: \quad A + B \left(\frac{q}{p}\right)^a = 0$

$$\Rightarrow \left[\left(\frac{q}{p}\right)^a - 1\right] B = -1$$

$$\Rightarrow B = \frac{-1}{\left(\frac{q}{p}\right)^a - 1} \quad \text{and} \quad A = \frac{\left(\frac{q}{p}\right)^a}{\left(\frac{q}{p}\right)^a - 1}$$

$$\Rightarrow r_n = \frac{\left(\frac{q}{p}\right)^a - \left(\frac{q}{p}\right)^n}{\left(\frac{q}{p}\right)^a - 1}$$

4 Sequences of random events

4.1 Will it rain tomorrow?

> **Would you expect a similar pattern (of *H*'s and *T*'s) for 120 tosses of a coin? Explain your answer.**

Though you would expect roughly equal numbers of *H*'s and *T*'s the long runs shown in the weather pattern would be very improbable. You will have noticed a run of 13 *W*'s, another of 12 *D*'s and several other runs of 5 or more of a kind. In Bernoulli trials with two equally likely outcomes, runs of such a length are very unlikely.

> **Relate the row and column totals to the numbers of wet and dry days.**

The row total of 56 *W*'s omits the first *W* of all, which has no predecessor. Similarly the column total of 62 *D*'s omits the final *D*, which has no successor.

> **Find P (*D* | *D*).**

$$P\,(D \mid D) = \tfrac{43}{62} \approx 0.69$$

Exercise 1

1. *A* and *B* are Ahmed and Belinda. *C* is Charlie the dog. They play with a ball. When Ahmed has the ball he is nine times as likely to throw it to Charlie as to Belinda. When Belinda has it she is four times as likely to throw it to Charlie as to Ahmed. When Charlie has it he plays with it on his own.

    You can probably do better than this!

2. Wet

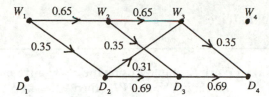

As in Example 1 the routes for W_1 to D_4 are

$W_1 - W_2 - W_3 - D_4$: probability $(0.65)^2 (0.35) = 0.148$

$W_1 - W_2 - D_3 - D_4$: probability $(0.65)(0.35)(0.69) = 0.157$

$W_1 - D_2 - W_3 - D_4$: probability $(0.35)(0.31)(0.35) = 0.038$

$W_1 - D_2 - D_3 - D_4$: probability $(0.35)(0.69)^2 = 0.167$

The total probability is the sum of the probabilities of these mutually exclusive events, namely 0.51.

The answer may be checked using Example 1, since 4 March must be either wet or dry. You will note that $0.49 + 0.51 = 1.0$.

3.

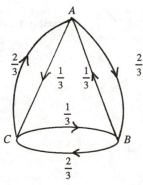

Routes finishing at A :

ABABA, ABACA, ACACA, ACABA, ABCBA, ACBCA

Routes finishing at B :

ABACB, ABCAB, ACACB, ACBAB, ACBCB

Routes finishing at C :

ABABC, ABCAC, ABCBC, ACABC, ACBAC

$$P \text{ (finish at } A \text{)} = 6 \times \left(\frac{2}{3}\right)^2 \left(\frac{1}{3}\right)^2 = \frac{8}{27}.$$

$$P \text{ (finish at } B \text{)} = \left(\frac{2}{3}\right)^4 + 4 \times \left(\frac{2}{3}\right)\left(\frac{1}{3}\right)^3 = \frac{8}{27}.$$

$$P \text{ (finish at } C \text{)} = 4 \times \left(\frac{2}{3}\right)^3 \left(\frac{1}{3}\right) + \left(\frac{1}{3}\right)^3 = \frac{11}{27}.$$

4.2　Stochastic matrices

(a)　Work Example 2 using the alternative method of calculating $V_1 = MV_0$, then $V_2 = MV_1$.

(b)　Note that the columns of M^2 are almost alike. What do you deduce?

(a)　$V_1 = MV_0 = \begin{bmatrix} 0.3 & 0.1 & 0.4 \\ 0.3 & 0.2 & 0.2 \\ 0.4 & 0.7 & 0.4 \end{bmatrix} \begin{bmatrix} 0 \\ 1 \\ 0 \end{bmatrix} = \begin{bmatrix} 0.1 \\ 0.2 \\ 0.7 \end{bmatrix}$

$V_2 = MV_1 = \begin{bmatrix} 0.3 & 0.1 & 0.4 \\ 0.3 & 0.2 & 0.2 \\ 0.4 & 0.7 & 0.4 \end{bmatrix} \begin{bmatrix} 0.1 \\ 0.2 \\ 0.7 \end{bmatrix} = \begin{bmatrix} 0.33 \\ 0.21 \\ 0.46 \end{bmatrix}$

(b)　The initial vector V_0 is not particularly important. For instance, if the family had a travel holiday in 1992 the probabilities for 1994 would be : activity – 0.30, seaside – 0.24, travel – 0.46; very little different from the answers actually obtained.

A further conclusion might be that the sequence $M^n V_0$ is probably tending to some limit in which all the columns of M^n are the same. You may like to check this.

Exercise 2

1.　(a)　$P(C_{k+1} | O_k) = \frac{2}{5}$.

(b)　With C, O in that order, the transition matrix is

$$T = \begin{bmatrix} \frac{2}{3} & \frac{2}{5} \\ \frac{1}{3} & \frac{3}{5} \end{bmatrix}$$

(c)　If $V_k = \begin{bmatrix} 0 \\ 1 \end{bmatrix}$ then $TV_k = \begin{bmatrix} \frac{2}{5} \\ \frac{3}{5} \end{bmatrix}$ and $T^2 V_k = \begin{bmatrix} 0.51 \\ 0.49 \end{bmatrix}$

		Year	
		$k+1$	$k+2$
Winner	C	0.40	0.51
	O	0.60	0.49

2.   The transition matrix is $\mathbf{M} = \begin{bmatrix} \dfrac{5}{11} & \dfrac{4}{11} & \dfrac{2}{9} \\[6pt] \dfrac{4}{11} & \dfrac{3}{11} & \dfrac{4}{9} \\[6pt] \dfrac{2}{11} & \dfrac{4}{11} & \dfrac{3}{9} \end{bmatrix}$

given that $\mathbf{V}_1 = \begin{bmatrix} 1 \\ 0 \\ 0 \end{bmatrix}$, $\mathbf{MV}_1 = \begin{bmatrix} 0.45 \\ 0.36 \\ 0.18 \end{bmatrix}$, $\mathbf{M}^2\mathbf{V}_1 = \begin{bmatrix} 0.38 \\ 0.35 \\ 0.27 \end{bmatrix}$

The probabilities in the column vectors are of win for Australia, draw and win for England, in that order.

3E.   From the product,

$$x = ap + bq \ , \ y = cp + dq \ ,$$

$$x + y = (a + c)p + (b + d)q = p + q = 1.$$

When an outcome probability vector, the sum of whose components is 1, is multiplied by a stochastic matrix the result is another outcome probability vector.

4.3   Gambler's ruin revisited

> **What feature of T shows the existence of absorbing states ?**

An entry of 1 in a transition matrix indicates an absorbing state.

> **Find the outcome vector after two tosses, $\mathbf{V}_2 = \mathbf{TV}_1$.**
>
> **How is $\mathbf{V}_2$ related to $\mathbf{V}_0$?**
>
> **What is the probability that G wins after two tosses?**

$$\mathbf{V}_2 = \begin{bmatrix} 0.5 \\ 0.25 \\ 0 \\ 0.25 \end{bmatrix} = \mathbf{T}^2\mathbf{V}_0 .$$

The probability that G wins is the probability of being in state S_4.

This is the final component of $\mathbf{V}_2$, i.e. $\dfrac{1}{4}$.

Exercise 3

1. (a) $T^2 = \begin{bmatrix} 1 & \frac{1}{2} & \frac{1}{4} & 0 \\ 0 & \frac{1}{4} & 0 & 0 \\ 0 & 0 & \frac{1}{4} & 0 \\ 0 & \frac{1}{4} & \frac{1}{2} & 1 \end{bmatrix}$, $T^3 = \begin{bmatrix} 1 & \frac{5}{8} & \frac{1}{4} & 0 \\ 0 & 0 & \frac{1}{8} & 0 \\ 0 & \frac{1}{8} & 0 & 0 \\ 0 & \frac{1}{4} & \frac{5}{8} & 1 \end{bmatrix}$, $T^4 = \begin{bmatrix} 1 & \frac{5}{8} & \frac{5}{16} & 0 \\ 0 & \frac{1}{16} & 0 & 0 \\ 0 & 0 & \frac{1}{16} & 0 \\ 0 & \frac{5}{16} & \frac{5}{8} & 1 \end{bmatrix}$

The matrices all have the same first and fourth columns. They also have half-turn symmetry.

(b) (i) $\frac{1}{4}$, (ii) $\frac{5}{16}$.

(c) As you may check, the sequence T^n tends to $S = \begin{bmatrix} 1 & \frac{2}{3} & \frac{1}{3} & 0 \\ 0 & 0 & 0 & 0 \\ 0 & 0 & 0 & 0 \\ 0 & \frac{1}{3} & \frac{2}{3} & 1 \end{bmatrix}$

Not unexpectedly, the probability of an eventual win by G is $\frac{1}{3}$.

2. (a) For states shown in the form (G's cash in £, O's cash in £) :

$S_1 : (0,5), \; S_2 : (1,4), \; S_3 : (2,3), \; S_4 : (3,2), \; S_5 : (4,1), \; S_6 : (5,0).$

The transition diagram would look like this:

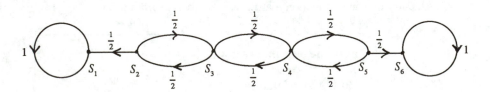

Transition matrix $\begin{bmatrix} 1 & \frac{1}{2} & 0 & 0 & 0 & 0 \\ 0 & 0 & \frac{1}{2} & 0 & 0 & 0 \\ 0 & \frac{1}{2} & 0 & \frac{1}{2} & 0 & 0 \\ 0 & 0 & \frac{1}{2} & 0 & \frac{1}{2} & 0 \\ 0 & 0 & 0 & \frac{1}{2} & 0 & 0 \\ 0 & 0 & 0 & 0 & \frac{1}{2} & 1 \end{bmatrix}$

(b)   The transition matrix is the $(n + 1) \times (n + 1)$ matrix

$$\begin{bmatrix} 1 & \frac{1}{2} & 0 & 0 & & \cdots & 0 \\ 0 & 0 & \frac{1}{2} & 0 & & \cdots & 0 \\ 0 & \frac{1}{2} & 0 & \frac{1}{2} & & \cdots & 0 \\ & & & \cdots & & & \\ 0 & \cdots & & & \frac{1}{2} & 0 & 0 \\ 0 & \cdots & & & 0 & \frac{1}{2} & 1 \end{bmatrix}$$

3.   The states, in the usual notation, are

$S_1 : (0,3), \quad S_2 : (1,2), \quad S_3 : (3,0).$

The game is over in one throw : transition matrix $\begin{bmatrix} 1 & \frac{2}{3} & 0 \\ 0 & 0 & 0 \\ 0 & \frac{1}{3} & 1 \end{bmatrix}$.

4E.   (a)   The states are simply labelled with the number of containers in the compound i.e. 0, 1, 2 or 3.

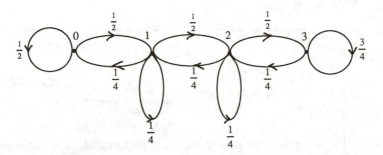

The problem differs from a gambler's ruin problem in that

(i)   the end states are not absorbing (they are said to be **reflecting**);

(ii)   it is possible to stay in the same state between one stage and the next.

(b)   The transition matrix is

$$T = \begin{bmatrix} \frac{1}{2} & \frac{1}{4} & 0 & 0 \\ \frac{1}{2} & \frac{1}{4} & \frac{1}{4} & 0 \\ 0 & \frac{1}{2} & \frac{1}{4} & \frac{1}{4} \\ 0 & 0 & \frac{1}{2} & \frac{3}{4} \end{bmatrix}$$

If the steady state vector is $\mathbf{V} = \begin{bmatrix} p \\ q \\ r \\ s \end{bmatrix}$

then, from the equation $\mathbf{TV} = \mathbf{V}$,

$$\frac{1}{2}p + \frac{1}{4}q = p$$

$$\frac{1}{2}p + \frac{1}{4}q + \frac{1}{4}r = q$$

$$\frac{1}{2}q + \frac{1}{4}r + \frac{1}{4}s = r$$

$$\frac{1}{2}r + \frac{3}{4}s = s$$

From these equations,

$$p : q : r : s = 1 : 2 : 4 : 8$$

$$p = \frac{1}{15}, \quad q = \frac{2}{15}, \quad r = \frac{4}{15}, \quad s = \frac{8}{15}.$$

These fractions represent the relative frequencies of days on which the compound contains 0, 1, 2 and 3 containers, respectively.

4.4   Run lengths

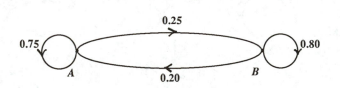

What sort of runs would you expect in a Markov chain with this transition diagram? What sort of frequencies for A and B would you expect in the long run?

Long runs of both A's and B's would be expected, those of B's being slightly longer than those of A's. Again, B would be somewhat more frequent than A. The probability of state A may be calculated using the formula

$$P(A) = P(A)\, P(A \mid A) + P(B)\, P(A \mid B).$$

If $P(A) = p$, this becomes

$$p = p \times 0.75 + (1-p) \times 0.20,$$

from which $p = \frac{4}{9}$, $1-p = \frac{5}{9}$.

Exercise 4

1. (a) $P \text{ (success)} = \frac{1}{6}$.

   The probability is $\left(\frac{1}{6}\right)^3 \left(\frac{5}{6}\right) \approx 3.9 \times 10^{-3}$.

   (b) The required probability is $\binom{5}{3} \left(\frac{1}{6}\right)^3 \left(\frac{5}{6}\right)^2 \approx 0.032$.

   (c) There are exactly two successes in the first four trials, then a further success in the fifth. The required probability is

   $$\binom{4}{2} \left(\frac{1}{6}\right)^2 \left(\frac{5}{6}\right)^2 \times \frac{1}{6} \approx 0.019.$$

   (d) One way of classifying the possible outcomes into mutually exclusive cases is as follows:

   $$P(SSSF \bullet) = \left(\frac{1}{6}\right)^3 \times \frac{5}{6} \times 1 \approx 0.00386$$

   $$P(\bullet SSS \bullet) = 1 \times \left(\frac{1}{6}\right)^3 \times 1 \approx 0.00463$$

   $$P(\bullet FSSS) = 1 \times \frac{5}{6} \times \left(\frac{1}{6}\right)^3 \approx 0.00386$$

   The required probability is the sum of these, 0.012 (2 s.f.)

2. $P \text{ ($k$th success in nth trial)} = P \text{ ($k-1$ successes in $n-1$ trials)} \times P \text{ (success)}$

   $$= \binom{n-1}{k-1} p^{k-1} (1-p)^{n-k} \times p$$

   $$= \binom{n-1}{k-1} p^{k} (1-p)^{n-k}.$$

3. (a) The possibilities are $(A)BBB \bullet$ or $(A)ABBB$.

   The probability is $0.25 \times (0.8)^2 \times 1 + 0.75 \times 0.25 \times (0.8)^2 = 0.28$

   (b) Possible cases: $(A)ABBB$, $(A)BABB$, $(A)BBAB$, $(A)BBBA$,

   The required probability is

   $$\begin{aligned} & (0.75)\,(0.25)\,(0.80)^2 + (0.25)\,(0.20)\,(0.25)\,(0.80) \\ + \ & (0.25)\,(0.80)\,(0.20)\,(0.25) + (0.25)\,(0.80)^2\,(0.20) \end{aligned}$$

   $$= \quad 0.172$$

4. The run is $(A)BBB \bullet$ or $(A)ABBB$ or $(A)CBBB$ with probability

   $$(0.7)\,(0.6)^2 + (0.2)\,(0.7)\,(0.6)^2 + (0.1)(0.5)\,(0.6)^2 = 0.3204.$$

4.5 In the long run

$$T^3 V_0 = \begin{bmatrix} 0.556 \\ 0.444 \end{bmatrix}, \quad T^4 V_0 = \begin{bmatrix} 0.567 \\ 0.433 \end{bmatrix}, \quad T^5 V_0 = \begin{bmatrix} 0.570 \\ 0.430 \end{bmatrix}, \quad T^6 V_0 = \begin{bmatrix} 0.571 \\ 0.429 \end{bmatrix}.$$

(a) Suppose now that John goes to the club on day 0. Calculate the first few members of the sequence $T^n V_0$ with a new V_0.

(b) Explain why, in the long run, John goes to the Youth Club on average on four evenings a week.

(a) If $V_0 = \begin{bmatrix} 1 \\ 0 \end{bmatrix}$ then $T^n V_0$ takes the successive values

$$\begin{bmatrix} 0.7 \\ 0.3 \end{bmatrix}, \begin{bmatrix} 0.61 \\ 0.39 \end{bmatrix}, \begin{bmatrix} 0.583 \\ 0.417 \end{bmatrix}, \begin{bmatrix} 0.575 \\ 0.425 \end{bmatrix}, \begin{bmatrix} 0.572 \\ 0.428 \end{bmatrix}, \begin{bmatrix} 0.571 \\ 0.429 \end{bmatrix}.$$

The sequence converges to the same limit as before, equally quickly.

(b) In the long run the probability that John attends on any evening is $\frac{4}{7}$, so on average he goes on 4 evenings per week.

Exercise 5

1. The transition matrix $T = \begin{bmatrix} 0.75 & 0.20 \\ 0.25 & 0..80 \end{bmatrix}$.

If the steady state vector $V = \begin{bmatrix} p \\ 1-p \end{bmatrix}$ then $TV = V$, i.e.

$$\begin{bmatrix} 0.75 & 0.20 \\ 0.25 & 0.80 \end{bmatrix} \begin{bmatrix} p \\ 1-p \end{bmatrix} = \begin{bmatrix} p \\ 1-p \end{bmatrix}.$$

Comparing the first row on the left with that on the right,

$$0.75\,p + 0.20\,(1-p) \;=\; p$$

$$\Rightarrow p \;=\; \frac{4}{9}$$

The steady state vector is $\begin{bmatrix} \frac{4}{9} \\ \frac{5}{9} \end{bmatrix}$

2.   The transition diagram for the team's result is:

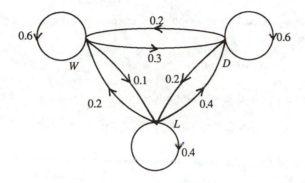

The transition matrix $\mathbf{T} \;=\; \begin{bmatrix} 0.6 & 0.2 & 0.2 \\ 0.3 & 0.6 & 0.4 \\ 0.1 & 0.2 & 0.4 \end{bmatrix}$ (order : W, D, L)

If the steady state vector is $\mathbf{V} = \begin{bmatrix} p \\ q \\ 1-p-q \end{bmatrix}$ then

comparing first and second rows in the equation $\mathbf{TV} \;=\; \mathbf{V}$,

$$0.6p + 0.2q \;+\; 0.2\,(1-p-q) \;=\; p$$

$$0.3p + 0.6q \;+\; 0.4\,(1-p-q) \;=\; q$$

These simultaneous equations have solution $p = \frac{1}{3}$, $q = \frac{11}{24}$.

The long term probabilities of win, draw and loss are respectively

$$\frac{1}{3}, \; \frac{11}{24} \; \text{and} \; \frac{5}{24} \;.$$

3.   (a) $\frac{4}{5}$ of obsolete data is recycled as unprocessed data.

The remaining $\frac{1}{5}$ remains classified as obsolete.

(b) If the limiting probabilities of categories I, II and III are respectively $p, q, 1-p-q$, then

$$\begin{bmatrix} 0.3 & 0 & 0.8 \\ 0.6 & 0.7 & 0 \\ 0.1 & 0.3 & 0.2 \end{bmatrix} \begin{bmatrix} p \\ q \\ 1-p-q \end{bmatrix} = \begin{bmatrix} p \\ q \\ 1-p-q \end{bmatrix}$$

Comparing first and second rows on left and right,

$$0.3p + 0.8(1-p-q) = p$$
$$0.6p + 0.7q = q.$$

From the second equation $q = 2p$. Substituting $2p$ for q in the first equation,

$$0.3p + 0.8(1-3p) = p,$$

giving $p = 0.258$. The limiting probabilities are:

category I – 0.258, category II – 0.516, category III – 0.226.

4. The transition matrix for the mouse's location is

$$\mathbf{T} = \begin{bmatrix} 0 & 1 & 0 & \frac{1}{2} \\ \frac{2}{3} & 0 & 0 & 0 \\ 0 & 0 & 0 & \frac{1}{2} \\ \frac{1}{3} & 0 & 1 & 0 \end{bmatrix} \qquad \text{(order : } A, B, C, D \text{)}$$

If the steady vector for $\mathbf{T}$ is $\mathbf{V} = \begin{bmatrix} p \\ q \\ r \\ 1-p-q-r \end{bmatrix}$ then

equating the rows in the equation $\mathbf{TV} = \mathbf{V}$,

$$q + \frac{1}{2}(1-p-q-r) = p$$
$$\frac{2}{3}p = q$$
$$\frac{1}{2}(1-p-q-r) = r$$
$$\frac{1}{3}p + r = 1-p-q-r.$$

From these equations, $p = \frac{3}{8}$. The mouse spends $\frac{3}{8}$ of the time in compartment A.

5. The mouse is now equally likely to go from A to B or D. The transition matrix of question 4 is changed by replacing each of the entries $\frac{2}{3}$ and $\frac{1}{3}$ in column 1 by $\frac{1}{2}$. Then, proceeding as before, you should find that the mouse spends $\frac{1}{3}$ of the time in compartment A.

5 *Simulation*

5.2 Pseudo-random numbers

> **Give two properties that random numbers generated by a computer should exhibit.**

You would expect, for example,

- each number to occur with (approximately) equal frequency;

- each number to be independent of the previous number.

> **What would happen if one number in the sequence was the same as an earlier number?**

The sequence would then repeat the same string of digits. It is important that your sequence of 'random numbers' has a long enough cycle (before it repeats) for the simulation to be completed before the numbers start repeating. The choice of c and N is therefore crucial. In particular, N should be large and c and N must not have any common factors. Try out a few examples to see what happens if these conditions are not satisfied.

> **How can you use your calculator to simulate the throw of a fair coin?**

Your calculator probably generates random numbers which are uniformly distributed over the range $0 \leq x < 1$.

You might consider

$$0 \leq x < 0.5 \sim \text{'heads'}$$
$$0.5 \leq x < 1 \quad \sim \text{'tails'}$$

Exercise 1

1. $x_1 \equiv 9 \times 0 + 13 \equiv 13 \pmod{32}$, $x_2 \equiv 9 \times 13 + 13 \equiv 2 \pmod{32}$ and so on. The sequence is 0, 13, 2, 31, 4, 17, 6, 1, 22, 19, 24, 5, 26, 23, 28, 9, 30, 27, 0, 13, ...

   The sequence repeats and will continue to cycle in this way. The run length of the sequence is so short that the formula is of little practical use.

2. The only possible numbers are 0, 1, 2, ... , 10. Division by 10 would produce numbers on the required interval to 1 d.p. only. Pairs of these numbers could, however, be used to generate numbers to 2 d.p. and so on.

153

3.   If your calculator generates numbers which are uniformly distributed over $0 \leq x < 1$:

$$0 \leq x < 0.143 \sim \text{Monday}$$
$$0.143 \leq x < 0.286 \sim \text{Tuesday etc.}$$

5.3   Empirical probability distributions

> **Explain the choice of the random numbers 00-39 in the table for component A.**

Since the probability of failure within 5 hours is 40% , 40 of the 100 possible numbers (i.e. 00-39) are assigned to this event.

> **Perform the above simulation a sufficient number of times to enable you to estimate the average time between failures of the unit. Calculate the average run time of the unit.**

The first few runs of a typical simulation are given below:

Random Number	Time to failure (A)	Random Number	Time to failure (B)	Time to failure for system
60	25	38	25	25
96	55	65	35	35
35	5	78	35	5
61	25	18	15	15
...	...	...	...	...
...	...	...	...	...

You should obtain an average time to failure of about 15 hours.

5.4   The Monte Carlo method

> **What would you expect to be the value of $\int_0^\infty f(t)\,dt$?**

This integral represents the probability that the time lies between 0 and $+\infty$.   This event is certain and so the integral must equal 1.

If a function is to be used to represent a continuous distribution in this way then the total area under its graph must equal 1. Furthermore, since probabilities can never be negative, the graph of such a function lies above the x-axis.

154

If X is uniformly distributed on [0, 1] then the appropriate variables to use are

(a)   2X;
(b)   6X − 3.

(a)   A Normally distributed variable with mean 0 and standard deviation 1 is almost certain to lie in the interval [−3, 3] and so 6*RND(1)−3 is used.

(b)   A short routine in BBC BASIC which can be used to estimate the mean time is as follows

```
10    SUM = 0
20    FOR N = 1 TO 100                          100 intervals are used
30    LET X = 10*RND(1) : Y = 0.5*RND(1)   ⎫ The Monte Carlo
40    IF Y > 0.5*EXP(−0.5*X) THEN GOTO 30  ⎬ method is used.
50    SUM = SUM + X                        ⎭ SUM is the total
60    NEXT N                                      of the time intervals.
70    PRINT SUM/100
```

A mean time of 2.19 minutes was obtained the first time the above simulation was run. Using 1000 samples, a mean of 1.99 minutes was obtained. The distribution of times given by $0.5e^{-0.5x}$ actually has mean 2 minutes. Your estimate should be reasonably close to this time period.

Tourism Impacts, Planning and Management

Peter Mason

AMSTERDAM   BOSTON   HEIDELBERG   LONDON   NEW YORK   OXFORD   PARIS
SAN DIEGO   SAN FRANCISCO   SINGAPORE   SYDNEY   TOKYO

Butterworth-Heinemann
An imprint of Elsevier
Linacre House, Jordan Hill, Oxford OX2 8DP
200 Wheeler Road, Burlington, MA 01803

First published 2003

British Library Cataloguing in Publication Data
A catalogue record for this book is available from the British Library

Library of Congress Cataloguing in Publication Data
A catalogue record for this book is available from the Library of Congress

ISBN 0 7506 5970X

For information on all Butterworth-Heinemann publications
visit our website at www.bh.com

Typeset by Newgen Imaging Systems (P) Ltd, Chennai, India
Printed and bound in Great Britain by Biddles Ltd, www.biddles.co.uk

To my Family and Friends in the North and Friends in the South

Contents

Part Three   Tools and Techniques in Tourism Planning and Management

Part Four   The Future of Tourism Planning and Management

Preface

Part One

The first six chapters of the book discuss the growth, development and impacts of tourism. It is assumed that all readers will have some understanding of the concepts of tourism. However, a brief discussion on the emergence and development of tourism is provided in Chapter 1. The reasons behind the development are also provided in this first chapter. The chapter attempts to establish the global significance of tourism, but it also points out some data limitations. Chapter 2 provides a discussion of key theories that are important within the context of tourism planning and management. Chapter 3 indicates that much tourism planning and management takes place in relation to tourism impacts. This chapter also considers factors that influence tourism impacts. The three chapters following Chapter 3 consider in turn, economic impacts, socio-cultural impacts and environmental impacts. Case studies are provided in each chapter to exemplify these different impacts. These studies are also employed to provide stimulus material for students and at the end of each chapter a number of student activities are suggested.

Part Two

Chapters 7–13 discuss concepts of, issues concerning and the players involved in tourism planning and management. Chapter 7 focuses on key concepts in tourism planning and management. It investigates the general relationship between planning and management before a discussion of tourism planning and management. This chapter also focuses on policy issues and introduces ideas in sustainability in tourism. Chapter 8 considers the major players in tourism planning and management and discusses visitors, host communities, the tourism industry and government. This chapter also discusses the role of the media and non-government organizations in tourism planning and management. Chapters 9–13 provide more detailed discussion of visitors, host communities and the tourism industry, as well as focusing on the environment as a key resource in tourism and the role of partnerships and collaboration in tourism planning and management. As with the first part of the book, this one uses a number of case studies. Here they are used to illustrate major concepts, themes and issues and once again a number of student activities are linked to the case studies in each chapter.

Part Three

This section is concerned with particular techniques used in tourism planning and management. It focuses on education and the role of interpretation (Chapter 14), self-regulation in tourism planning and management, and in particular codes of conduct, (Chapter 15) and the use of information technology as a tool in tourism planning and management. As with previous sections, case studies are an important feature of these chapters and as before they are included to provide stimulus material for students.

Part Four

The final part of the book is concerned with sustainability issues and tourism planning and management. A number of theoretical perspectives are discussed and a case study, with accompanying student activities, is presented to investigate some of these perspectives. A short concluding chapter is also provided and in addition this has ideas on the future of tourism. This final part of the book also uses a case study with related questions for students.

Acknowledgements

It is a truism that no book is the product of one person alone. I would like to thank the following for their help, either directly or indirectly, during the writing of this book.

The academics who informed the development of this book are numerous, but in particular, I would like to thank the following: at the University of Luton, Andrew Holden; in New Zealand, Sarah Leberman, Joanne Cheyne, Stephen Legg and Belinda Bonzon-Liu; and in Canada, Margaret Johnston and Dave Twynam.

Students at Massey University, New Zealand and the University of Luton, UK who tolerated, and may even have enjoyed, trial runs of some of the material contained in the book, deserve a special mention.

At Butterworth-Heinemann, I would like to express my thanks to Sally North, Holly Bennett and Rachael Williams for their advice on the practicalities of this book's production. I would also like to thank Mukesh V. S. at Newgen Imaging.

Last, but not least, I would like to thank my family, Patsy, Jess and Will, who put up with the long hours I spent at the computer.

The author and publisher would like to thank the following for permission to use copyright material:
Prosser, R., 'Tourism' Figure 7, in *The Encyclopaedia of Applied Ethics* (1998) Vol. 4, p. 381, published by Harcourt (Elsevier Science), New York. 'The Main Sectors of the Tourism Industry, Figure 4' in *Tourism Marketing* by Middleton V. (1994), published by Butterworth, London. 'Table 1 and Table 2' in *Tourism Collaboration and Partnerships* by Bramwell, B. and Lane, B. (2000), published by Channel View Publications, Clevedon, UK. Figure 1, p. 60, 'A classification of travellers and tourists' in *Travel, Tourism and Hospitality* by Ritchie, J. and Goeldner, C. (1994), published by John Wiley and Sons, New York, 'Some Important Dates in the Growth of Tourism. Figures 21 and 22 in *Tourism: Environment and Development Perspectives* by Mason, P. (1990), published by World Wide Fund for Nature, Godalming, UK. Figures 5.1 and 25.1, Table 13.1 and Boxes 13.1

and 13.2 in *Sustainable Tourism Management* by Swarbrooke, J. (1999), published by CABI, Wallingford, Oxford. All the photographs were taken by the author.

Every attempt has been made to trace all the copyright holders, but if any have been inadvertently overlooked the publishers will be pleased to make the necessary arrangements.

Part One

Tourism Growth, Development and Impacts

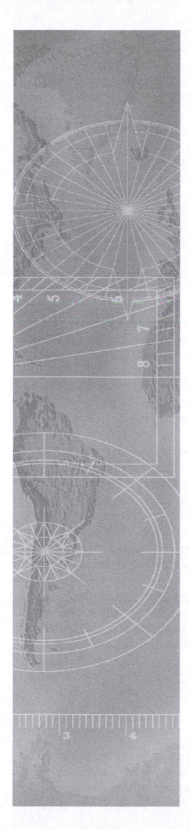

Social change and the growth of tourism

Learning objectives

At the end of this chapter you should:

- be aware of a variety of definitions of tourism;
- be aware of a number of dimensions and components of tourism, viz. the components of the tourism industry, motivations for tourism, tourism systems, data limitations in tourism;
- understand major social and economic changes that have contributed to the growth of tourism.

Introduction

Tourism is now a global industry involving hundreds of millions of people in international as well as domestic travel each year. The World Tourism Organization estimated (WTO, 2002) that there were 698 million international travellers in 2001 (this amounts to approximately 10 per cent of the world's population). Although some of this activity may comprise the same travellers involved in more than one journey per year and hence the precise scale of tourism as an industry is in some doubt

(Leiper, 1999), tens of millions of people globally work directly in the industry and many more are employed indirectly. Hundreds of millions of people are on the receiving end of tourism activity as they live in what are termed destination areas, in supposed 'host' populations. Millions of dollars are spent each year advertising and promoting holidays and tourism products.

For much of recorded history, travel was difficult, uncomfortable, expensive and frequently dangerous (Williams, 1998). Yet journeys were undertaken and this implies some strong motivating factors. However, it is only in the last 150 years, as travel has become more affordable and less difficult, that some of those who travelled were prepared to openly admit that pleasure was one of the motivations for their journeys.

As recently as the 1960s, tourism was an activity in which relatively few participated regularly, and was primarily confined to Europe, North America and a small number of locations in other parts of the world. International travel, prior to the 1960s, was still largely the preserve of a wealthy minority who had the time as well as money to afford long distance sea or air travel. Major changes in the second half of the twentieth century led to the rapid and massive growth of the phenomenon known as modern tourism. For example, these changes have contributed to the Pacific Region/East Asia becoming the fastest growing area for international tourism in the last quarter of the twentieth century. In 1975, East Asia and the Pacific Region accounted for only 4 per cent of international tourist arrivals, but by 1995 the share of world arrivals had increased to almost 15 per cent (Pearce, 1995). It should be noted that this change has occurred at a time when tourist numbers were growing globally. The increase in the share of international tourist arrivals in the Pacific Region therefore indicates a very significant increase in actual tourists between 1975 and 1995. There were approximately seventy-eight million visitor arrivals in the Pacific Region/East Asia in 1995 (Pearce, 1995). This compares with approximately 100 million in the combined area of North and South America and 305 million in Europe, which with almost 60 per cent of international arrivals remained, at the end of the twentieth century, the single most important region for international travel arrivals (Pearce, 1995).

This introductory chapter discusses what has made this growth possible. It involves discussion of a number of economic and social factors. This chapter also explores changing attitudes to travel, as well as presenting a discussion of how opportunities for travel have increased.

Key perspectives

Definitions of tourism and tourists

This book is an introductory text to tourism planning and management at undergraduate level, however, some understanding of the nature of tourism is assumed. Nevertheless, as there is not full agreement on the meaning of the term tourism, nor is there complete agreement on what a tourist is, this section contains a brief discussion of these concepts as they are clearly important in relation to the planning and management of tourism.

In the early 1980s, Matthieson and Wall (1982, p. 1) indicated that tourism comprised:

> The temporary movement of people to destinations outside their normal places of work and residence, the activities undertaken during the stay in those destinations, and the facilities created to cater for their needs.

A more recent definition – from the WTO in 1991 – was created, primarily to assist those whose responsibility it was to compile statistics in tourism. This definition reads as follows:

> The activities of a person travelling outside his or her usual environment for less than a specified period of time whose main purpose of travel is other than for exercise of an activity remunerated from the place visited   (WTO, 1991)

Neither of these two definitions makes reference to the impacts of tourism. Impacts are key to any discussion of the planning and management of tourism. However Jafari (1981), did include reference to impacts in his definition. Jafari (1981, p. 3) stated:

> Tourism is a study of man (sic) away from his usual habitat, of the industry which responds to his needs and the impacts that both he and the industry have for the host socio-cultural, economic and physical environments.

Most definitions of the term tourist are based on the concept of tourism. Usually, such definitions make reference to the need for the tourist to spend at least one night in a destination to which he or she has travelled. Tourists can be distinguished from excursionists in such definitions, as an excursionist is someone who visits and leaves without staying a night in a destination (Prosser, 1998). However, as Prosser suggested, it is relatively common today for the two terms to be combined. The term visitor is often used in preference to either tourist or excursionist. Theobold (1994), for example, used the concept of 'visitor' to combine the elements of a tourists and excursionist.

When discussing the impacts of tourism, a classification involving terms such as excursionist or tourist is not particularly helpful. For example, in relation to the environmental impacts of the feet of a walker on a natural or semi-natural landscape, it matters little whether the person involved is classified as a tourist or an excursionist; the feet will have the same effect! As the actions of day visitors (excursionists) and those of longer-stayers may be almost indistinguishable, the view that a definition of tourism does not need reference to an overnight stay has been become far more acceptable recently (Williams, 1998).

The distance travelled is often seen as important in definitions of both tourism and tourists. However, there is no commonly accepted international distance used in connection with definitions of tourism. As with the need of at least some definitions to include reference to an overnight stay, there is a good deal of debate and unresolved confusion about distance travelled and tourism definitions. In the United States, for example, the US Travel Data Centre reports on all trips with a one-way distance of 100 miles, the Canadian Travel Survey uses a lower than one-way limit of 50 miles, and the Australian Bureau of Industry Economics employs a one-way distance of 25 miles (Prosser, 1998).

One of the continuing problems caused by a lack of clear definition of tourism is that tourism studies are often poles apart in philosophical approach, methodological orientation or intent of the investigation (Fennell, 1999). Nevertheless, if there is no complete agreement on the definition of tourism, it is still important to understand the key aspects of the processes of tourism and the reality of being a tourist. Prosser (1998, p. 374) indicated that the central components of any definition of either tourists or tourism are as follows:

> movement, non-permanent stay, activities and experiences during the travel and stay, resources and facilities required and impacts resulting from the travel and stay.

Tourism is multi-dimensional and can be compartmentalized in a number of ways. According to Prosser (1998) there are two major variables. These are the origin–destination relationship and the motivation for travel. It is possible to create the following categories using Prosser's origin–destination relationship.

1 international tourism;
2 internal tourism;
3 domestic tourism;
4 national tourism.

Prosser indicated that international tourism involves overseas visitors to a destination, while domestic tourism relates to nationals of one country visiting that same country. Internal tourism can relate to a region within a country, while national tourism considers all forms of tourism within one particular nation or country.

Motivations for travel

In any tourism trip, there are likely to be a number of reasons which, when combined, can be considered as the motivational factors for the journey. These can be characterized as 'push' and 'pull' factors. The 'push' factors are a number of perceived negative factors about the context in which the potential tourist currently finds himself or herself. The 'pull' factors are perceived positive factors of a potential or real destination.

The nature, extent and significance of particular 'push' and 'pull' factors will vary according to the particular tourism context.

The classification of motivations into 'push' and 'pull' is linked closely with the psychological model of tourism motivation developed by Iso-Aloha (1980). The two dimensions in the model can be summarized as 'seeking' motives and 'escaping' motives (Pearce, 1993). In Iso-Aloha's model, individuals seek personal and interpersonal rewards and at the same time wish to escape personal and interpersonal environments.

The main criticism of Iso-Aloha's model is with only two dimensions it is limited by its level of aggregation (Raybould, Digance and McCullough, 1999). Hence, the use of the concepts 'push' and 'pull' may oversimplify a complex process. Nevertheless, investigating motivations in an attempt to understand the behaviour of tourists has become an important area of tourism research (Ryan, 1997). This can help with the categorization of tourists as well as provide a better understanding of their impacts. Tourist behaviour can be influenced by a number of factors including cultural conditioning, social influences, perception and education, but as Crompton and McKay (1997) indicated motives are the starting point of the decision making process that leads to particular types of behaviour.

It is particularly in the related fields of psychology and sociology that researchers (including Iso-Aloha, 1980) have developed significant theories on motivation. In the field of cognitive psychology, motives are seen as largely a function of the expected consequences of future human behaviour (Dunn-Ross and Iso-Aloha, 1991). In this sense, motives can be considered as internal factors that have initially aroused a person and then direct his or her behaviour (Iso-Aloha, 1980). The main components of a general psychological model of motivation are needs and motives, behaviour or activity, goals or satisfactions and feedback (Harrill and Potts, 2002). Mannell and Kleber (1997, p. 190) provide an example to indicate the links between the main concepts in this psychological model:

> People who have a strong need or desire to be with others (*motive*) may attempt to engage in leisure activities, such as going to bars and drinking that allow them to increase their interactions with other people (*behaviour*) in hopes of developing more friendships (*goal and satisfaction*).

This is an iterative model in that the feedback component leads back into the initial needs and motivations (Harrill and Potts, 2002). In other words, during an activity an individual interacts with the environment in which the activity takes place and possibly with others involved in the activity and this results in more, or perhaps, different motivation.

Several sociological theories have been put forward in the tourist literature in an attempt to explain motivation. One of the earliest was that of Cohen (1972) who sub-divided tourists into four types, based on motivation. Cohen asserted that the main variables forming the basis of his theory and hence leading to the four-fold classification were 'strangeness' versus 'familiarity'. Hence, at one end of his continuum was the 'organized mass tourist' seeking familiarity in holiday surroundings, while at the other end, the 'drifter' is willing to accept far more 'strangeness'.

Cohen developed his theory to investigate how various types of tourist might interact with host communities. This approach also influenced Plog (1973) who developed a continuum, using two concepts allo-centric and psycho-centric. Plog suggested that psycho-centric individuals are concerned primarily with the self, are inhibited and relatively non-adventurous. In terms of tourist behaviour, psycho-centrics want the familiar and are unlikely to travel great distances to explore new tourism destinations. Conversely, Plog asserted allo-centrics are confident, naturally inquisit-ive and seek out the unfamiliar when travelling. Both Cohen's (1972) and Plog's (1972) theories have been tested, but with varied success and have not met with universal acceptance. Nevertheless, they remain as key theories in tourism motiva-tion, although both are largely descriptive rather than explanatory (Harrill and Potts, 2002). Cohen's (1972) and Plog's (1972) theories are discussed in more detail in Chapter 2, which investigates important theories in tourism planning and management.

A number of sociological and psychological theories tend to imply that motivation is a fairly static concept. However, Pearce (1988) using the concept of a 'travel ladder' when investigating motivation for tourism, suggested that motivations are multivariate and dynamic, changing particularly as a result of ageing and life-cycle stage, as well as being influenced by other people. Pearce acknowledged that he was influenced by the work of the psychologist Maslow (1954), who created a hierarchi-cal range of needs, from low level, primarily physical needs to high level intellectual needs. Maslow termed these needs, in ascending sequence, 'physiological', 'safety', 'social', 'self-esteem' and 'self-development'. Pearce, using Maslow's (1954) ideas, proposed the following tourism moti-vation categories: 'relaxation', 'excitement and thrills', 'social interaction', 'self esteem and development' and 'fulfilment'.

In attempting to summarize the major motivations of tourists Ryan, (1991) drew on the work of Cohen (1972), Crompton (1979) and Matthieson and Wall (1982) and presented eleven major reasons for tourist travel. These are as follows:

- Escape;
- Relaxation;
- Play;
- Strengthening family bonds;
- Prestige;
- Social interaction;
- Sexual opportunity;
- Educational opportunity;
- Self-fulfilment;
- Wish fulfilment;
- Shopping.

This list of eleven motivations for tourist journeys can also be seen to be linked to the concept of 'push' and 'pull' factors with, for example, 'escape' clearly a push factor and 'prestige' clearly a pull factor. Ryan (1991) indicated that often, holidays choices are based on a combination of motivations that are seen as a set of priorities by the potential tourist at the time. These priorities may change over time and realizing some travel needs may be deliberately delayed (Ryan, 1991, 1997).

Chadwick (1987) provided a more simplified categorization of the reasons for tourist related journeys when he summarized the motivations for and purpose of travel under three main headings. These are as follows:

- Pleasure: leisure, culture, active sports, visiting friends and relatives.
- Professional: meetings, missions, business etc.
- Other purposes (study, health, transit).

The Annual International Passenger Survey carried out by the British Tourist Authority distinguishes five types of tourism-related visit (cited in Prosser, 1998):

1 Holiday independent;
2 Holiday inclusive;
3 Business;
4 Visiting friends and relatives (VFR);
5 Miscellaneous.

As Prosser (1998) indicated, the VFR segment is important in the United Kingdom and Europe and particularly significant within Australia and New Zealand with as many as 20 per cent of visitors to Australia being in the VFR category. Partly in relation to this high figure, Prosser (1998) suggested a threefold categorization of visitor motivation, as follows: (i) pleasure; (ii) business; and (iii) VFR.

With reference to attempts to classify tourist motivation, it should not be forgotten that many trips have multiple purposes and are likely to involve different forms of transport and accommodation types. Hence, this tends to limit the usefulness of any classification. Despite these limitations, Figure 1.1 is an attempt to classify tourists.

The Tourism Industry

An important issue in this book is the relationship between different sectors of the tourism industry. The book also investigates the relationships between tourists, tourism stakeholders and governments and industry representatives. A summary of different sectors of the tourism industry, referring to a travel sector, accommodation sector, leisure and entertainment sector and a sector concerned with tourism organizations is shown in Figure 1.2.

A slightly different summary of the tourism industry is shown in Figure 1.3. In this summary, based on Middleton (1994), there are five

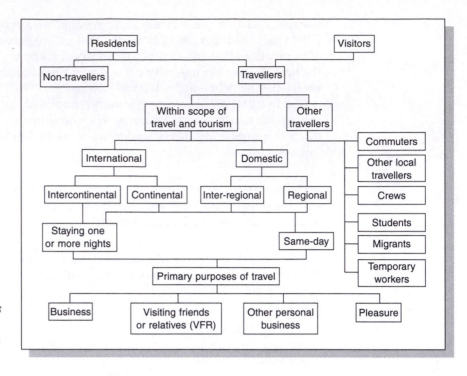

Figure 1.1
A classification of travellers and tourists (Adapted from Brent Ritchie and Goeldner, 1994.)

Figure 1.2
A summary of sectors of the tourism industry (Adapted from Lavery, P. *Travel and Tourism*, Elm Publications, 1987.)

(i) Travel:
Including travel agents, tour operators, airlines, cruise companies, coach companies, railways, taxis, tourist guides, couriers, reservations and sales staff

(ii) Accommodation, catering and related services to tourists:
Hotels with all their staff from receptionist to chambermaids, chefs and cooks, waiters, waitresses, bar staff, porters, caravan/camping site staff, self-catering enterprises, restaurants and cafes

(iii) Leisure facilities and entertainment:
These will include theatres, museums, art galleries, theme parks, zoos, wildlife parks, sports centres, gardens, historic houses, country parks, cinemas

(iv) Tourism organizations:
Whose aim is to market and monitor the quality and development of the tourist region. These will range from national and regional tourist organizations to staff at local tourist information centres

sectors and although these are similar to Lavery's sectors, there is more emphasis on tourism organizations and the attractions for tourists.

Tourism systems

The location of tourism activity is a major component of tourism (Mason, 1990). Leiper (1990) attempted to link the tourism destination with the tourism generating region. His model is shown in Figure 1.4.

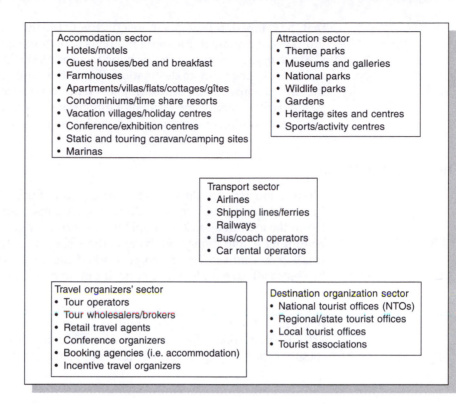

Figure 1.3

The main sectors of the tourism industry (Adapted from Middleton, 1994.)

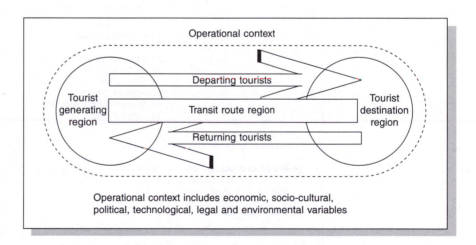

Figure 1.4

The tourism system: a spatial construct (Adapted from Leiper, 1990.)

Leiper's model is an attempt to view tourism as a form of system, in which there is an operational structure built up of interacting components. In the model there are three interactive components: (i) the tourism generating region; (ii) the destination region; and (iii) transit routes which link the two regions. However, Leiper's model has been criticized for being simplistic (Prosser, 1998). Prosser provided a more detailed model that, he claimed, represents more effectively the inner complexities of the tourism environment. Prosser's model is shown in Figure 1.5.

Much of the discussion in this book focuses on the location that tourists visit, that is, the tourism destination. It is in the destination (at the receiving end of tourism) that most impacts tend to be noted and may be felt particularly strongly by resident populations. Hence, there is a major need for planning and managing at the tourism destination.

The growth of tourism

Modern tourism developed largely as a result of urbanization in Western Europe. Prior to this, societal divisions, responsibilities and allegiances led to the great majority of people in Western Europe being born in small communities and living and dying in these same tightly focused relatively small communities. These people worked the land and were tied to this by seasonal demands for labour input and social relationships that required service to a land-owner and quite possibly the established church. Such people had little leisure time and what they had was often linked to family responsibilities. Recreation was largely a spiritual activity that took place through the Church, although festivals and religious holidays provided a few opportunities for leisure pursuits.

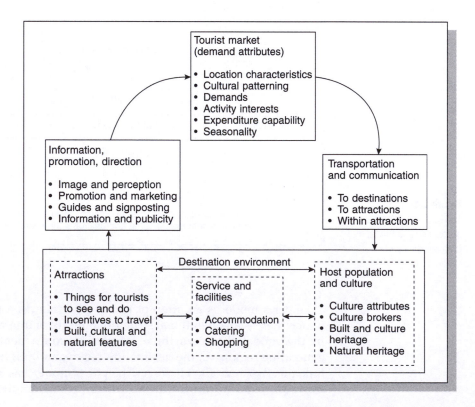

Figure 1.5
The tourism environment
(Adapted from Prosser,
1998.)

However, the great majority of people lacked the ability or desire to travel away from their birthplace (Mason, 1990). Frequent travel was confined to the small elite, the ruling class made up of large landowners, church leaders and monarchs and their entourage. For the majority of the masses, the only possibilities of long distance travel was likely to be linked to a pilgrimage, a religious crusade or time spent as a mercenary.

When urban settlements expanded from about 1750 in Europe, the old bond to land and land-owners was broken. Large numbers of people left their place of birth and moved to these rapidly growing settlements. Here, by 1800, employment opportunities were in factories, where for the first time workers received wages and despite long hours of work had both time and money to engage in leisure activities. Gradually, with the change in living environment and working relationships came new attitudes to life. Recreation was increasingly viewed as an important part of life and this could involve physical as well as mental activity.

Although an increasing number of people resident in Europe were able to travel, from the Middle Ages onwards up to the eighteenth century, it was still the preserve of a small wealthy elite. It was not until the era of the Industrial Revolution, and particularly after 1800, that travel became far more accessible to a significantly high percentage of the population. Greater access to travel was accompanied by certain other developments in society, and this contributed to the growth in demand for and provision of tourism experiences.

A variety of important factors contributed to the development of tourism during the nineteenth and early part of the twentieth century. Mason (1990) suggested five major reasons for the growth of tourism. These are as follows:

- A rise in industrial output associated with the Industrial Revolution that in turn led to an increase in the standard of living.
- Improvements in transport technology, which led to cheaper and more accessible travel. Railways and ocean liners appeared in the nineteenth century and cars and aircraft in the first half of the twentieth century.
- The introduction of annual holidays towards the end of the nineteenth century.
- Changing perceptions of the environment. Locations that were once viewed as hostile, were now seen as attractive.
- An increasing desire to travel. This was related partly to improvements in education and also to greater overseas travel, which was mainly the result of war. This created interest in foreign locations and also overseas business travel.

A number of the social and economic changes that had been occurring before the second half of the century continued and accelerated after the Second World War. Salaries and wages steadily increased and this meant more disposable income to spend on leisure pursuits. The amount of leisure time also went up as the working week decreased in terms of numbers of hours required at work, and the length of the annual holiday increased. This greater access to recreation activities was accompanied by a rapid rise in car ownership, particularly in North America in the 1950s and Western Europe during the late 1950s and early 1960s. Roads and motorway systems in Europe and North America were greatly improved during this period. For the first time, large numbers of potential tourists could plan their own trips without having to rely on either publicly or privately owned transport organisations. Aircraft also became more comfortable and sophisticated and an increasing number and range of passengers were flying; in this period flying to a distant overseas destination became a real alternative in financial terms to a journey by ship. During this period, public transport, in particular trains and coaches, improved in terms of comfort and comparative costs, hence allowing a wider range of users.

In the last quarter of the twentieth century, the relationship between demand and supply in tourism was based largely on the dynamics of people's perception, expectations, attitudes and values (Prosser, 1994). As Prosser argued, tourism had become very much a fashion industry, in which there were very close links between tourism demand and the concepts of status and image. This ensures that as societies that generate tourists frequently change their motivations, expectations and demands, tourism is a notoriously fickle industry. Therefore reasons for travel can change rapidly, although they may appear at any one time to be unchanging. For example, throughout much of the period from the late 1950s to the late 1980s getting a suntan was central to a large number of people's expectation of a holiday. This 'getting bronzed' mentality appeared endemic and eternal at the time. However, this desire only dated back to the lifestyle of leisured classes on the Cote d'Azur, France in the 1920s (Prosser, 1994). Prior to this, most Europeans kept out of the sun. This was especially so for women for whom a pale complexion was seen as more attractive. In the early twenty-first century, pale skin became once again fashionable, but this time the reason was more health related, with growing concerns about skin cancer caused by too much exposure to the sun.

Not only have people's motivations and expectations of holidays changed, but also there is an important geographical aspect to this. Where tourism experiences can be obtained is itself subject to variations in demand and, hence, supply. For instance, in the 1970s it was not sufficient just to get a suntan, but where one got it was vital (Prosser, 1994). In the early 1960s, in Britain getting a suntan in Brighton or Blackpool was sufficient, by the early 1970s to achieve the desired status the tan had to be brought back to Britain from Benidorm and by the 1980s it had to have been obtained in Belize! In Australia, Bondi Beach would have been good enough for most sun-seekers in the 1970s, but, by the 1980s, to really enhance one's status it was necessary to get the tan in Bali! However, reference to Bali emphasizes the unpredictability of tourism. Until October 2002, Bali was a major destination for sun-seeking tourists from many locations in the developed world. The terrorist attack at two night clubs in Kuta, a resort in Bali, on 19 October 2002, in which almost 200 young people from Australia, New Zealand, the United States, Canada, Britain and other European countries died, has resulted in a collapse of tourism numbers which has continued into 2003.

In the last 15 years or so of the twentieth century, changing attitudes also contributed to a re-evaluation of the nature of the tourist experience. Accompanying the growing realisation that tourism takes place in finite geographical space, was the notion that it consumes environmental resources (McKercher, 1993). Increasingly, tourists became concerned about the effects their activities were having on the environment (Fennell, 1999). This led to the growth of what some consider as more environment-friendly forms of tourism, such as ecotourism (Wearing and Neil, 1999). Additionally, some tourists sought experiences that would give them more contact with the population in the destination region and potentially contribute more to the local economy. In this way, these tourists demonstrated that they were concerned about the ethics of the tourist–host relationship and were seeking a more just and equitable form of tourism than was achievable in more conventional types of the activity (see Mason and Mowforth, 1996; Malloy and Fennell, 1998).

Data limitations

One of the key problems in assessing the scale, importance and hence impacts of tourism is the inconsistency and incomparability of figures collected. Leiper (1999) indicated that the WTO is frequently cited as a source of data on international tourism. Leiper quoted figures from 1996 that suggested there were almost 600 million international tourists, representing more than 10 per cent of the Earth's population at that time. Leiper stated that this figure was not truly tourists but 'arrivals.' He argued that WTO statistical data ignore patterns of trip frequency and multi-destination itineraries. He argued that a large proportion of these arrivals are by the same travellers not separate individuals. Therefore, Leiper suggested, nearer to 200 million individuals travelled internationally in 1996 – this is only one-third of the WTO figure.

Data problems can be found at all scales; international, national and internal (Prosser, 1998). As Theobold (1994) indicated, this is even a problem within one country. For example, in the United States, a tourist in Florida is 'an out-of-state resident who stays at least one night in the state for reasons other than the necessary lay-over for transportation connections or for strictly business transactions'. However, in Alaska a tourist is defined as 'a non-resident travelling to Alaska for pleasure or culture and for no other purpose' (Theobold, 1994).

Middleton (1994, p. 7) has indicated that despite efforts to create a degree of comparability of tourism statistics, achieving precision is very complex and:

> despite various guidelines, no uniformity yet exists in the measurement methods used around the world.

Case study
Tourism growth in Australia

Early European travellers to Australia were usually reluctant visitors. The commander of the First Fleet dispatched from Plymouth, England in 1787, to establish the colony of New South Wales described the 736 convicts on board as 'unwilling tourists'. For much of the nineteenth century European visitors to Australia were either convicts or business people. At this time, Australia suffered from the 'tyranny of distance' in terms of its links with Europe – it took several months to get to Australia by ship. The commentaries on Australian life which were published in Britain from the early nineteenth century, in order to attract settlers, were extremely important to the commencement of tourism. Australia was often pictured to the rural audience as an Arcadia where the fruits of the soil could be easily won. Such romanticised imagery was important in attracting both tourists and immigrants to Australia.

The Australian experience of Victorian attitudes towards leisure and recreation runs directly parallel to British developments. The North Shore Steamboat Ferry Service, that linked Sydney City with the then rural North Shore, and the ferries to take customers to Botany Bay Zoo may be regarded as the antipodean equivalent to the ferrying of city-weary Londoners to the coastal resorts of Margate and Southend. On land, however, perhaps the most significant event for making travel accessible to all social classes was the coming of the railway and with it came the development of mass tourism. The onset of rail led to a revolution in tourism and recreation activities. Prior to this, recreational travel was restricted to immediate areas surrounding population centres. The railways helped open up the hinterland for domestic travellers.

Mass tourism is usually acknowledged to have begun in 1841 when Thomas Cook, the world's first noted tour operator, conducted an excursion train from Leicester, England. Later Cook used a combination of rail and ship to organize and run tours to Europe, the Middle East and North Africa. By 1872, Cook offered a world cruise on steamboats that included glimpses of both Australia and New Zealand. The inclusion of Sydney and Melbourne in the itinerary marked the beginning of packaged international travel to Australia. Cook's significant role in relation to international tourism can also be noted in relation to his company's publishing of advice and a guide-book for travellers to Australia and New Zealand in 1889.

Accompanying the economic development of Australia were a number of social developments. Unlike British working practices, in Australia most urban trade unions adopted the principle of 8 h labour, 8 h recreation, 8 h rest. This ensured leisure was viewed in a positive way. The railways assisted in the pursuit of leisure as they made new destinations accessible and helped make travel a permanent part of Australian culture. The first railway lines were important in the establishment of Australia' national parks. These were initially set up as areas for recreational activity of city dwellers, rather than being for the protection of flora and fauna.

By the end of the nineteenth century, tourism and leisure were not just the regime of the wealthy. The railways, in particular, had made travel possible for the majority of the population. The railways helped open up the interior for domestic tourism, while the steamship brought Australia closer in terms of travelling time to Europe. Urban attractions such as museums, art galleries and parks, still important today, were already significant visitor attractions at the end of the nineteenth century.

The first true coastal resorts were also established by the end of the nineteenth century, in such places as Sandgate and Cleveland in Queensland, Glenelg in South Australia and Brighton and Sorrento in Victoria. However, at none of these places did swimming become legal until the early part of the twentieth century, as the original role of the coastal resorts was as places to take the sea air and waters as a cure for a variety of ailments. The railways helped boost inland tourism destinations in Australia that developed as health spas. After the building of the Sydney to Blue Mountain railway, the Blue Mountains became an area visited for the supposed health giving properties of their mountain air, as well as the spectacular scenery.

In the 1920s and 1930s, the expansion of mass transport enabled once remote beaches and attractions to come within easier reach. During this period a bush walking movement also developed in Australia. Several clubs were established, such as the Sydney Bushwalkers, set up by prominent walkers and conservationists Paddy Wallin and Myles Dunphy.

Regular airline services between Australia and overseas only began in the 1930s. The first airmail service from Britain to Australia was set up in 1934 and this provided the stimulus for the establishment of Qantas Empire Airways, the forerunner of the current Qantas Airlines.

After the Second World War, most people had greater disposable income as well as more leisure time, particularly as three weeks holiday became standard. Car ownership increased. This led to important changes in the accommodation sector as hotels and boarding houses declined in popularity and motels became more prominent. In the post war period of the 1950s, Qantas became the major Australian airline, and in 1958 Qantas introduced its first round-the-world service.

During the more recent period, particularly since the late 1970s, tourism activities became more closely linked with Australia's heritage. There was a recognition by the Australian public that tourists want to see Australia's past, and government and operators have also noted that heritage pays. Tourism has also assisted Australians in their search for social meaning in their environment, and

Photo 1 Ayers Rock: a symbol for modern Australia?

helped them better appreciate their national identity. As Horne (1994, p. 3) indicated: 'As the Swiss found national identity in the Alps, Australians have found identity in the red granite of Ayer's Rock.' (See Photo 1.)

(Adapted from Hall, C. M. (1995). *An Introduction to Tourism in Australia*, 2nd edn. Melbourne, Longman)

Summary

This chapter has considered the problems of trying to define tourism and tourists. It has briefly outlined the motivations for tourism, considered the nature of tourism as an industry and discussed tourism as a system. The chapter has also explored changing attitudes to travel, as well as presenting a discussion of how opportunities for travel have increased. The problems with and limitations of tourism data have been presented. The main focus has been an investigation of a number of important economic and social factors that have contributed to the growth of tourism in the last two centuries. Discussion has centred around changes in Europe since 1750 or so, but a case study of socio-economic change in Australia since Western colonization has indicated both similarities with and differences from the European experience.

Student exercises

1 What are the key social and economic changes suggested by the information in Figure 1.6?
2 Sub-divide the information shown in Figure 1.6, under the following headings:
   - transport changes;
   - leisure time changes;
   - tourist destination changes;
   - recreation/tourism activity changes.

- The first steam train, carrying passengers between Manchester and Liverpool, opened in 1830.
- On 5 July 1841, Thomas Cook chartered a train from Leicester to Loughborough and took 570 passengers at a round trip fare of 1 shilling (5p). In 1851, Cook organized rail trips from many parts of England to the Great Exhibition at the Crystal Palace, in London. In 1869 he organized the first trip to Egypt and the Holy Land.
- In 1911, there were 22 000 miles of railway in the United Kingdom.
- The first August Bank Holiday was on 7 August 1871. This was introduced by an Act of Parliament to make life more bearable for the working class.
- Seaside resorts expanded rapidly in the nineteenth century due mainly to the impact of the railways. In 1841 Blackpool's population was 2000, by 1901 this had risen to 47 000 and in 1921 had reached 96 000.
- The first holiday camp was established by Butlins at Skegness in 1939.
- In 1895 the National Trust was set up with the main aim of looking after 'places of historic interest and natural beauty'.
- In 1938, there were 2 million private cars in the United Kingdom, in 1949, 2.5 million, by 1969, 11 million, and by 1983 this had risen to 16 million.
- In 1982, more than 50 per cent of British people had taken a holiday abroad.
- In 1983, 6.8 million 'inclusive', or package tours, were taken by British tourists. This represents 55 per cent of all overseas holidays taken by British tourists.

Figure 1.6

Some important dates in the growth of tourism in the United Kingdom (Adapted from Mason, 1990.)

3 Study the information contained in both the case study of tourism growth in Australia and Figure 1.6. To what extent were the social and economic changes occurring in the United Kingdom: (a) similar to, and (b) different from those operating in Australia?

4 Consider a holiday that you have taken recently and attempt to classify your motivations for the holiday under the headings of 'push' and 'pull'. What are the limitations of this approach?

CHAPTER 2

Theoretical perspectives on tourism development

Learning objectives

At the end of this chapter you should be:

- aware of historical and geographical factors that have contributed to the growth of tourism and particularly the emergence of tourist resorts and areas;
- aware of important theories informing discussion about tourism planning and management, in particular those of Christaller, Plog, Cohen and Doxey;
- able to demonstrate awareness of factors influencing the development of Butler's life-cycle model of tourism destinations;
- able to demonstrate an understanding of Butler's life-cycle model of tourist destinations;
- aware of applications of Butler's model;
- aware of critiques of Butler's model.

Introduction

As travel for pleasure became a significant activity, so tourist destinations emerged. New forms of transport (such as rail in the nineteenth and road in the mid-twentieth centuries) linked the tourist generating regions with tourist resorts. Over time, due to factors such as geographical proximity to generating regions and climatic advantage, particular destinations and resort areas emerged and became popular with visitors. This popularity was maintained by return visits by tourists, as well as marketing of the resort attractions. A number of changes, some outlined in the previous chapter, such as those related to visitor motivations, transport and disposable income, and in addition negative consequences of tourism at the destination led, over a longer period, to some resorts declining as tourist attractions.

A major geographical focus of tourism planning and management is tourism destinations. It is here, in the destinations that tourists encounter and interact with the local community and the local environment. This interaction leads to impacts on the local population, the environment and also on the tourists themselves. As will be discussed in later chapters these impacts can be beneficial in relation to, for example, the local economy. However, the encounter between tourists and the destination they are visiting can also lead to, for example, damage to the local environment. It is in relation to these impacts that much tourism planning and management is targeted. Subsequent chapters invest these impacts. However, it is first necessary to understand how tourism destinations have emerged.

Hence, this chapter focuses on the development of tourism destinations and in particular is concerned with major theories in tourism that assist with our understanding of how destinations have emerged, grown and in some cases declined.

Key perspectives

The development of tourism destinations: important theoretical perspectives

One of the earliest writers to consider the development of tourism destinations was Christaller, who was a German geographer and planner. As Christaller worked as a planner during the Hitler era in Germany, his work was not well known in the English-speaking world until the post Second World War world. In 1963, an article by Christaller was published in which he suggested there was a process of continual development of recreation/tourist areas. He discussed how a location develops from one where, in his example, a group of painters visit. In a step-by-step process this becomes an artist colony. Later, poets, musicians and gourmets seek out this place. The place becomes fashionable and it is marketed. Members of the local community move into accommodation and food provision. Meanwhile the 'real' painters/artists move on and only those with commercial interests to sell to increasing numbers of tourists remain. Christaller (1963) suggested that elsewhere the cycle is beginning again.

Christaller's ideas were particularly influential on some later theorists of tourism planning and management. His ideas on how tourist areas develop over time can be summarized as follows:

- destinations develop and change over time;
- there are different types of visitors at different times;
- the tourist experience (the tourism product) changes over time;
- the impacts on the destination change over time;
- the involvement of locals in tourism destinations changes over time;
- new cycles involving new tourist destinations will occur.

The American researcher Plog developed ideas on the psychology of tourists and these were published in 1973. Plog's (1973) important contribution was the notion of allo- and pyscho-centric types of tourist. He argued that there are those psychological types who do not like unfamiliar environments or cultures, so when they select a holiday they will seek the familiar (these he termed psycho-centric). Plog argued that there are other groups in society who will be prepared to risk a far more uncertain holiday destination, and they actively seek out the strange or unfamiliar and these he termed allo-centric. Plog indicated that those whom he termed psycho-centric would not travel far from the local environment/region to take a holiday, while those he termed allo-centric would travel long distances to unfamiliar locations. Plog suggested the majority of tourists were neither fully psycho-centric nor fully allo-centric in relation to their holiday destination choices. In terms of his theory, the great majority of tourists were located close to a mid-point between the extremes of psycho-centric and allo-centric, Plog suggested. Nevertheless, Plog suggested in relation to their selected holiday destination, the majority of tourists seek the familiar and prefer not to travel great distances to get there.

Plog's theory was based on a study of New York residents. A major implication for destination development is that the majority of tourists will prefer to travel short distances to take holidays. Hence, the theory suggests that destinations, particularly in Developed countries, close to major population areas are likely to be developed and grow more quickly than those more distant, remote areas. Therefore, this will contribute to the growth of resorts/destinations close to the generating regions. However, Plog's theory was developed from relatively limited empirical research.

If Plog's theory was closely linked to the psychological make up of tourists, then Cohen's ideas related to the behaviour of tourists. Cohen (1972) developed a typology of tourists in which there was a fourfold classification. This classification is summarized below:

- *Organized mass tourists*. These tourists travel together in groups. According to Cohen, they take a packaged holiday (travel, accommodation and food are also arranged in advance of the trip, usually by a travel agent and/or tour operator).
- *Individual mass tourists*. This group uses the same facilities as the organized mass tourists, but make more individually based decisions about their tourist activity.

- *Explorers*. Such tourists arrange their own visit/trip. They go 'off the beaten track'. They wish to meet locals. However, they still tend to use the facilities of the mass tourist.
- *Drifters*. The drifter shuns contact with other tourists and 'goes native' by staying with locals. He/she stays longer than most tourists and does not regard himself/herself as a tourist.

It is possible to combine the key ideas of Cohen with those of Plog. In this way, it can be suggested that the majority of Cohen's 'mass tourists' and 'independent mass tourists' are likely to conform to Plog's category of psycho-centric tourists. At the time that both Plog and Cohen were writing, the early 1970s, this tended to suggest that significant tourism destinations, in Developed countries, would be developed in relative close proximity to the tourism generating regions. As most tourists prefer the familiar when choosing their holiday destination, the theories of both Plog and Cohen also suggested that relatively few tourists would come into contact with more distant and 'different' cultures.

During the mid-1970s, there was a growing concern about the potential and real negative impacts of tourism on destination regions. At this time, Doxey proposed what was termed an Irritation Index, or, in its shortened form, what was known as an Irridex. Doxey's (1975) Irridex considered the relationship between tourists and locals. The main idea in Doxey's Irridex was that over time, as the number of tourists increased, a greater hostility from locals towards tourists would emerge. The process by which this occurs is summarized in Figure 2.1.

Doxey's theory is built upon the premise that destinations will develop and grow over a period of time. However, an important implication of Doxey's theory is that destinations may not have the ability to grow without check. Doxey's Irridex suggests that, over time, as locals become more hostile to visitors, then visitor numbers will not continue to grow at the same rate as previously and may actually decline. Although regarded at the time as important and still seen as adding to our understanding of

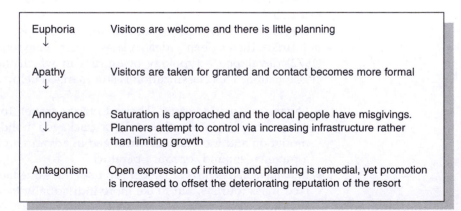

Figure 2.1
Doxey's Irritation Index

tourist–host interactions, Doxey's Irridex was not based on detailed empirical research, but mainly on conjecture.

Butler's theory

The geographer Butler built on the ideas of Christaller, Plog, Cohen and Doxey to create his theory, or model. Butler's model appeared in 1980 and he not only acknowledged that his ideas were linked to earlier theories, but he also indicated that they were based on the business/marketing concept of the product life-cycle. In summary, the product life-cycle is a theory in which sales of a new product are seen to slowly grow and then experience a rapid growth, before stabilizing and subsequently declining. When applied to tourism destinations, the model suggests that resorts develop and change over time and there are a number of linked stages: exploration; involvement; development; consolidation (shown in graph form in Figure 2.2). During these stages a tourism industry develops and the destination has an increasing number of tourists.

Figure 2.3 shows more detail on the processes occurring during each stage of Butler's model. After the consolidation stage there are a number of possibilities. The resort/destination could 'stagnate', without any increase or decrease in numbers; it could 'decline' or it could 'rejuvenate'.

In the 20 years or so since its creation, a number of attempts have been made to apply Butler's theory. Such an attempt is presented in the following case study, in which Agarwhal applies Butler's theory to the development of tourism in the Torbay area of South West England.

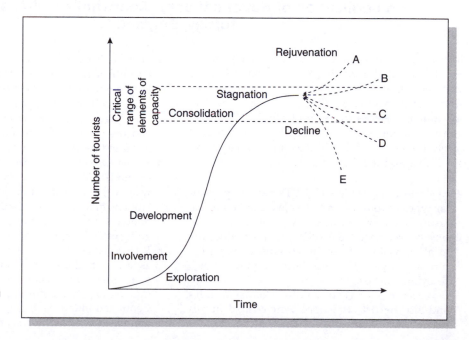

Figure 2.2
The resort cycle of evolution (Adapted from Butler, 1980.)

Stage	Characteristic
Exploration	• Few adventurous tourists, visiting sites with no public facilities
	• Visitors attracted to the resort by a natural physical feature
	• Specific visitor type of a select nature
Involvement	• Limited interaction between local residents and the developing tourism industry leads to the provision of basic services
	* Increased advertising induces a definable pattern of seasonal variation
	* Definite market area begins to emerge
Development	* Development of additional tourist facilities and increased promotional efforts
	* Greater control of the tourist trade by outsiders
	* Number of tourists at peak periods far outweighs the size of the resident population, inducing rising antagonism by the latter towards the former
Consolidation	* Tourism has become a major part of the local economy, but growth rates have begun to level off
	• A well-delineated business district has taken shape
	• Some of the older deteriorating facilities are perceived as second rate
	* Local efforts are made to extend the tourist season
Stagnation	* Peak numbers of tourists and capacity levels are reached
	* The resort has a well-established image, but it is no longer in fashion
	* The accommodation stock is gradually eroded and property turnover rates are high
Post-stagnation	* Five possibilities, reflecting a range of options that may be followed, depending partly on the success of local management decisions. At either extreme are rejuvenation and decline

Figure 2.3 Stages of resort development and associated features

Case study

An application of Butler's theory: Agarwhal's (1997) study of Torbay, England

Torbay is an important tourist destination in the South West region of England. The Southwest of England is the most important region of England for domestic British tourists (there were approximately 4.5 million visitors in 1995, of which 3.5 million were domestic visitors). Agarwhal attempted to apply Butler's model to Torbay. In summary form she indicated the following:

1 *Exploration stage* (1760–1920). There were particular types of tourists and these were linked to the health/medicinal virtues of sea water.
2 *Involvement stage* (1831–1950). In this period, the local provision of facilities/tourism infrastructure developed. This was in the form of hotels/boarding houses.
3 *Development stage* (1910–75). New tourist facilities and also tourist attractions were created in this period.

4 *Consolidation stage* (1950–75) A period of general take-off of trade. Visitor numbers exceeded the local population in this period and the economy was closely tied to tourism. However, antagonism began to grow between the local population and the tourists. The major causes of this were increased traffic problems and high local rates.
5 *Stagnation stage* (1975–86). Numbers peaked in the mid-1970s. Immediately following this, there was a great reduction in tourist numbers. Holidaymakers who had previously taken holidays in the Southwest were increasingly going elsewhere, particularly Spain and France.
6 *Post-stagnation* 1986+. There is some evidence of aspects of Butler's 'rejuvenation' phase. Attempts were made to regenerate tourism with new (indoor) facilities, for example, the Riviera Leisure Centre, an indoor shopping centre (the Pavilion) and the Hollywood Bowl, a ten-pin bowling alley.

Major differences between Agarwhal's study and the Butler model:

1 The stages of development were not discrete – there is an overlap in dates/periods.
2 In Torbay, unlike Butler's model, there was very early involvement of locals in tourism to try and provide tourist infrastructure.

3 In one part of the area (Paignton), the visitor type did not change over time, but stayed the same until very recently.
4 The decline of this resort area is not necessarily irreversible. Post-stagnation planning and management have attempted to overcome the downturn.

(Adapted from Agarwhal, S. (1997). The resort life cycle and seaside tourism. *Tourism Management* **18** (2), 65–73.)

In 1998, Butler reconsidered his model and indicated that, despite criticism, after almost twenty years there was also much support for his original model. In the paper, Butler indicated that the main criticisms of his theory were:

- doubts on there being a single model of development;
- limitations on the capacity issue;
- conceptual limitations of the life-cycle model;
- lack of empirical support for the model;
- limited practical use of the model.

In this same paper, he indicated a number of key points that he suggested confirmed the validity of his original theory. These were as follows:

- The key concept is *dynamism*. Hence resorts do change over time.
- There is a common *process* of development of tourist destinations.
- There are *limits to growth*. If the demand for visits exceeds the capacity of the destination, then the visitor experience will be diminished and visitors will subsequently decline.
- There are *triggers* – factors that bring about change in a destination.
- *Management* is a key factor. Management may be necessary, in particular, to avoid the 'decline' stage of the model.
- *Long-term viewpoint*. There is the need for a long-term view. Resorts need to look ahead for 50 years, not 5 years, to avoid some of the pitfalls suggested by the model.
- *Spatial component*. There is likely to be a spatial shift of tourism activity as the destination declines (i.e. tourists go elsewhere).
- *Universal applicability*. The model applies to all destinations.

Summary

There are a number of important theories relevant to tourism planning and management and a selection of these has been discussed in this chapter. The German geographer Christaller suggested a process through which tourism enclaves can develop. The American, Plog investigated the psychological make up of tourists and the effects on their destination choices and travel patterns, while Cohen created a typology of tourists. Doxey considered the likely reaction of host populations to increases in tourism numbers over time.

Probably the single most important theory in tourism contributing to planning and management is that of Butler. He suggested a model in which a tourism destination develops over time. He claimed that there were a number of processes that contribute to this. He also argued that resorts develop in particular stages over time. Butler claimed that the processes and stages of growth are applicable to all tourism destinations. However, applications of his model have not always found appropriate supporting evidence. Nevertheless, the importance of Butler's model for tourism planning is that he suggests that resorts are likely to go into decline unless remedial action is taken.

Student activities

1 Construct a table to indicate the major ideas within the theories discussed above of Christaller, Plog, Cohen and Doxey.
2 Use this table to show how the ideas Christaller, Plog, Cohen and Doxey are linked.
3 What are the key stages of Butler's theory?
4 What factors contribute to the changes noted in Butler's model?
5 With reference to Butler's model, what factors could lead to the rejuvenation of a destination?
6 How well does Butler's model fit the case study by Agarwhal?
7 What does Butler consider to be the main criticisms of his model?
8 To what extent does Butler consider his model to be applicable almost 20 years after it was first published?
9 How applicable do you think Butler's model is to resort development in other Developed countries such as Australia and New Zealand?

CHAPTER 3

An introduction to tourism impacts

Learning objectives

At the end of this chapter you should:

- have a basic understanding of the various impacts of tourism;
- be aware of a number of influences on tourism impacts;
- be aware of why tourism has the particular impacts that it has;
- be aware that tourism impacts can be considered as positive or negative;
- be aware of a range of perspectives on tourism impacts.

Introduction

Tourism takes place in the environment, which is made up of both human and natural features. The human environment comprises economic, social and cultural factors and processes. The natural environment is made up of plants and animals in their habitat. It is possible to make a distinction between the human environment and the natural environment and this is particularly useful when discussing the impacts of tourism. However, it is important to note that, in a real setting, the human environment and the natural environment are interwoven and human activity is both affected by and has effects on the natural environment.

Tourism, as a significant form of human activity, can have major impacts. These impacts are very visible in the destination region, where tourists interact with the local environment, economy, culture and society. Hence, it is conventional to consider the impacts of tourism under the headings of socio-cultural, economic and environmental impacts. This convention is followed in the three chapters that follow this introduction to tourism impacts. In fact, tourism issues are generally multi-faceted, often having a combination of economic, social and environmental dimensions. Therefore when considering each of the types of impact in turn, it should be remembered that the impacts are multi-faceted, often problematic and not as easily compartmentalized as is often portrayed. In other words, tourism impacts cannot easily be categorised as solely social, environmental or economic, but tend to have several inter-related dimensions. It should also be noted that much tourism planning and management is in relation to tourism impacts in destinations and resorts.

Key perspectives

The impacts of tourism can be positive or beneficial, but also negative or detrimental. Whether impacts are perceived as positive or negative depends on the value position and judgement of the observer of the impacts. This can be illustrated through the use of an example. In this case, only economic impacts are considered and the example relates to the building of a hotel in an area with currently little tourism activity. It is possible for one observer to express a view that the building of the hotel will create more jobs, both in the building and running of the hotel and the observer would consider this to be a positive impact. Conversely, another observer may claim although jobs will be created, they will only be part-time, semi-skilled, poorly paid and lacking a career structure, as well as taking people away from traditional forms of employment. This observer would view the building of the hotel as having a negative impact on the local economy.

Another example, in this case relating to environmental effects, may help with an understanding of the importance of attitudes and value positions in relating to tourism impacts. One observer may suggest that the creation of a footpath through a national park to cater for tourists can be viewed as a way of routing tourists and therefore limiting damage – a positive impact. Another observer may claim that this footpath routing will promote an increase in tourist numbers and hence the likelihood of more damage to the environment – a negative impact. Therefore, any discussion of tourism impacts needs to consider the value positions of observers and commentators and should be set within considerations of the wider context of tourism.

However, it is conventional for researchers and policy makers to note a number of both positive and negative effects of tourism. Positive economic benefits usually include contributions to the local economy and job creation. Positive social impacts of tourism can include the revival or boosting of traditional art or handicraft activity as a result of tourist demand. Positive environmental effects of tourism may include revenue generated from visits to sites of natural attraction being used to restore and maintain the attraction, as well as enhanced interest from visitors in the importance of the natural environment and therefore a greater willingness to support measures to protect the environment.

Negative economic effects of tourism may include food, land and house price increases in tourist destinations, which become particularly evident during the tourist season. Negative environmental consequences include pollution from vehicles, litter dropped by visitors, disturbance to habitats and damage to landscape features. Negative socio-cultural impacts may include the loss of cultural identity, particularly when tourists are from the developed world and the hosts are located in a developing country. This may be part of what is usually referred to as the demonstration effect. This occurs when inhabitants of a developing country imitate the activities of the visitors, who are from Developed countries. This may start off as what may be considered relatively innocuous behaviour, such as the desire to wear brand name jeans and consume branded fast food and drink, but can take the form of far more undesirable activities such as drug taking and prostitution.

Much research work on tourism impacts in the period since the late 1970s, has tended to suggest that negative impacts outweigh positive impacts (Jafari, 1990; Wall, 1997). However, large numbers of residents of destination areas have continued to want tourists to come and often want them very much (Wall, 1997). Jobs, higher incomes, increases in tax revenues and better opportunities for children are frequently stated reasons for wanting more tourists (Wall, 1997). Residents may be prepared to put up with some negative impacts in return for what they regard as desirable positive impacts. Thus, trade-offs are often involved in relation to tourism impacts.

As has been previously stated, it is often easy to see impacts in a uni-dimensional manner, when in reality they should be viewed within a wider context of not just tourism factors but also wider societal considerations. As Wall (1997, p. 2) stated:

> The situation is extremely complex … but impacts are often desired, are extremely difficult to assess, may require the acceptance of trade-offs and in a policy context, may involve the development of strategies to mitigate undesirable impacts.

Tourism impacts are likely to change over time as a destination area develops (Butler, 1980). According to Wall (1997), key factors contributing to the nature of the impacts are the type of tourism activities engaged in, the characteristics of the host community in the destination region and the nature of the interaction between the visitors and residents. Davison (1996) suggested a range of similar influences and also included the importance of time and location in relation to tourism impacts.

In stressing the importance of the 'where' and the 'when', Davison (1996) claimed these influences set tourism's impacts apart from those of other industrial sectors. In relation to tourism being concentrated in space, Davison indicated that tourism production and consumption, unlike many other industrial activities, take place in the same location. This means that the tourist consumes the product in the tourist destination. Therefore tourism impacts are largely spatially concentrated in the tourism destination.

In relation to tourism impacts being concentrated in time, Davison (1996) suggested it is because it is a seasonal activity that makes this important. The seasonality of tourism is largely due to two major factors: climate and holiday periods (Burton, 1992; Davison, 1996). Climate is a significant factor in that it controls important resources for tourism, such as hours of sunshine or amount of snow cover occurring at particular times of the year. Tourists' ability to visit a destination at a particular time of the year, for example, during a school holidays or an annual holiday, tends also to make it a seasonal activity.

In Australia and New Zealand, for example, the seasonality of tourism is closely related to climate. The summer period coincides with the traditional break at Christmas. In New Zealand, until relatively recently, the majority of businesses were closed during the last few days of December until late January. Although, changing social circumstances mean that more people now work over the Christmas and New Year break, as well as in January, the period from late December until late January is still the main school holiday time.

Some of tourism's impacts also occur beyond the destination. For example, transport from the tourist's home to the destination – the transit zone as shown in Leiper's tourism system (Figure 1.4 in Chapter 1) has an effect on the transit zone. Also, a package tour purchased in the tourists home region is likely to benefit the travel and tour operator based there, rather than one in the destination.

Tourism also has an impact on tourists themselves. These effects may be noted in their behaviour in destinations. The impacts may also become apparent when the tourist has returned from a visit. For example, the tourists' experiences may affect their decision on a future visit to the destination. In this case, some of the experiences gained would be in the actual destination, although the reflection on that experience and its effects on future tourism choices could take place elsewhere.

Major factors influencing tourism impacts have been synthesized and summarized below. These factors are based at least in part on the work of Davison (1996) and Wall (1997) and are set out in the form of questions, with some comment following the questions as examples or to provide explanation.

Major influences on tourism impacts

- Where is tourism taking place? (e.g. a rural/urban location, a coastal/inland location, a developed/developing country)
- What is the scale of tourism? (e.g. how many tourists are involved?)
- Who are the tourists? (e.g. what is their origin? Are they domestic or international visitors? Are they from Developed or Developing countries?)

- In what type of activities do tourists engage? (e.g. are these passive/active? Are these consumptive of resources? Is there a high/low level of interaction with the host population?)
- What infrastructure exists for tourism? (e.g. roads? sewage system? electricity supply?)
- For how long has tourism been established? [see particularly Butler's (1980) theory of the destination life-cycle]
- When is the tourist season? (time of year? importance of rainy/dry seasons)

McKercher (1993) argued that although the impacts of tourism are well documented, little research has been conducted into why impacts appear to be inevitable. He claimed that there are a number of what he referred to as structural realities – he used the term 'fundamental truths' – which explain why the various effects, particularly adverse effects of tourism, are felt, regardless of the type of tourism activity. McKercher's 'fundamental truths' can be considered as major influences on tourism impacts and hence are presented in a case study below (with comments added under the headings McKercher employed) and there a number of questions about these in the student activities that follow on from the case study.

Case study
Some fundamental truths about tourism

1 *Tourism consumes resources and creates waste.* Tourism is essentially a resource-based industry. These resources are either natural, man-made or cultural resources. Tourism is a voracious consumer of resources. The resources are typically part of the public domain, (e.g. woodlands, coasts, mountain regions) and hence tourism can be very invasive. Tourism is an industrial activity that creates waste with sewage, rubbish and car exhaust common by-products.

2 *Tourism has the ability to over-consume resources.* The natural, man-made and cultural resources that tourism relies upon are liable to be over-consumed. If threshold limits have been reached adverse effects over large areas can occur. This can be in relation to the natural, man-made or cultural resources.

3 *Tourism competes with other resource users and needs to do this to survive.* To survive it may be necessary for tourism to gain supremacy over competitors. Tourism and other non-tourism but leisure related activities often share the same resources. Hence, two people may be doing precisely the same activity (e.g. mountain biking) with one being classified as a tourist (because they are non-resident) the other (a 'local') as being only involved in recreation. Tourism may also compete with other non-leisure activities such as agriculture and forestry in rural locations.

4 *Tourism is private sector dominated.* As much tourism is private sector dominated, the profit motive is the key one. Investment is far more likely in profit centres (e.g. a swimming pool/leisure complex) than a cost centre (a sewage system). Governments have had a key role in promoting and developing tourism, but have been little involved in controlling it. Voluntary compliance of the industry with environmental protection is almost impossible.

5 *Tourism is multi-faceted and is therefore almost impossible to control.* Tourism is a very diverse industry including suppliers, producers, government agencies as well as a very large number of consumers. In Australia, for example, there were approximately 45 000 tourism businesses in the early 1990s. The great majority of these were small independently owned family businesses. Unity only comes through trade associations, which are usually voluntary organisations. This makes controlling tourism extremely difficult. It is however the most difficult challenge facing industry and government agencies. In a free

market system, a diverse and highly unregulated industry such as tourism will be very difficult to control and to restrict the expansion of.

6 *Tourists are consumers, not anthropologists.* Most tourists are consumers who want to consume tourism experiences. Tourists are pleasure seekers and except for a minority they are not anthropologists. Tourists are trying to escape their everyday life and hence tend to want to over-consume and are generally not interested in modifying their actions in relation to the host community or environment.

7 *Tourism is entertainment.* Most tourism products have to be manipulated and packaged to satisfy the needs of tourists to be entertained. This can lead to the commoditisation of local cultures and traditional activities. Existing products such as dances, festivals or even religious activities may need to be altered to satisfy the tourist demand.

Questions of authenticity are likely to be raised as a result.

8 *Unlike other industrial activities, tourism imports the clients rather than exports a product.* Tourism does not export products, but brings clients to consume the product *in situ*. This means tourism cannot exist in isolation from the host community. Tourism consumption usually takes place in concentrated geographical spaces. When planning for tourism, local regional and national governments should be aware of the stresses on the physical and social environment that an influx of visitors causes. Host communities also need to be aware that tourism is likely to cause a wide range of impacts.

(Adapted from McKercher, B. (1993). Some fundamental truths about tourism: understanding tourism's social, and environmental impacts. *Journal of Sustainable Tourism,* **1**, 6–16.)

Summary

This chapter has provided an introduction to the study of tourism impacts. It has indicated that although tourism impacts tend to be multi-faceted, it is conventional to subdivide them under the following headings: economic, socio-cultural and environmental. It is also conventional to present tourism impacts as either positive or negative. The chapter has indicated that such categorisation depends upon the value position of the observer. As impacts tend to be multi-faceted, often having a combination of economic, social and environmental dimensions, it may be not that straightforward to classify impacts at one particular tourism resort or destination under the heading of either solely 'positive' or 'negative'. It is quite likely that there is a combination of impacts of tourism in relation to a destination and some of these impacts may be viewed as positive, while others are seen as negative.

The nature of particular tourism impacts is related to a variety of factors, including what type of tourism is under discussion, where it is happening, when it is happening, the seasonality of tourism as well as the tourism infrastructure. Ideas put forward by McKercher (1993) on the commercial and entertainment aspects of tourism have also been introduced and these have been considered in connection with tourism impacts. The chapter has also suggested that is important to note that much tourism planning and management occurs in relation to impacts at tourism destinations.

Student activities

1 How do McKercher's 'fundamental truths' affect your views on tourism impacts?

2 To what extent do you agree with McKercher's 'fundamental truths'?

3 What are the major influences on tourism's impacts?

4 Consider a tourism activity/business in your local area and the impacts of this activity:

- Make a list of the impacts under the headings: 'positive' and 'negative'
- When complete, consider which of the two types of impacts are more important in relation to your example. NB: This does not necessarily correspond to the longer list of the two.
- Look again at the list and consider your own value position and indicate which of the impacts could be regarded in a different way, from your own assessment by another commentator, and how these impacts could be viewed.
- How important do you believe the nature of tourist activities are in relation to the impacts of tourism?

The economic impacts of tourism

Learning outcomes

At the end of this chapter you should be able to:

- describe in your own words the major economic impacts of tourism;
- demonstrate an awareness of a range of both 'positive' and 'negative' economic impacts of tourism;
- compare the economic impacts of tourism in Developed and Developing countries;
- discuss the implications of the economic impacts of tourism for the management of the tourism industry.

Introduction

The impacts of tourism have been historically the most researched area of tourism, and economic impacts have been more researched than any other type of impact. As Pearce (1989, p. 2) indicated:

> Studies of the impact of tourist development on a destination or destinations have been the largest single element of tourism research … much of this is predominantly the work of economists and has concentrated on the effects of income and employment.

Although, as has been stated in Chapter 3, economic impacts of tourism are linked to, and cannot easily be separated from, other types of impact, largely in an attempt to assist with understanding, economic impacts are discussed in this chapter separately from other tourism impacts.

Key perspectives

Chapter 3 provided a general indication of the key influences on the impacts of tourism, but of particular importance in relation to economic impacts are the following: scale of tourism activities, when tourism occurs (e.g. whether tourism is a seasonal activity) and the historical development of tourism (with a particular emphasis on infrastructure for tourism). It is also worth considering again Butler's (1980) model and criticisms of it (see Chapter 2) in relation to the economic impacts of tourism.

As was discussed in Chapter 3, impacts can be considered under the headings of positive and negative. In relation to economic impacts the following are usually considered to be positive effects:

- contribution to foreign exchange earnings;
- contribution to government revenues;
- generation of employment;
- contribution to regional development.
  (Lickorish, 1994)

Such benefits can usually be measured either at a national level or at the local or regional scale.

Negative consequences of tourism include, according to Pearce (1989) and Mason (1995), at least, the following:

- inflation;
- opportunity costs
- over-dependence on tourism.

Inflation relates to the increases in prices of land, houses and even food that can occur as a result of tourism. Prices for these commodities can increase when tourists place extra demands on local services at a tourism destination. Opportunity costs refers to the cost of engaging in tourism rather than another form of economic activity. For example, in a coastal area, with a predominantly rural hinterland, this could be the costs of investing in tourism instead of in arable farming, market gardening or fishing. Over-dependence on tourism can occur in, for example, small states where tourism is seen by the government as the best method of development. Over time, the emphasis on tourism becomes such that there is virtually no other approach to development. As a result, the country becomes dependent on tourism revenue to the extent that any change in demand is likely to lead to a major economic crisis.

One significant factor when discussing economic impacts of tourism is scale. Although similar processes may be operating, effects can be different as a result of them operating at different scales. The global economic importance of tourism has been briefly referred to above with discussion of employment and contribution to balance of payment and global gross domestic product. In addition to this data, is the projection that jobs in tourism are likely to increase steadily during the early part of this century, unlike jobs in other economic sectors. These macro-level figures however hide the unbalanced nature of global tourism. One continent alone, Europe, was the single most important tourist destination with over 60 per cent of all international visitor arrivals in the mid-1990s and most international arrivals of tourists in Europe were visits from other European countries.

The United States and Canada are also both important destination areas and tourism generating regions. Asia is an important region for tourists from Europe, North America and Australasia to visit, but is also becoming increasingly important as a source of tourists. These tourists, from Japan, Korea and Taiwan in particular, are visiting other parts of Asia and the Pacific Rim but are also making visits to Europe and North America. Two continents, in particular, reveal the uneven balance of international tourism. South America is a growing destination for tourists, but produces few visitors, relatively speaking, to other parts of the world. Africa shows this to an even greater extreme with increasing numbers visiting the continent, with the game reserves of East Africa, parts of the Mediterranean coast and South Africa becoming significant tourist attractions, but the percentage of world tourists originating in Africa is very low.

Economic impacts of tourism can be particularly marked in Developing countries. The Indonesian island of Bali provides a good example of both the gains and problems that can arise from tourism development in a destination located in a developing country. Since tourism began to grow in importance in the 1960s, a significant number of jobs have been created. These have been in the relatively obvious categories of hotel workers and bar staff, but also in perhaps less obvious areas such as boat hire, cycle hire and repair, car and motorcycle hire, food and drink selling and souvenir making and selling. Tourism is also said to have revived the arts and crafts activities of painting and wood carving, as well as the introduction of new arts activities, including batique making (Mason, 1995).

Residents have tried to benefit from tourism, either through direct involvement in tourism in hotel, restaurant and guide service jobs, as well as through the manufacture and sale of craft products, the undertaking of cultural performances and food production to feed tourists (Wall, 1997). Particular examples of ways in which Balinese have benefited from tourism include the provision of home-stays and the increase in those providing informal services to tourists (Wall, 1997). Home-stays are the Balinese equivalent of the Western bed and breakfast. The great majority of home-stays are run by local residents, rather than outsiders and hence almost all of the economic gain from the activity goes directly to the local population (Cukier and Wall, 1994).

A large number of young males (aged 15–25) work as street and beach vendors in Bali. They mostly lack formal education, but have substantial language skills. Although they worked long hours, and believed they had few alternative job opportunities, most of these vendors were relatively happy with their lifestyle and were well remunerated by Indonesian standards (Cukier and Wall, 1994). Tourism grew so rapidly in Bali in the period from 1970 that by 1995, if the associated craft industries were included, then tourism contributed over 30 per cent of the gross provincial product (Wall, 1997).

On the negative side, however, Bali provides evidence of tourism promoting inflation. Before 1968 (roughly the beginning of the growth of tourism) land prices had been steady for about 20 years, however, during the following 25 years land prices rose by nearly 100 per cent on average but by over 150 per cent in the tourist areas (Mason, 1995). Although it is difficult to calculate opportunity costs, there is some evidence from the large-scale development at Nusa Dua, on the southern coast of Bali (which was supported by the World Bank) that the money may well have been better spent on a smaller scale, less intrusive hotel complex. Something smaller would have been more in keeping with local values and may have contributed more to the local economy. It has been argued that the money would have been better spent on agriculture or forestry or locally based retailing rather than tourism that is primarily aimed at an up-market, international segment (Mason, 1995).

The future of tourism in Bali is far from clear after the terrorist bombings at Kuta in October 2002. Bali has become heavily dependent on tourism and the what happens after the events of October 2002 may indicate whether the island has become economically over-dependent on tourism.

Similar issues to those of Bali in its early stages of tourism development can be found in the Himalayan country, Nepal. As in Bali, tourism was relatively unimportant until the second half of the twentieth century, but more recently has come to be very significant to the economy of Nepal. Nepal, the fourth poorest country in the world, is a landlocked Himalayan kingdom relying on access to imports via India. Throughout the period of European global exploration, dating from about 1400 until as recently as the1950s, Nepal was almost inaccessible and hence it holds attractions for significant numbers of potential tourists. Tourism began in the early 1960s but took off in the 1970s. By 2001, there were in excess of 500 000 tourists per year. Particularly rapid growth took place in the 1980s. Between 1977 and 1988 there was a 60 per cent increase in tourist numbers and foreign earnings from tourism went up by 75 per cent. In the capital city Kathmandu, there were 2800 people employed in the accommodation sector in 1977 and 14 500 rooms for tourists, but by 1988 there were 4100 employers and 23 700 tourist rooms (Department of Tourism, 1990).

Nepal also shares some similarities with Bali in that violence there has had an adverse effect on tourist numbers and hence the economic contribution of tourism to the economy. Although not direct targets, tourists have been put off visiting by Maoist rebels who have become particularly active since the mid-1990s as well as the legacy of the, still not fully explained, killing of almost all members of the Nepalese royal family in June 2001.

As in Bali, jobs in Nepal's tourism industry are often outside the formal sector and hence difficult to measure but include part-time guide work (often undertaken by students/teachers and lecturers as this pays as much as US$ 10 a day compared with an average monthly wage of US$ 35). Souvenir producing and selling is also important in terms of job creation. Hand massage is a speciality of Nepal and there is a charge about US$ 1 a time. Those involved can make between US$ 15 and 20 a day.

The negative effects of the rapid expansion of tourism in Nepal can be seen at important Buddhist and Hindu temples. These temples are not just tourist attractions but are used for religious activities. Those who wish to use the temples for religious activities have to deal not only with the crowds of tourists who are causing physical damage to buildings but also with those who are becoming economically dependent on tourism. These include service providers such as the souvenir sellers, the drink hawkers and even beggars of all ages and both sexes who are there because of the reliance on tourist handouts (Mason, 1991).

Some parts of Europe are not completely unlike Developing countries in terms of being resource frontiers for tourism development. In the far north of Europe is the unlikely setting for the Santa Claus industry. This industry, a focal point for domestic and international tourism, is located in Finnish Lapland and is centred on the Santa Claus Village. The village opened in 1986, focusing on the concept of it being the home of Santa Claus. An account of its foundation and economic impacts is provided in the case study below.

Case study

Tourism in Lapland, the Santa Claus Industry

Lapland is the northern-most province of Finland and is the least populated region of the country. Traditionally, the region has attracted two major types of tourists. Lapland provides wilderness and solitude sought by those escaping from routine who wish to find solace in the forest. Many of this type of tourists come from within Finland. The other main type of tourist is interested in the indigenous culture of the Sami (Lapp) people.

The economy of Lapland has become increasingly dependent on tourism, with in excess of 6000 people in the industry in the early 1990s. The Finnish Tourist Board expected the number employed to rise to 9500–10 000 by the early part of the twenty-first century. The Board was particularly keen to encourage more foreign tourists. Despite the success of encouraging more domestic tourism during the 1980s when the number of overseas tourists appeared to be rising in the 1980s numbers then fell in the early 1990s. Overseas tourists made up about 20 per cent of all tourists to Lapland in the early 1990s. The main overseas generating countries were Germany, the Netherlands, Switzerland, Italy and France. Most tourists from these countries visited in summer. Many of these were in transit to the North Cape, the most northerly point of mainland Europe. Tourists from Britain and Japan come in winter to take part in winter sports, experience a 'white winter' or see reindeer.

In the late 1970s and early 1980s, the Board declared that the natural and cultural attractions of Lapland were not sufficient to attract tourists in the desired numbers and decided a new attraction had to be created. The idea of promoting Santa Claus as an attraction was appealing.

The Santa Claus industry

In 1985, the Governor of Lapland declared the entire state 'Santa Claus Land'. However, there

Photo 2 The Santa Claus Village, Rovaneimi, Finland, which has been specifically located on the Arctic Circle

were also a number of rival claims for the home of Santa Claus at this time; in Alaska, Norway, Sweden and Greenland. In 1989, the Santa Claus Land Association was founded by 16 Finnish companies and this was connected to the Finnish Tourism Board. This association had as its sole role the marketing of the Santa Claus idea. The Association operated the Santa Claus Postal service, coordinated Santa Claus visits overseas and promoted Santa Claus at various international gatherings.

The Santa Claus Village

The showpiece of Santa Claus Land is the Santa Claus Village. This is located exactly on the Arctic Circle a few kilometres north of the town of Rovaniemi, the capital of Lapland (Photo 2). The site was chosen as, prior to the establishment, tourists had stopped at the Arctic Circle sign to have their photograph taken. The village site is on the main North–South route through Lapland. The village was opened in 1985 and contains Santa's workshop, where he may be visited at all times of the year, Santa's Post Office, a reindeer enclosure, several restaurants and many gift and souvenir shops. The Santa Claus Village property is owned by a company based in Rovaniemi and individual businesses within the village are privately owned.

Of particular significance within the village is the Santa Claus Postal Service. In the 1950s, letters written to Santa Claus by European school children were received in Helsinki. In 1976, the Santa Claus Postal Service was moved to Lapland when some 18 765 letters were received. The number of letters steadily grew. Visitors to the Santa Claus Village were encouraged to sign their names in Santa's guest book and in 1990 over 550 000 letters were sent out at Christmas containing a free gift. By the early 1990s, letters were dispatched to 160 countries.

Nearby, Rovaniemi has an international airport and can handle international jet aircraft. The most famous international flight has been the regular flights by British Airways Concorde at Christmas between 1986 and 1992.

Economic impacts

In 1985, 225 000 visitors came to the village and the number of visitors increased rapidly from then until the late 1980s reaching 277 000 in 1989. In the early 1990s, related to the general global depression visitor numbers fell. However, in the second part of the 1990s visitor numbers once again increased and reached over 300 000 in 1995. In 1996, there were 1.6 million international and domestic visitors to Lapland and 325 000 visited the Village. Visitors to Lapland increased by 22 per cent between 1986 and 1994 and foreign earnings were up by 29 per cent and this was attributed mainly to the Santa Claus Village. The Village employed 290 people, which in 1990 was 7 per cent of total tourism employment in Lapland.

Although this development is a totally artificial creation, it is an attempt to bring tourists to an area perceived as lacking many natural attractions. The village has been heralded as a great success in bringing tourists to a relatively remote and inhospitable location, and that at present there is little recorded environmental or social damage there.

(Adapted from Pretes, M. (1995). Post modern tourism: the Santa Claus industry. *Annals of Tourism Research*, **22** (1), 1–15.)

Other relatively peripheral areas in terms of the global reach of tourism have also gained tourist in the past 25 years, or so. Hence, although New Zealand received only 0.2 per cent of international travellers in 1996, this percentage has increased in the last decade of the twentieth century and the economic impacts were highly significant. (Figures presented below are based on New Zealand Tourist Board data from 1996, 2000, 2001 and 2002.) From 1993 to 1996, the number of visitors increased by an average of 6.5 per cent per year. The average spend per trip in 1993 was NZ$ 2041, but in March 1996 this had increased to NZ$ 2776. By 2000, the average visitor spend per trip had risen to NZ$ 3222.

In terms of the main groups of tourists, Australia, Japan and the United States were the major origin areas. New markets areas were Taiwan and South Korea and in March 1996 these two areas made up 15 per cent of total visitors, which was an increase over 1995 of 3 per cent. Japanese, Taiwanese and South Koreans were the biggest spenders, averaging over NZ$ 200 per day. The importance of this expanding market can be seen in the following figures: there were 216 162 visitors from these three countries in 1996 with an estimated spend per head of NZ$ 234. By 2000, the average spend per head had increased to NZ$ 330 for Japanese visitors (the largest daily spend of any visitor group) and NZ$ 221 for Koreans. Only American visitors (averaging NZ$ 248 per day) in 2000 spent more than Koreans (Hall & Kearsley (2001)).

However, the economic crisis in Asia that occurred in late 1997/early 1998 affected the projected continued growth in this Asian market, and in 1998–9 the percentage of visitors from this region fell in relation to total visitors. Nevertheless, in 2000 visitor numbers from Asia recovered and there was a 13 per cent increase on the 1999 figure by the end of December 2000, a further 7 per cent increase during 2001 and an 8 per cent increase in 2002. By the end of 2002, visitors from Asia exceeded 500 000 for the first time, with Korea (104 000 in 2002) and China (71 000 in 2002) growing particularly rapidly in the first years of the new millennium.

At end of 2002 for the first time, New Zealand received more than two million visitors in 1 year. In relation to employment, in 1995 there were 155 000 jobs in New Zealand tourism and by the end of 2001 this had reached 176 000.

Summary

Economic impacts are one of the most researched areas of tourism. They have tended to be far more researched than other forms of impact. Economic impacts can be subdivided into both positive and negative groupings. Often, countries perceive positive economic benefits as the major type of tourism impact and hence are supportive of tourism development. Evidence suggests that a number of Developing countries have selected tourism as part of their approach to development. Such countries desire the positive economic benefits, however they tend to be less aware that their tourism may also bring some negative economic effects.

However, tourism is often one of a range of development options facing both Developed and Developing countries and regions. Tourism is often viewed as a preferred option, in relation to other possible choices. Hence, either, where there are old dying industries and the area is in need of revitalisation, or in related un-exploited locations seeking new developments, but with few choices, tourism can bring significant economic benefits. Nevertheless, this chapter has raised the issue, that to maximize economic benefits and minimize costs, tourism requires careful planning and management.

Student activities

1 Identify the positive and negative economic impacts of tourism from the perspective of a community affected by tourism that you know well.

2 Suggest what the economic impacts of tourism might be in small states, such as tropical islands or landlocked states.

3 How might the economic impacts of tourism in these small states differ from those in more Developed countries, such as those in Europe, North America or Australasia?

4 What factors could contribute to the impacts being different in these small Developing countries?

5 What factors (a) acting internally within a country and (b) acting externally (beyond the country) could affect the economic impacts of tourism, particularly in a negative way?

The socio-cultural impacts of tourism

Learning outcomes

At the end of this chapter you should be:

- able to describe in you own words the nature of socio-cultural impacts of tourism;
- aware of range of socio-cultural impacts of tourism and aware of the context in which these occur;
- able to discuss the implications that these impacts have for the good management of the tourism industry.

Introduction

Any discussion of socio-cultural impacts of tourism will require reference to and discussion of meanings of the terms society and culture. Sociology is the study of society and is concerned with the study of people in groups, their interaction, their attitudes and their behaviour. Culture is about how people interact as observed through social interaction, social relations and material artefacts. According to Burns and Holden (1995) culture consists of behavioural patterns, knowledge and values which have been acquired and transmitted through generations. They also indicate that 'culture is the complex whole which includes knowledge, belief, art, moral law, custom and any other capabilities and habits acquired by man as a member of society' (Burns and Holden, 1995, p. 113).

Key perspectives

This chapter is concerned with a study of the impacts of tourism on people in groups, and this includes both residents of tourism areas (such people are usually referred to as hosts) and tourists themselves. It also concerned with impacts on the culture of the host population (and also any effects on the culture of the visitors themselves). The way in which culture can be used and even packaged to promote tourism, and hence the subsequent effects this has on culture are also topics investigated.

Cultural attractions in relation to tourism include the following (Ritchie and Zins, 1978):

- handicrafts;
- language;
- traditions;
- gastronomy;
- art and music;
- history of the area/including visual reminders;
- types of work engaged in by residents;
- architecture;
- religion (including visible manifestations);
- education systems;
- dress;
- leisure activities.

Before proceeding with a discussion of socio-cultural impacts it is worth considering again the influences on the impacts of tourism once, which were presented in Chapter 3. All factors discussed there are important in relation to socio-cultural impacts. Clearly, a key influence is who is involved and the activities engaged in will be significant. Of particular importance, in relation to socio-cultural impacts of tourism, is the nature of both visitors and host populations. The interaction of the two groups will be a major issue in affecting the types of impact. As Burns and Holden (1995) argued when there is a large contrast between the culture of the receiving society and the origin culture then it is likely that impacts will be greatest.

Some of the more beneficial impacts of tourism on society include the following: the creation of employment; the revitalization of poor or non-industrialized regions; the rebirth of local arts and crafts and traditional cultural activities; the revival of social and cultural life of the local population; the renewal of local architectural traditions; and the promotion of the need to conserve areas of outstanding beauty which have aesthetic and cultural value (Mason, 1995). In Developing countries in particular, tourism can encourage greater social mobility through changes in employment from traditional agriculture to service industries and may result in higher wages and better job prospects.

However, tourism has the reputation for major detrimental effects on the society and culture of host areas. Tourism can cause overcrowding in resorts. This overcrowding can cause stress for both tourists and residents. Where tourism takes over as a major employer, traditional activities such as farming may decline. In extreme cases, regions can become over-dependent on tourism. Residents may find it difficult to co-exist with tourists who have different values and who are involved in leisure activities, while the residents are involved in working. This problem is made worse where tourism is a seasonal activity and residents have to modify their way of life for part of the year. In countries with strong religious codes, altered social values caused by a tourist invasion may be viewed as nationally undesirable.

One of the more significant socio-cultural impacts of tourism is referred to as the 'demonstration' effect. This depends on there being visible differences between tourists and hosts. Such a situation arises in many Developing countries. In the demonstration effect, it is theorized, that simply observing tourists will lead to behavioural changes in the resident population (Williams, 1998). Under these conditions, local people will note the superior material possessions of the visitors and aspire to these. This may have positive effects in that it can encourage residents to adopt more productive patterns of behaviour. But more frequently it is disruptive in that locals become resentful because they are unable to obtain the goods and lifestyle demonstrated by the visitors (Burns and Holden, 1995). Young people are particularly susceptible to the demonstration effect. Tourism may then be blamed for societal divisions between the young and older members. The demonstration effect may also encourage the more able younger members of a society to migrate from rural areas in search of the 'demonstrated' lifestyle in urban areas or even overseas.

The demonstration effect is most likely to occur where the contacts between residents and visitors are relatively superficial and short-lived (Williams, 1998). Another process, known as acculturation, may occur when the contact is for a longer period and is deeper. As Williams (1998, p. 153) noted:

> Acculturation theory states that when two cultures come into contact for any length of time, an exchange of ideas and products will take place that, through time, produce varying levels of convergence between the cultures; that is they become similar.

However, this process will not necessarily be balanced, as one culture is likely to be stronger than the other. As with the demonstration effect, it is in developed world/developing world relationships where the process is most likely to occur. As the Unites States has one of the most powerful cultures, it is usually the American culture that predominates over the one from the developing country in any such meeting of cultures. This particular process of acculturation has been dubbed the 'MacDonaldization' or 'Coca-colaization' of global cultures (Mason, 1992; MacCannel, 1995). One of the perceived negative effects of this acculturation process is the reduction in the diversity of global cultures.

At the beginning of the age of mass tourism in the early 1960s, it was possible for a number of researchers and commentators to view the relationship between tourists from the developed world and residents of Developing countries as a potentially positive one (see Tomlejnovic and Faulkner, 2000). Such writers considered that tourism could act a positive global force for the promotion of international understanding. An example of such a statement is presented in Figure 5.1.

Approximately a quarter of a century later, views on tourism's potential to contribute to greater global understanding had changed somewhat as is illustrated in Figure 5.2. As Figure 5.2 indicates, misunderstanding rather than understanding among different peoples was a more likely outcome of an encounter between visitors from the developed world and residents of the developing world.

Although acculturation became an important process towards the end of the twentieth century, the desire of many tourists to experience a different culture is still a major motivation for tourist visits (Ryan, 1997). The motivation is to see and experience, at first hand, the actual culture and its manifestation, in terms of art, music, dance and handicrafts. This

Figure 5.1
Tourism and international understanding
(Adapted from Hunziken, R. *Revue de Tourisme*. Bern, Switzerland, 1961.)

Tourism has become the noblest instrument of this century for achieving international understanding. It enables contacts among people from the most distant parts of the globe, people of various languages, race, creed, political beliefs and economic standing. Tourism brings them together, it is instrumental in their dialogue, it leads to personal contact in which people can understand attitudes and beliefs which were incomprehensible to them because they were distant. In this way it helps to bridge gaps and erase differences. Since its focal point is man and not the economy, tourism can be one of the most important means, especially in developing countries, of bringing nations closer together and of maintaining good international relations. This noble task is today more important than ever. It therefore overshadows all other means striving for international friendship.

Figure 5.2
The glasses of prejudice
(Adapted from Krippendorf, J. *The Holiday Makers*. Heinemann, London, 1987.)

'Travel in its current form hardly helps to bring people closer together and promote their mutual understanding. The dim glasses of prejudice are never taken off. Although there are studies of the subject, all indications are that travel, especially to countries with a totally different culture, does not diminish prejudice but reinforces it. The other people are poor but happy. Carefree, easy-going, and hospitable, but yes, a bit untidy, not so clean you understand, yes, even dirty and unhygienic, certainly unreliable, lazy too, and well, not so very intelligent. Well, that's exactly what one had expected, it's not surprising, that's what Africa's like – people say. The image we have of other nationalities is as distorted as their image of ourselves. For the native, the tourist's behaviour is typical of his country. In his eyes, for example, tourists are immensely rich and never have to work. Or because they walk around half-naked, they must come from "cold islands". "In the cold parts they cannot go to the beach because snow is falling and certain parts of the beach is frozen.' Neither the native nor the tourist knows what their respective worlds are really like. In this way travel confirms the clichés of both host and guest.

Misunderstanding instead of understanding among peoples. At times confrontation instead of meeting. In the worst case mutual contempt instead of esteem: tourists despise the "underdeveloped" natives, and natives in their turn despise the unrestrained foreigners."

desire has contributed to a revival of traditional crafts as well the development of new activities, in a number of locations, including, for example, Bali (Cukier and Wall, 1994; Mason, 1995). In Bali, this in turn has promoted the growth of a souvenir trade that has made a significant contribution to the local economy.

However on the negative side, the desire of visitors to experience the 'real' culture has brought into question the authenticity of the tourist experience. In some developing world locations, for example, Bali, the Solomon Islands and developed world locations with indigenous cultures, such as Canada, Arctic Norway and Finland, demand for cultural artefacts and performances has become packaged for convenient consumption by visitors. Such commoditization has led to challenges concerning the authenticity of the tourist experience. The commoditization has led to pseudo-events that share the following characteristics: they are planned rather than spontaneous; they are designed to be performed to order, at times that are convenient for tourists; and they hold at best an ambiguous relationship to real elements on which they are based (Mason, 1995; Williams, 1998). Also, of particular concern, as Williams noted, is that these pseudo-events eventually *become* the authentic events and replace the original events or practice.

As Mason (1995) reported, the keechak dance, part of a traditional religious ritual, performed originally only on special occasions in Bali's Agama Hindu culture, has been shortened, taken out of its religious context and performed on a daily basis, to paying tourist groups. Tourists observing such an inauthentic pseudo-event may feel cheated, although this assumes that they have the knowledge in the first place to comprehend the local traditions and they may not even be aware that they are watching a pseudo-event. It can be argued that this type of performance may actually relieve pressure upon local communities and even help to protect the performances real cultural basis from the tourist 'gaze' (see Urry, 1990). However, there is danger that the local performers, may, over time, forget the true meaning and significance of the practice or event now staged mainly for tourists. Likewise, traditional objects that are reproduced and marketed as tourist souvenirs may lose their meaning and value.

Much of the preceding discussion has focused on the interaction between tourists and residents of tourist destinations, with an emphasis on the effects on the resident population. However, contact between tourists and residents also will clearly have an impact on the tourists themselves. As is indicated in Figure 5.2, this can contribute to the reinforcing of stereotypes, rather then the broadening of the mind that, according to the aphorism, travel experiences are meant to bring about. Nevertheless, there is increasing evidence to suggest that the impacts of experiences on tourists themselves can lead to not only changes in their thinking and attitudes, but can also result in behavioural changes. A growing number of tourists visited the Antarctic continent in the last decade of the twentieth century. However, the continent still remains relatively inaccessible and expensive to visit; for many who travel there it is a once in a life time journey. Those who visit often have a profound interest in nature and the wildlife of the continent. It would appear that those who have visited return from the Antarctic with not only increased knowledge, but also a far greater awareness of the need to conserve this unique wilderness environment (Mason and Legg, 1999). Therefore, it is possible to conclude that the experience of their visit has had such a marked effect, to the extent that these tourist have become significant ambassadors for the continent.

A significant problem in assessing socio-cultural impacts is that it is difficult to differentiate these from other impacts and hence particularly difficult to measure them. This partly explains why these impacts have been regarded in the past as less significant than economic impacts. Much of what has been written about socio-cultural impacts of tourism has been based on research that has required those actually affected by these types of impact, to assess the impact on themselves or on others. This form of research tends to be more qualitative and subjective in comparison with the more quantitative approaches used to assess and measure economic impacts of tourism, such as the multiplier. For some commentators, this qualitative approach is less acceptable than quantitative approaches as it is argued that such an approach is less scientific. A number of criticisms of this position can also be made as those who support the more qualitative approach would argue, among a number of points, their techniques are more flexible, achieve a higher response rate and their data is likely to be richer, more detailed and hence more meaningful (see Tribe, 2000).

A number of theories have been put foward regarding socio-cultural impacts of tourism. One of the best known is Doxey's Irritation Index or Irridex and this was previously discussed in Chapter 2. As a reminder, in this theory, advanced in the mid-1970s, Doxey claimed that the resident population, or hosts in a tourist area, would modify their attitudes to visitors over time. Doxey suggested there are a number of stages in the modification of resident attitudes. When tourists first visit, Doxey argued, they will be greeted with euphoria and then over time as the tourist numbers grow, attitudes will move through stages of apathy, annoyance and finally to outright aggression towards the visitors.

A number of pieces of research have been conducted to apply theoretical perspectives on socio-cultural impacts of tourism. An important study was conducted, by Getz, in the Scottish Highlands, who attempted to apply Doxey's theory. The study was significant as it was, what Getz claimed to be, a longitudinal study. Getz study was in reality two snapshots taken at different dates. He investigated the Spey valley in the late 1970s and then again in the early 1990. However, such return visits to the same investigation site are very unusual in tourism literature and hence the findings are particularly important. The sample size and content for Getz' studies of 1978 and 1992 were fairly similar to each other, but there were different individuals involved on each occasion. Each used a sample of 130 households. The main findings were as follows:

- In both surveys residents were mainly supportive of tourism.
- Despite mainly positive views, by 1992 there was much more of a negative feeling towards tourism. This was partly related to the fact that tourism was not found to be as successful as had been hoped in the 1970s.
- Those directly involved in, and hence dependent on, tourism were more likely to be positive about tourism.

- There was some support for Doxey's idea that, over time, locals had become more negative towards tourism. However, the attitudes appeared more linked to a general feeling of economic depression. Getz suggested that if an economic upturn occured, then views would probably improve towards tourism. Also, it would appear residents were particularly concerned that there were few viable alternatives to tourism in the area, so despite the lower satisfaction with tourism's impacts it was still felt that it was the best alternative. Hence, the notion of 'trade-offs', discussed earlier in Chapter 3, was important here.

- The attitudes of locals had not greatly changed with the growth and change of the tourist industry. The number of tourists did not appear to have gone beyond a threshold in Speyside. This was not because of local's attitudes, but due to more general concerns with environmental impacts of tourism and restrictions on skiing development, although it would seem residents did not feel particularly concerned about environmental impacts.

In summary, the research by Getz (1978, 1994) suggested that, unlike the theoretical statements of Doxey, the attitudes of residents do not appear to change greatly over time. However, Getz noted some increase in negative attitudes to tourism in this time period, but not to the extent indicated by Doxey (1975). Getz, in fact, discovered that attitudes to tourism by the host population were closely linked to economic fluctuations, both nationally and locally, as well as to an awareness of the small range of other options to tourism in the local region.

In the mid-1990s, research was conducted into resident attitudes to tourism growth on the Greek island of Samos. The main results from this research are discussed in the following case study as these findings provide a particularly good example of the variety of perceived different positive and negative impacts of tourism, from the perspective of local residents.

Case study

Attitudes to Tourism on the Greek island of Samos

The study was concerned particularly with impacts of tourism on the host population in one town on the island of Samos (Pythagorean) and their attitude to visitors and tourism in general. In this study 20 per cent of households in the town were given a questionnaire. As many as 71 per cent of those questioned, were involved in a tourism-related business and 59 per cent had a member of the family involved in tourism. Most of those interviewed were relatively wealthy in comparison with the average Greek wage earner.

The main results were as follows (based on Haralambopolulos and Pizam, 1996):

- In general, residents favoured tourism (as high as 80 per cent strongly favoured tourism in their area).

- As many as 84 per cent indicated that the image of Pythagorean had improved since tourism developed.

- Residents were in favour of more tourism, indicating visitor numbers could increase.

- As many as 87 per cent of the residents perceived that tourists were different from them.

- Specific questions were asked about the perceived social impacts. The top three factors seen to improve as a result of tourism were: employment, personal income, standard of living.

- Factors that would worsen as a result of tourism, in order of importance, were as follows: drug addiction, fighting/brawls, vandalism, sexual harassment, prostitution and crime in general.

- A number of tests were conducted to investigate whether those with direct involvement in tourism had different views than those with no direct involvement. The researchers found, perhaps not surprisingly, that those with direct involvement in tourism did have more positive views on it. Even those with no personal involvement indicated that tourism had positive effects, but were generally less keen on the activity and they also had more neutral and negative views in relation to other effects.
- In terms of socio-demographic factors and attitudes, age was important; the young were generally more in favour of tourism. Length of time in the area was also important; the longer people had been resident, the less keen they were on tourism. Bigger family size also led to more positive views on tourism, and this was probably due to perceived job opportunities. More educated residents were more likely to have positive attitudes to tourism. Increasing sexual permissiveness was the only factor seen negatively by just about all groups, except the young.

(Adapted from Haralmbopolous, N. and Pizam, A. (1996). Perceived impacts of tourism: the case of Samos. *Annals of Tourism Research*, **2** (3), 503–26.)

The case study of the Greek island of Samos indicates that socio-cultural effect tend to be unbalanced in relation to different groups in society. In the Samos example, those who were more actively involved in tourism were more likely to be supportive of it. However, there is often a gender dimension to socio-cultural impacts of tourism.

There is now significant evidence to indicate that women are on the receiving end of different effects of tourism, particularly within the context of the developing world. The exploitation of mainly women (but also children – both male and female) through prostitution in the Developing countries was a feature of the last three decades of the twentieth century. Prostitution is only one form of sex tourism (massage parlours, sex shops, sex cinemas are other examples), but it is particularly strong in Developing countries.

In a number of Southeast Asian countries/destinations, prostitution and some form of sex tourism have been in existence for a long period. Such areas include Thailand, the Philippines, Korea, Taiwan and the Indonesian island of Bali. In such countries traditional attitudes, particularly of males towards females, means that the use of female prostitutes by males is a relatively common practice. This form of activity does not carry the same stigma as it would in a Western society and, if anything, is a relatively common practice. Hence, prostitution has become institutionalized in countries such as Thailand and the Philippines. However, prostitution is not necessarily legal in countries of Southeast Asia, but laws tend not to be always enforced.

What has been unusual in the last three decades of the twentieth century is the growing scale of sex tourism and that it increasingly involves international tourists. The great majority of these international tourists originate in Developed countries (O'Grady, 1980; Hall, 1992). One of the reasons for this has been the cost differential for sexual services in the developing world compared with the developed world (Hall, 1992). Other reasons include the difference in attitudes to women in Southeast Asian societies compared with Western societies, and the actual status of women in Western societies and Southeast Asian societies, respectively (Mason, 1995). Throughout much of the period from the 1970s until the late 1990s, sex tourism in, for example, the Philippines and Thailand, was also strongly promoted and marketed to mainly male tourists from Australia, the United States and Europe.

In an attempt to trace its history, Hall (1992) suggested that sex tourism in Southeast Asia passed through four stages. The first stage was indigenous prostitution, dating back several centuries, in which women were subjugated within the patriarchal nature of most Southeast Asian societies. The second stage came about as a result of militarization and economic colonialism. An example would be American service personnel satisfying their sexual needs in Thailand during 'rest and relaxation' from the Vietnam War. This was made possible as a result of the infrastructure that existed for indigenous prostitution. During this period, economic development was closely linked to the selling of sexual services. The third stage involved the substitution of international tourists for the military personnel. Hall suggested that the authoritarian nature of many Asian political regimes meant that sex was often considered as an important commodity that could be traded in an attempt to achieve economic growth. As a saleable commodity, little regard was actually given to individuals involved in providing the sexual services. This attracted media condemnation from Western societies, but also is likely to have stimulated increased sex tourism, as potential customers noted that the attitudes of the authorities were not condemnatory of the tourist's activities.

In the early 1990s, Hall suggested that standards of living in Southeast Asia had been improved, meaning less dependency on sex tourism as a means to economic development. However, it was too early to say whether attitudes to sex tourism as a saleable commodity had changed. Nevertheless, in the last decade of the twentieth century, there was growing awareness of the spread of AIDS via prostitutes in Developing countries (Mason, 1995). This, coupled with the attempts of some politicians and influential members of Thai society to move the image of the destination away from one where sex tourism is a key activity, may reduce the dependency on sex tourism in the first decade of the twenty-first century.

Summary

There is a range of both positive and negative socio-cultural impacts of tourism. Much has been written about the supposed negative impacts, including the demonstration effect, cultural damage, authenticity and specific issues such as increases in drug taking, prostitution and crime in general. The negative consequences have been noted, particularly where there is a major cultural difference between the tourists and the local population.

Assessing and measuring socio-cultural impacts is not straightforward. Most research has relied on the attitudes of a range of respondents, particularly local residents, but also tourists themselves and other players in tourism. As local communities are not homogenous, socio-cultural impacts are perceived differently by different individuals.

A good deal of research has also been an attempt to apply various theories, such as that of Doxey (1975) to specific contexts. Empirical research tends to suggest that local residents in many locations are willing to consider trade-offs in relation to tourism – they are willing to accept some negative consequences as long as tourism is perceived as bringing some benefits. This is particularly so where tourism is one of a small range of choices.

Student activities

1 In relation to a tourism development/activity in your area identify the main types of socio-cultural impact. What characteristics do they exhibit? Arrange these impacts under the headings of positive and negative. Look again at the lists you have prepared and consider whether someone else asked to carry out this task would put the impacts under the same headings.

2 Consider an aspect of your culture that could be packaged and commoditised for tourist consumption. What would be the likely reaction of tourists? What would be the likely impacts of this commoditization on the aspect of culture you have selected?

3 Under what conditions would Doxey's theory apply? Can you think of any locations in your region/country where Doxey's theory is applicable?

4 What would you suggest are the main reasons for the responses obtained in the survey conducted on the Greek island of Samos? How well do these findings relate to Doxey's theory?

5 Getz's findings from his research in the Spey Valley, Scotland were not closely related to Doxey's theory? What reasons would you give for this?

6 Why has sex tourism become so important in society in countries such as the Philippines and Thailand?

7 Hold a class/group debate in which the main proposition is as follows: 'As a female citizen of Thailand, I believe it is better to be involved in prostitution than trapped in poverty'.

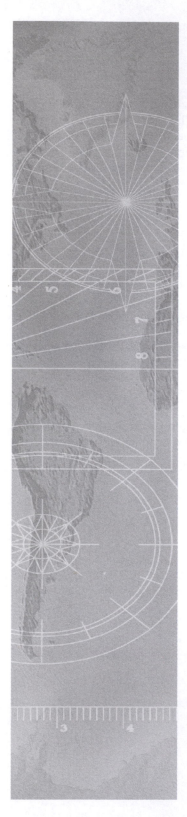

CHAPTER 6

Environmental impacts of tourism

Learning outcomes

At the end of this chapter you should be able to:

- describe in your own words the main types of environmental impacts of tourism;
- be aware of the various meanings of the term carrying capacity in relation to environmental effects of tourism;
- describe in your own words the key tourism management and planning issues that result from the environmental of tourism;
- discuss the implications that these issues have for the good management of the tourism industry.

Introduction

This chapter is concerned with the impact of tourism on the environment. The environment is made up of both natural and human features. Human settlements set within the countryside may contain a large number of attractions for tourists. Often the natural environment is referred to as the physical environment. The natural or physical environment includes the landscape, particular features such as rivers, rock outcrops, beaches and also plants and animals (or flora and fauna).

Key perspectives

The environment is being increasingly recognized as a key factor in tourism. In the last decade of the twentieth century, it was noted that tourism depends ultimately upon the environment, as it is a major tourism attraction itself, or is the context in which tourism activity takes place (Holden, 2000). However, tourism–environment relationships are complex. There is a mutual dependence between the two, which has been described as symbiotic. Williams (1998) explains this relationship as one in which tourism benefits from being in a good quality environment and this same environment should benefit from measures aimed at protecting and maintaining its value as a tourist resource.

In the post Second World War period and especially since the beginning of mass tourism in the 1960s, it has become clear that the relationship between tourism and the environment has become unbalanced. Tourism has become a major cause of environmental damage to the environment rather than a force for enhancement and protection in the past 50 years.

The term environment is often assumed to mean no more than the physical or natural features of a landscape. However, as Figure 6.1 shows, according to Swarbrooke (1999), there are five aspects of the environment. These are: the natural environment, wildlife, the farmed environment, the built environment and natural resources. Figure 6.1 indicates the components of each of these five. It should also be remembered that these five aspects are not separate entities, but linked. For example, a bird of prey, an example of wildlife, may nest in a mountain area (the natural environment), will certainly consume water – a natural resource, is likely to visit

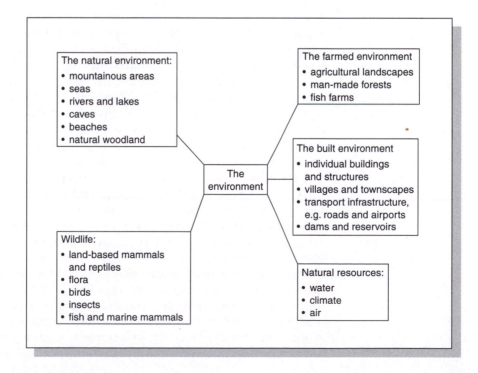

Figure 6.1
The scope of the concept of environment (*Source:* Swarbrooke 1999.)

farmland in search of live prey and nest material, and may even go to a town (the built environment) in search of carrion.

Chapter 3 indicated the main factors influencing tourism impacts and it is advisable to reconsider these again. However, in relation to environmental impacts the following are particularly significant:

- The 'where' factor is important. Some environments are more susceptible to tourism impacts than others.
- The type of tourism activity.
- The nature of any tourist infrastructure will also be important.
- When the activity occurs, particularly any seasonal variation.

In relation to the 'where' factor, an urban environment is likely to be affected differently, in comparison with a rural environment. An urban environment, being a largely built one, can usually sustain far higher levels of visiting than most rural environments. This is not just because a city has, for example, roads and paths, but is also the result of the nature of the organizational structure such as the planning process (Williams, 1998). However, tourists are also particularly attracted to sites that are coincidentally fragile, such as cliff-tops, coasts and mountains (Ryan, 1991; Williams, 1998).

The nature of the activities tourists are engaged in will greatly influence the impacts they have. Some activities lead to minimal impact on the environment and are not resource consumptive. Sight-seeing from a bus will have little effect on the actual environment travelled through (although the bus may contribute to pollution and traffic congestion). Off-road vehicles in a mountain or dune environment will have far more direct impact. Tourism involving hunting and fishing can also be heavily resource consumptive if not carefully controlled and as indicated in Chapter 3, McKercher (1993) argued that tourism tends to over-consume resources.

The nature of the infrastructure that exists for tourism is significant in relation to impacts. It would appear that the effects of those involved in mass tourism on the French and Spanish Mediterranean coastal areas are potentially far greater than a small number of walkers in the Himalayan Mountains. However, if this form of mass tourism is well planned and the groups controlled, this can limit impacts to a minimum. Paradoxically, a small group of trekkers visiting a relatively remote area of Nepal, where there is little preparation for tourists, could be far more damaging to the environment (see Holden and Ewen, 2002).

In many parts of the world, tourism is a seasonal activity. Under these conditions, tourism may only affect the environment for part of the year. During the rest of the year the environment may be able to recover. However, in some areas despite only seasonal tourism affecting the environment, this impact is so serious that there is little chance for recovery. For example, there are certain areas of the Swiss Alps that are so heavily used for ski tourism that they cannot recover fully during the summer period. Over time the inability of a slope to re-grow sufficient vegetation means it is more susceptible to erosion (Krippendorf, 1987).

In relation to tourism's impacts on the physical environment, an important term is ecology. Ecology is the study of animals in their habitat (this includes plants and other organisms, but usually excludes humans). Therefore, ecological impacts of tourism include impacts on, for example, plants as result of trampling by visitors and modifications to animal behaviour as a result of tourists being present in their habitat.

There is a relatively long history of the environment acting as a significant attraction for visitors, but there is also growing evidence of conflict between tourism activity and the wish to conserve landscapes and habitats. As with other impacts it is possible to sub-divide environmental impacts under the headings positive and negative. Although, as with other impacts the value position of the observer, or commentator on environmental impacts, will affect their assessment of whether these impacts are classified as positive or negative.

Conventionally, the following may be regarded as positive impacts:

- tourism may stimulate measures to protect the environment and/or landscape and/or wildlife;
- tourism can help to promote the establishment of National Parks and/or Wildlife Reserves;
- tourism can promote the preservation of buildings/monuments (this includes for example UNESCO's World Heritage Sites);
- tourism may provide the money via, for example, entrance charges to maintain historic buildings, heritage sites and wildlife habitats

Conventionally, the following have been regarded as negative environmental impacts:

- tourists are likely to drop litter;
- tourism can contribute to congestion in terms of overcrowding of people as well as traffic congestion;
- tourism can contribute to the pollution of water courses and beaches;
- tourism may result in footpath erosion;
- tourism can lead to the creation of unsightly human structures such as buildings (e.g. hotels) that do not fit in with vernacular architecture;
- tourism may lead to damage and/or disturbance to wildlife habitats.

Figure 6.2 shows a number of impacts of tourism on the environment and it indicates a somewhat more complex situation regarding the effects of tourism than the lists above. Here, by comparing the positive and negative effects of tourism in relation to particular key themes, a form of balance sheet has been created. Figure 6.2 shows a far greater number of negative effects than positive effects, but this does not mean that negative effects are more important as quantity of impacts does not necessarily equate with quality of impacts.

One of the key concepts in relation to environmental impacts of tourism is *carrying capacity*. This can be viewed as a scientific term, and it is therefore possible to measure carrying capacity. When used in a scientific sense it may relate to, for example, a plant or animal species that is threatened

Area of effect	Negative impacts	Positive Impacts
Biodiversity	Disruption of breeding/feeding patterns Killing of animals for leisure (hunting) or to supply souvenir trade Loss of habitats and change in species composition Destruction of vegetation	Encouragement to conserve animals as attractions Establishment of protected or conserved areas to meet tourist demands
Erosion and physical damage	Soil erosion Damage to sites through trampling Overloading of key infrastructure (e.g. water supply networks)	Tourism revenue to finance ground repair and site restoration Improvement to infrastructure prompted by tourist demand
Pollution	Water pollution through sewage or fuel spillage and rubbish from pleasure boats Air pollution (e.g. vehicle emissions) Noise pollution (e.g. from vehicles or tourist attractions: bars, discos, etc.) Littering	Cleaning programmes to protect the attractiveness of location to tourists
Resource base	Depletion of ground and surface water Diversion of water supply to meet tourist needs (e.g. golf courses or pools) Depletion of local fuel sources Depletion of local building-material sources	Development of new/improved sources of supply
Visual/structural change	Land transfers to tourism (e.g. from farming) Detrimental visual impact on natural and non-natural landscapes through tourism development Introduction of new architectural styles Changes in (urban) functions Physical expansion of built-up areas	New uses for marginal or unproductive lands Landscape improvement (e.g. to clear urban dereliction) Regeneration and/or modernization of built environment Reuse of disused buildings

Figure 6.2 'Balance sheet' of environmental impacts of tourism (Adapted from Hunter and Green, 1995.)

by the damage caused by visitors, and any increase will lead to more damage. In this way, it can be seen as a threshold measure, beyond which damage and possibly irreversible change may occur.

Carrying capacity also has a less purely scientific connotation, as it can be viewed as a term linked to perception. In this sense, the perceptual carrying capacity is in 'the eye of the beholder', for example, what one observer views as a landscape virtually free of human activity, for another may be already too full with the evidence of people, past and present. This point about varying perceptions of carrying capacity is also important in relation to damage/disturbance in the environment. One commentator may perceive loss, or damage, or perhaps unsightliness, while another 'sees' none of these impacts.

Whatever the nature of perception by different individuals, it is clear some landscapes are more susceptible to damage from tourism than others. In an attempt to overcome this problem of differing perceptions, environmental or physical impacts can be separated from ecological impacts when discussing carrying capacity. As has been suggested there is a third type of carrying capacity, perceptual carrying capacity. These three forms of carrying capacity are summarized below:

- Environmental (or physical) carrying capacity usually refers to physical space and the number of people (or the number of cars) in a particular place.
- Ecological carrying capacity is a threshold measure, which if exceeded will lead to actual damage of plants/animals habitat.
- Perceptual carrying capacity; this is the level of crowding that a tourist is willing to tolerate before he/she decides a particular location is too full and then goes elsewhere.

The first two terms refer to actual measures and, in particular, ecological carrying capacity would be used in a scientific approach to tourism environmental impacts. Both environmental carrying capacity and ecological carrying capacity can be measured with scientific equipment and are likely to be significant measures in determining the point at which negative environmental impacts will occur. As perceptual carrying capacity is a subjective assessment of environmental effects, it is not a strictly scientific term as it requires individuals' views. The ways in which it would be assessed in a given setting is through the use of a questionnaire survey or interview. The case study of Waitomo Caves in New Zealand indicates the significance of perceptual carrying capacity.

Case study

Waitomo Caves, New Zealand

Waitomo Caves are located in the North Island of New Zealand. They are a part of a system of limestone caves and underground rivers. The key feature of the system is the Glowworm Cave. The area is part-owned by a local Maori group, but is also part-government owned and the responsibility of the Department of Conservation (DOC). The Glowworm Cave itself and a number of associated commercial activities are currently leased to a commercial operator Tourism Holdings Ltd (THL) and form part of the village of Waitomo (population approximately 500). The site is regarded as one of considerable aesthetic and ecological significance and, with over 450 000 visitors per year in the mid-1990s, is one of the most important visitor attractions in New Zealand.

The Glowworm Cave operates as a 'traditional' attraction in which tour groups are guided through various parts of the cave system. The high point of the visit (for the great majority of tourists) is the viewing of the glowworms from a small boat on an underground river in almost complete darkness. As the glowworms hang from the roof of the cave they look like overhead stars in the night sky.

Tours of the Glowworm Cave lasts approximately 40 min and visitation is subject to diurnal and seasonal fluctuations. The peak season is November–April and 11 AM–2 PM is the busiest time of day. In the mid-1990s, the main visitor groups were as follows: 27 per cent Japanese, 26 per cent Korean, 9 per cent Taiwanese, 8 per cent Australian and 7 per cent New Zealanders.

THL regards the Glowworm Cave very much as a 'money maker', and it is considered by most speleological (caving) circles as a 'sacrificial' site, that is, it concentrates activity so that other more environmentally significant sites remain relatively undisturbed. An important environmental problem of the cave is carbon dioxide, as excessive amounts of it leads to corrosion of the limestone. The cave license specifies that carbon monoxide should not exceed

2400 parts per million. This is equivalent to 300 people per hour. There is no accurate measurement of visitor numbers at the cave, but anecdotal evidence suggests that the limit of 300 people per hour is regularly exceeded. It would appear that the glow-worms are unaffected by visitor numbers (although the use of flash photography can change behaviour). However, a perception that commercial interests were over-riding ecological and experiential factors led to DOC conducting research. This study focused on visitor experience with respect to crowding, and whether perceptions of crowding were affecting the experience and hence its sustainability.

The results of the study indicate a number of differences in perception of crowding and satisfaction with the visit between New Zealanders and various international visitor groups. New Zealanders, for example, registered the highest perception of crowding, although they were generally not dissatisfied with the visit. Although Koreans registered amongst the lowest levels of crowding, they were dissatisfied with the number of groups in the cave at any one time and having to wait for other groups. As many as 71 per cent of visitors in summer registered some form of crowding, but this fell to 40 per cent in winter. Australian and Japanese visitors tended to view the cave system as relatively crowded, more so than the Korean visitors, but less so than the New Zealanders. Another important finding was that domestic visitors were being 'squeezed out' by high-volume international short-stay visitors. This was largely a result of aggressive marketing to the 'Asian market'.

In conclusion, this study suggested that the search for social carrying capacity at the Glowworm Cave necessitates the introduction of the issue of who decides on appropriate levels of crowding and for which visitor groups should it be applied. The research also revealed that the concept of social or perceptual carrying capacity was unworkable without some clearly defined value positions that management could employ. This study therefore shows the potential and real conflict facing a tourism operator when market driven management and a strong marketing policy clash with the localised sensitivities of culture and heritage.

(Adapted from Doorne, S. (2000). Caves, culture and crowds: carrying capacity meets consumer sovereignty. *Journal of Sustainable Tourism*, **8** (4), 34–42.)

The Waitomo study indicates that perceptual carrying capacity is difficult to assess, however even in relation to ecological and environmental carrying capacities, measuring is far from straightforward. Capacities are also likely to vary according to whatever management strategies are in place. To overcome this problem, other measures have been developed and applied. The limits of acceptable change (LAC) technique, was developed in the United States. This has been used in relation to proposed developments. It involves establishing an agreed set of criteria before the development and the prescription of desired conditions and levels of change after development (Williams, 1998). However, LACs suffer from technical difficulties in agreeing some of the more qualitative aspects of tourism development. They also assume the existence of rational planning. Another technique is that of the environmental impact assessment (EIA), which has become a particularly common process in the last 20 years or so. In relation to assessing tourism's impacts, the EIA is similar to the use of the LAC and the key principles of EIA are summarized in Figure 6.3. EIAs are also used in relation to other industries and they provide a framework for informing the decision making process. A number of different methods and techniques can be used in an EIA, including impact checklists, cartographic analysis simulation and predictive models (Williams, 1998).

Discussion of carrying capacities, LACs and EIAs raises one of the key factors in relation to environmental impacts. This is the importance of scale. Footpath erosion, for example, may appear a small-scale impact and may easily be alleviated by re-routing. In this case, both impacts and management attempts to alleviate will be limited to a small area. However,

Figure 6.3
Key principles of
environmental impact
assessment
(Adapted from Hunter and
Green, 1995.)

- Assessments should identify the nature of the proposed and induced activities that are likely to be generated by the project
- Assessments should identify the elements of the environment that will be significantly affected
- Assessments will evaluate the nature and extent of initial impacts and those that are likely to be generated via secondary effects
- Assessments will propose management strategies to control impacts and ensure maximum benefits from the project

in the case of coastal pollution that has been caused by raw sewage being pumped into the sea from a hotel complex, this is very likely to spread widely and attempts to alleviate this will require access to an extensive area.

As the Waitomo Caves case study indicates, a key tourism draw in New Zealand, is the environment. It is certainly a major tourist attraction, if not the major attraction. This is linked to the idea of the 'clean green image', which is used in marketing New Zealand to international tourists. For a relatively long period until the early 1980s New Zealand felt sheltered from negative impacts of tourism on the environment.

Part of the reason there is a growing concern about environmental impacts of tourism in New Zealand, is that the country needs to maintain its 'clean green image' to sell holiday experiences. The New Zealand Tourism Board (1992) indicated that, in 1991, natural attractions accounted for 29 per cent of visits to New Zealand and 55 per cent of all overseas tourists visited a National Park in that year. Natural attractions accounted for almost one-third (32 per cent) of all visits to New Zealand in 2000 (New Zealand Tourism Board, 1999). There are two important ideals in the relationship between tourism and the environment in New Zealand: these are the notions of wilderness and equality of access to the countryside. However, with increasing numbers of both domestic and international visitors these ideals may become incompatible.

Coastal areas and offshore islands, lakes and rivers and high country and mountain areas have been identified as the most environmentally sensitive areas in New Zealand (New Zealand Tourism Board, 1996). In relation to impacts on ecosystems, native bush areas are threatened by introduced species, native animals are vulnerable to disturbance and construction of facilities can cause problems particularly if too much vegetation is removed as poor drainage of sites results and the ground becomes unstable.

The role of Maori people is important, as they own more than 50 per cent of native bushland in New Zealand that is in private hands. However, many Maori people see growth in environmental concern as being detrimental to them. This can lead to conflict as a result of different Maori attitudes to the environment compared with white (*pakeha*) views. Nevertheless, there is some evidence in New Zealand that tourism can promote preservation and, of particular relevance to Maori values, tourism can help promote protection of sites of cultural significance.

Large areas of Australia are often regarded as wilderness or semi-wilderness. Their use for all forms of development in the past has tended to ignore that such areas are finite resources. However, coastal areas are the most developed in Australia and the case study of Julian Rocks considers the growing scale of environmental impacts of tourism in Australia in a marine environment.

Case study
Julian Rocks, Australia

The Julian Rock Aquatic Reserve is close to the township of Byron Bay and located approximately two kilometres off the northern part of the New South Wales (NSW) coast in Australia. This is a popular holiday spot on the NSW coast and the main attraction is the surfing beach. Scuba diving is also a very significant activity. The great majority of visitors are Australian domestic visitors. Backpackers comprise the fastest growing visitor segment and there are increasing numbers of international backpackers.

Julian Rocks comprise a nature reserve and the surrounding waters (within a 500 m radius) have been an aquatic reserve since 1982. The aims of the aquatic reserve are to protect, manage and conserve the environment and existing uses of the area and to ensure ecological diversity and significance are maintained. Julian Rocks has been described as one of the best diving locations on the east coast of Australia. Although not part of the Great Barrier Reef, over 10 per cent of the reserve is made up of coral. The area contains a diverse range of habitats including rock reefs, caves, tunnels, steep rocky slopes and sandy areas. There are many fish species, some of which breed here as well as marine turtles and grey nurse sharks.

Julian Rocks is a popular and heavily used scuba diving site. The peak diving season is November–January (the southern hemisphere summer) and also at Easter. Diver numbers in December are double those of June. There were in excess of 20 000 dives in 1993, 86 per cent of which occurred in two specific locations. These sites are used as intensively as all but two of those on the Great Barrier Reef, but they are smaller in area than the leading two on the Great Barrier Reef. The number of divers has increased steadily since the mid-1980s. In 1985, there were only two dive operators who ran normally three, or at most four vessels. By 1994, there were four operators using up to ten boats. Each of these vessels can carry up to twelve divers. In 1994, the vessels made 3800 launches at the local boat launch ramp. This suggests that there was the potential for over 40 000 dives per year (double the actual usage in 1993).

By the mid-1990s there were report that the site had declined since the early 1980s. Damage was largely attributed to boat anchors, although this was not only from dive vessels but also fishing boats. Research in the early 1990s indicated that a key contributor to environmental damage was overcrowding at the two most visited sites. Some of the damage was inflicted directly by divers coming into contact with sensitive sub-marine material, in particular coral. Fins, coming into contact with living coral, were a cause of damage, although most of this was not serious damage, hard coral suffered more than other organisms. This research also noted that the majority of damage resulted from inexperienced divers. There was conflict between divers and recreational anglers. Divers complained about damage caused by anchors, destruction of corals by snagged lines, the catch of non-target fish and the incidence of turtles and sharks with fish hooks in their mouths.

It is very difficult to define the carrying capacity for an area such as Julian Rocks. There is a lack of baseline data on the ecology of the area. There is also a lack of information on attitudes of divers to crowding. Nevertheless, a study conducted at a site in the Caribbean with some similarities to Julian Rock, although with more sensitive coral, suggested an upper limit of 5000 dives per year. Each of the two most popular sites at Julian Rocks had double this number in 1993. Because of this lack of baseline data it is also difficult to assess the limits of acceptable change. However, anecdotal evidence would suggest that the great majority of divers would conclude that no change was acceptable. Apparent or potential degradation was a primary reason for declaring Julian Rocks a marine preservation area, implying that any further change was unacceptable. User perception of the area suggests that levels of change related to social values such as crowding are likely to be as significant as environmental change. Hence, even if management practices led to an improved environment, social factors might impose an upper limit on user numbers that could be below a threshold limit above which environmental damage would occur.

(Adapted from Dervis, D. and Harriot, V. (1996). Sustainable tourism development or the case of loving a place to death. In *Practising Responsible Tourism* (L. Harrison and W. Husbands, eds), pp. 422–44. New York, John Wiley & Sons.)

Summary

The environment is a key resource for tourism. It is possible to subdivide the environment into the human (or built environment) and the natural environment. To a great extent the environment provides the significant attractions for visitors. Hence, any damage to the environment may contribute to a reduction in visitor numbers.

Tourism can have important negative impacts on the environment, including footpath erosion, river and marine pollution, litter, traffic congestion, overcrowding and the creation of unsightly structures. However, it can have beneficial impacts by contributing to an awareness of the need to conserve valued landscapes and buildings and revenue generated from visitor charges can be used to preserve and maintain threatened sites.

In relation to assisting with planning and management of environmental impacts, the concept of carrying capacity is particularly useful. Environmental and ecological carrying capacity are both scientific terms and hence lend themselves to scientific forms of measuring. The concept of perceptual carrying capacity is no less important in relation to management of environmental impacts, although it may be more difficult to assess in a given context, as it is a more subjective term.

As visitor numbers continue to increase and virtually nowhere on the earth remains free of tourists, the need for carefully planned and managed tourism in relation to environmental impacts has become, and continues to be, a critical issue.

Student activities

1 In relation to a tourism activity in your area, identify the environmental impacts. Classify the impacts under the headings 'positive' and 'negative'. Note which of these two lists of impacts is the longer. Why do you think there are differences in the content and length of these two lists?

2 Which areas of your region/country are particularly susceptible to environmental impacts of tourism?

3 What are the major types of environmental impact of tourism in your country/region?

4 How might environmental impacts on a heavily visited small tropical island vary from those on the interior of the mainland of Europe?

5 Explain why carrying capacity is an important concept, but a problematic one.

7 What does the case study of Waitomo Caves reveal about the concept of carrying capacity and its practical application?

8 What are the environmental impacts of tourism at Julian Rocks, Australia and why is tourism difficult to control here?

9 Select a location in your area and indicate how you would assess the following:
environmental carrying capacity;
ecological carrying capacity;
perceptual carrying capacity.

Conclusions to part one

The three preceding chapters (Chapters 4–6) have indicated the importance of different types of tourism impact. These impacts have been classified under the headings: economic, socio-cultural or environmental. However, as stated in Chapter 3, in a real setting, impacts are not that easy to separate and classify under these headings. Tourism impacts are, in fact, multi-faceted. A number of the case studies in Chapters 4–6 may have suggested this, although this may not have been asserted overtly.

In any given situation, it is likely that there will be a combination of different impacts, with some being considered more significant than others. It is also likely that the impacts of tourism will vary overtime. The theories of Butler and Doxey suggest how tourism' impacts may change over time. It is therefore possible and indeed very likely that, for example, where economic gain is noted at the earliest stages of tourism, it will be the case, several years later that socio-cultural effects are becoming more apparent and environmental consequences may also be noted. By this stage in the development of tourism, the initial positive economic impacts of tourism may be replaced or diminished by growing social unease between the residents and tourists as well as mounting concern about tourism's environmental impacts.

It is important to note that when considering tourism' impacts, the environment in which impacts is taking place usually comprises complex systems in which there are inter-relationship between the so-called environmental, social and economic aspects. Impacts often have a cumulative dimension in which 'secondary processes reinforce and develop the consequences of change in unpredicted ways, so treating individual problems in isolation ignores the likelihood that there is a composite impact that may be greater than the sum of the individual parts' (Williams, 1998, p. 102). Williams argued for a holistic approach to tourism impacts and, in addition to the point made above, he suggested that such an approach enables a more balanced view of these impacts to be obtained and in this way positive aspects of tourism impacts will be recognised as well negative views.

Adopting a holistic approach also makes us aware that the word environment embraces a diversity of concepts – built environments, physical environments, economic environments, social environments, cultural environments and political environments – and tourism has the potential to influence all of these, albeit in varying degrees.

Part Two

Tourism Planning and Management: Concepts, Issues and Players

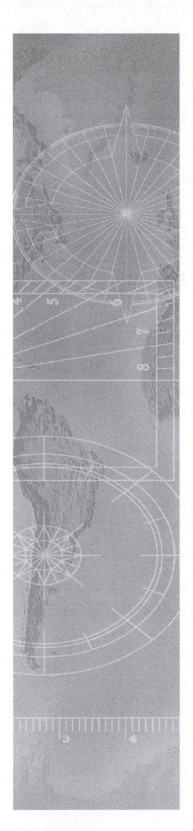

Tourism planning and management: concepts and issues

Learning objectives

At the end of this chapter you should be able to:

- understand the meaning of planning;
- understand the meaning of management;
- understand the relationship between planning and management;
- understand meanings of tourism planning and management;
- understand the meaning of policy and the nature of tourism policy;
- understand some preliminary ideas on tourism planning, management and sustainability.

Introduction

The first section of this book considered the growth, development and impacts of tourism. This chapter and following chapters consider planning and management issues in relation to the development and impacts of tourism. This first chapter in the second part of the book discusses, initially, the nature of planning and management in general terms. It focuses on tourism planning and management and considers the relationship between tourism planning, policy and management.

Modern Western-style planning can be traced back at least 200 years to town planning in the United Kingdom (Gunn, 1988; Williams, 1998). However, the physical planning of the layout of urban areas dates back to the Greek era (Gunn, 1988). Modern town planning emerged when the population became increasingly urbanized and was, largely, a response to the increasing 'evils' of urban living in terms of social and environmental impacts (Gunn, 1988). Those involved in planning for utopian cities to replace the rapidly built unplanned creations of eighteenth century Britain, however, were still concerned primarily with the physical appearance of cities.

To create order in response to social and environmental degradation is still an important rationale for planning today. As Williams (1998) suggested, without planning there is the risk that an activity will be unregulated, formless or haphazard and likely to lead to a range of negative economic, social and environmental impacts. Gunn (1988) made a similar point when he claimed that the absence of planning may result in serious malfunctions and inefficiencies.

In its early stages, modern planning may have been largely reactive, but, as Gunn (1988) suggested, by the late twentieth century it was far more proactive and future oriented. Although planning experiences vary across the globe, some form of official planning has taken place almost everywhere.

Key perspectives

The nature of planning

Williams (1998) suggested that the aim of modern planning is to seek optimal solutions to perceived problems and that it is designed to increase and, hopefully, maximize development benefits, which will produce predictable outcomes. Williams (1998, p. 126) claimed planning 'is an ordered sequence of operations and actions that are designed to realise one single goal or a set of interrelated goals'. Hence, according to Williams, planning is, or should be, a process: for anticipating and ordering change: that is forward looking: that seeks optimal solutions: that is designed to increase and ideally maximize possible development benefits and: that will produce predictable outcomes.

However, planning is a very difficult term to define. The term planning can be used in a variety of contexts; it can be used in connection with individuals, groups, organizations and governments. It can be used in relation to different geographical settings, such as urban and rural, as well as being applied at different scales such as local, regional and national. A plan can mean little more than partially thought through ideas that are barely articulated, or a complex, carefully considered and presented document. Hall, P. (1992, p. 1) suggested that this is where part of the problem with the concept of planning arises. As he stated:

> Although people realise that planning has a more general meaning, they tend to remember the idea of the plan as a physical representation or design

This focus on the plan as a physical design has probably contributed to the failure to recognise the importance of the processes involved, the processes that have led to the creation of the actual physical plan. However, a focus on planning as a process, rather than with a consideration of its product, can lead to planning being considered rather vague and abstract (Gunn, 1988). Nevertheless, it is the process element of planning that is particularly important. McCabe et al. (2000) argued strongly that planning is a process when they suggested a plan provides direction. As they indicated:

> A plan ... enables us to identify where we are going and *how to get there* (emphasis added) – in other words it should clarify the path that is to be taken and the outcomes or end results. It also draws attention to the stages on the way and ... helps to set and establish priorities that can assist in the scheduling of activities
>
> (McCabe et al., 2000, p. 235)

One of the key elements of the process of planning is decision-making (Veal, 1994; Hall, 2000). As Veal (1994, p. 3) stated 'planning can be seen as the process of deciding'. Hall (2000a) suggested that this process is not straightforward, as he claimed these decisions are interdependent and systematically related and not just individual decisions. The process of planning involves 'bargaining, negotiation, compromise, coercion, values, choice and politics' (Hall, 2000a, p. 7)

Hall (2000a) suggested that decision-making is part of a continuum that follows directly from planning and this in turn is followed by action. Gunn (1988) believed that action was a very important part of planning and employed the ideas of Lang (1985) to differentiate between strategic planning and conventional planning. Lang (1985) suggested that conventional planning separates the planning from the implementation stage, has only vague goals, is reactive rather than proactive, periodic rather than consistent and fails to consider the values of those individuals and organizations involved. Strategic planning, however, according to Lang is action oriented, focused, on-going, proactive and considers the values of those involved.

Wilkinson (1997) suggested that a plan provides the rationale for and details of how implementation will take place within a country or region, and sets this within a wider economic and social context. He also indicated that planning involves not only the formulation of plans and their implementation, but also their supervision and review.

Hall (2000a) argued that the most important aspect of planning is that it is directed towards the future. He used the ideas of Chadwick to support this. As Chadwick (1971, p. 24) suggested 'planning is a process, a process of human thought and action based upon that thought – in point of fact, forethought, thought for the future, nothing more or less than this is planning'. Gunn (1988, p. 15) also indicated that planning is clearly forward looking when he stated it requires 'some estimated perception of the future'.

Planning and policy

Planning and policy are closely related terms. Wilkinson (1997) linked planning and policy when stating planning is a course of action, while policy is the implementation of the planned course of action. Policy is usually created by and emanates from a public body or organization. Such public policy is a major concern of government activity. As Wilkinson (1997) indicated, policy is a course of action adopted by an agency, such as a government body. Public policy is, therefore, what governments decide to do or not to do (Dye, 1992).

However, it is important to note that planning is not just a process conducted by government. Private sector organizations, (in tourism this would include, e.g. tour operators and airlines), prepare careful plans and usually have a number of policies through which they operationalize these plans. Hence, as Elliot (1997) indicated, planning covers private as well as government and public enterprise.

Public policy, by definition is in the public domain, while the policies of individual organizations are often protected because of commercial concerns and may not be so easily discerned. In relation to public policy, it is important to recognize that it is not created in a vacuum, but is greatly influenced by the social, economic and environmental context in which it is created, as well as the governmental structures and nature of the political regime. Therefore, it is important to realize that policy results from political structures, value systems, institutional frameworks, the distribution of power and the decision making process (Simeon, 1976; Hall and Jenkins, 1995).

Values and planning

The section above on policy and planning suggested that values are important in planning. As Hall (2000a) argued, the standpoint or value position in relation to planning must not be ignored. A similar view was put forward by Healey (1997, p. 29) who indicated that public policy and planning are 'social processes through which ways of thinking, ways of valuing and ways of acting are actively constructed by participants'.

Both Gunn (1988) and Veal (1994) suggested that planning for recreation and tourism relies heavily on values, and each argued that community values are particularly important. Therefore, it is important, they claimed, that a recreation and/or tourism policy should reflect the values of stakeholders and interested parties.

However, if planning is to intended to represent the views of all stakeholders and interested parties, then it should be obvious that there will not automatically be unanimity and homogeneity in values and views. Nevertheless, Wilkinson (1997) claimed that much thinking and writing about planning tends to assume that it is a straightforward, virtually value free, scientific process. He noted in relation to conventional definitions of planning that:

> emphasis (is) on a straightforward approach that accepts the (positivist) possibility of comprehensive rationality. Such a process

> assumes several factors: consensus on objectives, lack of uncertainty, known alternatives, a high degree of centralised control, and ample time and money to prepare a plan.
>
> (Wilkinson 1997, p. 24)

Wilkinson argued such factors rarely exist in any planning situation, and are unlikely to be found in tourism planning. Similar views were put forward by Cullingsworth (1997) who indicated the implications of the meeting of differing value systems in the planning process. As Cullingsworth (1997, p. 5) claimed:

> Rational planning is a theoretical idea. Actual planning is a practical exercise of political choice that involves beliefs and values. It is a laborious process in which many public and private agencies are concerned. These comprise a wide range of conflicting interests. Planning is a means by which attempts are made to resolve these conflicts.

Wildavsky (1987) also stressed the importance of recognising that planning is not a rational activity. Hall, P. (1992) argued very strongly that planning is not a tidy process as posited by theorists of the activity. He indicated that a key problem is trying to predict the future when there are conflicts of values. He added to this that there is the problem of the interaction of decisions made in different spheres of public policy, and there is the clash of organised pressure groups with the defence of vested interests. Hence, Hall, P. (1992, p. 246) argued: 'The systems view of planning is therefore a condition to which planners aim but will never be the reality'.

Several of the processes referred to by Hall are related to conflict resolution and can be seen as very much as part of a wider political process. Jenkins (1997) also indicated that planning is very much a political process. As he stated, a plan is: 'a document that has been the focus of political debate and is available to the public' (Jenkins 1997, p. 25). The relationship between planning and policy in relation to differing values and the wider political context is discussed in the next section.

Planning and policy in leisure, recreation and tourism

Leisure planning • • •

As tourism is a recreational activity that takes place in leisure time, planning in the leisure area usually includes both recreation and tourism (Veal, 1994; Spink, 1994; Hall and Page, 1999). Therefore, tourism planning can be seen to fit within the wider context of leisure planning and the planning framework for tourism can be seen to fall within leisure. However, traditionally there has been a split between outdoor recreation and tourism provision, with the former being provided by the public sector and the latter by the private sector (Hall and Jenkins, 1995). However, from the mid-1980s onwards this distinction began to disappear in Western countries (Hall and Page, 1999). Today, in relation to tourism provision, there is much overlap between the public and private sectors in many countries, however this tends to create complications in terms of responsibilities for planning.

The planning process adopted in the leisure field tends to display the same characteristics as those found in planning more generally in that it is often disjointed and reactive. However, it is complicated by the fact that the process may involve a variety of land-owners, public bodies and private providers, as well as different user groups (Veal, 1994; Williams, 1998; Glyptis, 1994). This means that the process is complex and at times difficult to operationalise. Within the British context, Veal (1994) identified three phases of leisure planning. The 'demand phase' (1960–72) which was in response to a rapidly growing population base. The 'need phase', (1973–85) which saw the focus on the needs of particular groups. The 'enterprise phase' (from 1985 to the mid-1990s) which saw the rise of private providers, with the government seeking to distance itself from leisure provision.

Spink (1994) introduced the concept of leisure action spaces, which range from the home, through the local neighbourhood and the region, to national and international levels. Within these spaces, individuals have the choice of pursuing various leisure options, including visiting heritage sites, resorts and the countryside. With a focus on the United Kingdom, he argued that most leisure/recreation activities take place within urban areas, including the urban fringes such as country parks, green-belt areas, footpaths and bridleways.

However, by definition, those classified as involved in leisure/recreation activities in their home area will be residents of the area, those who have travelled into an area will be classified as tourists (see Mason, 1995; Cooper et al., 1998). Therefore, planning for tourism is likely to be targeted at different visitor groups and involve different processes (Mason, 1995). The nature of tourism planning is discussed below.

Tourism planning • • •

Approximately 20 years ago, the key aims of tourism planning were summarized in the following way: 'to ensure that opportunities are available for tourist to gain enjoyable and satisfying experiences and at the same time to provide a means for improving the way of life for residents and of destination areas' (Matthieson and Wall, 1982, p. 186).

More recently, Williams (1998) suggested a number of general aims for tourism planning. He indicated that it can help to shape and control physical patterns of development, conserve scarce resources, provide a framework for active promotion and marketing of destinations and can be a mechanism to integrate tourism with other sectors. More specifically, Williams (1998) suggested that tourism planning has a number of key objectives. These are, he suggested, as follows:

- The creation of a mechanism for the structured provision of tourist facilities over quite large geographic areas.
- The coordination of the fragmented nature of tourism (particularly in relation to accommodation, transport, marketing and human resources).

- Certain interventions to conserve resources and maximise benefits to the local community in an attempt to achieve sustainability (usually through a tourism development or management plan).
- The redistribution of tourism benefits (the development of new tourism sites or the economic realignment of places that tourists have begun to leave).

Williams also considered that tourism planning, as part of an integrated plan involving other human activities, gives tourism a political significance and hence provides legitimacy to an activity, which has not always been accorded this status. Planning can also be an attempt to match supply and demand for tourism services/activities (Williams, 1998).

Much early tourism planning was very site specific and linked to the supply side (or destination end) of tourism activity (Gunn, 1988). This geographical focus helps to explain the rationale often provided for tourism planning. Williams (1998) provided such a rationale when he stated that there is now enough evidence around the world to suggest that unplanned tourist destinations are those associated with negative impacts. In seeking to justify a rationale for tourism planning, Jenkins (1991) argued that all countries should have a planning process in place, to make use of resources in a wise and efficient manner.

However, planning for recreation and tourism is not necessarily a straightforward process (Gunn, 1988; Spink, 1994; Veal, 1994; Coccossis, 1996; Williams, 1998). A major problem is that tourism planning operates at a range of scales, from national, through regional to the local level. This can contribute to problems of coordination. Williams (1998) suggested another major problem of tourism planning is that it encompasses many activities and although it may address physical, economic, environmental and business concerns it does not necessarily blend these together well. Coccossis (1996) concurs with this view and argued that until very recently one of the activities relating to tourism planning, environmental conservation was seen as being a threat to economic and social development. Similar concerns are associated with outdoor recreation planning, where the increasing pressures on limited environmental resources have led to environmental degradation (Chavez, 1997; Hammitt and Cole, 1998) and conflict between different user groups (Moore, 1994; Hendricks, 1995; Ramthun, 1995; Watson, 1995). Reference to conflict infers that tourism planning is a political process. Hall (2000a) supported this view when he argued that tourism policy is what governments decide to do or not do about tourism. Gunn (1988) and Veal (1994) also confirmed that tourism planning is very much a political process.

Fennell (1999) argued that tourism planning requires a policy, which states the aims and objectives to be implemented in the planning process. In addition, Gunn (1988) suggested that for plans to be implemented governance is required and Fennell (1999) stated that implementation is usually done by governments. However, Lickorish (1991) claimed that government has often viewed the responsibility of tourism policy as lying with the private sector. Williams (1998) and Hall and Jenkins (1995) also discussed this problem, and indicated that recreation and tourism planning increasingly involves both public and private sector bodies. Gunn (1988) suggested that this mix of private and public sector responsibility for planning is one of several reasons why tourism planning has not been as effective as planners may have wished.

As with policy in generic terms, tourism policy involves a number of ideas and statements that can be implemented via a tourism plan (Wilkinson, 1997). However, Hirschmann (1976) suggested tourism policy is different from many other policies created by government. Hirschmann (1976) suggested that one of the reasons tourism policy is different from other forms of policy is that unlike agrarian reform and some industrial policies that are forced on government, tourism policy is chosen. It is also different from policies like industrial policy because there tends to be little conflict, at least not in the initial early stages. An industrial policy of restructuring may involve job losses, environmental change and attempts to relocate industry. This will clearly lead to at least controversy and possible conflict and strife. This is not the way tourism policy has been perceived (Hirschmann, 1976). Unlike industrial policy, tourism policy is not linked to major problem solving such as the economic and social changes associated with, for example, the closure of a coal mine or steel works Hirschmann claimed.

Almost 70 years ago, Lasswell (1936) indicated that the core issues in politics are who gets what, where, when, how and why. This view is still highly relevant today, but Richter (1989) argued that tourism policies have rarely been conceived of and scrutinized in terms of Lasswell's core political issues. Hence, tourism policy may be viewed as 'simple' by those whose job it is to create and implement it (Wilkinson, 1997). The following case study on planning in New Zealand provides an indication that the process of policy-making is not that simple.

Case study

Tourism planning in New Zealand

Planning in New Zealand

The key piece of legislation relating to planning in New Zealand is the Resource Management Act (RMA), which became law in 1991 and replaced fifty-nine previous resource and planning statutes. The RMA provides a legislative framework for planning for and managing land, air, water, coastal, geothermal and pollution issues under one umbrella. The overall aim of the RMA is to promote sustainable management, whilst at the same time it is developing and protecting resources which enable social and economic well-being (Gow, 1995).

Under the RMA, planning for and the management of natural and physical resources is delegated to regional and local authorities. Locally, the district or city councils are responsible for developing a district plan, which identifies community objectives over a ten-year period and specifies the processes for achieving these (Page and Thorn, 1997). The Conservation Act 1987 requires the Department of Conservation (DOC) to prepare management plans for all the land under its jurisdiction, which currently is around one third of New Zealand. This is important because a significant amount of outdoor recreation and tourism takes place on the DOC land. In some areas of New Zealand, DOC land is adjacent to local or regional council land, which may require some cooperation between agencies in terms of the policies and practices adopted in each area.

Leisure planning and tourism in New Zealand

Much leisure planning in New Zealand has been associated with the provision of sport and recreation facilities in the form of playing fields, recreation centres and swimming pools (Department of Tourism, Sport and Racing, 1994). However, whilst local government allocates money to managing these recreation facilities and open spaces, only a small amount tends to be invested in planning. This has resulted in an ad hoc approach to leisure planning, rather than one which involves integrating a number of information sources, so as to ensure policy decisions are based on informed decisions (Department of Tourism, Sport and Racing, 1994). Since the early 1990s, issues associated with sustainability have emerged in recreation planning. Accompanying the socio-economic and political changes occurring in urban and regional areas of New Zealand, have come questions of not only environmental, but also social and economic sustainability. It is argued, therefore, that leisure planning needs to be seen in the wider political context and integrated with local and regional planning, rather than be regarded as an optional extra (Department of Tourism, Sport and Racing, 1994).

Most initial approaches by recreation and tourism providers are made to local councils, as they are responsible for determining the effects of land use under their jurisdiction according to the RMA. Page and Thorn's (1997) study suggested that research with respect to tourism is undertaken by over half of all councils in New Zealand. The majority of this research focused on visitor numbers, with little being conducted in the area of resource sustainability or visitor satisfaction. Dymond (1997, p. 289) came to similar conclusions in his research and his findings suggested that 'local resident satisfaction is only being measured within a third of local authority areas ... indirect sources are dominant, for example local authority strategic plan consultations and resident satisfaction surveys'. He concluded that more research needed to be centred on supply-related issues, which consider the sustainability of the tourism resource base.

In relation to tourism planning, it is often regarded as something that appears to be conducted retrospectively rather than in a proactive manner. In the New Zealand context, Page and Thorn (1997, p. 70) suggested 'that tourism is identified as an activity requiring promotion, rather than something which requires strategic planning'. Similar approaches to tourism planning have been noted in other parts of the developed world

(see Butler, 1991; Dymond, 1997). Furthermore, the RMA encourages a focus on individual project impacts, which in turn has meant that local recreation and tourism planning often takes place on an 'as required' basis, rather than as part of an integrated approach (Page and Thorn, 1997).

Of particular importance in New Zealand is that the nature of regional and local planning rarely falls squarely into either urban or rural contexts. More often than not local councils have to address planning issues associated with semi-rural or semi-urban environments. This in itself requires councils to take a broader approach to planning issues associated with their area, than may be the case in, for example, the United Kingdom or other European countries.

Whether the planning issue under consideration in New Zealand is recreation or tourism focused, urban or rural it appears that there is a need for an integrated proactive approach to planning. The RMA has only been in existence for just over a decade, but may be the appropriate vehicle for more integrated planning. As Page and Thorn (1997, pp. 64–5) suggested 'the RMA should encourage public sector planners to adopt a more holistic view of development and the way in which tourism affects the environment and population within a sustainable framework' (see Photo 3).

Photo 3 The Lido, Palmerston North, New Zealand. Swimming pools are usually designated as part of the remit of planning in leisure. They tend to be in public ownership and serve a local market. However, they also cater for tourists and may be in private ownership. This indicates just one of the problems of planning for the leisure/tourism field

(Adapted from Mason, P. and Leberman, S. I. (1998). *Mountain Biking in the Palmerston North Area: Participants, Preferences and Management Issues.* Report to the Recreation and Community Development Unit of the Palmerston North City Council, June. Department of Management Systems, Massey University, New Zealand.)

Planning and management

The case study of New Zealand gives an indication of links between tourism planning and tourism management. This section discusses the links between planning and management in generic terms, and is followed by a discussion in greater detail on tourism planning and management.

As with the term planning, management also has a number of different definitions. Gilbert et al. (1995, p. 8) defined the activity in the following way: 'Management is a goal-oriented process that involves the allocation of resources and the co-ordination of the talents and efforts of a group of people'.

Gilbert et al. (1995) indicated a major link between planning and management. As they noted, one of the key activities involved in managing is planning. They suggested that managing is the first part of a process that also involves organising, empowering and controlling. They further elaborated their ideas on managing by suggesting that it is in reality a cyclical process, with a link back from controlling to planning. They also argued that each of activities in any given situation may be on-going simultaneously and therefore each is not an entirely discrete processes.

Similar views on the nature of management and its links with planning have been expounded by Doswell (1997). Doswell suggested that there is well-established way of looking at the functions of management, and this is based on one of the earliest thinkers in management theory, the French writer Fayol. Doswell indicated the functions of management are as follows: planning, organising, giving direction, providing coordination and monitoring. Doswell claimed planning is about what one is trying to achieve, organisation is concerned with mobilising and deploying resources, giving direction relates to the provision of leadership and maintenance of a sense of purpose, while coordination is the provision of a unifying force and monitoring is a control function achieved through the reporting and analysis of results.

Hall and Page (1999) also recognized this link between planning and management. They suggested that strategic planning can be regarded as a process that involves concurrently integrating planning and management. In essence, this means that the proactive approach of planning should be intertwined with the, frequently, reactive reality of management. However even this relationship is not that straightforward. As Mason and Leberman (2000) indicated, there is evidence that planning policies have been put in place without considering the issue in detail beforehand. Hence, they noted, planning, in many cases, is reactive rather than proactive, particularly when policy documents are often prepared for a 5 to 10-year period. This means that the information in the plan is dated by the time it takes effect and new issues may have arisen in the interim.

If management is perceived as a goal-oriented process, then it is necessary to have some measure of its effectiveness in relation to these goals (Gilbert et al., 1995). The performance of management is therefore part of the management process and is in effect a measure of the quality of management. As Gilbert et al. argued, there are two factors that should be measured in relation to the quality or effectiveness of management. These are as follows: how well has the process been aimed at appropriate goals? and how well has the process been managed in terms of use of resources? (Gilbert et al., 1995, p. 19)

Tourism management

Many standard works on management make reference to the focus of the activity as being about people. Such works are usually concerned with the management of businesses or companies. One important aspect of tourism management has a specific focus on people who work in tourism. This is usually referred to as functional management and can be seen as a part of strategic management (see Moutinho, 2000).

However, tourism management is also concerned with ways to manage the resources for tourism, the interaction of tourists with physical resources and the interaction of tourists with residents of tourist areas (Mason, 1995). This focus of tourism management is concerned primarily with tourism impacts in resorts areas or tourism destinations. It is in such areas that the supply side of tourism (physical resources, built environment and resident population) interacts with the demand side (often summarized as the market side, but made up of tourists, travel agents, tour operators, transport operators, tourist boards and tourism developers). It is this aspect of tourism management, the management of tourism impacts, rather than the management of people in tourism businesses, with which this book is primarily concerned.

The definition of tourism management that is particularly useful in this book is that produced by Middleton (1994). Middleton's definition is as follows: 'Strategies and action programmes using and co-ordinating available techniques to control and influence tourism supply and visitor demand in order to achieve defined policy goals' (Middleton cited in Middleton and Hawkins, 1998, p. 84).

To a great extent, it is possible to say that tourism management is what tourism planners are, or should be, engaged in (Doswell, 1997). However, as Doswell indicated tourism planning and tourism management are often treated as separate activities. Doswell claimed that this is due to planning being linked to physical planners. In this case, planning is not seen as an ongoing process of management, but a one-off activity which precedes the construction of whatever was planned (Doswell, 1997). In the context of Developing countries, Doswell indicated that such a one-off plan is likely to be a master plan. Doswell distinguished between master plans and ongoing planning. He argued that a master plan is created prior to construction and may not involve any ongoing monitoring. Doswell argued that only ongoing planning in tourism is likely to be satisfactory in relation to tourism management. As he stated:

> The whole concept of a planning process means there is no end as such, only a beginning. It means that things, once studied and agreed, can start to be implemented. Action can be taken from the start. It also means that committees and working groups,

organised to consult on an initial plan, can be left in place to play an ongoing role.

(Doswell, 1997, p. 184)

In practical terms, Middleton and Hawkins (1998) indicated tourism management is concerned with procedures to influence five variables that are as follows: location, timing, access, products and education. Middleton and Hawkins suggested in relation to location that there may be too few or too many visitors and tourist businesses in a particular destination. In relation to timing, they indicated there may be too many or too few visitors at particular places at particular times of the day, week or month. They indicated that access relates to the relative ease or difficulty and associated cost of reaching chosen places. They suggested that there could be too many or too few products in a particular location and perhaps a lack of infrastructure to support certain products. Education is concerned with the awareness of the cumulative behaviour of visitors and tourism businesses and awareness of resident's wishes for the destination, Middleton and Hawkins indicated.

Middleton and Hawkins (1998, p. 85) provided a good summary of tourism management in practice when they stated: 'Tourism management focuses on ways and means to influence visitors' choices of location, access, timing and product provision, and to develop local understanding and knowledge'. The reality of 'influencing visitors' choices' means ways to persuade tourists and tourism businesses to voluntarily change their naturally occurring behaviour where 'naturally occurring behaviour' is what people do when exercising their instincts and choices in a free society (Middleton and Hawkins, 1998). Changing this behaviour may require selected inducements, or by obliging people and businesses to change through the imposition of regulations, controls, taxes or penalties of various types (Mason and Mowforth, 1996; Middleton and Hawkins, 1998).

In most countries, controlling visitor numbers at destinations is beyond the influence of either public sector bodies, such as tourist boards or private sector organizations. In some cases control can be exerted by such methods as high entrance charges to attractions and/or limited car parking spaces. However in the majority of destinations, such draconian measures are not employed. Instead, what Middleton and Hawkins (1998, p. 85), term 'selective influences and control' are used. These are designed to achieve stated and quantified objectives at destinations. They are as follows:

- making judgements on carrying capacity;
- selecting and targeting particular market segments or groups;
- identifying partner organizations in planning and marketing for tourism;
- developing a variety of management techniques for visitor segments and products;
- systematically monitoring results and making any required changes.

These selective influences and controls are shown in Figure 7.1. The left-hand column shows examples of mainly public sector resource

Resource constraints (supply orientation) mainly public sector	Market forces (demand orientation) mainly commercial sector
Regulation of land use	Knowledge of visitor profiles, behaviour, needs and trends
Regulation of buildings	Design of visitor products (quality and satisfaction)
Regulation of environmental impacts	Capacity (products marketed)
Provision of infrastructure	Promotion (image/positioning)
Control by licensing	Distribution of products/ access for customers
Provision of information	Provision of information
Fiscal controls and incentives	Price

Figure 7.1

Resource constraints and market forces – tourism management controls and influences at destinations (Based on Pearce, 1989 and Middleton, 1994.)

constraints, while the right-hand column shows controls as market forces, which are primarily associated with the private sector.

A major concern in relation to the use of selective influences and controls is having the relevant information to make appropriate decisions. Research information for targeting and monitoring at the local level is vital (Mason and Leberman, 2000; Leberman and Mason, 2002). However, much planning and management in the recreation and tourism fields seems to take place without the required information (Mason and Leberman, 2000). Mason and Leberman argued that it is necessary to start the planning process by gathering information about the issue concerned. This process should involve conducting proactive wide-ranging research and in particular consulting with relevant stakeholders, which then enables a decision to be made based on the information collected, they suggested. The gathering of data as a significant part of tourism management is also advocated by Middleton and Hawkins (1998).

In the early 1990s, the English Tourist Board produced an influential report on the relationship between tourism and the environment (ETB, 1991) The report included a triangle which can be considered to be at the heart of all approaches to tourism management. This triangle is shown in Figure 7.2 and indicates that the three major components to be taken into consideration in tourism management are as follows: the visitor, the host community and the environment. Figure 7.2 shows how these three factors are inter-related and significantly impact upon each other. Although the triangle is relatively simplistic, it does 'neatly encapsulate the three main focal points for management decisions' (Middleton and Hawkins 1998, p. 86).

However, the situation is somewhat more complex than this. There are more than just visitors and residents interacting with the environment (Middleton and Hawkins, 1998). In addition, there are elected representatives and appointed officials, as well as tourism-related businesses that need to be taken into account. The elected representatives and appointed officials are responsible to residents for the goals and management of

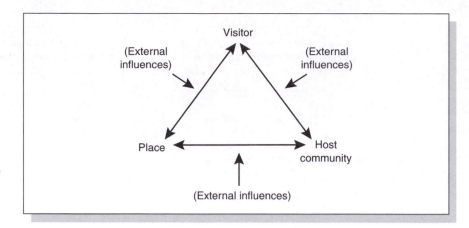

Figure 7.2
The triangle of three major components in tourism management (Adapted from ETB, 1991.)

a destination. Businesses involved include accommodation providers, cafes, restaurants and hotels as well as transport providers and visitor attractions. Middleton and Hawkins also indicated that residents will be made up of different interests groups and visitors will possibly comprise a number of different market segments. They stressed the importance of recognizing this variety of stakeholders or the nature of the 'players' in tourism, particularly with reference to attempts to achieve sustainable tourism practices.

Swarbrooke (1999) produced a very similar set of stakeholders in tourism management to that suggested by Middleton and Hawkins. In addition to the 'players' provided by Middleton and Hawkins, he also included the voluntary sector, particularly pressure groups and professional bodies, as well as the media.

Much of this discussion concerning tourism management has implied a major separation between the public and the private sector. However, there is mounting evidence of the growing importance of partnerships in tourism management (Bramwell and Lane, 2000). Such partnership may involve the voluntary sector as well as links between private organizations and public bodies (Mason, Lebermann and Barnett, 2000). Partnerships are likely to be particularly significant in future attempts to achieve sustainable tourism practices (Bramwell and Lane, 2000). While the private sector is likely to have the best information about demand and also influential marketing techniques, the public sector should be most aware of acceptable levels of tourism impacts and be able to apply sanctions in relation to agreed resource capacities.

Tourism planning, management and sustainability

Many publications and much research in the last decade of the twentieth century focusing on tourism planning and management were concerned with issues relating to planning, management and sustainability. The concept of sustainability emerged from ideas on sustainable development (Fennell, 1999; Holden, 2000). One of the more influential statements came at the World Conference on Environment and Development (WCED) in

1987 in which it was stated that sustainable development 'meets the goals of the present without compromising the ability of future generations to meet their own needs' (WCED, 1987, p. 43).

One of the first public action strategies on tourism and sustainability came from the Globe 90 conference held in Canada. Conference delegates suggested five goals of sustainable tourism. These are as follows: (a) to develop greater awareness and understanding of the significant contribution tourism can make to environment and economy; (b) to promote equity and development; (c) to improve the quality of life of the host community; (d) to provide a high quality of experience for the visitor; and (e) to maintain the quality of the environment.' (Fennell, 1999, p. 14).

However, the concept of sustainable tourism changed during the last decade of the twentieth century. Emphasis has been placed on environmental factors, social factors or economic factors depending on the author, the target audience and the context in which statements have been made. For some commentators, sustainable tourism relates primarily to community issues, for others it is about jobs and the tourism industry, yet others are more concerned with conserving threatened environments. These changing approaches have contributed to a realisation that attempting to sustain jobs, host communities and the local environment are potentially conflicting aims and hence are not necessarily achievable (Mason, 1991, 1995).

The concept of sustainability has also been applied in tourism at a variety of scales and in both the public and private sectors (Holden, 2000). Therefore, there is now a significant literature on sustainable tourism but much of this is theoretical and there is often a large gap between theory and practice. Butler (1991) made a sobering observation when he argued that whatever its origins and aims, all tourism tends towards mass tourism and as Fennell (1999) argued, despite the rhetoric, it would appear that few sustainable tourism projects have withstood the test of time. Adding to this is the contribution that disasters (either natural or man-made) can make to supposedly carefully constructed tourism plans (see Faulkner, 2001) that may challenge concepts of long-term sustainability. The significance of crises and disasters in relation to planning and management is examined in Chapter 17, which focuses on sustainability issues, as despite concerns raised above they remain a key focus for much writing and research in tourism.

Summary

This chapter has indicated that planning is a forward-looking, future-oriented activity. In the past, planning was often a largely reactive process in response to perceived problems. Recently, planning has become a more proactive activity. Tourism planning is concerned specifically with ideas on the future of tourism and is, or at least should be, a coherent process of ordering change with the intention of deriving maximum benefits, while minimising negative effects. Tourism policy is the implementation of a tourism plan. Tourism management involves the day-to-day, ongoing overseeing and monitoring of the effects of a tourism plan and tourism policy. This may suggest a linear relationship, which begins with planning, is followed by policy and this in turn is succeeded by management. However, the relationship between planning and management is somewhat more complex. One of the key roles of managers and therefore important as a major process of management is planning. Hence, planning activities and management processes are likely to be taking place simultaneously in a given context.

Tourism planning and tourism management take place in the real world, where there are different individuals and groups, different value systems, varying and often conflicting interests and the processes of negotiation, coercion, compromise and choice all conspire to ensure that these activities are not necessarily rational or straightforward.

In the last decade of the twentieth century, planning and management in tourism were linked with ideas on sustainability. Despite a growing literature in this field, there is currently a significant gap between theory and practice.

Student activities

1 What is the relationship between planning and management?
2 What is the relationship between planning and policy?
3 How is tourism planning and management (a) similar to planning and management in general; (b) different from planning and management in general?
4 Study the case study material and indicate why tourism planning in New Zealand is not a straightforward process.
5 Use local media to investigate a planning issue in your local area that has a tourism dimension. Consider the following:
   What are the main issues?
   Who is involved?
   What are the views of those involved?
   What are the planning processes?
   How does the tourism dimension fit?
   What are the links between policy and planning?
   What are the links between planning and management?
   What are the possible outcomes?
   What is your preferred option?

The key players in tourism planning and management

Learning objectives

At the end of this chapter you should:

- be aware of the key players in tourism management;
- be aware of a number of introductory issues in relation to the key players in tourism planning and management; viz. tourists, the host community, the tourism industry, government agencies, the media and non-government organizations (NGOs).

Introduction

Discussion of tourism management requires consideration of a number of factors, including:

- Who is managing?
- What is being managed?
- How is it being managed?
- Where is it happening?
- When is it happening?

These questions are clearly linked and it may be difficult to separate, for example, the 'who' from the' how' and the 'when' and the 'where'. This chapter concentrates on 'who' is involved.

In relation to those involved, consideration needs to be given to individuals and organisations acting as managers, including government bodies, as well as members of the tourism industry. Tourism management clearly relates to the tourists themselves and will need to consider the host or resident population. Later chapters present in-depth discussions on the management of tourism, in relation to players and related issues focusing on:

- the management of tourists/visitors;
- the role of the host community;
- the management of resources for tourism (in particular environmental, social and cultural resources);
- the management of the tourism industry;
- partnerships in tourism planning and management.

Key perspectives

Key players in tourism management

It is possible to suggest that the key players in tourism planning and management are as follows:

- the tourists themselves;
- the host population;
- the tourism industry;
- government agencies (at local, regional, national and international level).

Less obvious players, but nevertheless having very important roles, are voluntary organizations/NGOs (including charities and pressure groups) and also the media (Swarbrooke, 1999).

The 'ETB triangle' (ETB, 1991) (see Figure 7.2) stresses the importance of both the tourist and the local or host community when discussing the factors influencing management issues in tourism. This chapter provides initially a discussion of tourists in relation to planning and management of tourism prior to a discussion of host communities. This is followed by a consideration of the role of government agencies and the tourism industry itself. Brief consideration is then given to the media and non-government organizations.

The tourists

Tourists are obviously of key importance in the management of tourism. Unfortunately, tourists are often viewed as the major cause of the problems of tourism. If they are perceived as an homogenous group, then tourists are a relatively easy target for the so-called evils of tourism. They are 'outsiders' and can be blamed by 'insiders' (the local people) for

Basic responsibilities

- The responsibility for obeying local laws and regulations.
- The responsibility for not taking part in activities which while not illegal, or where the laws are not enforced by the local authorities, are nevertheless, widely condemned by society, such as sex with children
- The responsibility for not deliberately offending local religious beliefs or cultural norms of behaviour
- The responsibility for not deliberately harming the local physical environment
- The responsibility to minimize the use of scarce local resources

Extra responsibilities of tourists in relation to sustainable tourism

- The responsibility not to visit destinations which have a poor record on human rights
- The responsibility to find out about the destination before the holiday and try to learn a few words of the local language, at least
- The responsibility to try to meet local people, learn about their lifestyles, and establish friendships
- The responsibility to protect the natural wildlife by not buying souvenirs made from living creatures, for example
- The responsibility to abide by all local religious beliefs and cultural values, even those with which the tourist personally disagrees
- The responsibility to boycott local businesses which pay their staff poor wages, or provide bad working conditions for their employees
- The responsibility to behave sensibly, so as not to spread infections such as HIV and hepatitis B
- The responsibility to contribute as much as possible to the local economy

Figure 8.1

Responsibilities of the tourist (*Source*: Swarbrooke, 1999.)

negative consequences of tourism. When the appearance of tourists and their behaviour is in marked contrast to that of the local population, it is also easy to point the finger of blame at them. However, this is rather a simplistic picture. It is possible to argue that the tourist has both rights and responsibilities (Swarbrooke, 1999). Figure 8.1 indicates a number of basic responsibilities of tourists and also some others that are linked to the concept of sustainability in tourism, while Figure 8.2 suggests some tourists' rights.

Although there are a number of laws and regulations relating to the operational aspects of the tourism industry, there are few regulations pertaining directly to the behaviour of tourists (Mason and Mowforth, 1996). Hence, the notion of tourists' responsibilities can be seen as rather an alien concept. However, there have been a number of attempts to influence the behaviour of tourists. These usually take the form of voluntary codes of conduct (Mason and Mowforth, 1996) and/or the use of more overt educational approaches (see Orams, 1995 on the efficacy of such approaches).

Attempts to educate tourists have frequently been linked to concerns about the real and potential impacts that they are perceived to have on the environment and/or the community at the destination. Such attempts have been usually closely linked to what has been termed 'alternative' or 'responsible' tourism, which was developing in the late 1980s (Mowforth, 1992). Creating more responsible tourism was also linked with the growth

The rights of the tourist	Those who are responsible for protecting these rights
The right to be safe and secure from crime, terrorism and disease	• The host community • Government agencies, e.g. security services and health authorities
The right not to be discriminated against on the grounds of race, sex or disability	• The host community • The tourism industry • Government agencies, e.g. immigration departments
The right not to be exploited by local businesses and individuals	• The tourism industry • The host community • Government agencies, e.g. police
The right to the fair marketing of products through honest travel brochures and advertisements	• The tourism industry • Government agencies, e.g. the advertising regulators
The right to a safe, clean, physical environment	• The host community • The tourism industry • Government agencies, e.g. environmental bodies and policy departments
The right to free and unrestricted movement providing that they cause no damage	• Government agencies, e.g. security services
The right to meet local people freely	• Government agencies, e.g. security services
The right to courteous and competent service	• The host community • The tourism industry

Figure 8.2 The rights of tourists and the responsibilities of the host community, government agencies and the tourism industry (*Source*: Swarbrooke, 1999.)

of ecotourism in the late 1980s (Mason and Mowforth, 1995; Fennell 1999), which can itself also be viewed as a form of alternative or responsible tourism (Mowforth, 1992).

The use of the term alternative requires an explanation of to what it is an alternative. However, this is not always made clear. Generally the term is attached to forms of tourism that are an alternative to large-scale mass tourism. Hence, alternative tourism would be small scale, non-packaged and involving relatively few people. Such tourism has also been referred to as 'good' tourism (Wood and House, 1991). In the early 1990s, being a 'good' tourists involved travelling independently, out of season, to relatively unknown areas, buying local produce, enjoying local traditions and cultural activity and getting to know local people, as well as taking an interest in the local environment and wildlife (Wood and House, 1991)

An important problem arises here in that such notions of 'good tourism' and responsible tourism (including ecotourism) frequently claim, either overtly or implicitly, that the form of tourism under discussion is *better* than mass tourism. Clearly a value judgement is being made here. There are a number of criticisms of this anti-mass tourism, pro-'good' tourism stance. As Swarbrooke (1999) claimed, if there is a good tourist then there must be an 'evil' tourist to contrast with the 'good', who either intentionally or accidentally causes harm. In this way, the concept is divisive. Further criticisms include the suggestion that the type of tourism favoured by the good tourist, or at least commentators on good tourism, only appeals to a minority (Wheeler, 1993). Additionally it is argued that as a minority activity, such tourism offers little to established destinations where many are already employed in tourism (Swarbrooke, 1999). Wheeler (1993) also suggested in relation to ecotourism, which he renamed 'egotourism', that it is more likely to make the ecotourist feel better about their involvement than actually bring about benefits to the environment and local communities. Also, as yet, there is little compelling evidence to support the idea that supposed 'good' tourism is anymore sustainable in the longer term than mass tourism. Indeed, as Butler (1998) suggested all forms of tourism tend over time toward mass tourism. Therefore, terms such as responsible tourism and ecotourism may be little more than convenient labels which appeal to certain self-righteous consumers and this in turn may help sell more holidays (see Mason and Mowforth, 1996; Fennell, 1999). If this is so, it runs entirely contrary to the principles upon which these forms of tourism are based.

An important factor that this discussion of various forms of tourism has demonstrated is that, unlike what is stated in much popular commentary on tourism, tourists are far from one homogenous group. There are important demographic variables; for example, it is only necessary to consider 'seniors' travel in comparison with '18–30' activities to grasp this point. Tourism marketing media reveals that different types of holidays are targeted at male and female, heterosexual and homosexual tourists. Tourists engage in very different types of pursuits. Some forms of tourism are very active – sport tourism, for example – while other types are relatively passive, such as sight-seeing from a coach. Some activities consume resources and have marked economic, socio-cultural or environmental impacts, while others have minimal consequences. Tourists to one resort may vary according to seasonal factors; skiing in winter and walking in summer in a mountain environment, for example. Additionally, an individual tourist may appear in one particular holiday location or a number of destinations in a variety of guises over a period of a week, a month, a year or a life-time.

Regulation of tourist behaviour, the application of codes of conducts, the use of tourist education within tourism planning and management and the nature of ecotourism are discussed in more detail in subsequent chapters.

The host community

Such terminology as the host community may be somewhat misleading as it implies that there are guests to complement the supposed hosts. However, as tourists are not always welcome, a more appropriate term could be local community, resident community or destination community. Nevertheless, the term host community is now commonly used in tourism literature and so it is employed here.

As has been indicated in Chapter 5, the host community can act as a major attraction for tourists. More often than not, it is the cultural manifestations of the community, including craft and art works, as well as less tangible factors such as music, dance and religious festivals that act as important attractions. In some cases, actually meeting members of a particular community and staying with them is a key motivation for certain types of tourist. However, as several of the earlier case studies and discussions have indicated there are a number of dangers that may result from the contact between tourists and host communities, particularly in terms of erosion of host community values and possible loss of cultural identity.

An important aspect of any discussion of host communities is that it would wrong to assume that there is such a thing as *a* host community. As with tourists, the host community is heterogeneous not homogenous. A host community can be made up of long-term indigenous residents and recent domestic as well as international migrants. In addition to obvious variations in gender and age, a host community is likely to have individuals and groups with several different value positions, political persuasions and attitudes to socio-cultural phenomena, including tourism.

Some definitions of host communities refer to a specific geographical area. This would seem a sensible way to define a host community. However, there are problems with this. The geographical extent of the community has to be decided upon. It may be relatively simple when considering a small town or village. In this situation, a local political boundary may serve as the boundary of a community, but even here it is quite possible for one community to spread over several geographical and political boundaries. For example, in New Zealand it is possible to talk about the 'Maori community', which could be all of those with some Maori ancestors in New Zealand. However, the term could refer only to those living in a specific settlement. At the international level, all Maori in the world could be viewed as part of the 'Maori community'.

This discussion may lead to the conclusion that it is easier to define a community by the values and behaviours that it shares. This approach is however problematic as many geographical settlements are made up of majority and minority groups in any one community. Hence, geographical settlements, including many tourist destinations, exhibit variations of community in terms of ethnic background, length of residency, age of residents and levels of income.

In relation to tourism planning and management, if it is acknowledged that communities are heterogeneous, then the importance of different interest groups and vested interests needs to be recognized. The acceptance of the notion of heterogeneous communities brings with it the realisation that the planning and management of tourism is a more complex and yet even more necessary task (see Mason and Cheyne, 2000). In accepting that communities are heterogeneous, Swarbrooke (1999, p. 125) suggests that they could be divided up in terms of:

- elites and the rest of the population;
- indigenous residents and immigrants;
- those involved in tourism and those not involved;
- property owners and property renters;
- younger people and older people;

- employers, employees, self-employed;
- those with private cars, those relying on public transport;
- affluent and less well-off residents;
- majority communities/minority communities.

The preceding discussion may have implied that host communities are passive recipients of tourists. This is not necessarily the case. There are many examples, particularly in Developed countries and increasingly in the developing world, where local residents in a tourist destination are actively involved in the provision for tourism and also its planning and management.

By the late 1990s, there was a groundswell of opinion that communities should be involved actively in planning for tourism (Middleton and Hawkins, 1998). However, this is not a particularly recent development. In fact, as long ago as the mid-1980s Murphy (1985) had argued that as tourism makes use of a community's resources, then the community should be a key player in the process of planning and managing tourism. Swarbrooke (1999) suggested that the rationale for community involvement in tourism is as follows: it is part of the democratic process; it provides a voice for those directly affected by tourism; it makes use of local knowledge to ensure decisions are well informed; and it can reduce potential conflict between tourists and members of the host community.

Nevertheless, the actual involvement of a community in tourism planning and management will depend on a number of factors. These include the following; the nature of the political system at national and local level; the degree of 'political literacy' of the local population; the nature of the particular tourism issue; the awareness of the tourism issue in the community; how the tourism issue is perceived by members of the community; the history of involvement (or lack of it) in tourism related issues; and the attitudes and behaviour of sections of the media.

Discussions of the involvement of communities in tourism planning and management and illustrations through case studies are provided in subsequent chapters that are concerned with, respectively, host communities, natural resources for tourism and codes of conduct.

Government agencies • • •

Government agencies are frequently referred to as the public sector of tourism. They are not commercial organisations intent on making a profit, but are meant to represent the views of tax payers and electors. Government agencies are funded from taxes and in most Developed countries are run by democratically elected representatives supported by paid civil servants. In some parts of the world, particularly some Developing countries, governments are headed by un-elected dictators or military rulers and in such cases the rationale suggested for the involvement of the public sector in tourism is not necessarily that provided below.

However, there are a multiplicity of government bodies that have a bearing on tourism planning and management. These bodies exist at different scales from national, through regional, down to local. A number of countries in Europe, such as France and Spain, (the two most important destinations globally in 2001 by number of international visitors), have national bodies for tourism in the form of a Ministry or Department of Tourism. The United Kingdom, a major tourism destination, has a Minister for Tourism but subsumes this relatively minor role and its public sector national tourism functions with the Department of Culture, Media and Sport. At the local and regional level, in the United Kingdom as well as many other Developed countries, there are not necessarily government agencies focusing specifically on tourism or government representatives with tourism knowledge and experience (Middleton and Hawkins, 1998). Such factors will have a significant impact on the ability of the public sector to influence the course of tourism development in a particular tourist destination.

The main reasons for the involvement of the public sector in tourism are as follows (Swarbrooke, 1999, p. 87):

- The public sector is mandated to represent the whole population and not just one set of stakeholders or interest group.
- The public sector is intended to be impartial, with no particular vested or commercial interests.
- The public sector can take a longer-term view of tourism development than, for example, the private sector.

The public sector in many Developed countries has what may appear at face value to be contradictory roles. Governments may attempt to regulate tourism, but they also have a role in marketing tourism (Mason and Mowforth, 1995; Seaton and Bennett, 1996). Marketing is usually associated with promoting tourism, that is, not controlling or regulating it. However, there are examples when marketing is used as a controlling measure. Such an example is that employed by the government agency, English Heritage and the non-government organization the National Trust of England. These organizations work together in the marketing and management of two prehistoric sites in England. Stonehenge is the most visited prehistoric stone circle site in the United Kingdom. Approximately 30 km away is a similar prehistoric stone circle at Avebury. Stonehenge received approximately one million visitors per year in the last decade of the twentieth century, while Avebury received only 50 000 visitors per year. The main reason for this great difference in visitor numbers is that Stonehenge is very strongly marketed to both domestic and international tourist groups. However, Avebury is deliberately not marketed to overseas visitors and there is also only a limited attempt to market it within the United Kingdom. There is further discussion of the management of Stonehenge and Avebury in Chapter 9.

In the discussion below, it is also suggested that the ability of the public sector to regulate tourism is relatively restricted. This is due partly to the fact that there is only a limited amount of legislation directly affecting tourism. Governments in a number of European countries, such as the United Kingdom, for example, have legislation relating to land use and also building controls. Such governments may also have certain official standards and these may be backed by international standards established by the International Standards Organization (ISO). The ISO has standards in relation to, for example, vegetarian food and there are likely to be national standards in relation to, for instance, food hygiene or hotel accommodation.

Governments tend to operate at a number of different levels in any one country. Hence, there are at least national, regional and local level government bodies. For example as is revealed by the case study in Chapter 7, in New Zealand the main legislation relating to land use planning is the Resource Management Act (RMA). The RMA was introduced in 1991 and provides a legislative framework for managing land, air, water, coastal, geothermal and pollution issues under one umbrella in New Zealand (Mason and Leberman, 2000). As the case study reveals, the overall aim of the RMA is to promote sustainable management whilst at the same time developing and protecting resources which enable social and economic well being. Under the RMA the management of natural resources is delegated to regional and local authorities. Locally, the district or city councils are responsible for developing a district plan. The Department of Conservation (DOC) in New Zealand is also charged with the preparation of land management plans, and currently such plans cover approximately one-third of the New Zealand land area.

Governments in most Developed countries and increasingly in Developing countries are also involved in setting aside areas that are designated for special protection for environmental or cultural reasons. This has led to the creation of National Parks in individual countries and when countries collaborate internationally, this has led to the establishment of World Heritage Sites, such as Kakadu National Park in the Northern Territory of Australia and the Tonagariro National Park on the North Island of New Zealand. Governments may also require Environmental Impact Assessment (EIA) to be conducted when a new tourism venture is to be developed. As Middleton and Hawkins (1998) suggested, an EIA is an attempt to prevent environmental degradation by giving decision-makers information about the likely consequences of development actions. EIAs usually require the completion of an evaluation form prior to a development. This would cover a number of environmental resources and the likely impact of the tourism development upon them. The EIA would consider not only whether there is likely to be an impact but also its intensity.

However, as Swarbrooke (1999) indicated, there is virtually no tourism legislation concerning certain key areas of significance to tourism planning. These key areas include: socio-cultural impacts of tourism, environmental impacts of tourism; impacts of tourism on wildlife; the carrying capacity of areas and sites, tourists behaviour and the wages and working conditions of tourism industry employees.

This has meant that public bodies and government organisations have tended to rely on the tourism industry regulating itself. However, there is no reason to believe that the tourism industry will be anymore responsible for its actions in regard to the environment and social impacts than any other industry (Mason and Mowforth, 1996).

The public sector has also tended to rely on the education of tourists in an attempt to modify their behaviour in relation to potential and real impacts. Such voluntary efforts often involved codes of conduct targeted at visitors or sectors of the tourism industry in an attempt to regulate behaviour. Educating tourists through interpretation at visitor sites is another commonly adopted approach. The use of codes of conduct and the education of visitors as tourism management approaches are discussed in some detail in later chapters. However, there is increasing evidence that these attempts at self-regulation are only achieving moderate success and there is likely to be a need for the introduction of externally imposed, government-backed legislation pertaining to certain sectors of tourism (Mason and Mowforth, 1996; Swarbrooke, 1999). Government legislation aimed at controlling tourist behaviour is also a possibility.

The preceding discussion has centred around the public sector playing a mainly reactive role in terms of attempting to regulate and control tourism. However, public bodies can be proactive and play a positive role in tourism planning and management. Governments may own or at least administer certain key assets for tourism, such as valued natural or semi-natural environments, as well as built environment attractions such as museums and historic buildings. These can be marketed and/or regulated in such a way that they provide models for private operators. Governments can also develop the infrastructure necessary for both public and private sector tourism activities. If the public sector can do this in a way that is more sustainable than previous attempts, it may give a lead that is then followed by the private sector tourism operators.

There are increasing number of international links and intergovernmental treaties that are attempting to create more sustainable forms of tourism. One important development at the international level at the end of the twentieth century was the application of Agenda 21 (developed at the 1992 Rio Environment Summit) to tourism. Figure 8.3 shows the actions identified for travel and tourism companies from Agenda 21. It is possible that such intergovernmental cooperation, as envisaged by Agenda 21, will lead to fairer, more equitable and more sustainable forms of international tourism.

Figure 8.3
Agenda 21 for the travel and tourism industry (*Source*: Press release of February 1997 issued by WTTC/WTO/Earth Council.)

Actions identified for travel and tourism companies, with the main aim of establishing systems and procedures which incorporate sustainable development at the core of the decision-making process for business operations. (Applies also to public sector business operations.)

   (i) Waste minimization, re-use, and recycling.
  (ii) Energy efficiency, conservation, and management.
 (iii) Management of fresh water resources.
 (iv) Waste water management.
  (v) Management of hazardous substances.
 (vi) Use of more environmentally friendly transport.
(vii) Land-use planning and management.
(viii) Involving staff, customers, and local communities in environmental issues.
 (ix) Design for sustainability.
  (x) Developing partnerships for sustainable development.

The tourism industry • • •

The tourism industry is not easy to define. It is complex and has many dimensions. As Middleton and Hawkins (1998) argued, the industry is so large and diverse that some tourism companies would not see themselves as part of the same industry. In Chapter 1, Leiper's system's model of tourism is shown in Figure 1.4. This shows three sectors: the generating zone, the transition zone and the destination zone. Each of these zones or sectors contains tourism industry organizations. In the generating zone are travel agents, tour operators and marketing agencies. The travel media also operates from here. The transition zone contains the carriers such as airlines and rail companies. The destination zone contains the greatest variety of tourism industry organizations as there are various types of accommodation including hotels, and there are restaurants and other food providers. The destination zone also has the forms of hospitality and entertainment providers as well as visitor attractions, transport providers tourist information offices and other infrastructure organisations that support tourism. It should be noted that some of the so-called industries within tourism, such as Tourist Information Centres are in fact public sector organizations. However, one of the key differences between the private sector of the tourism industry and the public sector is that the private sector responds directly to market forces (Middleton and Hawkins, 1998).

The tourism industry is often blamed for causing damage to destinations and showing little willingness to be involved in planning for long-term viability of tourism development (Mason and Mowforth, 1995). However, the complexity of the tourism industry makes it difficult to point the finger of blame directly at the cause of problems. Nevertheless, the tourism industry has been accused of (Swarbrooke, 1999, pp. 104–5):

- Being mainly concerned with short-term profit, rather than long-term sustainability.
- Exploiting the environment and local populations rather than conserving them.
- Being relatively fickle and showing little commitment to particular destinations.
- Not doing enough to raise tourists awareness of issues such as sustainability.
- Only getting on the sustainability wagon when it is likely to achieve good publicity.
- Being increasingly owned and controlled by large trans-national corporations, who have little regard for individual destinations.

Despite the fact that there are a large number and range of tourism businesses, there are many linkages between apparently different sectors. For example, travel agents and tour operators often work closely together, and some agents may be owned by operators. Under these circumstances, agents may strongly market the brands of the operator they are linked with. Operators may also have a stake in hotels and carriers. Linkages in the industry are becoming more common. Even apparently competing organisations may be linked. In the 1990s, for example, Qantas linked with British Airways and other international airlines to offer a global service. In an attempt to gain customer loyalty they established 'Frequent Flyer' (an 'air miles' scheme) which provides 'free' travel as reward for collecting sufficient points.

The major way in which members of the tourism industry manage their operations is through what is known as the marketing mix (Middleton and Hawkins, 1998). The marketing mix can be summarized under four headings, each of which begins with a 'p'. These are as follows: product, price, promotion and place. Middleton and Hawkins (1998) add one other 'p' to this list, that of people. The marketing mix can be used by the tourist industry to manage the consumer, in this case the visitor or tourist.

The private sector provides the bulk of most tourist products at tourist destinations. This is particularly so with visitors staying in commercial accommodation. However, even those staying with friends and relatives are likely to make some purchases in a destination. The number and type of visitors in a destination is therefore strongly influenced by decisions taken by commercial tourism operators in terms of the products they have to offer there. However, this is only partially the case as a major part of the tourism product is the tourist experience and the public sector has a role here. This experience is obtained within the wider context of the destination environment. Evidence suggests that few tourism operators in a destination have paid much regard to the wider environment in which tourism takes place. Small businesses, in particular, expect visitors to be provided with free access to the environment around them, but such operators have not accepted any responsibility, for example, for increased traffic congestion, pollution and litter that tourists may cause (Middleton and Hawkins, 1998). However, if the quality of the environment falls, customers may go elsewhere. It is more often than not, the public sector that makes attempts to improve the quality of the environment, which tourists purchasing from the private sector have contributed to damaging.

The strongest influence that the private sector has for determining the level of demand for their product is price (Middleton and Hawkins, 1998). The price of a holiday is largely determined by commercial judgements of what the market will bear. Hence, the private sector largely determines products and prices, the segments to be targeted and the volume of products to be offered. When commercial decisions on product and price are made, there has been until very recently little attempt to factor in environmental costs or socio-cultural impacts (Swarbrooke, 1999). As Middleton and Hawkins (1998) argued it would require some form of external regulation and/or private sector collaboration to ensure that such factors applied equally across all those competing in the same market.

Commercial operators can influence the behaviour of tourists by promotion. Promotion involves publicity and usually this is an attempt to increase product awareness and ultimately sell more holiday experiences. The promotion of products is often seen as the key marketing role of commercial operators (Seaton and Bennet, 1996). However, the public sector also has an important role in marketing destinations (Middleton and Hawkins, 1998). It is frequently carried out by local council officials and staff at Tourist Information Centres as well as via a number of publicity media. As promotion is a key way that both the private and public sector can influence tourists behaviour, it can be a very important tool in tourism planning and management.

The fourth 'p' in the marketing mix is place. In tourism marketing terms, place means the point at which tourists can gain convenient access to information about the various tourist products on offer. The obvious place to obtain this is the destination itself, but another place is a travel agency. Distribution of information ensuring the appropriate potential consumer receives the material is important. Increasingly, tourists are gaining access to marketing information via the World Wide Web.

As indicated above, Middleton and Hawkins (1998) added a fifth 'p' to the traditional marketing mix. They suggested that people are vital within marketing. They referred specifically to those providing tourist services, both within the destination and beyond. Clearly, the relationship between hotel staff and visitors can greatly influence a tourist's view of a destination. There are also people who have very little or no direct involvement in tourism, such as bank staff and health workers who can influence a tourist's experiences of a resort.

As has been previously stated, few operators, until very recently, have been concerned with the impacts of taking tourists to destinations on the environment or society of the destination. However, in the last decade of the twentieth century a number of tourism companies became involved in initiatives and this suggests a growing awareness and concern with such impacts. These include recycling, promoting 'green' holidays, providing information on environmentally sound activities for tourists and donating money to local charities. Some operators are also using guides selected from local communities and are involved in partnerships with local community groups.

It would appear that most industry action to date has been designed to indicate that the industry can regulate itself. One interpretation of this could be that industry does not wish for external control and regulation and hence voluntary self-regulation is preferable (Mason and Mowforth, 1996; Swarbrooke, 1999). Another interpretation is that the industry is aware that regulation will eventually come and that it wishes to appear proactive rather than reactive, as this may soften the blow of external regulation (Mason and Mowforth, 1996). Some industry bodies have taken voluntary self-regulation to the point of designing and implementing voluntary codes of conduct. These operate at the individual company level – the Canadian Chateau Whistler Hotel Group has such a code of operation. Voluntary codes are also found at supra-national level and examples include the Pacific Asia Travel Associations Code for Environmentally Responsible Tourism (Mason and Mowforth, 1996). Such codes are generally welcomed by commentators on tourism (Mason and Mowforth, 1996; Malloy and Fennell, 1998), but may be, in reality, little more than clever marketing devices which succeed in providing tourists with a 'feel good' factor, while doing little to change industry practices in relation to the environment and society of tourist destinations.

Other players

Two other sets of actors are important in terms of tourism planning and management. These are voluntary sector organizations and the media. The voluntary sector is made up of a number of different groups. These include pressure groups, voluntary trusts, some of which have charitable status, and industry associations. Pressure groups can be further sub-divided into those, whose membership is primarily public and those, whose members come largely from within the tourism industry.

A major pressure group in the United Kingdom is Tourism Concern. The original members of Tourism Concern were individuals who were concerned mainly about the social impacts of tourism, particularly in Developing countries. Tourism Concern has mounted and run campaigns targeted at, for example, child prostitution and the enforced displacement of local people as a result of tourism development. Tourism Concern has widened its focus to encompass economic and environmental issues and now has many members who are academics and students, but it has few members from the tourism industry. It has, however, frequently found itself in conflict with the industry. Given this lack of involvement of industry, its effectiveness has been limited, although it has almost certainly raised levels of awareness.

There are also organizations that act as pressure groups, but are not part of the voluntary sector. However, neither are they part of the tourism industry. Such organizations are termed non-government organizations, or NGOs, and they usually have a far wider brief than just tourism, but run events/campaigns and/or plan projects that have important tourism dimensions. In the United Kingdom, one NGO, the World Wide Fund for Nature (WWF) has been active since the early 1990s in campaigning for more 'environmentally friendly' forms of tourism. WWF has been active in connection with tourism issues in several areas globally and a particular project of theirs, the WWF Arctic Tourism Project, is discussed in Chapter 13. Another NGO, Friends of the Earth, has also campaigned for preservation of the environment in relation to tourism development. In the United States, the Audobon Society has performed a somewhat similar role to that of WWF in terms of tourism issues.

A number of non-profit-making trusts exist in Developed countries and they are targeted at one particular issue or purpose. In the United Kingdom, for example, the National Trust is a non-profit-making organisation involved in conserving historic buildings and heritage landscapes. In New Zealand, the organization Forest and Bird fulfils a similar role in terms of landscape conservation. At the local scale, a non-profit-making trust aimed at heritage preservation in New Zealand is the Napier Art Deco Trust. Due largely to rebuilding after the 1931 earthquake, the New Zealand North Island town of Napier has one of the most complete set of art deco buildings anywhere. The trust was established in 1985 to both conserve this heritage and make it available to visitors.

The tourism industry also has a number of pressure groups. The World Travel and Tourism Council (WTTC) is such a pressure group and is supported by major tourism companies. It lobbies on behalf of the tourism industry. There are also a number of professional bodies that represent the tourism industry. In the United Kingdom, for example, there is the Association of British Travel Agents, and also the Association of Independent Travel Operators. In relation to Australia and New Zealand, the Pacific Asia Travel Association is a major regional professional body for the tourism industry.

The media has potentially a key role in tourism planning and management issues. Much of the media deals directly or indirectly with tourism. In Australia, New Zealand and the United Kingdom, a number of the main terrestrial television channels regularly show 'travel shows'. These tend to be relatively uncritical 'travelog' style programmes, whose aim is to promote holidays to particular destinations. A number of newspapers in each country also use a similar approach. There are also significant numbers of travel-related magazines and radio programmes and much travel information is now available on the World Wide Web. Probably the oldest form of literature concerned with travel is the guidebook. Many types of television programme and several magazines have an indirect travel component; those focusing on wildlife and natural history are within this category. The media has even created tourist attractions as the following case study indicates.

Case study

How the media can create a tourist attraction

Ian reckons he has got a lot to thank his 10 000 sheep for. On his rolling 500 hectare farm in the heartland of the Waikato region of the North Island of New Zealand, he says it was his woolly flock and the way that they kept the pasture trimmed that attracted the interest of the 'Lord of the Rings' film scouts. The scouts were searching for the tranquil green shire, the mythical land of the hobbits in Tolkien's famous trilogy.

Three main attributes attracted the scouts: the farms neat pastures, the lack of visible signs of modern human settlement such as houses, roads and power lines and the big pine tree on the edge of a lake that became the Shire's party tree.

The film-makers finally decided to use the farm in March 1999. But from then on it was a case of tight security as Ian and his family were sworn to secrecy. However, word that the farm was the secret location for filming quickly spread. Media interest grew, with newspapers phoning repeatedly only to be told that Ian could not say a thing! The army was then contracted by the film company to build a road into the Shire. This was followed by the film crew digging hobbit holes, planting gardens and landscaping the area. Filming of the 'Lord of the Rings' finally got under way in late 1999, but was not completed until early 2001.

The first part of the trilogy, 'The Fellowship of the Ring' was shown to cinema audiences in late 2001 and just before the second part, 'The Two Towers', was reaching cinemas in December 2002, Ian was released from his contract with the film-makers. He is just beginning to offer guided tours of the remnants of the set.

Although some visitors would like to see the site restored to how it was in the movie, Ian says this is unrealistic. However, the virtually bare site, (there are a dozen or so hobbit holes, including the remains of Bag End) has not deterred fans like Dave and Di from Hampshire, who booked for the 2-h tour at NZ$50. 'I knew all about it from the book and the film and I thought the tour was very good. Excellent', said Di.

(Source: The Manawatu Evening Standard, 18 December 2002)

95

The Waikato region is just one of many in New Zealand that were used in the making of the 'Lord of the Rings' film trilogy. The first two parts of the trilogy have been very successful at the 'box office'. This success was used to gain publicity for tourism to New Zealand during 2002 and was set to continue during 2003 prior to the release of the final part of the trilogy. One way in which the film trilogy and tourism have been closely linked is through the publication of a book, in late 2002, which specifically identifies and promotes just under one hundred locations in New Zealand that were used in the filming.

Until recently, most media concerned either directly or indirectly with tourism was largely promotional and lacked a critical perspective. In the last two decades of the twentieth century this situation was gradually changing. Consumer 'watchdog' television and radio programmes have investigated travel and tourism 'stories', while some newspapers, such as *The Independent* in the United Kingdom, have focused specifically on important issues such as those relating to tourism sustainability. Guidebooks have also tended to become more discerning and critical in the past decade or so. The 'Good Tourist' series (see Wood and House, 1991) discussed above is one indication of this attempt to provide alternative perspectives.

It is likely with advances in satellite and cable television and as the World Wide Web reaches more potential consumers the power of the media will grow. Nevertheless, there is no real reason why the media should adopt a critical perspective to tourism issues and assist in planning and management through the promotion of more sustainable forms of tourism.

Summary

This chapter has introduced a discussion of the key players in tourism planning and management. The major players are the tourists themselves, members of host communities, representatives of the travel industry and government agencies. NGOs and the media are also important players in relation to tourism planning and management.

In relation to tourists and host communities, it is important to note that neither group is homogenous. However, the heterogeneity of tourists and host communities is often ignored in much tourism literature, including that on planning and management. This heterogeneity contributes to the complexity of planning and managing tourism. The government role in tourism is often viewed as promotional rather than regulatory, although government at various levels fulfils both these roles. The tourism industry, although it is multi-faceted, is frequently viewed as being in need of external regulation in relation to tourism impacts. However, recently, some sectors of the industry have made attempts to regulate themselves. NGOs and the media have been important in relation to tourism planning and management. Historically, the media has tended to act in a largely promotional role, but more recently, particularly through its focus on issues and the mounting of campaigns on tourism themes, a more critical stance has been developed.

Student activities

1 Consider the key players in tourism planning and management and produce a table that summarizes the key roles of each player.

2 Consider how the key players in tourism planning and management are able to interact with each other in a formal context. What obstacles exist in relation to both formal and informal interaction between the key players?

3 How influential are the media in tourism?

4 Consider a location that you know well that has been used by the media in terms of a TV programme, film or radio production. How has this been exploited for tourism purposes and what further could be done? What are the potential issues, resulting from the media's involvement in promoting specific locations for tourism?

5 Conduct a group debate with the motion 'Tourists comprise the single most important players in tourism planning and management'.

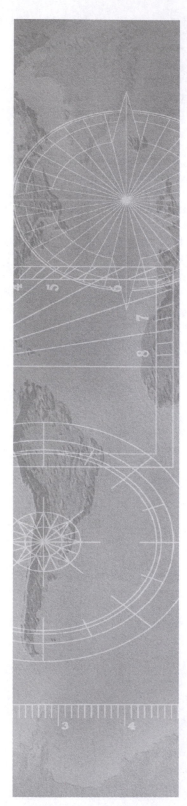

Visitor management

Introduction

Managing visitors is one of the important ways of managing the impacts of tourism, particularly impacts on the environment, but in addition managing socio-cultural and economic impacts. Visitor management has been viewed in the past 20 years or so as a significant way to attempt to reduce the negative impacts of tourism. Often, this has been through attempts to divert tourists from areas with large volumes of tourists, the so-called 'honey pots'. Another approach has been to minimise the negative impacts at a popular site by 'hardening' (e.g. resurfacing paths and footpaths), or by schemes such as 'park and ride' which keep cars out of the immediate environment of a popular attraction. However, there is a danger that by attempting to improve the site, this only encourages more visitors who in turn cause more damage (Swarbrooke, 1999).

This introductory statement indicates that visitor management can be viewed as a way to regulate visitors. Hence, regulation may relate to such factors as preventing (or indeed allowing access) to particular areas or sites. Regulation is also likely to involve the provision of information and instructions on what can and cannot be done. In most cases, regulations relating to tourism are likely to be voluntary, of a self-regulatory nature, and unlikely to be backed up with laws. There are, however, legal regulations of relevance to tourism relating to transport, health and safety and hygiene.

As well as regulation, managing visitors can also involve education. Education frequently involves the process of interpretation. This educational process may involve the dissemination of information about a particular site, but is also likely to involve more general education about social and environmental factors. In certain situations, a combination of education and regulation is used in an attempt to manage visitors. Education and regulation in relation to visitors are discussed in greater detail in Part Three of this book. This chapter considers the overall framework in which visitor management takes place and presents a number of management issues via an investigation of selected examples.

Key perspectives

Visitor management has been used by a number of different agencies and organisations, at different scales and in a variety of locations. In some countries, it has become a major tool in an attempting to control visitor flows. In the United Kingdom, for example, a government task force produced a tourism report that had visitor management as a key strategy. This report, *Maintaining the Balance*, from the UK Ministry of Environment/Department of Employment and published in 1991 focused on the relationship between the environment and the visitor and suggested there are three main ways of managing visitors. These are as follows:

- controlling the number of visitors – either by limiting numbers to match capacity, or spreading the number throughout the year, rather than having them concentrated in time in a focused 'tourist season';
- modifying visitor behaviour;
- adapting the resource in ways to enable it to cope with the volume of visitors, and hence become less damaged.

In relation to the first of these three methods, that of controlling the numbers of visitors, the report suggested that the initial task is to determine the carrying capacity. The report then cites the following thresh-old levels at which the ambience and character of the place is damaged and the quality of the experience is threatened. These are as follows:

- a level above which physical damage occurs;
- a level above which irreversible damage occurs;
- a level above which the local community suffers unacceptable side-effects.

In addition to this approach to controlling the number of visitors, the report also discussed ways of managing traffic. It argued for positive rout-ing of vehicles, clear parking strategy, park and ride schemes, the use of public transport, road closures, traffic calming and traffic control systems.

The report also made a number of suggestions on modifying visitor behaviour. These are as follows:

- marketing and general information provision;
- promotion to bring visitors out of season, to help spread the load;
- promotion of alternative destinations;
- niche marketing, to attract particular types of visitors;
- providing visitors with specific information;
- the use of signs, Travel Information Centres and information points/ boards;
- the use of codes of conduct to enable a combination of education and regulation in the interpretation process.

In addition, the report made suggestions on modifying/adapting the resource as a part of the process of visitor management. It indicated that this approach acknowledges there will be some wear and tear of the tourism resource. Minimizing damage through an adaptation of the resource in an attempt to promote protection is the key aim of this approach. The report suggested the following approaches:

- the use of wardens, guides and even guards to watch over and/or superv-ise. This is to prevent unruly behaviour, theft or deliberate damage;
- restrict the use of the site (by e.g. cordoning off areas, to prevent access, allow re-growth);
- protective measures (e.g. coverings over valuable carpets, stones, reinforce-ment of footpaths, the wearing of slippers/shoe covers to protect floors);
- the building of replicas (e.g. there has been a suggestion to create a Foam Henge to prevent damage to Stonehenge, a prehistoric monu-ment in the south of England. This is discussed in more detail in a case study in this chapter).

New Zealand provides a good example of possible conflict in relation to visitor management. The potential for real conflict is linked closely to traditional New Zealand attitudes to use of the environment (these were discussed briefly in Chapter 6). The New Zealand Government Ministry, the Department of Conservation (DOC), produced a report in 1994 and according to DOC there are potential points of conflict. These are as follows:

- The majority of New Zealanders view the environment as one to which they have free access and this is particularly so with the backcountry (remote mountain areas), even though they may visit such areas only infrequently. New Zealanders are therefore generally opposed to attempts to limit access.
- The New Zealand tradition of self-reliance means opposition to improving existing accommodation and increasing the number of huts and other facilities in the backcountry.
- International visitors generally demand easy access to facilities and these need to be of a relatively high standard, particularly toilets and washing facilities. International visitors also demand good signage, clear notice boards, good maps and sufficiently well serviced camp-sites. International visitor numbers are likely to increase significantly in the next 10–15 years, while domestic visitors will remain almost constant. Hence the pressure will be to improve and increase facilities for the international visitor, but this is likely to be opposed by domestic visitors.
- There will come a point when the visitor experience/satisfaction declines. This will occur when numbers reach a certain (as yet unknown) level. At this point there may well be conflict between, for example, international hikers and domestic mountain bikers.
- There is pressure for visitors to make a greater contribution and to pay more to help maintain the environment they are visiting.
- There is an increased desire by local communities and Maori communities to have a greater say in environment/conservation decision-making.

A major problem in relation to all types of visitor management is the lack of data about the impacts of tourism at particular sites that attract visitors (Shackley, 1998). In certain locations, site records relating to details of visitors may not be kept at all, or records from one site may be combined with others. Some sites attracting visitors are not neatly contained within a limited geographical area. Given the problems of measuring visitor numbers, site managers may resort to guesswork (Shackley, 1998). However, as Shackley asserts, it is clear that visitors to many visitor attractions are increasing. Nevertheless, visitor numbers are not spread evenly throughout the year in many destinations, but there are usually seasonal peaks and troughs. At the micro-scale, even during the peak period of visits, there is a variation in visitor numbers at a given site. Often, the weekly (and even daily peaks and troughs) are linked to the schedule of tour operators and carriers. Those organizing such visits seldom take into account issues of crowding, visitor preferences or visitor satisfaction levels (Shackley, 1998).

An extreme case of this 'periodicity' of visits is that of a cruise ship. Visits by cruise ships to relatively remote attractions, for example, to Antarctica or the Arctic region may take place infrequently. Several weeks may elapse between visits and when a ship arrives, the visit may have a duration of less than 1 h (Mason, Johnston and Twynam, 2000). During this time, up to 10 per cent of annual arrivals may occur, creating enormous pressure on all shore-based facilities.

At particularly popular 'honey pots', crowding may not only contribute to low satisfaction levels, adversely affect the natural and/or built environment, but also may create safety problems. Photo 4 shows the aftermath of the problems caused by queuing to enter the Eden Project in Cornwall, England. The Project, involving the creation of biomes (plant worlds) in large domed glasshouses in a disused quarry, was first opened in March 2001.

Photo 5 was taken a month later at Easter 2001. The attraction was planned to take a maximum of 5000 visitors per day. On the day the

Photo 4

Road rage at The Eden Project, Cornwall. Police carrying out an arrest for dangerous driving at the Eden Project at Easter 2001

Photo 5

The Eden Project in Cornwall. The attraction opened in early 2001. During the Easter week of 2001, visitor numbers exceeded the planned maximum day targets by more than double. This caused huge traffic jams and contributed to the incident shown in the accompanying photograph

photograph was taken, over 13 000 visitors came to the site. Queuing time for the car park at the attraction averaged 1.5 h and the pedestrian queue added another 1 h on average to a proposed visit. On this particular day, as is shown in Photo 5, police arrested a driver for alleged dangerous driving. The car was seen to overtake a line of queuing cars and drive in a hazardous manner narrowly avoiding a car park steward and running over traffic cones. This form of tourism-related 'road rage' is clearly an undesirable consequence of overcrowding at an attraction and needs careful consideration in relation to future management strategies at the Eden Project.

Even relatively remote 'wilderness areas' including several in Australia are not without their visitor management problems. Issues relating to growing numbers of visitors and related visitor management strategies are discussed in the following case study that focuses on the World Heritage Site of Kakadu National Park in Australia.

Case study

Visitor mangement in Kakadu Park

Kakadu Park is a World Heritage site in the Northern Territory of Australia. It was established as a National Park in the late 1980s. The establishment of the Park was an attempt to reconcile the interests of conservation, mining, Aboriginal land rights and tourism. Kakadu achieved World Heritage status in 1992.

Kakadu has a tropical climate, with high temperatures all year round (with a mean between 30 and 37°C). It has two seasons; a wet season from October to March and dry season from April to September. Heavy rain falls, particularly in January and February, and this causes widespread flooding in the riverine floodplains. The area has several large rivers and streams.

The climate supports a complex tropical ecosystem and the only recent arrival of Europeans and European descended settlers means Kakadu is a major habitat for a large range of wildlife. Over one-third of Australia's bird life is found here, over 120 reptiles and amphibians, 50 different fish species, 55 types of mammal, 300 species of ants, 1500 types of butterfly and moth and over 1600 botanical species. In addition to the bird life, for many visitors the key attraction is the saltwater crocodile.

Aboriginal settlements in Kakadu date back at least 50 000 years. One of the major cultural components of the park is the large number of Aboriginal rock paintings. There are least 5000 known sites of rock paintings and, probably, another 5000 yet to be itemized. These are important living parts of Aboriginal culture, they are a repository of local knowledge, a source of teaching, manifestations of the

spiritual made physical and a link between Aboriginal Dreamtime and the present. A number of these rock paintings are tourist attractions.

The discovery of gold in the nineteenth century and uranium in the 1950s led to the creation of a framework in which the interests of Aborigines, conservation and mining could be encompassed. The result was that title was invested in Aboriginal peoples under the 1976 Aboriginal Land Rights Acts. Jabiru town was established at this time as a mining centre.

Visitor management issues

Initially, tourism development was denied in some areas including Jabiru. By the late 1970s, with the establishment of the area as a National Park, tourism infrastructure was allowed. Visitor numbers increased rapidly in the period from the early 1980s to the mid-1990s (46 000 in 1982 and 220 000 in 1994). Visitors tend to be well educated, better paid than the average Australian. The average length of stay was 3–4 days in the mid-1990s. One of the major destinations is Yellow Rivers with over 75 per cent of tourists visiting. Here, the main tourist product is a wildlife experience, the opportunity to go bird watching and a scenic boat ride. Aboriginal involvement in tourism is significant, although not always direct. The most famous hotel in the area, the Gagudju Crocodile Hotel, is Aboriginal owned. The hotel owners also own Yellow Rivers Boat tours, motels and camping grounds. In addition to the group that own the

Gagudju Crocodile Hotel, there are two other Aboriginal associations actively involved in tourism. Aboriginal groups obtain significant economic benefits from tourism. Considerable amounts of this benefit are ploughed back into sustaining the Park and maintaining the traditional lifestyle.

The original intention when creating the Park was to prevent tourism development in the town of Jabiru. However, Jabiru grew as shops, services and a town infrastructure developed and as a result it was decided to concentrate tourism here. Nevertheless, the town is zoned, with some areas focusing on tourism and in other areas tourism is excluded.

On the rivers in the park, there is recommendation that boats should not travel faster than 10 km/h. This restricts bank erosion to only a minor scale. While the larger tour boat run by the Yellow River operation tend to comply with the recommendation, smaller craft have been reported as travelling faster.

Evidence was emerging in the late 1990s that tourism is affecting wildlife in the park. A number of bird species including the red-winged parrots, sulphur-crested cockatoos and shining flycatchers were recorded as being 'highly disturbed' when tourist boats passed them. This means they flew away but it was not known whether they re-grouped after the departure of the tourists.

In Kakadu, it is possible for tourists to see rock art *in situ*. Sites are managed through the use of mainly Aboriginal guides. Guided walks are a popular part of the tourist experience in the Park. Guides act as interpreters and also in an unofficial policing role, monitoring any unintentional damage or vandalism at sites. The Park authorities also have a record of the sacred sites in the Park, but these are not generally known to tourists or any other member of the public. The Park authorities also have the power to deny access to certain sites.

In conclusion, in Kakadu National Park there has been an attempt to allow local indigenous people to retain their traditional lifestyle, promote their culture in the way they see fit, obtain employment and to allow tourists to see wildlife in a natural setting within the context of Aboriginal culture.

(Adapted Adapted from Ryan, C. (1998). Visitor management in Kakadu National Park. In *Visitor Management at World Heritage Sites* (M. Shackley, ed.), pp. 178–92. London, Butterworth-Heinemann.)

The study of Kakadu National Park indicates a number of issues concerned with managing World Heritage Site visitors going to a relatively remote area that contains important natural attractions. However, some world heritage sites are based upon built attractions and the United Kingdom's attraction Stonehenge is such a site. It is the most visited prehistoric site in the United Kingdom and is one of the world's most important archaeological remains. The location of the site amongst other factors contributes to significant visitor management problems. These are presented in the following case study.

Case study

Visitor management at Stonehenge

Stonehenge is a stone monument dating back at least 4000 years and possibly as far back as 4000 BC (hence, it may be nearly 6000 years old). What the monument was used for has caused much controversy over a period of several hundred years. This, in turn, has generated much literature, which has been a form of marketing to potential tourists. A number of theories exist:

- it is a prehistoric temple or religious site;
- it is a prehistoric calendar;
- it has astronomical significance helping to mark position of stars;

- more fancifully, it is part of an earlier landscape which helped alien beings locate themselves from space.

It seems likely that it was probably a combination of the first three above, with compelling evidence that it was a calendar. The stones at Stonehenge mark the position of the sun at different times of the year, with mid-summer's day (June 21) and mid-winter's day (December 21) given particular prominence in the stone circle.

Stonehenge is a World Heritage Site. It had approximately 800 000 paying visitors in 2001 (plus at least

200 000 who looked from the road but did not pay). It is the most visited prehistoric site in the United Kingdom and has been consistently in the top ten UK visitor attractions since 1990. In 2001, as high a proportion as 73 per cent of visitors were from overseas (41 per cent visitors from the United States) and 98 per cent visitors arrived by car/coach. Most visitors stay for only 20–30 min and about half of these do not get beyond the visitor centre/or car park so they do not actually go to the stones. It has been estimated that up to 500 visitors per hour could be accommodated in the stone circle if access was allowed, but there were up to 2000 visitors per hour in the peak summer season of July and August. The facilities include a Visitor Centre, a souvenir shop, a take away café/restaurant, toilets and a large car park.

Stonehenge is owned by English Heritage, an independent body set up in 1984 by Parliament to protect England's archaeological and architectural heritage. It is marketed globally, but particularly in the United States, by English Heritage and the British Tourist Authority. The interpretation of the Stonehenge is almost exclusively by hand-held mobile phone-sized electronic device. This operates in a number of languages and provides a basic interpretation of the site, but has the option of more details. There are numbered stopping off points with a linked commentary in English, four different European languages and also Japanese.

There are a number of key management issues. These are as follows:

- The sheer number of visitors (there is likely to be increase to over 1 million paying visitors by 2006).
- There is the problem of possible damage to the monument. To prevent damage to the stones they are normally roped off. One of the reasons given is the potential damage caused by too many hands and feet. But another reason is that alternative groups in Britain, those who claim to be Celtic priests (Druids) and others including so-called 'hippies' and travellers have tried to use Stonehenge for festivals and quasi-religious ceremonies. Recently, access has been granted for the use by 'Druids' on the summer solstice (21 June). But as most visitors cannot get this type of access they may feel cheated.
- Authenticity of the experience and related tourist satisfaction is a key factor.
- Entrance costs are relatively low at £4.40 pounds for adults and £2.20 pounds for children in 2003, and with other concessionary fares for groups and senior citizens and students which may encourage large numbers of visitors.

- The site is between two relatively major roads linking London with Southwest England. The traffic noise, particularly in summer, is disruptive to the experience of the site. In December 2002, after many years of discussion, plans were finally accepted by the Secretary of State for Transport, to build a 2 km tunnel, that will house the main A303 trunk road that passes very close to the site. This will remove the road from the sight of Stonehenge, although noise may still be intrusive.
- The Visitor Centre is currently underground and there is an under-road by-pass to get to the site. This is for safety reasons as there were road accidents in the past. The Visitor Centre was called 'a national disgrace' by the House of Commons Select Committee on Heritage in 1994. A new visitor centre is planned for a location approximately 3 km away, just to the north of Amesbury, the nearest town. This centre will provide an interpretation of the site of Stonehenge over a 10 000-year period. Visitors who wish to will then be able to walk to the actual site of the stones from this visitor centre. However, siting a visitor centre away from Stonehenge has raised authenticity issues.
- Who actually owns the site and for what purposes it should be used, is a major area of controversy. In the past 20 years or so, various groups have claimed that they should have access to the site, including 'hippies' for festivals and 'Druids' for religious purposes. As these groups have been viewed until very recently as outside the main stream of society, it has been relatively easy for the police and authorities to get the support of locals to restrict access. However, in the mid-1980s, a number of clashes between police and 'hippies/travellers' led to serious injury to persons and property. Eventually, the police had to pay compensation and access to the site has been on the agenda again. In the early part of the twenty-first century, it is roped off most of the time, although there have been occasions, such as mid-summer's day, when access has been allowed. Increasingly, private access is being allowed outside normal opening hours particularly for educational purposes. An important issue for future management relates to who is allowed regular access. Is it fair, for example, that scientists/archaeologists can gain easy access, but not those who claim they want to use the site for religious purposes?

Stonehenge is located in the county of Wiltshire in the United Kingdom. This county has more prehistoric sites than any other in the United Kingdom. Only 30 km away from Stonehenge, at Avebury, is another stone circle, albeit with a much larger diameter than that at Stonehenge. Another difference in appearance between Stonehenge and Avebury is that the site of Avebury includes a village located within the stone circle. The site has been used for continuous habitation for probably 5000 years. This means there are somewhat different visitor management issues.

The site is owned by the National Trust (NT). This is a body set up about 100 years ago (1895) as a charitable organization to preserve both natural and built heritage. It owns areas of land and many old country houses. Rather confusingly, the site is in the guardianship of English Heritage (EH) and is managed by the National Trust. Avebury, like Stonehenge, is a World Heritage Site (Photo 6).

Because of the nature of the site, with a living community inside the stone circle, there are different management issues. These are as follows:

- There is no entrance charge because a road cuts through the site and hence it would very difficult to have one.
- There is a car park (Photo 7) at some distance from the site, so visitors have to walk to the site itself, but there is no charge here either.
- There is a museum that is also a visitor centre. There is no charge for this but there are many NT and EH publications, plus souvenirs are on sale here. There is no café, takeaway or restaurant. However, there are a number of public houses and cafes in the village, mainly catering for tourists.
- The stone circle is easily accessible and the stones can be touched. However, the land is also used for sheep grazing, dog walking and the circle is cut in two by a busy, relatively dangerous road. The road passing through raises questions of authenticity/satisfaction of tourists.

Photo 6 Prehistoric Avebury is a World Heritage Site in the care of the National Trust

Photo 7 Parking at Avebury (and at nearby Stonehenge) is a major visitor management issue

- It is a living community, so there is potential conflict, in particular the feelings of locals in relation to the satisfaction of visitors.
- Periodically in the last two decades, a number of stones have been defaced by graffiti. This has led to arguments over whether there should be continued free access, or if the area should be roped off like Stonehenge.
- Unlike Stonehenge, there is no security team. This is viewed as not desirable as the site is part of a living community.

The site at Avebury, unlike that at Stonehenge, is not marketed directly either to domestic or overseas visitors. It is largely by word of mouth and a small range of publications that it is known. This is part of a deliberate visitor management strategy, which has been used in the past in an attempt to limit the number of visitors (R. Henderson, personal communication, 8 January 2003). The strategy to date appears to have been successful, as Avebury received only 54 000 visitors in 2000. However, these were visitors recorded in the Avebury museum and it is likely the number of visitors to the stone circle will have been at least three or four times this figure (R. Henderson, personal communication, 8 January 2003). Nevertheless, Avebury has not had the visitor management problems of Stonehenge and the different approach here suggests that such problems are unlikely to occur in the near future. Despite the low visitor numbers and scale of activities at Avebury, there is a cost to maintaining the site. Hence, a key question for the future remains: 'What economic contribution does the site make to its own upkeep?'

Summary

Visitor management involves regulating and often educating visitors. Controlling visitor numbers and/or modifying their behaviour are important approaches. Adapting the resources used by tourists is another approach in visitor management. Various techniques, including interpretation and the use of codes of conduct can be used in relation to these visitor management approaches.

In some locations, New Zealand is one such example, managing visitors is not straightforward. This relates to the attitudes to the use of the environment amongst domestic visitors – they expect to have free unhindered access to virtually all areas. Increasing numbers of international visitors will place greater strains on even the remote wilderness areas. At currently heavily visited attractions such as Stonehenge, in the United Kingdom, there are serious issues in relation to visitor satisfaction. Radical solutions, including preventing site access, the creation of replicas and the building of visitor centres at a distance from attractions are being seriously considered. However, as the example of Avebury in the United Kingdom suggests, a deliberate policy of not marketing a site can assist in the process of visitor management.

Student activities

1 What are the three main methods of controlling visitors suggested in the 1991 ETB report *Maintaining the Balance*? Consider each of these methods in turn and discuss how effective they would be in the longer term.

2 Why are there particular problems in relation to visitor management in New Zealand?

3 With reference to the case study of Kakadu National Park, produce a table with three columns headed as shown below and then complete the table:

Visitor Management Issue	Possible Solution	Likelihood of Success of Solution
(a)		
(b)		
(c)		
(etc)		

4 What are the main differences in terms of management issues between Stonehenge and Avebury?

5 What plans are there to improve the visitor experience at Stonehenge? What factors may affect the success of these plans?

6 What are the possible long-term problems/issues with the visitor management approach adopted at Avebury?

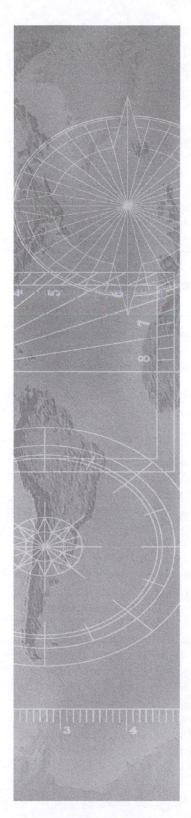

10

Managing the natural resources for tourism

Learning outcomes

At the end of this chapter you should:

- understand the nature of natural resources and semi-natural resources for tourism;
- understand how the nature of natural resources and semi-natural resources for tourism can be managed;
- have a better understanding of the term ecotourism;
- be aware of a range of different definitions of the term ecotourism;
- understand how ecotourism can operate in practice.

Introduction

As Figure 6.1 indicates (see Chapter 6), the environment has five components: the natural environment, natural resources, wildlife, the farmed environment and the built environment. The focus of this chapter is the natural environment, natural resources and wildlife and how these together act as tourist attractions. In summary, the type of tourism discussed in the chapter can be termed nature-based tourism. According to

Blamey (1995), nature-based travel is now generally referred to as eco-tourism. This chapter focuses on the relationship between tourism and nature, discusses the concept of ecotourism and considers a number of management issues in relation to ecotourism.

Key perspectives

The natural environment and tourism are inextricably linked. In the last decade of the twentieth century, the environment was increasingly viewed as the key resource for tourism. Therefore, ensuring that the environment is not over exploited, suffers irreversible damage or becomes excessively polluted as a result of tourism, will be major tasks for tourism planners and managers in the twenty-first century. However, management of the environment, is not just about maintaining the status quo, or not letting the environment decline. In fact, as Middleton and Hawkins (1998) reported, many consumers are demanding a better quality environment for their tourism experiences.

In the fairly recent past, the aims of environmental conservation and tourism development were viewed as incompatible (Coccossis, 1996). To benefit the environment and in turn provide higher quality tourism experiences, it would seem vital that the relationship between tourism and the environment should be improved.

Swarbrooke (1999) made a number of suggestions on ways to improve the relationship between tourism and the environment. He argued that it is vital to take a holistic view of the environment. He indicated that it is necessary to see the environment as a complex web of inter-relationships that are best expressed through the concept of the ecosystem. Such a view is also supported by Fennell (1999), Hall (2000b), and Holden (2000).

A way to avoid repeated damage to the environment is to raise awareness amongst tourists and also the tourism industry. However, as has been argued in Chapter 7 there is also a need to regulate, through land-use planning and building controls, to avoid or reduce some types of negative environmental impact. However, it is necessary to keep a sense of proportion, as some negative environmental impacts of tourism are not that serious and can be remedied relatively easily. Nevertheless, it has been argued there should be greater acceptance that tourism does damage the environment and that it costs money to ameliorate or solve the problems (Hall, 2000b; Holden, 2000). Hence, it may be sensible to argue that holidays should have a built in charge to the tourist, which is used to remedy the damage they have caused. Swarbrooke (1999) suggested that good practice does indeed exist and this should be promoted to tourism developers. In the long term, he says, it is important to maintain a balance between conserving the environment and its development for tourism purposes, although this may not be a simple, straightforward task.

The following case study of the Great Barrier Reef provides an indication of the problematic relationship between tourism and the environment and in particular, it also presents some of the management approaches in response to the environmental impacts of tourism.

Case study

The Great Barrier Reef, Australia

The Great Barrier Reef is made up of some 600 islands, 300 cay (reef islands) and almost 3000 submerged reefs. It is one of the largest coral reefs in the world. It is home to 15 000 species of fish, 400 sponges, 4000 molluscs and it is made up of 350 different types of coral. Because of its location at a distance offshore on the North East coast of Queensland, Australia it has remained relatively undeveloped in terms of tourism.

However, in the last quarter (and particularly the last decade) of the twentieth century tourism began to expand on the Reef. Between 1975 and 1990, charter boats numbers grew from 135 to 300 and registered speed boats in the area increased from 15 000 to 24 000 in this period. In 1982, large high-speed catamarans were introduced and these offered much easier access to the reef. In the period 1982–92 there was a 35-fold increase in visitors and they were going to four times as many sites on the reef by the end of this period. In 1988 over 900 000 tourist visited the area, but this had risen to just under 2 million by 1996.

The standard trip to the reef did not change very much in the last 20 years of the twentieth century. Most visitors take a day trip by large catamaran and this is moored to a pontoon anchored close to the ridge. Some visitors travel to islands that are part of the reef. In addition to the overall growth there has been a substantial increase in international visitors. In the late 1990s, the Japanese formed the largest single international group of visitors, with increasing numbers from Taiwan, Hong Kong, and Singapore. The chief activity on the reef is scuba diving and snorkelling. Sight-seeing from semi-submersible and glass-bottomed vessels is also popular.

By the late 1990s, there was evidence of increasing environmental impacts. These include physical destruction of reefs by anchors and divers' feet and hands. Divers can even cause damage to the coral merely by resting on it, as it is so sensitive. There has been localized water pollution from sewage and boat fuel. Some divers feed and/or touch fish. This seems an innocuous form of activity but can lead to the modification of fish behaviour. Many of the catamaran operator's crew also feed the fish from the back of the boat as part of the tourist experience. This may also have an impact on the behaviour of the fish, as they become accustomed to being fed at particularly times in specific places to entertain visitors. The removal of coral and fish specimens has also been reported.

The Great Barrier Reef Marine Park was set up in 1975, partly in response to growing environmental problems, but also on an attempt to provide a framework to deal with the effects of increasing number of tourists. The main strategy within the Park management is a zoning system. There are three main categories in this zoning system:

(a) a general use zone (about 80 per cent of the park in the late 1990s) where most activities are permitted, provided they are ecologically sustainable.
(b) National Park zones that allow only activities that do not remove living resources.
(c) Preservation Zones which permit only scientific research.

Tourism is permitted in two of the zones but not the Preservation Zone. However permits are required in both the General Use and National Park Zones. Factors considered in the issuing of permits are: the size, extent, and location of usage, access conditions, likely effects on the environment in general and ecosystems in particular and likely effects upon resources and their conservation. In relation to any large-scale development, proponents are encouraged to produce Environmental Impact Assessments and follow this with Environmental Impact Statements as a routine part of the development process. Tourists are targeted via a number of educational strategies including pictorial symbols on the reef, leaflets, guides and codes of conduct. These are backed up with local controls and prohibitions depending on particular circumstances. Combined together, these are an attempt to encourage responsible behaviour to conserve the marine environment.

(Adapted from Williams, S. (1998). *Tourism Geography*. London, Routledge; Moscardo, G., Woods, B. and Pearce, P. (1997). Evaluating the effectiveness of pictorial symbols in reef visitor education. CRC Reef Research Centre Technical Report No. 15, Townsville, Australia.)

An example of a potentially beneficial relationship between tourism and the natural environment is that of ecotourism. The term ecotourism has emerged in the last 10–15 years and, during the last decade of the twentieth century, this form of tourism grew very rapidly. Unfortunately, there is little agreement on what, precisely, it is. It has emerged as an alternative (to mass tourism) form of tourism (Mowforth, 1992). However, terms such as 'responsible' and 'sustainable' have also been linked closely with the term ecotourism (Cater, 1994).

What is clear, however, is that ecotourism is a form of nature-based tourism (Boo, 1990). The concept of ecotourism appears to have emerged from the work of the Mexican researcher Ceballos-Lascurain in 1987. He indicated that nature tourism could be defined as:

> Tourism that consists in travelling to relatively undisturbed or uncontaminated natural areas with the specific objectives of studying, admiring and enjoying the scenery and its wild plants and animals, as well as any existing (both past and present) cultural manifestations.
>
> (Ceballos-Lascurain, cited in Boo, 1990)

Ceballos-Lascurain also used the term 'ecological tourist' (this was probably the first time the term had been used) and said such a person was interested in a scientific, aesthetic or philosophical approach to travel. The concept of ecotourism developed and changed in the last decade of the twentieth century, as the following statements, which are set out in chronological order, indicate:

- A form of tourism inspired primarily by the natural history of an area, including its indigenous cultures. The ecotourist visits relatively undeveloped areas in the spirit of appreciation, participation and sensitivity. The ecotourist practises a non-consumptive use of wildlife and natural resources. (Ziffer, 1989, p. 60).
- Ecotourism is travel to relatively undisturbed natural areas for study, enjoyment or volunteer assistance. It is travel that concerns itself with the flora, fauna, geology and ecosystems of an area, as well as the people (caretakers) who live nearby, their needs, their culture and their relationships to the land. It is envisioned as a tool for both conservation and sustainable development – especially in areas where local people are asked to forego the consumptive use of resources for others. (Wallace and Pierce, 1996).
- Ecotourism is low-impact nature tourism which contributes to the maintenance of species and habitats either directly through a contribution to conservation and/or indirectly by providing revenue to the local community sufficient for local people to value and therefore protect, their wildlife heritage (Goodwin, 1996, p. 228).
- Ecotourism is a sustainable form of natural resource based tourism that focuses primarily on experiencing and learning about nature, and which is ethically managed to be low-impact, non-consumptive and locally oriented (control, benefits and scale). It typically occurs in natural areas and should contribute to the conservation or preservation of such areas (Fennell, 1999, p. 43).

As these four definitions indicate, ecotourism is an alternative form of tourism. Figure 10.1 is an attempt to indicate how ecotourism is related to other alternative forms of tourism.

(a)	1st level		Alternative		
	2nd level	Eco-/Nature	Cultural	Adventure	Specialist
	3rd level	Safari	Anthro-	Risk	Academic
		Wilderness	Archeo-	Safari	Agro-designer
		Wildlife	Contact	Sport	Scientific
			Cottage	Wilderness	
			Ethnic		
(b)	1st level		Alternative		
	2nd level	Eco-/Nature	Cultural	Adventure	Specialist
	3rd level	Safari	Anthro-	Risk	Academic
		Wilderness	Archeo-	Safari	Agro-designer
		Wildlife	Contact	Sport	Scientific
			Cottage	Wilderness	Solidarity
			Ethnic		
(c)	1st level		Eco-/alternative		
	2nd level	Nature	Cultural	Adventure	Specialist
	3rd level	Safari	Anthro-	Risk	Academic
		Wilderness	Archeo-	Safari	Agro-designer
		Wildlife	Contact	Sport	Scientific
			Cottage	Wilderness	Solidarity
			Ethnic		

Figure 10.1
Hierarchies of terms relating
to ecotourism
(*Source*: Mowforth, 1992.)

In their attempt to define ecotourism, Wearing and Neil (1999) discussed what can be considered as essential travel aspects of this form of tourism. The travel essentials they considered are summarized below:

- Ecotourism encourages an understanding of the impacts of tourism
- Ecotourism ensures a fair distribution of benefits and costs.
- Ecotourism generates local employment, both directly in the tourism sector and in various support and resource management sectors.
- Ecotourism stimulates profitable domestic industries – hotels and other lodging facilities, restaurants, transportation systems, handicrafts and guide services.
- Ecotourism generates foreign exchange and injects capital and new money into the local economy.
- Ecotourism diversifies the local economy, particularly in rural areas.
- Ecotourism seeks decision-making among all segments of the society including local populations, so that tourism and other resource users can co-exist.
- Ecotourism incorporates planning and zoning, which ensure tourism development appropriate to the carrying capacity of the ecosystem.
- Ecotourism stimulates improvements to local transportation, communications and other community infrastructures.
- Ecotourism creates recreational facilities which can be used by local communities as well as domestic and international visitors.
- Ecotourism encourages and helps pay for preservation of archaeological sites, and historic buildings and districts.

Feature	The rough ecotourist	The smooth ecotourist	The specialist ecotourist
Age	Young to middle aged	Middle-aged to old	Young to old
Travelling	Individually or in small groups	In groups	Individually
Organization	Independent	Tour-operated	Independent + specialist tours
Budget	low: cheap hotel/ b&b; local/fast food; uses buses	High: 3–5 star hotels; luxury cafes; uses taxis	Mid–high : cheap– 3 star hotels; mid– lux. cafes; as necessary
Type of tourism	Sport and adventure	Nature and safari	Scientific investigation/ hobby pursuit

Figure 10. 2
A classification of ecotourists (*Source*: Mowforth, 1992.)

● Ecotourism monitors, assesses and manages the impacts of tourism, develops reliable methods of environmental accountability and counters any negative effect.

Mowforth (1992) synthesized a number of statements on ecotourism and produced a classification of ecotourists. This is shown in Figure 10.2.

There is a real danger that the term ecotourism can be misused or abused. If ecotourism is perceived by potential tourists as a more desirable form of tourism, then using the term as a marketing ploy has significant advantages for tour operators and other sectors of the tourism industry. This is compounded by the lack of agreement on the meaning of ecotourism. Therefore, it is possible for unscrupulous operators to use the label of ecotourism to draw in potential customers, increase the price of the holiday and in turn raise their profits while providing an experience which does nothing for environmental or cultural conservation (see Mason and Mowforth, 1996; Fennell, 1999). Research into the nature of ecotourism operators in New Zealand has been conducted by Bonzon-Liu (1999) in an attempt to reveal if companies practised what they preached. The results from this research are presented in the case study below.

Case study

Ecotourism operators in New Zealand

Bonzon-Liu (1999) conducted a survey of eco-tourism operators in New Zealand. The response rate was somewhat over half the known operators at the time of the survey. The study investigated the particular practices of the operators in relation to sustainability issues. Bonzon-Liu was particularly interested to discover which practices were regarded as sustainable by operators and were adopted by them and which activities were regarded as unsustainable. Bonzon-Liu used open-ended questions and then created categories from her data. The following were found to be the major response categories in relation to sustainability and each includes further comment/examples from the data:

Ethical matters. Operators should publicly display codes of conduct and guidelines, they should indicate that they put the environment before profit, they should provide leadership in conservation efforts, they need to promote conservation, and put into practice their sustainable philosophy.

Education. Enhancing visitor knowledge, providing written and verbal information, using knowledgeable and competent interpretation staff and guides are key components of education within ecotourism. The education component has a strong conservation message, and clients should leave with a greater concern for environmental matters.

Focus on nature. Interpreting the environment is at the centre of ecotours. However, ecotourism neither requires consumptive activities such as fishing, nor is it necessarily environmental activity such as skiing, rock climbing or adventure tourism. Ecotourism involves appreciating the environment in the context of the environment, but does not necessarily involve intensive use of it.

Minimising impacts. Ecotourism should minimize all forms of tourism impact. This can be achieved through limiting group size, leaving wildlife alone, keeping noise level to a minimum, minimising the use of fuel, minimising visual impacts, restricting over-development, attempting to prevent litter and other forms of pollution.

Proactive measures. Ecotourism is not just about restricting activities but promoting certain types of behaviour/activities. Ecotours should: contribute financially to protection and conservation of the environment, make use of environmentally friendly products, recycle, re-use and reduce waste, actively involve participants in conservation projects, be actively involved in research and act as an advocate for the environment.

Bonzon-Liu asked about unsustainable practices and classified the responses she received under three headings:

Ethical matters. A short-term focus, profit put before environmental concern, the lack of codes of conduct, growth orientated rather than enhancement orientated.

Environmental impacts. Damage to flora and fauna, overcrowding, poor waste disposal disturbance to wildlife habitats, the use of vehicles which create too much noise and/or damage the environment.

Organizational problems. Lack of an adequate infrastructure for tourism, poor communication channels, poor education provision, lack of fees gathered to assist in maintenance of tracks and huts, failure to recognise significance of codes of conduct, poor planning and management of natural areas, uncontrolled and rapid growth of tourism.

(Adapted from Bonzon-Liu, B. (1999). *An Accreditation Scheme for Ecotourism in New Zealand.* Masters Dissertation, Victoria University, Wellington, (unpublished).)

Summary

Natural resources include the natural environment and wildlife. Nature-based tourism has become very important in the last ten or so years. A particular type of nature based tourism that emerged in the late 1980s was ecotourism. Initially concerned primarily with the environment, ecotourism had changed by the end of the twentieth century to include cultural factors. Education is viewed as a key component of ecotourism and increasingly the host community is seen as having an important role to play. However, it is possible that ecotourism may tend towards mass tourism in terms of its impacts. Ecotourism may also be used as a convenient label, which may in fact lead to the promotion of more tourism. In this way, it can been argued that ecotourism may also contribute more to a feeling of satisfaction amongst participants in the activity than conservation of the environment.

Student activities

1 What are the visitor attractions of the Great Barrier Reef? What issues are there in relation to the planning and management of tourism to the Great Barrier Reef?

2 List the key components of ecotourism.

3 Summarize how the concept of ecotourism developed and changed during the 1980s and 1990s. How would you summarize the concept of ecotourism today? What is different about the concept of ecotourism today compared with the original definition from the 1980s?

4 Why do some tourists view ecotourism as a preferable option to mass tourism?

5 What reasons might tour operators give for their involvement in ecotourism?

6 Study the case study of New Zealand ecotourism operators. How does ecotourism differ from more conventional tourism according to the information in the study?

Tourism planning and management and the host community

Learning objectives

At the end of this chapter you should:

- understand the role that host communities have in tourism planning and management;
- be aware of obstacles that impede the involvement of host communities in tourism development;
- be aware of opportunities for local participation in community tourism development;
- be aware of the attitudes of members of host communities to proposed tourism development.

Introduction

Increasingly, the host community is being recognised as a major player in decision-making about tourism management and the future direction of tourism. However, as has been previously stated, the term host community is not necessarily appropriate as tourists are not always welcome in a destination and a more appropriate term could be local community, resident community or destination community. However, the term is employed below as it is now commonly used in tourism literature.

Key perspectives

It is very important to note that as with tourists, the host community is heterogeneous not homogenous and hence there is no such thing as *a* host community. In addition to obvious variations in gender and age, any host community is likely to be a mixture of individuals and groups with varied political persuasions and attitudes to tourism, and will include those with a vested interest in tourism.

This heterogeneity is not always recognized, particularly by tourists. Tourists, particularly from wealthy, Developed countries, are often attracted by the products of a host community in a developing country, such as arts and craft as well as less tangible factors, including music and dance. Such manifestations may be the product of what is perceived as the 'traditional community' and tourists may be far less interested in other aspects of a heterogeneous community and also individual members of the community who are not viewed as being within the realm of the 'traditional'. Nevertheless, making direct contact with members of a particular community and staying with them can also be a major attraction for some tourists. However, as the earlier discussions have indicated, there are a number of problems that may result from the contact between tourists and members of host communities, particularly in terms of the demonstration effect, erosion of host community values and possible loss of cultural identity.

Partly as result of the problems that result from contact between such international tourists and communities in Developing countries, and in an attempt to ensure greater benefits to host communities, there has been a focus, recently, on community participation in tourism planning and development. As Mowforth and Munt (1998) argued, one of the criteria often agreed as essential to achieving sustainability in any new tourism scheme, is the participation of local people. However, until recently, most tourism development lacked the direct involvement of local people (Mowforth and Munt, 1998). As Pretty (1995, p. 4) stated in relation to development projects in general:

> The terms 'people participation' and 'popular participation' are now part of the normal language of development agencies.

However, as Pretty claimed, participation can mean different things to different people. Pretty created a typology of participation and this is shown in Figure 11.1. Pretty also included a critique of each form of participation. Figure 11.1 shows that in some forms of participation, such as 'manipulative participation', actual power lies with groups beyond the local community. In fact, in this typology, it is only under the headings of 'interactive participation' and 'self-mobilization' that local peoples are actively involved in decision-making.

Involving local communities in decision-making about development projects does not necessarily ensure their success (Mowforth and Munt, 1998). Holden (2000) cited two examples in which local participation in decision making led to the choice of a tourism project with significantly more damaging environmental effects than some other rejected possibilities. As Mowforth and Munt suggested, criticism of the failure of local

Typology	Characteristic of each type
1 Manipulative participation	Participation is simply a pretence: 'peoples' representatives on official boards, but they are unelected and have no power
2 Passive participation	People participate by being told what has been decided or has already happened: involves unilateral announcements by project management without any listening to people's responses: information shared belongs only to external professionals
3 Participation by consultation	People participate by being consulted or by answering questions: external agents define problems and information-gathering processes, and so control analysis: process does not concede any share in decision-making: professionals under no obligation to account for people's views
4 Participation for material incentives	People participate by contributing resources (e.g.labour) in return for food, cash or other material incentive: farmers may provide fields and labour but are not involved in testing or the process of learning: this is commonly called participation, yet people have no stake in prolonging technologies or practices when the incentives end
5 Functional participation	Participation seen by external agencies as a means to achieve project goals, especially reduced costs: people may participate by forming groups to meet project objectives. Involvement may be interactive and involve shared decision-making, but tends to arise only after major decisions have already been made by external agents; at worst, local people may still only be co-opted to serve external goals
6 Interactive participation	People participate in joint analysis, development of action plans and strengthening of local institutions: participation is seen as a right, not just the means to achieve project goals; the process involves interdisciplinary methodologies that seek multiple perspectives and use systematic and structured learning processes. As groups take control of local decisions and determine how available resources are used, so they have a stake in maintaining structures and practices
7 Self-mobilisation	People participate by taking initiatives independently of external institutions to change systems: they develop contacts with external institutions for resources and technical advice they need, but retain control over resource use; self-mobilization can spread if governments and NGOs provide an enabling framework of support. Self-mobilization may or may not challenge existing distributions of wealth and power

Figure 11.1 Pretty's typology of participation (*Source*: Pretty, 1995.)

people to make appropriate decisions about their future, may come from those with a vested interest in a project such as government officials or even development agencies. Nevertheless, as Middleton and Hawkins (1998) suggested, there is little evidence that effective community-led tourism has been implemented. They argued that even in Canada, where Murphy (1985) suggested affluent local communities are better placed than many others in the world, this has not happened. Middleton and Hawkins suggested that there are those who will argue that community-led planning has never worked because it has never really been tried. They reject this and argued that the main reason that community-led planning has failed is due to the fact *a community* does not really exist and hence obtaining a consensual view on tourism development is virtually impossible.

As Murphy (1985) indicated, it is relatively easy for a community to unite in opposition to a tourism development. However, it is far more difficult for a community to:

> Conceptualise, agree and then achieve its own long-run tourism future.
>
> (Middleton and Hawkins, 1998, p.127)

Within the context of New South Wales, Australia, Jenkins (1993) indicated why this is a difficult process. He suggested that there are seven impediments to local participation in tourism planning. In summary, these are as follows:

- The public generally has difficulty in understanding complex and technical planning issues.
- The public does not necessarily understand how the planning process operates or how decisions are made.
- The problem of attaining and maintaining the representation of all views in the decision-making process.
- Apathy amongst some, if not a majority, of citizens.
- The increased cost in relation to staff time and money.
- The fact that decision-making takes much longer as result of community participation.
- The overall efficiency (particularly in terms of time/money and the smooth running) of the decision-making process is adversely affected.

The following case study indicates some of the issues raised by Jenkins (1993). The case study is based upon research that was conducted prior to the emergence of substantial tourism activity and is used to indicate how residents of an area view the potential impact of tourism on their community. The case study focuses on a relatively remote rural area in the North Island of New Zealand. Here, in the mid-1990s, there was little evidence of organized tourism, and hence it was possible to provide some form of benchmark of local residents' attitudes to the likely effects of a new tourism development.

Case study

Residents attitudes to tourism development in the Pohangina Valley, New Zealand

The Pohangina Valley (photo 8) is a North Island New Zealand rural backwater, which has generally remained off the beaten track. The location could be described in tourism marketing language as 'undiscovered and unspoilt'. The area, originally native bush, was settled by Europeans from the late nineteenth century onwards. A number of small settlements (each with only dozens rather than hundreds of people) grew up and the region reached its peak population in the 1930s and then declined until the early 1980s.

The development, which was the focus of the field research, caused much local interest and controversy. In July 1996, a proposal to develop an old

Photo 8 The isolated Pohangina Valley, New Zealand, setting for the controversial planned tourism development

Photo 9 The café/bar in the Pohangina Valley which was the focus of much controversy prior to development in 1997

school house in the township of Pohangina was put forward. After some opposition to the use of a local community facility for a private enterprise, the proposal was withdrawn. However, community sentiment had been disturbed. A new proposal was submitted in January 1997. This involved the establishment of a cafe/bar using an existing private house at a distance of 6 km from the Pohangina township. However, this proposal led to death threats for some of the intended developers, a group of eight local individuals. This, in turn, contributed to much media interest, particularly from the local evening paper which for several days ran front page stories about the proposal and related issues. The proposal was submitted to the local district council and after a 1-month objection period had elapsed it was granted planning permission. The questionnaire survey, which was the main research instrument, was distributed in the week following the granting of planning permission. The response rate of 47 per cent provided a demographically representative sample according to local council staff. The results of the survey were as follows:

- As tourism was at such an early stage, residents could not even be considered to be at the euphoria stage of Doxey's (1975) Irridex theory. Generally, residents were in favour of the proposed development, but a significant minority (approximately one fourth) were opposed to it. The study indicated that this community, like many others, is made up of groups and individuals with mixed views in relation to the perceived impacts of tourism. In other words, the community was heterogeneous not homogeneous in its views on tourism.

- Respondents provided their views on the development based on perceived impacts. They tended to view these impacts from their own perspective, without necessarily any reference to tourism, which is probably not surprising given the general lack of tourism development in the area. Residents suggested perceived positive impacts would be the establishment of a meeting place, provision of a place close to home to obtain a meal and drink and the related reduction in travelling time to such locations. Some responses made reference to tourism when indicating the proposed development would create jobs, attract other businesses and promote the area for tourism. The negative impacts of the development were that it would contribute to more drunken driving, generally cause traffic problems and create more noise.

- There was some indication of gender differences in response to a number of survey questions. Women tended to be more opposed to the establishment of the café/bar (photo 9) and gave as reasons such concerns as increases in drunkenness and issues of road safety. Men were more in favour of the development. In relation to tourism dimensions, a number of women who supported the development gave consideration to impacts in a rather different way from the men who supported it. The women indicated the proposal would create tourism-related jobs and business opportunities more than the men. Such differences may be a product of the different world-views of the male and female respondents to the survey (see Pearce, Moscardo and Ross, 1996).

- The survey revealed a high degree of community attachment to the area. However, the length of residency did not appear to affect the strength of views held. The research supports the findings of McCool and Martin (1994) and Williams et al. (1992) that both 'old-timers' and new comers can have strong attachments to an environment and their views are more 'place dependent' than based on social networks.
- The research suggested as has been found by several other studies that the smaller the community the more visible the tourism development and the stronger the views held.

- The research provided a benchmark of community views as it took place prior to any significant tourism development and hence should be helpful in the planning process.
- The study suggested that the large-scale studies of tourism impacts and attitudes to tourism conducted in New Zealand in the last two decades of the twentieth century, mainly by the New Zealand Tourist Board, which produced largely positive attitudes to tourism, should be read with particular care and be subjected to more critical interpretation.

(Adapted from Mason, P. and Cheyne, J. (2000). Resident attitudes to tourism development. *Annals of Tourism Research*, **27** (2), 391–412.)

Despite the mixed views of respondents in the Pohangina study, there is some evidence to suggest that local communities can be actively involved in tourism development and achieve benefits. One of the longest running tourism projects which has actively involved the local community is in Lower Casamance, Senegal, West Africa (De Kadt, 1979, 1988). The original aim of the project was to create a more meaningful exchange between local people and tourists than was then being experienced along the Senegalese coast. Here, there were large hotel resorts built with foreign capital, and the resorts were protected by security guards and high walls. By the early 1990s, thirteen tourist camps had been built with loans from l'Agence de Co-operation Culturelle et Technique (Gningue, 1993). The tourist accommodation is simple lodges, built in local architectural styles with local materials by local people. The number of guests is limited to a maximum of forty at any one time in any lodge. Lodges have only been constructed in villages with over 1000 inhabitants. Tourists eat local food cooked using local recipes. Public expenditure of the revenue gained from tourism is controlled by village cooperatives. The scheme has been viewed as a success as it has aided development and social stability, improved health care and education facilities, and of great importance provided jobs for the young which has discouraged them from migrating to the larger towns in search of work (Gningue, 1993).

Within the context of nature-based tourism, Drake (1991) suggested a model of local participation in tourism development. Drake argued that local participation referred to the ability of local communities to influence the outcomes of development projects that had an impact upon them. Drake created a nine-phase model, which is presented in Figure 11.2.

There is more chance of community development projects being accepted by local people if it is realized that there are different groups in a community with different views (Fennel, 1999). As Jurowski (1996) suggested, resident's individual values need to be recognized, and based on the different values, he identified a number of unique groups in a community.

Jurowski was particularly interested in trying to get tourism developers to recognize that there are a variety of individual values in a community and tourism developers will only be successful in developing a

- Phase 1: Determine the role of local participation in the Project. This includes an assessment of how local people can help
- Phase 2: Choose research team. The team should include a broad multi-disciplinary approach
- Phase 3: Conduct preliminary studies. The political economic and social conditions of the community should be studied, via documents and surveys. The following should be identified: needs, local leaders, community commitment to the project, media involvement/interest, traditional uses of land, role of women, type of people interested in the project and why, likely managers and financiers of project, land ownership and cultural values
- Phase 4: Determine the level of local involvement. This will be somewhere along a continuum from low to high intensity
- Phase 5: Determine an appropriate participation mechanism. This is linked to the intensity of involvement, the nature of existing institutions and characteristics of local people. It is likely to involve consultation and sharing
- Phase 6: Initiate dialogue and educational efforts. The use of the press is important in this phase as a means by which to build consensus through public awareness. Key community representatives can be used in this process. The team should explain the goals and objectives of the project, how the project will affect the community, the values of the area, and history of threats and the benefits of the project. Workshops or public meetings could be organized to identify strengths and weaknesses of the project
- Phase 7: Collective decision-making. This is a critical stage that synthesizes all research and information from the local population. The project team present the findings of their research to the community, together with an action plan. Community members are asked to react to the plan, with the possible end result being a forum through which the team and local people negotiate to reach a final consensus based on the impact of the project
- Phase 8: Development of an action plan and implementation scheme. In this phase, the team and community develop an action plan for implementing solutions to identified problems. They may develop a variety of positions to be occupied by local people including gift shops, research positions, park management positions and private outfitting companies for the local people. This local action plan must then be integrated into the broader master plan of the project
- Phase 9: Monitoring and evaluation. Monitoring and evaluation, although often neglected, should occur frequently and over the long term. The key to evaluation is to discover whether goals and objectives set out early in the project's life-cycle have been accomplished or not

Figure 11.2 Local participation in nature-based tourism: Drake's (1991) nine-phase model

project if they are aware of this and act accordingly. Jurowski noted three major groups and the first he termed 'attached residents'. These were either long-term residents or older community members who loved the community because of its social and physical benefits. They also liked to have control over the form and function of the community. Jurowski suggested that tourism planners can gain the support of this group in a community if they emphasize heritage themes, indicate that the project has social and ecological benefits to the community and establish a focal point and common theme for a tourism project. The second type of community members that were identified by Jurowski are 'resource users'. Such people are typically recreationists. They are ambivalent about the economic benefits of a tourism development. Developers can gain their support by providing opportunities for their interests, supporting schemes that provide skill development for young people in the community, protecting 'their sites' for participation and allocating some tourism funds to support facilities and service these people want. Jurowski's third group he termed 'environmentalists'. He acknowledged that this group will tend to see negative impacts of any development. Jurowski suggested that developers should however pay specially heed to this group. Hence, developers should provide information on the following: how the project will protect the environment; how to build in ecological education programmes; how to actively involve environmentalists in the development; and how to inspire community members to develop education programmes for tourists.

According to Fennel (1999), leadership is a key principle in the process of community development. However, as Mabey (1994) suggested, this is not 'old style' leadership but an approach that requires power to be devolved to others in the community and will involve collaboration and partnerships. In this situation, the leadership is not held constantly by one individual or a small group, but passes between different community members and these people will play the role of leader or follower according to circumstances. Fennel (1999) stated that this will occur if there is a shared common purpose and under these conditions, community members will be empowered. He argued that this is the situation in which community members will be 'holding the will, resources and opportunity to make decisions within the community' (Fennel, 1999, p. 221). Under such conditions, Fennell asserted, it will be possible for people both internal and external to a community to provide assistance, while local people will actually be able to shape and control the pace of tourism development.

Summary

Until approximately 15 years ago, little regard was paid to the views of host communities in relation to tourism development. By the end of the twentieth century, host communities were viewed as having an increasingly important role in tourism planning and management. There are however a number of obstacles to the involvement of host communities in tourism planning and management. In addition to a community's possible lack of understanding of the complexity of the planning process, there is the problem of obtaining the representation of a range of views. Also, involving the community takes time and thus is costly and may adversely affect the overall efficiency of the planning process. Nevertheless, if tourism is to be a more sustainable activity it would seem essential to involve host communities in planning and management processes.

Student activities

1 Why have local communities not been actively involved in tourism planning and management until comparatively recently?

2 Apply the Drake nine-phase model (Figure 11.2) to the case study of the Pohangina Valley, New Zealand. Which phases of the model appear to have been employed and which not applied in the project?

3 Identify a tourism project in your local area or one elsewhere of which you are aware. Apply the Drake nine-phase model to this project and indicate which phases of the model appear to have been employed and which not applied in the project. Explain why the model applies or does not apply as the case may be.

Tourism planning and management and the tourism industry

Learning objectives

At the end of this chapter you should:

- understand the role of the tourism industry in tourism planning and management;
- understand the role tour operators play in improving tourism management;
- understand the problems of and potential for tourism organiz-ations to develop more sustainable forms of tourism.

Introduction

As suggested in earlier chapters, the tourism industry is made up of a great variety of both private and public sector organizations and businesses. For example, there are travel agents, tour opera-tors, carriers such as airlines and rail companies, as well as various types of accommodation including hotels, restaurants and other food providers, the latter being found largely in the destination area. The destination zone also has entertainment providers as well as visitor attractions, transport providers, tourist information offices and other infrastructure organizations that support tourism. Here in the destination are also located Tourist Information Centres, which are public sector organizations. This chapter provides a case study of the attitudes of representatives of a number of sectors of the UK outbound tourism industry and also focuses on tour operators and accommodation providers.

Key perspectives

As stated above, there is no clearly definable 'tourism industry'. As a result, one of the key problems that has restricted the involvement of the 'industry' in tourism management and in the development of more responsible forms of tourism, is that tourism businesses in specific sectors of the industry have not seen this as their responsibility. In fact, the 'industry' has tended to view government as being responsible for any regulations relating to tourism. Also, particular tourism businesses while operating in a free market situation have shown little inclination to impose upon themselves, or wish to have imposed on them, anything they perceive as preventing them from having a competitive edge over other tourism businesses. Many businesses therefore perceive that regulation for environmental or social protection will interfere with business performance (Forsyth, 1995).

Either as a result of the tourism industry not seeing it as an industry responsibility, or because of the perception that the industry does not care about the environment in which it operates, but only its profits, the industry is often viewed as causing significant negative impacts.

Tour operators are a key element in the tourism system but are an example of an industry sector that has a reputation for causing negative impacts and creating problems. Mass market operators tend to have only low profit margins per customer so need to ensure there are large volumes of tourists. Mass market tour operators usually send tourists to the 'honey pots' (the more popular destinations). As Middleton and Hawkins (1998) argued, mass package tourism has been traditionally 'supply side' or 'product-led' tourism. Holidays developed under such conditions in the past were done so on an understanding of customer needs, but with virtually no regard for the so-called externalities (i.e. the impacts of the activity).

Large-scale operators in the United Kingdom, for example, work according to three basic concepts: maximum aircraft loads, lowest possible prices and perceived advantage of market share (Middleton and Hawkins, 1998). This approach could be summarized as 'pile' em high and sell 'em cheap', in other words, financial viability of the operator lies in selling more holidays. Generally, tour operators working under these conditions have paid little regard to the environment of the destination. In fact, the environment frequently suffered as result of the activities of these operators. If, at one point in time, they sent large numbers of tourists to particular destinations, then, the only way they could maintain or possibly increase their profits at a future point was to send even more, was the prevailing view.

However, as discussed in the first part of this book, destination areas have finite resources and compounding the problem of too many tourists is that large tour operators also have the reputation for not staying loyal to specific destinations. Hence, when a resort becomes no longer popular (which may be the direct result of too many tourists visiting in the past), the tour operator shifts allegiance to other locations. Such tour operators have also tended to use their own employees as guides rather than hire local staff. Not only does this deprive the locals of jobs, but also the knowledge of the foreign employees is likely to be far less than that of the locals. Therefore, tourists may often be misinformed about the places they are visiting. Large tour operators also negotiate contracts with local suppliers to keep cost low for the tourists, but this gives little economic return for the locals.

There are a number of ways in which tour operators can assist in the better management of tourism, particularly at destinations. Swarbrooke (1999) suggested what he termed a three-pronged strategy to help tour operators play a more effective role in the development of more sustainable forms of tourism. He suggested the following: local communities should develop their own tour operation enterprises; destinations should try to ensure that as much as possible of their inbound tourism be handled by small specialist operators; and mass market operators should be encouraged to act more responsibly.

Travel agents can also make significant contributions to better planned and managed tourism. In Australia, a prominent body is the Australian Federation of Travel Agents (AFTA). This body, formed in 1957, represents the distribution agents of Australia. In the late 1990s it had almost 2000 members, comprising 1500 travel agencies and almost 500 allied members. This organization has emphasized professionalism amongst travel agents. Professionalism here refers to effective management, ethical behaviour and fair trading (Pearce et al., 1998). AFTA has a code of conduct that is intended to bind all its members and protect the interests of the consumer. As Pearce et al. (1998) indicated, this code is a long-standing initiative in the world of travel. Its details are as follows:

- *Accuracy*: AFTA members will be factual and accurate in the information they provide and will not use deceptive practices.
- *Affiliation*: AFTA members will not falsely represent a person's affiliation with their firm.
- *Compliance*: AFTA members will abide by all federal, state and local laws and regulations.
- *Confidentiality*: AFTA members will treat all client transactions in confidence.
- *Conflict of interest*: AFTA members will not allow any preferred relationship with a supplier to interfere with interests of their clients.
- *Consumer protection*: AFTA members will use every effort to protect their clients against all attempts at fraud, misrepresentation or unethical practices
- *Cooperation*: AFTA members will cooperate with any inquiry conducted by AFTA.
- *Delivery*: AFTA members delivering tours will provide all components as stated in their brochure, or written confirmation, or provide alternative services if required.
- *Disclosure*: AFTA members will provide details about terms and conditions of travel service including cancellation fees, before accepting payment for bookings.
- *Notice*: AFTA members will promptly notify clients of any changes in price itinerary of service provided.
- *Qualifications and professionalism*: AFTA members must employ staff with appropriate qualifications and are committed to continuing professional development.

In the last decade of the twentieth century, there was some evidence that tourism businesses were starting to manage their operations with the concept of sustainability in mind. For example, Forsyth (1995) conducted research into the practices of tourism enterprises in Britain, and their attitudes to sustainable tourism. Forsyth's sample comprised sixty-nine tourism businesses including tour operators, travel agents, hotel chains, airlines, tourism associations, national tourism offices, consultancies and also included one sea cruise operator. He used key informants in each organisation and conducted semi-structured interviews with them. The aims of the research were as follows: to identify the awareness of environmental and social problems resulting from tourism and practices adopted to overcome these; to identify the main obstacles to the adoption of such practices as perceived by the industry; and to find out what the industry saw as priorities for future action for sustainable tourism. A selection of the results are shown in the case study below. The results presented in the case study are those Forsyth obtained from the tour operators, travel agents, hotels, carriers, tourism associations and consultancies. In each of these categories, responses were ranked and only the more important from Forsyth's research are shown here.

Case study

Business attitudes to sustainable tourism: practices (Table 12.1), obstacles (Table 12.2) and priorities (Table 12.3)

Tour operators ($n = 36$)
(1) Providing 'ecotips' and advice in brochures (13)
    Giving donations to local charities and schools (13)
(2) Sponsoring research into impact/management of tourism (9)
(3) Promoting specialist 'green' holidays (8)
    Lobbying of destinations to improve infrastructure, etc. (8)
    Recycling brochures (8)

Travel agents ($n = 6$)
(1) Recycling paper and brochures (6)
(2) Providing specialist knowledge about responsible tourism (2)

Hotels ($n = 3$)
(1) Abiding to the International Hotels Environment Initiative (recycling, waste management, etc.) (3)

Carriers ($n = 5$)
(1) Monitoring fuel emissions, noise, sea waste management (5)
(2) Providing tourists with 'ecotips' and information in magazines (2)

Tourism associations ($n = 6$)
(1) Advising members on sustainable tourism (6)
(2) Developing links with research charities (5)
(3) Liasing with government to increase awareness (3)

Consultancies ($n = 8$)
(1) Advising companies on short- and long-term basis (8)
(2) Training or briefing industry representatives (6)
    Conducting research (6)

* Responses are ranked by frequency of response.

Table 12.1 Practices of sustainable tourism currently adopted*

Tour operators (*n* = 36)
(1) The belief that others are responsible, especially governments (18)
(2) The fear of taking steps not matched by competitors (12)
    Difficulties in educating tourists (12)
(3) The belief that operators are powerless to produce change (8)
    Apparent lack of demand for sustainable tourism in the British market (8)
    Perceived intransigence and corruption amongst host authorities (8)

Travel agents (*n* = 6)
(1) The belief that travel agents are powerless to produce change (6)
(2) The apparent lack of demand from the British market (3)
    The fear that introducing new measures may upset the fragile balance of business (3)

Hotels (*n* = 3)
(1) The belief that hotels are powerless to produce sustainable tourism (3)
(2) The desire not to preach to high-spending guests (2)

Carriers (*n* = 5)
(1) The belief that carriers are marginal to the main tourism industry and hence powerless to change it (4)
(2) The lack of power resulting from owning no land or resorts in destinations (2)

Tourism associations (*n* = 6)
(1) The widely held view that holidays have to be cheap (5)
(2) The low margins and high fragility of profits amongst tour operators (4)
(3) The belief that governments will not listen to tourism companies (3)

Consultancies (*n* = 8)
(1) The simplistic marketing of holidays to promote only one aspect of holiday locations (7)
(2) The false idea that sustainable tourism much be a niche product (6)
(3) The lack of respect for environmentalists by the tourism industry (4)

---

* Responses are ranked by frequency of response.

Table 12.2 Perceived obstacles to adopting practices of sustainable tourism*

Tour operators (*n* = 36)
(1) Increase awareness of sustainable tourism amongst tourists (13)
    Increase awareness amongst host governments (13)
(2) Increase the quality and therefore value of holidays (9)
(3) Train staff in tour operators, hotel and travel agents (7)
    Enforce government controls on tourists and tourism development (7)

Travel agents (*n* = 6)
(1) Increase the awareness of tourists, therefore increasing the range of holidays currently valued by the market (6)

Hotels (*n* = 3)
(1) Introduce new designs for hotels (3)
(2) Increase public awareness of sustainable tourism (3)

Carriers (*n* = 5)
(1) Educate tourists about cultural and environmental diversity at destination (5)
(2) Put pressure on suppliers for quality products (3)

Tourism associations (*n* = 6)
(1) Increase awareness of tourists (6)
    Increase awareness of governments (6)
(2) Provide guidelines for operators to use for contracting (3)

Consultancies (*n* = 8)
(1) Increase awareness of tourists (8)
    Increase awareness of governments (8)
(2) Long term marketing to achieve a differentiation in the standard holiday
    package to allow competition on more than price (7)
(3) Develop mechanisms to attract re-investment in destinations by tour operators (5)

---

* Responses are ranked by frequency of response.

Table 12.3 Perceived priorities for action*

Forsyth's results indicate that although members of the tourism industry are prepared to act to bring about more sustainable tourism, the obstacles they perceive to achieving this fit well with the generally held views about them. It would seem that industry representatives view it as largely somebody else's role and responsibility to create more sustainable tourism. In particular, it is tour operators and travel agents that would seem to want others to take responsibility and they suggest this should be primarily government, although tourists and host communities are also perceived as having a key role here by industry representatives.

Some accommodation providers in a number of countries have been in the forefront of attempts at more environmentally friendly, better planned forms of tourism. The Chateau Whistler Hotel Group in Canada, for example, was one of the first hotel chains to develop a code of conduct for its staff members in relation to environmental issues. In the United Kingdom, a major chain, Travel Inn, part of the Whitbread Group, who own and operate low-cost overnight hotel/motel style accommodation is one of several organizations attempting to minimise resource consumption. They provide the following information in each hotel room:

> Going for Green. As you know, a huge amount of washing is done every day, using large amounts of water and washing powders, which can pollute our rivers and seas. If you are staying another night and don't mind using towels again, please leave them on the towel rail and help us help the environment ... Help Travel Inn to help the environment. By acting in this small way, we can safeguard clean, unpolluted water for the future.

Club Mediterranee is a large global hotel chain. It has operations in many countries worldwide, including Australia. The following case study focuses on one particular Club Mediterranee development that was established in the early 1990s on one of Australia's Whitsunday Islands.

(Adapted from Forsyth, T. (1995). Business attitudes to sustainable tourism: self regulation in the UK outgoing tourism industry. *Journal of Sustainable Tourism*, **3** (4), 210–31.)

Case study

Club Mediterranee Lindemann Island, Australia

The Club Mediterranee Group's core business is resort villages, of which it had 106 in 35 countries in 1995. Its Club Mediterranee Lindemann is one of the organization's more recent developments. Lindemann Island is part of the Whitsunday Islands, which are themselves within the Great Barrier Reef Marine Park. Most of the island is a National Park, controlled by the Queensland Department of Environment and Heritage (DEH). Lindemann Island has coral sand beaches and parts of the interior eucalyptus forest and rain forest were modified by pastoral farming, that continued into this century. The first resort was built here in 1936 and the Club Mediterranee resort in 1992.

Although Club Mediterranee had no structured approach to environmental matters in the mid-1990s, there was significant awareness within the organisation of the need to factor in environmental concerns at the development stage of the operation on Lindemann Island.

At the start of the development, Club Mediterranee established a close working relationship with DEH.

A major initiative requested by Club Mediterranee was the establishment of a golf course. DEH eventually granted permission but with two major conditions. First, Club Mediterranee could only develop areas that had previously been for pastoral usage and that work was to be supervised by DEH staff. Second, an agreement was signed between DEH and Club Mediterranee providing compensation for land used during the golf course development. This agreement also led to the provision of a full-time park ranger position on Lindemann, the construction of a ranger station and an interpretation centre and the making available of a Club Mediterranee staff member to work half time for 1 year at a time with DEH.

Lindemann Island Resort has a number of features that are an attempt to create a more sustainable resort facility. The details are as follows:

Resort buildings. The resort was built to blend with the natural environment in terms of visual appearance, building materials, colours and its has also used some recycled materials.

Power. Power is generated by an on-site generator, which has several noise limiting features. The system is computer monitored to note demand peaks and troughs. This system also controls the resort's sewage and water delivery systems. Energy minimization systems operate in the guest rooms with lights/power automatically turned off when guests leave.

Water resources. Water is stored in a dam built in the 1930s. On average, there is sufficient water for 2 years, but usage is carefully monitored. Dam water is used to irrigate the resort area. There is a physical limit on the amount used each day, as the day's rations are physically stored in a tank.

Waste management. All waste that decomposes quickly is crushed. Glass cardboard, plastics and metals are separated from other waste. All waste is shipped backed to the mainland on a weekly basis. Waste levels are monitored by Club Mediterranee staff.

Chemical usage. All cleaning products are phosphate free. Fertilizer usage is limited. Only occasionally is herbicide used. Chlorine is currently added to pool and drinking water.

Staff. Staff are told their environmental responsibilities during their induction. Each staff member is given a copy of the Environmental Charter issued by the company. This charter has detailed statements in the form of a code of conduct, with supporting guidelines under general headings including: The web of life; The living world and specific headings concerned with their work, including 'in the kitchens', 'laundry', 'rooms', 'boutiques' and there is also reference to 'wildlife', 'marine and land based sports', 'special events' and the 'clubs organized for children'.

Guests. Guests receive information upon their arrival and are advised during their orientation session of the need to adopt a responsible attitude to their activities within the national park area. They are also informed about the availability of printed brochures on the national park.

(Adapted from Harris, R. and Walshaw, A. (1995). In *Sustainable Tourism: An Australian Perspective* (R. Harris and N. Leiper, eds). Chatswood, Butterworth-Heinemann, Australia.)

Summary

The term tourism industry is rather a misnomer as there is not one industry, rather a collection of both linked and also unrelated activities that make up what is termed 'the industry'. Partly as a result of this, the tourism industry has until very recently not viewed the planning of tourism as its responsibility. Tour operators are one key component in the industry that could make an important contribution to tourism planning and management. In the past tour operators have had a bad reputation in terms of the impacts of tourism. More recently, as the research of Forsyth (1995) suggests, some tour operators are taking more responsibility for their actions. The case study of Club Mediterranean Lindemann Island development provides evidence of what can be done, particularly in relation to environmental management. A number of industry representatives, such as accommodation providers and travel agents, have recently become more actively involved in tourism planning and management.

Student exercises

1 How do tourism operators cause problems and how can they assist in the better management of tourism?

2 Study Table 12.1 in the case study of 'business attitudes'. What similarities are there between the different sectors of the tourism industry in their responses?

3 Study Table 12.2 in the case study of 'business attitudes'. What similarities are there in terms of obstacles to sustainable tourism practices between the different sectors of the tourism industry in their responses?

4 Study Table 12.3 in the case study of 'business attitudes'. Produce a list of the top six priorities of the tourism industry for achieving sustainable tourism.

5 What are the advantages of Club Mediterranee pursuing its current policy on Lindemann Island? What could be the disadvantages?

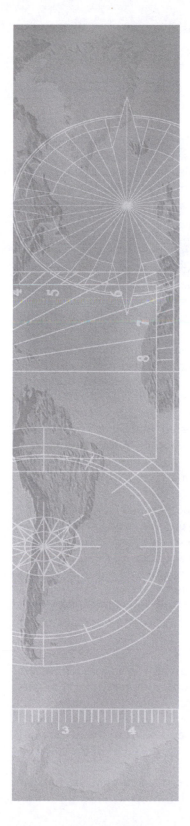

CHAPTER 13

Partnerships and collaboration in tourism

Learning objectives

At the end of this chapter you should be:

- understand the meanings of collaboration and partnerships in tourism;
- understand how collaboration and partnerships in tourism are important within tourism planning and management;
- understand the nature and significance of the processes involved in collaboration and partnerships in tourism.

Introduction

The importance of involving different stakeholders in tourism planning and management is receiving growing recognition (Bramwell and Lane, 2000). As they claimed, 'stakeholder collaboration and partnership has the potential to lead to dialogue, negotiation and consensus building of mutually acceptable proposals about how tourism should be developed' (Bramwell and Lane 2000, p. 1). Clements, Schultz and Lime (1993) suggested that it is vital partnerships are developed in tourism to ensure that a high quality of product is delivered, and because tourism experiences rely on all aspects of the community.

This chapter considers advantages and disadvantages of collaboration and partnerships. It presents a case study of a partnership between a number of tourism industry representatives, government officers and a non-government organization (NGO).

Key perspectives

A number of different terms are used to describe the variety of collaborative arrangements that exist in tourism. These include coalitions, forums, alliances, private–public partnerships and also task forces. The term collaboration is particularly common in academic literature, while in government and practitioner circles the term partnership is especially popular (Bramwell and Lane, 2000).

Tourism partnerships are now relatively common in the United States and United Kingdom. It has been suggested that a major reason for the development of such partnership is to give destinations a competitive edge (Kotler, Haider and Rein, 1993). Broadly based ownership of tourism policies can also bring 'empowerment and equity, operational advantages and an enhanced tourism product' (Bramwell and Lane, 2000, p. 2).

A partnership has been described as 'an on-going arrangement between two or more parties, based upon satisfying specifically identified mutually needs (and) such partnerships are characterised by durability over time, inclusiveness, co-operation and flexibility' (Uhlik, 1995, p. 14). Middleton and Hawkins (1998) discussed partnerships in relation to achieving sustainable tourism. They suggested that such partnerships should be jointly negotiated and agreed approaches to tourism management in which the goals are mutually defined and endorsed and the techniques designed to achieve matching of demand and supply are jointly operated.

Collaboration occurs 'when a group of autonomous stakeholders of a problem domain engage in an interactive process, using shared rules, norms and structures, to act or decide on issues related to that domain' (Wood and Gray, 1991, p. 146). As Bramwell and Lane (2000) argued, this statement by Wood and Gray is particularly useful as it encompasses the diversity of partnerships forms that are likely to be found in practice. It also makes no assumptions about who is involved, how much power they may have, how representative they may be, and even how many stakeholders are involved.

Collaborative relationships can have many forms and the processes involved in the partnerships can also vary greatly. It is possible to conceptualize the relationships along a continuum from very formal to very informal. It is also possible to view the relationships as a complex web between the various stakeholders. This complex web will be greatly dependent on the nature of social, economic and political forces, but may also vary according to the particular issue that is the focus of the collaborative relationship.

Collaboration and partnerships have been advocated in tourism because of the perceived benefits they can bring. One of the major benefits, it has been suggested, is that collaboration can avoid the adversarial conflicts between different interest groups (Bramwell and Lane, 2000). There are also a number of problems with collaboration. These include mistrust and misapprehension between the interest groups, embedded power relations which favour certain interests over others and perceived and real barriers that may restrict access by some groups to partnerships entirely. Figure 13.1 provides more detail on the potential benefits of collaboration, while Figure 13.2 provides a number of potential problems. As Figure 13.1 indicates, the potential benefits of collaboration can be a greater democratization of tourism decision making, with the involvement of a range of players, the sharing of a range of views and the possibility of synergy and creative solutions to tourism problems. However, as Figure 13.2 suggests, collaboration may be costly, time-consuming, not representative of some views and involve unbalanced power relationships.

The following case study discusses the World Wide Fund for Nature (WWF) Arctic Tourism Project. This project involved a number of different players, including local government officials, tour operators, researchers/academics and environmental non-government organizations in developing a framework and guidelines for linking tourism and conservation in the Arctic region. The study indicates a number of the potential benefits and problems of tourism partnerships.

- There may be involvement by a range of stakeholders, all of whom are affected by the multiple issues of tourism development and may be well placed to introduce change and improvement.
- Decision-making power and control may diffuse to the multiple stakeholders that are affected by the issues, which is favourable for democracy.
- The involvement of several stakeholders may increase the social acceptance of policies, so that implementation and enforcement may be easier to effect.
- More constructive and less adversarial attitudes might result in consequence of working together.
- The parties who are directly affected by the issues may bring their knowledge, attitudes and other capacities to the policy-making process.
- A creative synergy may result from working together, perhaps leading to greater innovation and effectiveness.
- Partnerships can promote learning about the work, skills and potential of the other partners, and also develop the group interaction and negotiating skills that help to make partnerships successful.
- Parties involved in policy-making may have a greater commitment to putting the resulting policies into practice.
- There may be improved coordination of the policies and related actions of the multiple stakeholders.
- There may be greater consideration of the diverse economic, environmental and social issues that affect the sustainable development of resources.
- There may be greater recognition of the importance of non-economic issues and interests if they are included in the collaborative framework, and this may strengthen the range of tourism products available.
- There may be a pooling of the resources of stakeholders, which might lead to their more effective use.
- When multiple stakeholders are engaged in decision-making the resulting policies may be more flexible and also more sensitive to local circumstances and to changing conditions.
- Non-tourism activities may be encouraged, leading to a broadening of the economic, employment and societal base of a given community or region.

Figure 13.1 Potential benefits of collaboration and partnerships in tourism planning (*Source*: Bramwell and Lane, 2000.)

- In some places and for some issues there may be only a limited tradition of stakeholders participating in policy-making.
- A partnership may be set up simply as 'window dressing' to avoid tackling real problems head on with all interests.
- Healthy conflict may be stifled.
- Collaborative efforts may be under-resourced in relation to requirements for additional staff time, leadership and administrative resources.
- Actors may not be disposed to reduce their own power or to work together with unfamiliar partners or previous adversaries.
- Those stakeholders with less power may be excluded from the process of collaborative working or may have less influence on the process.
- Power within collaborative arrangements could pass to groups or individuals with more effective political skills.
- Some key parties may be uninterested or inactive in working with others, sometimes because they decide to rely on others to produce the benefits resulting from a partnership.
- Some partners might coerce others by threatening to leave the partnership in order to press their own case.
- The involvement of democratically elected government in collaborative working and consensus building may compromise its ability to protect the 'public interest'.
- Accountability to various constituencies may become blurred as the greater institutional complexity of collaboration can obscure who is accountable to whom and for what.
- Collaboration may increase uncertainty about the future as the policies developed by multiple stakeholders are more difficult to predict than those developed by a central authority.
- The vested interests and established practices of the multiple stakeholders involved in collaborative working may block innovation.
- The need to develop consensus, and the need to disclose new ideas in advance of their introduction, might discourage entrepreneurial development.
- Involving a range of stakeholders in policy-making may be costly and time-consuming.
- The complexity of engaging diverse stakeholders in policy-making makes it difficult to involve them all equally.
- There may be fragmentation in decision-making and reduced control over implementation.
- The power of some partnerships may be too great, leading to the creation of cartels.
- Some collaborative arrangements may outlive their usefulness, with their bureaucracies seeking to extend their lives unreasonably.

Figure 13.2 Potential problems of collaboration and partnerships in tourism planning (*Source*: Bramwell and Lane, 2000.)

Case study

The WWF Arctic Tourism Project

The WWF Arctic Tourism Project was established by The WWF Arctic Programme in 1995 with the aim 'to make Arctic tourism more environmentally friendly and ... to generate support for conservation projects' (Pedersen, 1998, p. 3). The specific goals of the Project are:

1 To identify common interests of tourism and conservation and use these to reduce environmental problems and maximise the advantages for the Arctic environment and the local people.
2 To develop guidelines for Arctic tourism that not only educate tourists about conservation and

appropriate behaviour, but that also generate political support from the tourism industry and tourists for WWF's conservation objectives.
3 To develop competition among tour operators concerning compliance with the guidelines, which will require a form of evaluation/certification that can be used for marketing purposes, and that will be awarded to those tour operators who comply with the guidelines.
4 To increase recognition of the global significance of the Arctic.
5 To increase recognition of local needs in the Arctic and its cultural diversity.

Brief project history

The WWF Project was established largely as a result of the polar tourism conference held in St Petersberg in 1994. The first meeting of the Project took place in January 1996 in Longyearbyen, Svalbard, Norway. The chief aim of this meeting was the drafting of basic principles for Arctic tourism. The forty-three participants, covering most, but not all, of the Arctic countries attended, included tour operators, members of conservation organizations, representatives of indigenous peoples' organizations, government representatives and scientists. Most of these had been specifically invited, by the WWF Arctic Programme Director, on the basis of their expertise.

The meeting produced a Memorandum of Understanding which made reference to minimizing negative impacts of tourism, optimizing benefits to local communities and promoting the conservation of nature. It suggested that cooperation between tour operators, as well as competition, could be in their interests. The memorandum recommended the creation of guidelines and codes of conduct for Arctic tourism. It indicated the need for local involvement in tourism and advocated the use of a contract between local communities and tour operators. It also contained suggestions for operators to reduce the use of resources, to recycle and to minimize damage. It recommended a wide dissemination of the guidelines/codes and suggested that financing for the development of these should be sought from Arctic tour operators.

The next phase of the project was held in September 1996 in Cambridge, UK. Those present here comprised a number of participants from the Svalbard conference and several new collaborators, and it transformed the Memorandum of Understanding into ten basic principles for Arctic tourism. Working group members also produced draft codes of conduct both for tour operators and tourists, and recommendations for communities involved in tourism. In March 1997, the WWF Arctic Programme, working jointly with the Norwegian Polar Institute and the Svalbard Tourism Board held a second workshop on Svalbard. A number of those present at earlier meetings attended this meeting. Those who attended represented a variety of communities of interest and came from twelve different countries, including all the Arctic nations. The objective of the workshop was to develop a process to implement the principles and codes of conduct that had been developed at earlier meeting, and to refine those principles and codes of conduct.

To support implementation, the workshop participants decided to create an eight member Interim Steering Committee which would guide the project in the coming year. The Steering Committee members were elected by the meeting participants to represent indigenous peoples (2), destination tour operators (1), international operators (1), local tourism NGOs (1), conservation NGOs (2), and the research community (1). Individuals were also selected to ensure geographical representation among the Arctic countries. In order to enable participation of observers, such as members of the Arctic Council or the Nordic Council of Ministers, it was intended that an accreditation procedure be established.

It was decided that a number of pilot projects would be established to evaluate the usefulness of the various components of the guidelines project. Evaluation of the pilot projects was to take place one year later, at which point a new Steering Committee would be elected and the office of the permanent secretariat would be formalized.

In December 1997, the WWF Arctic Programme published *Ten Principles for Arctic Tourism, A Code of Conduct for Tour Operators* and *A Code of Conduct for Arctic Tourists*. These documents were the first to put this material into a widely available published form. Five thousand copies of this document were distributed to tour operators, tourist boards, environmental management organizations and government officials as well as to the general public. The intention was to promote awareness of the principles and codes and to encourage further discussion on their content.

In February 1998, a workshop was held in Iceland to bring together the Interim Steering Committee, interested tour operators, and tourism researchers. The purposes of the meeting included: developing methods to measure compliance with codes; developing a structure for future implementation; examining funding sources; and, identifying appropriate pilot projects to evaluate various aspects of the principles, codes and implementation.

The project used the processes of negotiation and consensus building in an attempt to achieve its aims. A key problem was the lack of continuity, as not all participants at early meetings could make follow-on meetings. English was not the first language of most participants but was the main language of the project. Although many views were represented, not all voices were heard and some were more powerful than others.

Meeting structures were relatively informal, but gave a good deal of ownership to participants, although may have contributed to a lack of direction at times. Despite these shortcomings, the project did build consensus and had notable achievements not the least being the codes of conduct and the introduction of pilot projects to apply the codes and guidelines.

(Adapted from Mason, P., Johnston, M. and Twynam, D. (2000). The World Wide Fund for Nature Arctic Tourism Project. *Journal of Sustainable Tourism*, **8** (4), 305–23.)

The case study of the WWF Arctic Tourism Project reveals a number of issues in relation to collaboration and partnerships in tourism planning and management. One of the major issues in the case study was the nature of the arrangements for collaboration. In the WWF study, it is clear that not all of the parties who wanted to play a part were able to do so consistently. This problem of inclusion (or lack of it) is significant. As the WWF study indicated, some stakeholders were unable to make it to all meetings, partly because of a lack of travel funds, others had problems communicating between meetings because of technical difficulties and some may not have participated because of the politics of WWF.

Although the WWF project had overall aims and reasonably clear objectives for each of the meetings, the arrangements were relatively loose and ad hoc and did not have the highly institutionalized structure such as a task force (see Hall, 2000b). This appeared to suit most participants in that they were to some extent empowered and given a degree of ownership of the agenda and products. However, the project arrangements contributed to a problem of a lack of direction and leadership at times. Hence, the WWF project was more 'networked' than 'centred' around a highly institutionalized structure (see Parker, 2000). There is the possibility that this 'loose' structure may have negative effects in terms of the long-term viability of the project.

However, the WWF project appeared particularly good at building a consensus. Due to the nature of arrangements for the project, this process took the form of negotiated consensus building. Although not all participants agreed with everything that took place, their commitment to the idea that such a project was necessary took them beyond individual concerns to accept a majority view in order to keep the whole process moving.

The WWF project presented a major problem of co-ordination. As the focus was the Arctic region, it was by definition an international project. Participants came from many different countries as well as a variety of backgrounds and represented different views and stakeholders. On one level, this led to potential communication problems, although attempts to resolve this involved the use of English as the key language. On another level, the implementation stage was difficult to operationalize. Nevertheless, by the latter part of 1999, codes of conduct had been created and a number of pilot projects had been put into action. It is still not clear what measurable success the WWF project has achieved, as these pilot projects and other initiatives still remain to be evaluated.

The issues presented in relation to the WWF Project are not unusual. In fact, as Bramwell and Lane (2000) argued, such issues are to be expected. Hence, these issues need to be taken very carefully into consideration when considering collaboration and partnerships as part of tourism planning and management.

Summary

Tourism partnerships are now relatively common in both the United States and United Kingdom and are growing in importance in developed and developing areas of the world. Partnerships (or collaboration) are attempts to bring together different players in tourism. They may take a number of different forms, from loose, informal, ad hoc arrangements, to tightly structured, time-tabled, formalized groupings. Partnerships are important in relation to tourism planning and management as they have the potential to lead to dialogue and consensus building between potentially adversarial participants, around mutually acceptable proposals about how tourism should be developed. Information on the WWF Arctic Tourism Project has been presented and discussed and this has revealed some of the advantages of collaboration, as well as indicating the nature and impacts of obstacles.

Student activities

1 What are the major advantages of tourism partnerships?
2 What are the major disadvantages of tourism partnerships?
3 Who was involved in the WWF Arctic Tourism Project?
4 What do you think each of the parties involved in the WWF partnership hoped to get out of their involvement?
5 What factors have contributed to the relative success of the WWF project?
6 What factors have acted as obstacles to the success of the WWF project?
7 What tourism proposals/developments in your area would benefit from a partnership approach?
8 Figure 13.3 provides greater detail on the processes that operated in the WWF Arctic Tourism Project. Please study Figure 13.3 and then answer the questions below.
   a How was consensus building achieved?
   b What part did group dynamics play in the project meetings?
   c How did a lack of continuity of participant involvement affect the project?
   d What were the advantageous of WWF involvement and what problems did this cause?
   e The project has been considered a success. By what criteria could it be viewed as successful and what reasons would you give for its success?

The main processes involved in the project meetings were consultation and negotiation. Although activities varied from meeting to meeting, common to all was a process in which participants were involved actively in preparing and presenting their own material and, in addition, commenting on and questioning the work of other participants. Hence, this was an interactive process of consultation, and as the Arctic Programme Director indicated at the first project meeting, the aim was to achieve a consensus of views. This process of consultation had the advantage that it gave ownership of the tasks to participants. At the early stages, an individual's interpretation of the direction of the project was important as it formed the foundation for the particular activity. A consultative approach can contribute to a general feeling of involvement and the belief that one's views are significant. Individuals had a substantial degree of involvement in the early stages of the project. This also worked to motivate participants and contributed to a generally high level of commitment. Allowing a high degree of control appears to have been a successful strategy as the meetings generally achieved the tasks suggested.

Group dynamics were important in the working groups. In these situations there were individuals with very different backgrounds, experiences, interests and concerns. Workshops were held in English, which was not the first language of many participants. This gave an advantage to some participants over others. A combination of factors contributed to varying levels of participation: some individuals expressed well-articulated views while others contributed little in formal discussions. At some meetings there was evidence of what has been reported elsewhere in similar circumstances, with 'strong voices' dominating and 'weaker voices' not being listened to, as well as there being unarticulated views. Despite this, it was evident that although there were differences of opinion on details, there was a general feeling that such an initiative was necessary and hence individuals gave way to a majority view to keep the project moving.

Attempting to develop consensus among a diverse and widely scattered group of individuals with varying levels of resources (such as computer access, translation services, funds for travel) has meant that some individuals' ideas were not incorporated until late in the process or were not incorporated at all. The direction taken by earlier participants formed the foundation and also informed subsequent revisions of project work. This continues to be a factor in the development of the initiative. An example of communication difficulties is the problems that develop in transferring information between computer network programmes. A more fundamental problem arises from the inability of some participants to return to later meetings, and the complete absence throughout the process of participants from various segments of the communities of interest. The latter problem means that some views were never heard while the former means that continuity was disrupted. Both are almost inevitable in such a project, but they have important implications for the process and the final product.

A number of tourism operators may have resented the possibility of the imposition of external evaluation and some may have disliked the inclusive focus on all Arctic tourism, others may have felt left out of the process, and yet others may have disagreed with the nature of the initiative. Some operators may also have taken issue with the politics of the lead organisation, although the Project Director indicated that a number of operators were very willing to be linked with the WWF panda logo, presumably for the marketing advantage it would bring. At various points during the development stages comments were made that the very involvement of WWF could hinder operator and community participation in the project. The acceptance of WWF varies from place to place in the Arctic, and by interest group. However, local operators and community representatives will have at least a chance to hear the aims of the project and make their view known in the locations involved during the community consultation parts of the Project. For example, a series of community meetings in Nunavut (the newly created Inuit territory in Canada) in 1999 brought the programme to local residents to seek their input into draft guidelines.

Nevertheless, in summary it is possible to state that during consultation and negotiation, despite some evidence of disagreements, dissatisfaction and delays, the major aims of avoiding conflict and building consensus, were generally successful. The success reflects a number of related factors. These are as follows:

- having meetings open to whoever displayed an interest and attempting to advertise such meetings widely;
- encouraging discussion of presentations and positions papers at meetings;
- using working sessions to focus participation and the development of 'products';
- seeking input via the World Wide Web for versions of the guidelines and codes;
- giving feedback to participants in the form of summaries and documents.

The processes outlined above were used in an attempt to hear people and incorporate their ideas. While it is clear that not everyone agreed with everything, it would seem that most project participants agreed with the basic principle that a project like this was necessary. Therefore, they were willing to have their own interests subsumed in order to keep the project moving. Hence, this was a form of negotiated consensus building that required participants to accept a majority rule approach in the interest of moving forward. That this negotiated consensus happened should be viewed as a major accomplishment of WWF.

This project demonstrates an important role for environmental NGOs such as WWF in making a significant contribution to attempts at developing sustainable tourism. In this project, WWF provided its organizational skills in initiating the project, in seeking funding to continue the project and in conducting several international meetings to accomplish particular tasks. In bringing together individuals with differing perspectives ed a willingness to listen and respond, and also the ability to usefully inform the debate. WWF staff indicated that the project required action, not only words, and that the organisation was committed to acting quickly to facilitate the achievement of the Project aims. The success to date of this project also suggests that, despite some opposition, WWF had an important advantage over an industry-based organization: a genuine and credible concern for the key resource for sustainable tourism, the environment.

Figure 13.3 The processes involved in the WWF Arctic Tourism Project

Part Three

Tools and Techniques in Tourism Planning and Management

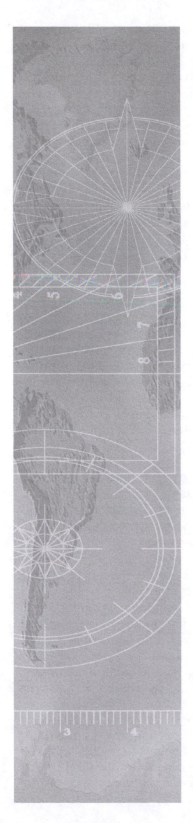

CHAPTER 14

Education as a technique in tourism planning and management

Learning objectives

At the end of this chapter you should:

- aware of the meaning of education in relation to tourism planning and management;
- aware of educational techniques that can be used in tourism planning and management;
- able to critically evaluate educational techniques in tourism planning and management;

Introduction

Education can be used in tourism planning and management in a variety of ways. Education is used often in relation to providing information to visitors, hence education here is used being used as a technique in visitor management. There are many situations in which it is necessary to give visitors information. This educational process can take the form of a relatively formal lecture, for example, on board a cruise ship about a specific destination or a topic such as a particular wildlife species. A guide accompanying a coach tour giving information about the likely time of arrival is providing information and is therefore engaging tourists in an educational process, although this will be less formal than a lecture. Education also takes place when a prospective tourist reads a guidebook or even reads signs in, for example a museum, or a zoo. It is possible to distinguish different types of educational process by the media used (e.g. oral, written), the information content of the activity and the style of presentation, in terms of degrees of informality and interactivity. It is conventional to discuss the presentation of information to visitors in a tourism context using the term 'interpretation' (see Tilden, 1957; Stewart et al., 1998; Moscardo, 1999).

This chapter discusses and critically evaluates the concept of interpretation. It investigates how tour guides act as interpretation agents and presents a case study of zoo-keepers as interpreters.

Key perspectives

Interpretation

One of the earliest commentators on heritage interpretation, Tilden (1957) suggested interpretation is an educational process that employs objects, illustrative media and the use of firsthand experience. The aim of interpretation, Tilden claimed, is to reveal meaning and relationships. A variety of 'objects', such as urban monuments, works of art and flora and fauna, as well as media such as print and photographs can be used to achieve this. Prentice (1995, p. 55) defined interpretation in the following way (Photo 10):

> a process of communicating to people the significance of a place so that they can enjoy it more, understand its importance and develop a positive attitude to conservation. Interpretation is used to enhance the enjoyment of place, to convey symbolic meaning and to facilitate attitudinal or behavioural change.

Interpretation can therefore be seen as part of the process of making places accessible to a public audience and providing visitors with insights into places. The more specific aims of an interpretation programme are 'to stimulate, facilitate and extend people's understanding of place so that empathy towards conservation, heritage, culture and landscape is developed' (Stewart et al., 1998, p. 257).

As Stewart et al. (1998) indicated, a major aim of interpretation is to stimulate interest and develop understanding in visitors. It has been argued that visitors can respond to interpretation in two major ways. Moscardo (1996) suggested that visitors have two modes of response for dealing with new social situations: 'mindless' or 'mindful'. A 'mindless' state is characterized by mental passivity and behaviour, while 'mindful' means a state marked by active mental processing (Moscardo and Pearce, 1986; Moscardo, 1996). Moscardo (1996) argued the importance of promoting 'mindful' tourism through interpretation programmes.

Photo 10
Interpretation can take a variety of forms. Here it is on a sign at the Citadel in Halifax, Nova Scotia in Canada

Only a limited amount of research has been conducted into the effectiveness of interpretation. Stewart et al. (1998) indicated that what evaluation studies of interpretation exist usually determine their effectiveness by how much factual information visitors can recall. Such studies, however, provide little idea of how people use interpretation to help them understand places they are visiting, they argued.

Orams (1994, 1995) suggested that interpretation programmes are usually designed not just to inform, but to change visitors' behaviour. There is little evidence, however, to suggest that interpretation programmes will necessarily lead to a change in the behaviour of visitors, Orams (1995) indicated. He suggested the need to conduct evaluation to ascertain any changes in behaviour and advocated the use of 'cognitive dissonance' as a way to get visitors to modify their behaviour. Orams (1994) argued that cognitive dissonance can be used in interpretative programmes to challenge people's belief systems. Such programmes would be an attempt to throw people off balance and put questions in their minds. Orams suggested that the eliciting of emotional responses from visitors, as part of a strategy involving cognitive dissonance, may be the way to counter the problems inherent in educating tourists.

As suggested in the introduction to the chapter, interpretation can involve formal or informal educational processes as well as a variety of media and presentational forms. The following section discusses the use of tour guides in the process of interpretation.

The role of the tour guide and interpretation

Tour guides may be the most maligned people in the world of travel. They are blamed for the problems of travel such as bad weather and traffic jams. They are also called the shepherds of the industry, as they herd tourists around safely and try to ensure that they return with fond memories of their holiday (Ang, 1990). As Ang (1990, p. 171) indicated 'they exist not merely as a mouthpiece, mindlessly rattling information or as a merciless shopping sales person ... The job calls for commitment, enthusiasm and integrity as the entire experience of the tourist lies in their hands'.

Early tour guides were usually unpaid, but had a strong motivation and a desire to share the feelings and values they held with others (McArthur, 1996). They also wanted to promote a conservation ethic in order to ensure what they had first experienced was maintained in the same state.

Pond (1993, p. 76) suggested that a tour guide has five roles: leader; educator; public relations representative; host; and conduit. Pond (1993, p. 78) indicated that these are in practice 'interwoven and synergistic'. Pond also suggested that the roles of tour guide and adult instructor are very similar. She suggested an adult educator has four key roles: a programmer who sets up the conditions to facilitate learning; a guide; a content resource; and an institutional representative. Pond argued, however, that the roles of teacher and guide, although similar, are not identical. Guides must focus on the diversity of an audience, be more flexible and be more aware of their other roles (leader, host, public relations and conduit) than teachers.

The main interaction involved in tour guiding is between the visitor and the guide. Hence, tour guiding, with its key role to inform and educate visitors, is a part of the process of interpretation (Pond, 1993; Knudson, Cable and Beck, 1995; Prentice, 1995). The guide's role in relation to the visitor is as follows: telling (provision of information); selling (interactive communication that explains and clarifies); participating (being a part of activity); and delegating (giving responsibility to some future behaviour) (Howard, 1997). The role of the tour guide in this situation can be viewed as assisting in the interpretation of the site for the visitor.

Those who participate in guided activities are doing so to meet certain of Maslow's hierarchy of needs (Howard, 1997). Maslow (1943) indicated there is a five-tier hierarchy of needs. These needs are, at the lowest level, physiological followed by safety then ascending to a feeling of belonging and being accepted as a friend, through status and self-respect needs at the fourth level, to the highest level of self-development, accomplishment and growth. Maslow suggested that a need creates a tension, pleasant or unpleasant that has to be resolved. The goal of people's behaviour is therefore to reduce the tension.

The decision to participate in a guided tour may be based on the expectation that certain needs will be fulfilled and these are likely to be relatively high level needs of seeking friendship, personal development and recognition. Many visitors find it necessary to satisfy their lower-level needs and the need for refreshment, relief and details on the length of stay are often uppermost in people's minds (Knudson, Cable and Beck, 1995). To maximize the experience of visitors and minimize discomfort, Howard

(1997) suggested three principles should be employed. These are as follows (Photos 11 and 12):

- minimize the threat to safety or to psychological needs;
- satisfy social esteem, self-actualization needs;
- avoid mixing groups with different needs.

Photo 11
The Acropolis in Athens is one of the most visited attractions in the world

Photo 12
A tour guide at work on the steps leading to the Parthenon on the Acropolis in Athens

Photo 13

Zoos can convey their messages in a variety of ways. Here at Wellington Zoo, New Zealand is a sign that is species specific

Photo 14

This sign at London Zoo, is not species specific, but is communicating a wider message on the importance of ecosystems

Zoos are an example of a particular type of visitor attraction that uses guides. The guides do not usually accompany the visitors as they make their way around the zoo, but give presentations at particular locations in relation to specific animal attractions (Broad, 1996) (Photos 13 and 14). The following case study examines the nature of this process of interpretation and considers the role of interpretation in visitor management.

Case study
Keeper talk at Wellington Zoo

The keepers at Wellington Zoo, New Zealand give talks on a number of the animal exhibits. Talks concerning the following were observed: chimpanzees, 'big cats', Malaysian sun bears, giraffes and exhibits in the Nocturnal House. The results from these investigations provide an insight into the issues of presenting and interpreting wildlife under zoo conditions.

- Chimpanzees: The keepers offered audience members the opportunity of feeding the chimpanzees. This enabled interaction between the audience and the animals. Audience members were offered the opportunity to feed the animals if they could answer questions. It appeared a successful strategy as many children put up their hands and wanted to become involved in feeding. The keeper questions in this talk were also useful as they helped point out differences between monkeys and other primates. The talk was predominantly specific to chimps, but also raised the bigger issues of conservation, habitat loss and ideas on endangered species.
- Big cats: The 'tiger talk' was very informative and engaging because the animals were fed and talked about at the same time. The keeper fed one tiger by hand, from outside the cage. Hence, the audience could get close, still feel safe and yet also be aware of the 'presence' of the animals. The behaviour of the different tigers in the zoo was discussed. This was linked to conditions for tigers there, and the animals' preference for different activities. Hence, this was a story of animals that have strong links with Wellington Zoo and New Zealand and was not just another talk concerned with 'animals in captivity'. However, the type of talk observed (part of the Zoo School activities) is not generally available to Zoo visitors and during a subsequent visit it was reported by several visitors that the animals were generally rather docile and difficult to see. This is of importance, as for many visitors the 'big cats' are their favourite zoo exhibit, hence they may feel cheated if they do not see 'cats' in action.
- Nocturnal House: Talks observed here were very detailed and informative, but tended to be very exhibit specific. However, the size and layout of the Nocturnal House makes it difficult to engage a large audience. In particular, this is a problem at the entrance and exit and means it is difficult to give a presentation. Problems of presentation here also relate to the dark. Some young children are frightened of the dark. Also, the darkness means it is less easy for the audience (or at least some) to concentrate. Some exhibits here are very static, for example, tuatara, bats. Hence, the time spent here is quite likely to be short.
- The Malaysian Sun bears: One talk observed lasted just over 20 min and amplification was used. This talk was given to an audience of approximately 60, about one-third of whom were parents with young children. However, it seemed that this tended to make the audience less attentive. A number of parents with younger children left after about 8–10 min, and by the end there were virtually no parents with young children left. On a later visit, it was revealed that two cubs had been born and these provoked a strong audience reaction and a number of questions at the end of the talk. The audience during this talk was smaller, had slightly fewer younger children and was generally more attentive.
- Giraffes: The audience on each occasion was made up of approximately one-third children (aged 3–13). This exhibit appeared particularly interesting for children as they could directly feed the animals. The arrangements at the zoo are good as visitors are at the same height as a giraffe's head. However, the physical area under cover and where there is direct access to feed the giraffes is rather small. A small number of people left during one of the talks observed as it appeared they could not get close enough to feed/see the giraffes adequately. The talks were focused on these giraffes and also links with other zoos in New Zealand. The comparison between giraffes and people appeared to provoke a high level of response from the audience, including questions.

The investigation of keeper talk at Wellington zoo also revealed some general issues in relation to interpretation. All talks were very detailed in relation to the particular animal exhibit presented. A large proportion of the talks was about feeding and breeding and other bodily functions. In relation to particular animals, for example, the Malaysian Sun bears, much of the talk focused on the young.

All talks made some reference to conservation issues, usually in relation to the specific animal in the talk. However, not all talks made more general comments, that is, going from the specific talk to larger issues.

Most of the talks observed were given by one keeper. However, one of the talks in relation to the Sun bears and one of the chimpanzee talks involved, in each case, two keepers. For these talks, a microphone and loud speaker system were used, all other talk were given without any audio aid. Some problems were caused by the amplification system.

The great majority of the talks were to audiences of mixed age groups. Young children, (those under age 5) made up 10–30 per cent of such groups. Their attention span was very short. The audience usually contained the parents of these children, as well as some unaccompanied children (usually older 8–13). Other adults not accompanied by children made up 30–50 per cent of the audience. The audiences were predominantly female. The composition of the audience creates particular problems for the keeper in terms of the content of a talk and methods of presentation.

Trying to keep the audiences attention is not always easy, but is clearly an important role of the zoo-keeper. In all talks observed, except those given in connection with the Zoo School, a proportion of the audience left during the talk. Those with young children tended to leave first.

(Adapted from Mason, P. (1999). *Wellington Zoo: Visitor Survey and Keeper Evaluation. An Interim Report to the Zoo Management Committee*, Department of Management Systems, Massey University, New Zealand.)

Summary

Education can be used as an important technique in tourism management. The use of education for tourism management is within the context of what is termed interpretation. Interpretation is an educational process, which involves not only the transfer of knowledge, but also the development of values to the environment and culture of the site visited and has been used extensively in visitor management. Interpretation can be via oral presentation, the printed word or even other media such as film, video or computer. Tour guides act as site interpreters and zoo-keepers are a specific form of interpreter used by zoos to help manage the educational experience for visitors.

Visitors to a site have particular needs and interpretation can be used to meet these. Interpretation can also be used to transform visitors' thinking and behaviour, with the intention that they become 'mindful' tourists. However, there is little evidence, to date, that education programmes within interpretation necessarily lead to changes in behaviour. Nevertheless, programmes that provoke an emotional response may lead visitors to modify their attitudes and behaviour.

Student activities

1 What do you understand by the term 'interpretation'?
2 How can interpretation be used in tourism management?
3 What is the role of the tour guide in interpretation?
4 Produce a matrix with four boxes, in the format shown below, to compare the activity of a tour guide in comparison with that of a printed guide book:

Advantages of a tour guide   Disadvantages of a tour guide

Advantages of a printed guide   Disadvantages of a printed guide

5 What is the role of a zoo-keeper?

6 What are the advantages of a zoo-keeper over a printed zoo guide?

7 Summarize the response of visitors to their experience of interpretation by zoo-keepers at Wellington Zoo under the headings: *positive responses* and *negative responses*

8 In relation to the study of Wellington Zoo discussed above, a number of recommendations relating to ways to improve the keeper talk were made. These recommendations are presented below.

- The keeper talk should be viewed as a performance in front of, and potentially involving, an audience. It should not be viewed solely as presenting information. Therefore, thought should be given to issues such as how to maintain audience attention, as well as ways to get the audience involved and/or to respond.

- Presenting some form of 'story' about the animals would seem an appropriate way to keep audience attention. This could involve reference to the animal's life at the zoo, or a discussion of similarities between the animal and other animals/humans.

- The process of the keeper asking questions and offering rewards (such as feeding the chimpanzees) appears a successful way of keeping the audience attention, particularly children, and could be used in a variety of different talks.

- If the zoo's chief role is to educate, then the 'bigger picture' issues about the need for conservation, in general, need to be given in addition to discussion of matters relating to the individual species.

- If animals can be taken from cages or brought close to the audience (e.g. through feeding) this will help maintain the audience interest. However, consideration should also be given to the stress that this puts on the exhibit.

- If amplification is required, then hand-held microphones are probably not a good idea, as they limit the overall 'performance'. It would be better to use small clip-on microphones.

- Using two keepers rather than one to present a talk would appear more successful than using just one in certain circumstances. This worked well with the Malaysian Sun bears and the chimpanzees. In this context, one person does 'the talk', the other interacts with the audience and the animals.

- An announcement, via a tannoy system, a few minutes prior to a keeper talk would probably increase the audience size, although this could disturb animals. Alternatively, an announcement by loud-hailer in the area in which the talk will be given 5–10 min beforehand could help.

  (a) Suggest possible constraints to the application of these recommendations.

  (b) Do you agree with the recommendations?

  (c) Suggest what else could be done to improve keeper talks at the zoo.

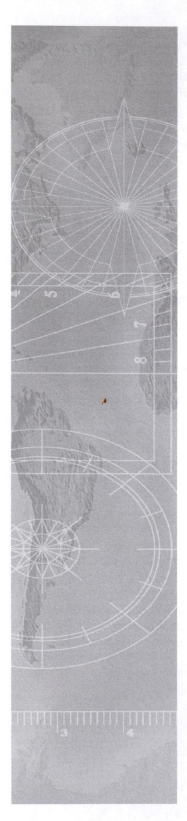

Self-regulation as a technique in tourism planning and management

Learning objectives

At the end of this chapter you should:

- be aware of the meanings of regulations, self-regulation, guidelines and codes of conduct in relation to tourism;
- understand what tourism codes of conduct are;
- be aware of the different authors and target audiences for codes of conduct;
- be aware of critical perspectives on the use of tourism codes of conduct in tourism planning and management.

Introduction

This chapter discusses regulations, self-regulation, guidelines and codes of conduct in tourism planning and management. Although often linked, there are important differences between these three terms. As Stonehouse (1990) indicated regulations usually have some form of legal status while codes of conduct, codes of practice and guidelines, although attempting to regulate tourism, do not. Guidelines, however, are usually based on well-considered precepts, indicating a course of action to be followed with the reasoning behind it, while codes of conduct provide sets of rules for behaving in certain circumstances (Stonehouse, 1996). Codes of conduct are usually voluntary, tend to be self-imposed and are designed to act as a form of self-regulation (Mason and Mowforth, 1996). There are few examples of legally backed regulations pertaining specifically to tourism but a variety of tourism codes of conduct have been existence for at least the last 20 years (Mason, 1997). This chapter therefore focuses on codes of conduct in tourism and the guidelines that often accompany them.

Key perspectives

A number of earlier chapters have made reference to codes of conduct. The use of codes of conduct in tourism is a relatively recent phenomenon, although there are examples, such as the English Countryside Commission's Country Code, which date back to the 1960s (Mason and Mowforth, 1996). In the past few years, codes have been developed by governments, the private sector, concerned individuals as well as NGOs.

The main aim of codes is to influence attitudes and modify behaviour (Mason and Mowforth, 1996). Codes are usually designed to improve environmental quality and minimize negative impacts of tourism. Hence, codes of conduct are used in an attempt to regulate behaviour. Codes of conduct are usually part of a process involving attempts to regulate tourism and are often used in conjunction with guidelines.

A number of discrete target groups for tourism codes of conduct have been identified. These groups are as follows: visitors, the tourism industry and members of host communities (UNEP, 1995; Mason and Mowforth, 1996). The most significant target audience in terms of sheer number of codes is the visitor; the WTTRC (1995), for example, listed almost eighty visitor codes in use around the world in 1994 and this has risen to several hundred by the end of the twentieth century. A number of codes have also been prepared for use by those directly involved in the tourist industry and more recently codes have been prepared for the use of host populations.

In addition to a variety of target audiences for codes of conduct, there are a range of different authors. A significant number of codes have been written by concerned individuals and NGOs while government bodies and the tourism industry itself have not been until recently very active in producing codes (Mason and Mowforth, 1996).

However, codes of conduct frequently fail to specify either their broad aims or more specific objectives (Mason, 1994). Nevertheless, UNEP, having conducted a survey of voluntary environmental tourism codes in 1992 and received information on thirty codes used by countries and international associations, was able to deduce a number of specific objectives (UNEP, 1995). UNEP (1995, p. 8) produced, in summary form, five objectives of such codes, which are as follows:

- to serve as a catalyst for dialogue between government and other bodies involved in tourism;

- to create an awareness in government and industry of the need for sound environmental management;
- to heighten awareness amongst tourists of the need for appropriate behaviour;
- to make host populations aware of the need for environmental protection;
- to encourage cooperation between government agencies, host communities, industry and NGOs.

In that they provide information, advice and frequently instructions, it should be clear that in their attempt to regulate, codes of conduct also aim to educate.

It would appear from the UNEP summary of the aims of tourism codes above that they are primarily concerned with environmental impacts and improving environment management, however, the message of tourism codes is not just confined to environmental issues. A number of visitor codes, for example, make reference to socio-cultural matters, such as respect for local religious beliefs. Codes with industry as the audience, frequently refer to the need for appropriate training and honest marketing of tourism products (Mason and Mowforth, 1996).

Although many codes are impressive in terms of the range of issues that they cover and in their depth of discussion and information, there are a number of significant problems with them. Mason and Mowforth (1996) suggested four major problem areas. First, codes must be practised as intended, but as UNEP (1995) indicated most codes tend to be poorly implemented. An indication of whether codes are well implemented can be derived from monitoring.

However, until very recently, the great majority of codes were not monitored, so it is very difficult to evaluate their effects (UNEP, 1995). Clearly, there is little point in having a code unless it achieves its desired impact.

Second, several codes may be found operating in the same location but they may be written by different authors and aimed at targets existing at different scales, from local to national or even international. This suggests a much greater need to coordinate codes and there is perhaps a related need to reduce variability between codes. However, as Valentine (1992) suggested most codes are targeted at visitors, hence he argued that in any given situation it is necessary to employ simultaneously a number of codes of conduct with different target audiences. For example, a code aimed at visitors should be used in conjunction with another aimed at operators, as a code for one group on its own would not be as effective. However, this may lead to a proliferation of codes that could appear to contradict the argument for less variability in codes, but would nevertheless appear to further support the need for greater coordination between code authors.

Third, and of particular importance, codes may be little more than clever marketing devices, rather than genuine attempts to promote more sustainable forms of tourism (Mason and Mowforth, 1996). Under such conditions, a code is used in an attempt to persuade potential customers that a tour operator adheres to a set of environmental and/or socio-cultural principles. The reality may be that the principles are not adhered to, but this is, in fact, a cynical attempt to get a customer to part with their cash, believing they are buying an ethical/green tourism product.

Fourth, codes are voluntary; they are a form of self-regulation (Mason and Mowforth, 1996). As such, they can do little more than exhort the target audience to respond to the requests/instructions contained within the code. Virtually no codes are backed up by actual legally binding documents, which of course limits their effectiveness. Evidence from a number of locations, suggests that external regulation may be far more effective than self-regulation (Mason et al., 2000a,b). However, Mason and Mowforth (1996) argued that the motivation for self-regulation industry, is either the tourist industry wishing to appear to be acting responsibly in advance of imposed regulation to weaken the force of this regulation, or is an attempt to stave off external regulation entirely.

Examples of codes of conduct in tourism are shown below. Figure 15.1 (the Countryside Commission's Code) is a visitor code. Figure 15.2, *Tourismus mit Einsicht* is a code for the tourism industry and Figure 15.3, a form of code for the Ministry of Tourism. Figure 15.4 provides a summary of key elements of codes of conduct.

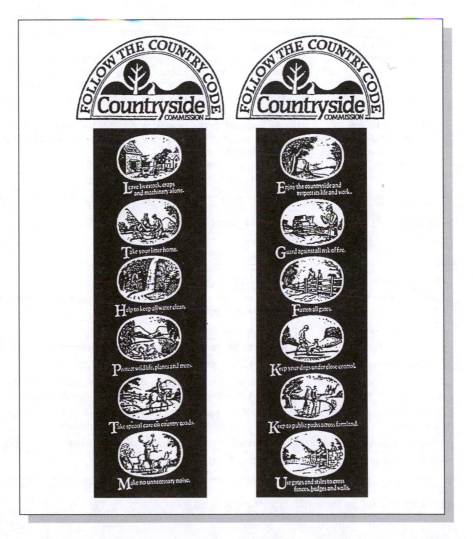

Figure 15.1
The Country Code

We, the travel business

1. We act as a business organized on commercial principles, which tries to meet the travel needs of its Clients while achieving reasonable economic results. We can reach this goal in the long run only if we succeed in making better use of the opportunities of travel and simultaneously reducing its dangers. We shall therefore promote such forms of tourism which are economically productive, socially responsible and environment-friendly.
2. We see our clients as people who enjoy life and who want their holidays to be the 'most pleasurable weeks of the year'. We also know that there is an increasing number of interested, considerate and environment-conscious tourists. We shall try to respond to and encourage this trend without preaching to our guests.
3. We shall bear in mind the interests, independence and rights of the local population. We shall respect local laws, customs, traditions and cultural characteristics. We shall always remember that we as travel agents and as tourists are guests of the local population.
4. We want to collaborate as partners with the service industry and the host population in the tourist areas. We advocate fair business conditions, which will bring the greatest possible benefit to all partners. We shall encourage active participation of the host population wherever possible.
5. Our efforts to improve travel should include a careful selection and continuous training of our staff at all levels, as well as development and supervision of our services.
6. We want to provide our clients with expert and comprehensive information about all aspects of the country they want to visit through catalogues, travel information and guides. Our advertising must be not only attractive but honest and responsible. We shall try to avoid the usual superlatives and cliched texts and pictures. Special emphasis will be placed on a respectful description of the population in the host areas. We shall desist from any advertising with erotic enticements.
7. Our guides and social directors will have a particular responsibility in promoting tourism with insight and understanding. We shall provide special, and continuous, training for personnel working in these areas.
8. We shall not organize travel, trips or expeditions to ethnic groups who live apart from our western civilisation. We shall not promise our clients 'Contact with untouched peoples' because we know that they are vulnerable and must be protected.
9. All our activities and those of our business partners will have to meet the same strict quality standard. We want to make our business partners aware of the fact that they too should contribute to an environment-conscious and socially responsible tourism.
10. We are prepared to formulate within our professional associations a set of principles encompassing – the ethics of the tourist trade – which shall be binding for all members.

Figure 15.2 *Tourismus mit Einsicht:* code for the travel business

Include aspects of nature tourism in national tourism policy

Carry out marketing programme for nature tourism, including product identification, inventory of nature tourism attractions, and visitor surveys to determine demand

Design a mechanism, with the park service, for collecting entrance fees

Change tourism laws as needed to include environmental protection clauses for natural areas

Develop mechanisms to record statistical information about nature tourists

Work with private sector and international funding agencies to develop adequate tourism infrastructure at each site not only to accommodate tourists but also to provide opportunities for tourists to spend money

Create training programmes, with the park service and tour operators, for all park personnel and tour guides. Training should include natural resource education and tourism management skills

Develop mechanisms to channel a portion of tourism revenue back into maintenance and protection of the park

Monitor the quality of nature tourism services and facilities

Figure 15.3 Checklist for the ministry of tourism (Boo, 1990.)

Type of codes	Authorship	Audience	Message
Visitor codes	Predominantly NGOs and concerned individuals, but also some government bodies such as Ministry of the Environment.	Domestic visitors and international visitors, especially overseas visitors to Developing countries.	Minimize environmental and socio-cultural damage to area visited. Maximize economic benefit to host community. Encourage more equality in relationships between visitors and hosts. Promote more responsible and sustainable forms of tourism.
Industry codes	Predominantly coordinating bodies such as WTO and IATA; also governments and to a lesser extent NGOs and concerned individuals; and exceptionally tourism companies, e.g. Chateau Whistler Hotel Group.	Tourism industry in general, and some codes for specific sectors such as the hotel industry.	Appropriate training/education for staff. Honest marketing of product. Develop awareness of environmental and socio-cultural impact of tourism. Promote more responsible and sustainable forms of tourism. Promote recycling.
Host codes	Predominantly NGOs and concerned individuals; some host communities in both developed and Developing countries; and a small number of host governments.	Mainly host communities, especially in Developing countries.	Information and advice about visitors. Minimize environmental and socio-cultural damage. Maximize economic benefits to host community. Encourage more equality in relationship between host and visitors. Advocate more democratic and participatory forms of tourism development.

Figure 15.4 Key elements of codes of conduct in tourism (*Source*: Mason and Mowforth, 1995.)

Summary

Codes of conduct and guidelines are part of the attempt to regulate tourism. However, codes of conduct and guidelines are not the same as regulations as these usually have legal status while codes and guidelines are voluntary and a form of self regulation. Codes of conduct have a range of authors, including governments, NGOs, industry representatives and concerned individuals.

Codes are targeted at tourists, industry, government and host communities. The message of most codes involves statements, or more usually instructions about environmental matters and increasingly cultural factors. However, codes are not without problems. Few codes are monitored, there is a great variability among codes and a general lack of coordination. Codes can also be misused. For example, an unscrupulous operator can claim that it meets certain requirements of a code written by say an environmental group (with no evidence to support this) in an attempt to sell more holidays. Codes of conduct also suffer from that fact that they are largely voluntary. This has led to the conclusion amongst some commentators that external regulation is required.

Student activities

1 What are the main differences between codes of conduct, regulations and guidelines?
2 Take the examples of codes of conduct supplied, in Figures 15.1–15.3, and say how well you think they meet the objectives produced by UNEP.
3 Study each of the examples of codes of conduct (Figures 15.1–15.3) and also the summary shown in Figure 15.4, then read the following:

The scenario:
A new resort hotel with 120 beds, an indoor and outdoor swimming pool, restaurant and gift shops is about to be built in a developing area for tourism on the coast of a Mediterranean island. The main customers, it is hoped, will be from overseas, but significant numbers of domestic tourists will be attracted. The hotel will appeal to a broad cross section of visitors including business travellers, families with and without children, but will be tending to aim slightly upmarket. In your study groups, create a code of conduct in relation to the hotel development for each of the following target audiences:

visitors;
the industry (hotel owners);
the local and regional government.

Compare the completed codes for each sector and examine and comment both on similarities between them and possible points of conflict.
4 What has this activity taught you about tourism development?
5 Repeat the activity but this time set the hotel in Eastern Europe and once again compare and contrast the codes of conduct you have created.

CHAPTER **16**

Information technology and tourism planning and management

Learning objectives

At the end of this chapter you should be:

- aware of the use of a range of information technology (IT) in tourism;
- able to demonstrate a general understanding of what Geographical Information Systems (GIS) are;
- able to demonstrate an awareness of how GIS can be used in tourism management.

Introduction

Tourism is a complex, global industry and information is its life-blood. Information about the tourism product is vital to assist the consumer in making choices. This is particularly so given that the tourism product is intangible. Selling the product requires representations and descriptions by the travel trade. Electronic forms of messages about tourism products have certain advantages over printed sources. Electronic forms can be more up-to-date and hence topical, they can be more visual and colourful and in relation to computerized systems such as the

Internet can provide tour operators and tourism providers with access to large numbers of potential customers simultaneously. Increasingly, consumers are using Internet sites for planning, searching, reserving and purchasing tourism products.

There is increasing use of IT in tourism. Various types of IT are being used by industry, government departments, operators and even potential and actual customers to seek out data on holidays and tourist destinations. IT is also being used to display data in a tourism context. IT has been defined as follows:

> The collective term given to the most recent developments in the mode (electronic) and the mechanisms (computers and communication technologies) used for the acquisition, processing, analysis, storage, retrieval, dissemination and application of information.
>
> (Poon, 1993)

It is a common assumption that IT equates with computers. However, IT covers a large range of electronic devices including videotext, teletext, faxes, telephones, teleconferencing, satellites, mobile phones, computer network and the Internet (Cooper et al., 1998). IT can be used in tourism planning and management and one particularly significant use is with GIS. This chapter discusses GIS in detail.

Key perspectives

Until very recently, IT, and in particular computerized systems, were not being used extensively in relation to tourism planning and management. However, in the early 1990s, Destination Management Systems (DMS) were applied to tourism destinations and this involved the coordination of the activities of all partners involved in the production and delivery of the destination tourism product (Cooper et al., 1998). Although still in their infancy, advanced forms of the DMS:

> can rationalise destination management and marketing by supporting promotion, distribution and operation, while also offering innovative tools for strategic management, product differentiation and amelioration of tourism impacts by better balancing the needs and expectations of tourists and locals.
>
> (Cooper et al., 1998, p. 441)

A particularly useful type of IT that can assist in the planning and management of the resources for tourism is the GIS. GIS are basically computerized systems for handling and processing data. They deal with geographical and other types of data, processing it to produce maps, graphs, tables and statistics. GIS can deal with information on the natural resources, human settlement and cultural resources for tourism (Doswell, 1997). GIS can either print maps as overlays or generate computer images as virtual overlays. Sophisticated GIS can also perform statistical and complex computational tasks. GIS can show clearly spatial relationships and other forms of relationship. In this way, they can show how activities, both tourism and non-tourism may conflict. GIS can be used at a variety of scales and are particularly useful in integrating data from local, regional and national sources. They can also simulate a number of possible future scenarios that can assist in the planning and management process (Doswell, 1997).

GIS can be used for many tasks, and have been used by a number of government departments in many countries since the mid-1980s. GIS are particularly useful when a large amount of data needs to be manipulated. GIS are being used and reported on in an increasing number of tourism context including the Central American state of Belize, in the United Kingdom and in New Zealand.

In Belize, which is a small developing country, there was a need to map areas that could be established for a number of different uses, both tourism and non-tourism (BBC, 1991). The coastal area is suitable for tourism development, but also has a number of important wildlife habitats. GIS were used as a planning tool to create areas in the form of zones for the development of ecotourism. The planned ecotourism areas were in locations that were not likely to be damaged easily by visitors.

In New Zealand, GIS have been used in connection with the Resource Management Act (RMA), which was introduced in 1991 (Watkins, Cocklim and Laituru, 1997). In relation to planning and management, GIS have been found to particularly useful in New Zealand in the following areas:

- making a contribution to environmental monitoring and the state of the environment;
- assisting with the assessment of the effectiveness of regional policy statements;
- helping with decisions on resource consents (planning permission).

MacAdam (1999) investigated the use of GIS by consultants in tourism in the context of the United Kingdom. In summary, MacAdam indicated that GIS is particularly useful for: data analysis; modelling; and forecasting. More specifically MacAdam indicated that GIS had an important tourism planning and management role in terms of:

- the production of environmental statements;
- qualitative/quantitative data collection (particularly in terms of community involvement);
- the use of system analysis techniques/audit trails;
- the interviewing of local representatives and local people;
- the interpreting of sites using the result of visitor surveys;
- feasibility studies for a tourist facility;
- strategy programmes, including an action plan;
- traffic modelling from highway engineer's data;
- wildlife data given by English Nature for the management of ecology in local areas;

- infrastructure audit in the context of hotels, restaurants;
- policy studies.

Hasse and Milne (1999) investigated the use of GIS in relation to tourism in New Zealand. The particular focus of their study was on the potential use of GIS for community involvement in tourism. Their findings are summarized in the case study below.

Case study

GIS and community aspects of tourism in New Zealand

Hasse and Milne (1999) investigated the uses of GIS in a tourism context and its potential for community involvement. In summary, they indicated that GIS could be used to:

- compare different sources of data/information;
- identify gaps and shortcomings in data;
- link different systems of understanding;
- analyse spatial patterns;
- highlight choices/preferences.

The particular community aspects of their findings were as follows:

- Data collected from the community using GIS (maps and diagrams) were used in a questionnaire survey and interviews.
- Data were presented visually to the community using GIS (particularly maps and diagrams).

The rationale for this was that the community were likely to find it easier to understand maps/diagrams than figures/ numbers.

- GIS can become a means to community participation in tourism decision-making.
- GIS can aid in analysing data, explaining key concepts and presenting findings and information.
- GIS can therefore contribute to the stronger possibility of more sustainable tourism, as the community is more involved.

(Adapted from Hasse, J. C. and Milne, S. (1999). *Tourism and community development: stakeholder participation and GIS*. Paper presented at the *Tourism Policy and Planning Conference*, 12 September 1999. Oamaru, University of Otago, New Zealand; MacAdam, P. (1999). Geographical information systems and their application within tourism. *Journal of Sustainable Tourism*, **7** (1), 62–74.

Summary

IT is being used increasingly in tourism planning and management and of particular importance is the use of computers. DMS are one such use of computers. A particularly useful computerized tool in tourism planning and management is a GIS. GIS are computerized systems that handle and process geographical data. GIS can also handle other forms of data. GIS can be used for a wide variety of tasks in tourism planning and management, including the production of environmental statements, data collection, the interviewing of local people, sites interpretation, feasibility studies for a tourist facility and policy studies.

Student activities

1 What do you understand by GIS?
2 How can GIS be used in relation to resource evaluation?
3 How can GIS be used in a tourism management context?
4 How could GIS contribute to more sustainable tourism?

Part Four

The Future of Tourism Planning and Management

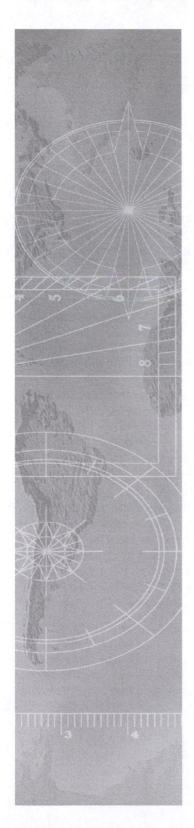

Tourism planning and management and sustainability

Learning outcomes

At the end of this chapter you should:

- be able to define sustainability in you own words;
- understand how sustainability has arisen as a concept;
- be able to discuss the link between sustainability and the impacts of tourism;
- understand how sustainability needs to be addressed in the planning and management of tourism.

Introduction

Sustainability is a concept used with increasing frequency in tourism development, planning and management circles. It is often linked to terms such as 'green' tourism and/or 'eco-tourism'. The term, however, is not well defined, and tends to be used as a 'buzz' word by commentators, researchers and those in marketing. To a certain extent, sustainability is now an over-used term and is open to abuse, particularly from those operators who wish to indicate that their product is worthier than another's, and even by academics who see that their careers could be advanced through work in this area of tourism!

Key perspectives

The modern usage of the term 'sustainability' would appear to date from the Brundtland Report of 1987 (Holden, 2000). In this report, the term sustainable development was used. The Brundtland Report focused on the Earth's environment and was concerned about unsustainable resource use associated with what was seen as too rapid development. This report also made the link between environment and development very clear.

At what was known as the Earth Summit, held in 1992 in Rio de Janeiro, the concerns that were expressed in the Brundtland Report were once again present. This conference set forward a programme for promoting sustainable development throughout the world. This came to be known as Agenda 21. Agenda 21 is an: 'action plan laying out the basic principles required to progress towards sustainability' (Holden, 2000, p. 164). The particular approach of Agenda 21 is to involve local communities in a 'bottom-up' approach to their own development.

However, the concept of sustainable development was not fully defined in either the Brundtland Report or at the Rio Summit. This means that for example, private organizations, governments, NGOs and academics may have very different views on its meaning. Nevertheless, the Brundtland Report stressed that sustainable development does not mean preservation of the environment, but sustainable development of it (Holden, 2000) and the focus is thus on conservation and not preservation.

Holden (2000) suggested that although there is a diverse range of views on sustainable development, they can be classified, generally into two camps; there are 'technocentric' views and 'ecocentric' views. The technocentric view insists that problems can be quantified and solved largely through the application of technology. The ecocentric view places great emphasis on 'quality of life' rather than 'standard of living' and the measurement of economic growth in quantitative terms has little value. The opposite ends of the spectrum of the technocentric and ecocentric are shown in Figure 17.1. Here the ecocentric view is represented under the 'deep ecology' heading which follows from the ideas of Doyle and McEachern (1998). The technocratic view is recognized by most commentators as being the dominant one globally (see Bartelmus, 1994), hence is represented as such in Figure 17.1. However, it should be remembered that this is a *spectrum* and there are many views lying between the extremes.

Sustainable tourism

Mirroring the range of views on sustainable development there is also a number of different views on sustainable tourism. One perspective on the meaning of sustainable tourism is that of a sustainable industry of tourism (Coccossis and Papairis, 1996). In this view of sustainable tourism, the development of tourism is one alternative and seen as more acceptable than other more environmentally damaging activities such as logging or mining (Holden, 2000). However, little allowance is made in this view for the cumulative impacts of tourism on the environment (Hunter, 1996).

Hunter (1996) suggested a number of other perspectives in which the environment is more, or less, central in concepts of sustainable tourism.

Dominant world-view
- Strong belief in technology for progress and solutions
- Natural world is valued as a resource rather than possessing intrinsic value
- Believes in ample resource reserves
- Favours the objective and quantitative
- Centralization of power
- Encourages consumerism

Deep ecology
- Favours low-scale technology that is self-reliant
- Sense of wonder, reverence and moral obligation to the natural world
- Recognizes the 'rights' of nature are independent of humans
- Recognizes the subjective such as feelings and ethics
- Favours local communities and localized decision-making
- Encourages the use of appropriate technology
- Recognizes that the earth's resources are limited

Figure 17.1
Differences in views of development between the 'dominant world-view' and 'deep ecology' (Adapted from Bartelmus, 1994.)

There is another position in which the environment is given more consideration than in the previously discussed perspective. However, even in this position the environment comes second to attempts to develop tourism. Hunter stated this position may be defensible in communities that are heavily dependent on tourism and where changes would lead to significant threats to the community. Hunter suggested a third form of sustainable tourism that he termed 'environmentally led tourism'. In this form, a quality tourism experience is equated with a high quality environment. In this scenario, there would be a strong link between the success of the tourism industry and environmental conservation. Unlike the former example of product-led tourism, here the environment is prioritized and forms of tourism are developed that are not damaging to it (Holden, 2000). Hunter suggested a fourth scenario, which he termed 'neotenous' tourism, in which very little or actually no tourism is permitted. This would be in relation to particularly environmentally sensitive areas.

Much of the preceding discussion has not made explicit that statements on sustainable tourism need to be related to value judgements. Hence, the interpretation of the term sustainable tourism is very closely related to the political context in which the term is being applied. Butler and Hall (1998) argued strongly that it is actually impossible to separate concepts of sustainable tourism from the value system and political context in which these are being used.

If in early definitions of sustainable tourism the environment was central, then during the late 1980s and early 1990s socio-cultural factors were linked closely to the concept. By the last decade of the twentieth century, sustainability was usually assumed to refer to the specifically environmental and cultural aspects of the visitor destination area. However, it is possible to suggest that it is rather artificial to consider only these aspects from the total of all elements that make up the tourism experience. Hence, tourism sustainability has an economic and organizational dimension as well as socio-cultural and environmental aspects.

One of the early thinkers who set concepts of tourism sustainability within the context of tourism planning and management was Innskeep. His views give an indication of how sustainable tourism was conceived at the beginning of the last decade of the twentieth century. The case study of leisure and tourism planning later in the chapter gives an indication of some of Innskeep's ideas in action.

Innskeep (1991) suggested that, in relation to practical applications of concepts of sustainable tourism, there are a number of assumptions that underpin these concepts. These assumptions and further comments are presented in the case study below.

Case study

Innskeep's (1991) concept of sustainable tourism

Innskeep's assumptions underlying the concept of sustainable tourism include the belief that:

- it is possible to *actually define and achieve* the type of tourism you want;
- it is possible to *establish and sustain* appropriate levels of visitor flow;
- it is possible to *define and promote equity* in development and to reconcile any conflicts arising between the stakeholders involved – the tourist, the resident, the industry agent and the government – and that an appropriate balance of interests can be achieved between host and guest and between private interest and public good.
- sustainability is *maintainable* over the long term.

A number of comments can be made in relation to Innskeep's claims.

1 In relation to the statement about equity, this implies equal rights and equal gains, or certainly a balance of interests and benefits that sustains all parties to the relationship. Such equity is established through a mix of formal rules and implicit understanding of the limits, directions and the boundaries of the development game. Development decisions, however, often involve more than just specifically tourism issues, but extend into wider physical resource issues and culture relationships that bring whole communities of interest together.

2 It is possible to sustain integrity/authenticity in the host tourism product. This has to do with keeping the original 'indigenous values' intact without any appreciable modification to accommodate its 'touristic' values. Product modification to suit tourism use, it is usually claimed, is to be avoided except where it accords with a natural restoration or compatible extension of the original function or purpose. This is not always easy. For example, controversy currently surrounds the degree of legitimate restoration allowable for such historic places, monuments, buildings as the ruins of Pompeii, the Sphinx in Egypt, the frescoes of Venice and the art and ruins of Ankhor Wat.

3 It is possible to ask the question: Does sustainable tourism actually work to improve the quality of life of the host community? It is possible that the outcome of contact between the host and the guest may be positive and both gain and negative aspects are minimal in the long term. However, the host community is generally poorly represented as a direct voice in tourism industry policy groups. It is usually non-existent at the national level of government and forms only part of the ratepayers perspective at the local and regional levels. The surveys by Getz and Haralambopolous and Pizam in Chapter 5 and the study of the Pohangina Valley in Chapter 11 give an indication of local communities stake in tourism development, and awareness of the costs and benefits of tourism.

(Adapted from Innskeep, E. (1991). *Tourism Planning*. New York, Van Nostrand.)

Drawing on the work of Innskeep, a model of sustainable tourism can be created. This model can be represented as being: non-intrusive, non-depleting and renewable, scaled to the particular environment, natural in material make-up and presentation and well integrated into the local physical, social, cultural and economic environments. The characteristics of Innskeep's (1991) model are as follows:

- non-depleting in its use of local resources;
- non-intrusive in the way it fits with the local physical, social, cultural and economic environments;
- a user of natural resources that are minimally transposed or re-configured;
- integrated with the local physical, social, cultural and economic environment rather than being shut-in on itself;
- more focused on the high-quality–high-yield end of the commercial product spectrum in contrast to the high-profit rapid turnover model;
- more centred on the qualitative aspects of individual experience than a quantitative 'been there done that' model of many group-centred options;
- one in which the balance of market power lies with the host community and in which the resident has a recognized voice in the definition and management of the tourism product and its context;
- one in which the industry is managed by an appropriate blend of public sector good and enlightened private sector self-interest.

The UK Department of Environment/ETB (1991) in the Report referred to in a number of earlier chapters, (it produced the triangle of environment, visitor and host, see Figure 7.2) developed some guiding principles for sustainable tourism. These are as follows (ETB, 1991):

- The environment has an intrinsic value that outweighs its value as a tourism asset. Its enjoyment by future generations and its long-term survival must not be prejudiced by short-term considerations.
- Tourism should be recognized as a positive factor with the potential to benefit the community and the place as well as the visitor
- The relationship between tourism and the environment must be managed so that the environment is sustainable in the long term. Tourism must not be allowed to damage the resource, prejudice its future enjoyment or bring unacceptable impacts.
- Tourism activities and development should respect the scale, nature and character of the place in which they are sited.
- In any location, harmony must be sought between the needs of the visitor, place and the host community.
- In a dynamic world, some change is inevitable and change can often be beneficial. Adaption to change, however, should not be at the expense of any of these principles.
- The tourism industry, local authorities and environmental agencies all have a duty to respect the above principles and to work together to achieve their practical realization in achieving sustainable tourism.

These guidelines stressed the need for a balance between the place, the visitor and the host community. However as Holden (2000) suggested the ETB Report is somewhat simplistic in that implies tourists are one homogenous group. Nevertheless, the report does emphasize the important role of the local community in sustainable tourism and the role of communities has been discussed in a number of earlier chapters.

The ETB guidelines clearly indicate the central importance of the environment, and increasingly it is being argued that community control over tourism is necessary, particularly by those who advocate greater democracy in tourism decision-making. However, even with tourism decision-making under local control there is no guarantee, that sustainable forms of development will be selected. Indeed, Holden (2000) reported two examples in which local communities in Scotland and South Africa, respectively, supported development that was damaging to the environment because of the perceived economic and social benefits. The following case study of local planning in New Zealand discusses local community stakeholder participation and indicates the possible contribution of such groups and individuals to more sustainable forms of tourism. This study also stresses the importance of gathering and using relevant data in making planning decisions.

Case study

Leisure and tourism planning in the Manawatu Region of New Zealand

This case study is based on research that involved two projects investigating recreation and tourism issues. One study involved mountain biking in the Manawatu region and the other the use of an urban walkway in Palmerston North, both in New Zealand.

The first stage of the mountain biking research consisted of a postal questionnaire, which was sent to all current members of the Manawatu Mountain Bike Club. One important recommendation made by respondents was the establishment of a mountain biking forum, to provide an opportunity for on-going discussion of mountain biking issues. The first meeting of this mountain biking forum, hosted by the Palmerston North City Council (PNCC), and chaired by staff from the Recreation & Community Development Unit, was held in September 1998. A number of stakeholders were invited to the meeting, including the two Recreation & Community Development Unit staff, two members of the Manawatu Mountain Biking Club, a member of a local tramping (hill walking) club (also a mountain biker), a representative from the environmental organization, Forest and Bird and a couple who owned and ran one of the four bicycle shops in Palmerston North. A particular focus at the meeting was on whether there should be a dedicated mountain bike area or multiple use tracks in the Palmerston North area. It was decided to investigate the possibility of sites within Palmerston North for a dedicated mountain biking area.

Resulting from this research, the authors were asked to comment on the PNCC's Recreation Plan for the Manawatu Region 1998–2003. It was noted in this report that only a limited amount of research had been conducted on user groups, different types of activities and potential management issues associated with a key recreational resource, the Manawatu Riverside Walkway and Bridle Track (MRWBT). The MRWBT research involved a questionnaire survey to a sample of the 'walkway' users, conducted on the MRWBT itself via face to face contact between researchers and respondents. The high response rate would indicate a strong interest from the community concerning the recreational and tourism use of the MRWBT.

Figure 17.2 is an attempt to summarize the approach used in the mountain biking and the MRWBT research projects, set against the apparent PNCC response to planning decisions in the recreation/tourism area prior to this. Column A, in Figure 17.2, shows the PNCC (Council) approach. It is suggested in Figure 17.2 that such a policy is unsatisfactory for the following reasons:

1 This approach appears to lack an explicitly stated rationale for the management of recreation/tourism issues.
2 The actions of the council can be seen as reactive, not proactive, and decisions have been made without the necessary data to support them.
3 The consequences in terms of views not being heard, needs not being met and the potential for user group conflict are indicated. The Manawatu based research suggested the importance of acquiring the views of stakeholders.

	A	B	C
	Council approach	Mountain Bike Research approach	Walkway Research approach
		Need for policy	
Initial planning response	Create policy without data	Independent research: questionnaire and focus groups (one user group involved)	Independent research: questionnaire and focus groups (a number of user groups involved)
Initial consequence	Policy inaccurate?	Recommendations based on research findings	Recommendations based on research findings from a larger sample of user groups
Long-term consequences	(a) User group conflict (b) Needs not met (c) Lack of consultation (d) Lack of involvement	(a) Establishment of a forum (b) Informed discussion (c) Views heard (d) On-going involvement	(a) Establishment of a forum? (b) Informed discussion (c) Greater variety of views heard? (d) On-going involvement
Time dimension	Quick? (quick fix)	Slow? (continuous monitoring)	Potentially slower? (continuous monitoring)
Cost dimension	Cheap?	Expensive?	More expensive
Local political dimension	Satisfies elected council	Satisfies user group	Potentially satisfies more user groups

Figure 17.2 Recreation and tourism planning approaches in the Manawatu

The only perceived advantage of such an approach is that, as it does not involve detailed consultation, it is relatively inexpensive. However, the political process often requires the compilation of strategies within tightly defined time frames, which is not necessarily accommodating of the suggested 'research approach' shown in columns B and C of Figure 17.2.

In contrast to column A, column B in Figure 17.2, summarizes the approach used in the mountain bike research. This 'research approach' is viewed as a more desirable approach to planning for the following reasons:

1 The decision-making was based on the gathering of data relevant to the issue.
2 Informed discussion took place. The views of one user group, the Manawatu Mountain Biking Club were stated via the questionnaire survey and the focus groups. The views of the club were also reiterated at the mountain biking forum meetings. Additionally, some indication of the views of other users groups, stakeholders and interested parties, were heard at the mountain biking forum meetings.

Such an approach, as indicated in column B of Figure 17.2, suffers the disadvantage, however, of being slow and hence perceived as expensive.

Column C exemplifies the evolutionary stage of an applied recreation and tourism planning model,

and it is possible to indicate the following:

1 The research approach adopted has generated responses from a number of user groups, which, it is hoped will provide detailed data to inform the planning and management decision making process.
2 The research approach involving personal contact on the MRWTB during the questionnaire survey has enabled users to express their preferences and concerns. Traditionally, on issues such as this, consultation with the public has taken place via public submissions and interactive public. These place the onus on the participant.
3 A significant number of respondents indicated their willingness to participate in follow-up focus groups, providing further opportunities for opinions to be expressed.

However, a disadvantage of the process shown in column C is that it is likely to be more time-consuming and more costly.

Nevertheless, as the research has sought to involve the community in the planning process, it is suggested that a variety of views will have been heard. Hence, it is hoped that any decision relating to the future recreation and tourism use of the MRWBT will reflect a number of community values. Ideally, the process outlined in column C will ensure that recreation and tourism planning does not occur in isolation from its social context. It is hoped that the planning process adopted in column B and, to a greater extent in Column C of Figure 17.2, may lead to more sustainable forms of recreation and tourism, as the views of user groups are heard and heeded, rather than these groups having decisions forced on them.

(Adapted from Mason and Leberman, 1998; and Leberman and Mason, 2002)

Discussion on sustainable tourism in this chapter, so far has concentrated, largely, on the impacts of tourism itself and how tourism can become more sustainable in terms of, for example, the environment or local communities. However, this ignores the fact that tourism like many other human activities is affected by events beyond the control of those directly involved in it, (such as tourists, host communities and even members of the tourism industry). In other words, tourism is subject to important external forces, both natural and man-made.

However, much thinking in tourism planning and management has ignored external factors. If these are ignored, then it is relatively easy to believe that tourism activities are the result of known factors and are generally predictable. The assumption that causal relationships can be discerned easily and hence that events are predictable is based on a view of the world that is often described as reductionist (Capra, 1982). In this view, which is largely influenced by the ideas of scientists such as Galileo and Newton, objects and events can be understood in terms of their constituent parts and these parts fit together like cogs in a machine and hence every event is determined by initial conditions that are, in principle, predictable (Faulkner and Russell, 1997). This view has held sway in the natural sciences until the early part of the twentieth century and has also been greatly influential in the social sciences, including tourism studies until very recently.

However, particularly in the second half of the twentieth century, the ideas of Einstein on relativity and Heisenberg's uncertainty principle, meant a revolution in scientific thinking in which it was accepted that the universe is more complex and chaotic than originally conceived. Faulkner and Russell (1997) have applied the idea of chaos to the social sciences and specifically to tourism studies. They suggested that in science, the language used involving linear concepts and machine analogies is now being replaced by a world of non-linearity, spontaneity and surprise and these concepts are being set alongside attributes normally associated with living organisms, such as adaptation, coherence and organization (Faulkner and Russell, 1997).

In terms of tourism, Faulkner and Russell put forward a number of key ideas based on the application of the notions of chaos and complexity and these are shown in Figure 17.3. In Figure 17.3, a number of examples are provided, and several of these, such as changing of gambling laws in Nevada and the development of new forms of transport, indicate that there are changes from outside that have influenced tourism.

Figure 17.3 does not, however, indicate that natural events can greatly influence tourism. For example the eruption of a dormant volcano on the Caribbean island of Montserrat in 1997, severely disrupted the tourism economy, not only because of the perception created, that the island was a dangerous place to visit, but because it actually permanently covered some of the island's tourism resources in lava and ash. Storms, floods and tsunamis

Concept	Tourism elements/examples
Bottom-up synthesis: individual agents driven by simple rules of transaction give rise to complex, dynamic systems.	• Host–guest relationship between visitors and residents. • Client–service provider relationship between tourist and tourism industry. • Competitive relationships between providers of similar services/product. • Cooperative relationships between vertically integrated providers or coalitions of providers at a single destination. • Regulator–regulatee relationship between public and private sector agents.
Butterfly effect: initial small random change or perturbation induces a chain reaction that precipitates a dramatic event or shift of considerable magnitude.	• Relaxation of legal restrictions on gambling in Nevada initiates development of Las Vegas as major tourist destination. • Terrorist activities in Europe in the 1980s boost international arrivals in safe destinations such as Australia (Faulkner, 1990).
Lock-in effect: where accidents of history have a lasting effect long after the conditions that influenced their initial impact have subsided or where innovations have a lasting effect despite being superseded by new technology.	• The Las Vegas example (i.e. in the sense that this destination has maintained and enhanced its position inspite of Nevada no longer being the only state in the US to have legalized gambling).
Edge of chaos (phase shift): a state of tenuous equilibrium whereby small changes ('mutations') involving individual agents may be enough to precipitate evolutionary change in the system through mutual adaptation of its constituents.	• Displacement of railway-based system of tourist services by car-based network. • Phase shifts in the life-cycle of destinations.

Figure 17.3 Basic concepts of chaos and complexity and corresponding examples in tourism (Adapted from Faulkner and Russell, 1997.)

are other natural events that can cause major disruptions to tourism activities. Although it is generally known when these might occur and even where, the specifics of force of individual events, precisely when and exactly where they will occur is still not possible to accurately predict. Hence, such events do not fit neatly into the scientific linear conceptualization of tourism activities.

It has been argued that if we accept that we live in an increasingly complex world then, the type of natural or man-made disasters referred to above will become more common (Faulkner, 2001). However, the impacts of disasters on tourism activities (and hence by implication their relevance for tourism planning and management) have been little researched. Faulkner, in attempting to create an agenda for this type of research, tried to distinguish between disasters and crises. He indicated that it is commonly accepted that crises tend to be associated with on-going change that an organisation has failed to respond to and not adapted, while a disaster is the result of a sudden event (or events) that an organization has failed to respond to at all.

Nevertheless, both crises and disasters may have very similar features and, in particular, generate similar impacts (Faulkner, 2001). Fink (1986) attempted to distil the main ingredients of disasters and crises and came up with the following aspects:

• There is usually a triggering event, which is so major that it challenges existing structures, routines and even survival of an organization.

- They are characterized by fluid dynamic situations.
- There is an element of surprise with a high threat and short decision time.
- For at least part of the event, a feeling of an inability to cope.
- A turning point, when a decisive change will happen which may have both negative and positive dimensions, to the extent that even if the event is well managed, the organization will experience great change that may be irreversible.

In the early part of the twenty-first century, despite the general belief that life on earth is becoming more complex, there is as yet insufficient evidence to indicate whether crises and disasters are becoming more common, than in earlier epochs. Neither is it clear, yet, the effect that such events may have on tourism and the various attempts to make the activity more sustainable. Nevertheless, chaos theory provides important perspectives on tourism planning and management. In the final chapter of the book, a number of important events that have occurred in the early part of the twenty-first century, and in particular, global terrorism are discussed in relation to global complexity and chaos.

Summary

Sustainability is a term that is used often in relation to tourism planning and management. Concepts of sustainable tourism have been derived from concerns with sustainable development. A number of statements on sustainable development appeared in the 1980s. The first major statement on sustainable tourism appeared in 1990. Since then the concept has developed and changed. Early ideas on sustainable tourism usually focused on environmental sustainability. More recent statements have been concerned with socio-cultural and economic factors. The role of host communities has also featured significantly in recent comments on sustainable tourism. It is possible to subdivide comments on sustainable tourism into groupings such as 'technocentric' or 'ecocentric'. It is very likely that concepts of sustainable tourism will continue to evolve over the next decade, and that tourism planning and management will reflect these changing notions.

Student activities

1 What do you understand by the term sustainability?
2 What is sustainable development?
3 What is sustainable tourism?
4 Why could it be difficult to achieve sustainable tourism?
5 How did views on sustainability and sustainable tourism develop in the last decade of the twentieth century?
6 With reference to the case study, how can the involvement of the local community contribute to more sustainable tourism? What problems may arise as the result of greater involvement of local communities in tourism development?
7 What do you think will be the chief components of sustainable tourism in the year 2021?

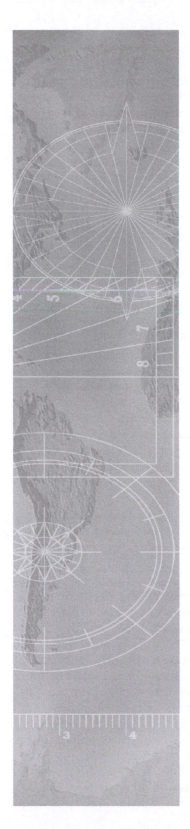

Conclusions and the future of tourism planning and management

This book has discussed social and economic factors that have contributed to the rise of modern mass tourism. It has considered a variety of tourism effects under the headings of economic, socio-cultural and environmental impacts. It has also tried to show that although it is conventional to sub-divide these impacts in any given situation under a number of headings, it is most likely that the impacts will be multi-faceted and not that easily separable.

The fact that tourism impacts are multi-faceted contributes to them being difficult to plan for and manage. There are a number of different organisations, groups and individuals that have an important role to play in tourism planning and management. These key players, in the form of tourists, host community members, industry members, government representatives, and to a lesser extent the media and voluntary organizations, are involved in the day to day problems of tourism. In most demo-cratic countries, at least, these individuals, groups and organi-zations are in a position to play an active part in tourism planning and management.

The book has considered a number of different approaches and techniques for managing tourism. Managing visitors is clearly an important part of managing tourism. The natural resources for tourism, the environment and landscape require particular approaches and techniques. The use of both educa-tion, through interpretation, and regulation, particularly in the form of guidelines and codes of conduct are assuming greater importance as tools in tourism management. Information technology, particularly the use of various forms of GIS is also becoming a significant factor in tourism management.

The different sectors and players in tourism have tended, traditionally, not to work together. In the last 10–15 years of the twentieth century, this situation was changing as partnerships between the public and private sector and collaboration between individuals, groups and organization became not only more common but also perceived as generally desirable. A major reason for this desire for collaboration has been the wish to achieve more sustainable forms of tourism. Despite a lack of full agreement on their meanings, sustainability and tourism were almost inextricably linked concepts in the last decade of the twentieth century.

Influences on the future of tourism

A number of issues are pertinent to the future direction of tourism and there are various influences on these possible future directions. Consumer choices and preferences will be a key factor in this future direction of tourism. In the past, the 'pile' em high sell 'em cheap' approach secured a market made up of the great majority of tourists. In the last decade of the twentieth century, there was a growing number of tourists who appeared to be willing to pay a premium for a high quality tourist experience. For some, ecotourism is the chosen option when seeking out what they as a high quality holiday. However, confusion still surrounds the exact nature of ecotourism and it has been suggested that, over time, it will become merely a variant of mass tourism, rather than a true alternative to it.

It is clear that the resources for tourism, particularly the natural and semi-natural environmental features, but also man-made components of the environment that have become attractions, are actually finite. This has led to calls to make these resources in particular, but also the field of tourism generally, more sustainable. With reference to specific destinations, a complete halt to tourism development may be considered desirable by some members of the community, and in a number of cases this may be a majority view, but it is unlikely that tourism growth will be stopped. In fact, the reverse of this looks more likely as all types of tourist travel continue to grow. In the near future, virtual tourism using electronic media such as the world wide web is likely to become more popular. In early 2001, the first space tourist orbited the Earth on a Russian rocket and, it and may soon be possible for (albeit a small elite group of very wealthy) travellers to leave this planet and take holidays in space on a more regular basis.

Evidence from the previous century, particularly the last 40 years of it, would seem to suggest, that neither virtual tourism, nor space tourism, is likely to offset longer term growth trends for tourism on planet earth. However, a number of critical incidents in the early part of the twenty-first century have called into question whether this growth will continue as rapidly as previously, or may indeed even fall away.

In the United Kingdom, the outbreak of Foot and Mouth Disease in early 2001, led to the almost complete closure of large parts of the UK countryside until late summer 2001. This caused major disruption not only to the farming community, but also more importantly, in terms of the focus of this book, led to significant impacts on tourism in the UK countryside. Lack of access during the outbreak of Foot and Mouth Disease, for both domestic and international visitors was the key effect on UK rural tourism and visitor numbers were down throughout most of 2001. However, impacts in terms of visitor numbers were geographically patchy, as UK coastal and urban areas appear to have been far less affected during the summer of 2001 than rural areas, and may even have benefited from the restrictions on access to rural areas.

In the early part of the twenty-first century, other global tourism destinations also suffered from localized problems affecting visitor numbers, including the effects of natural phenomenon such as volcanic eruptions, storms and flooding. But these were not particularly unusual in terms of the history of global tourism development. However, the events of 11 September 2001 in the United States and other related terrorist attacks appear more unusual and may have long-term effects on the global tourism industry. The terrorist attacks are seen as different, as they are being viewed as part of a global, not local threat. In terms of tourism, in the United States particularly, the terrorist attacks have had a significant impact on potential and real travellers. The impacts of the events of 11 September 2001 have also continued well after the event. In terms of consequences for the tourism industry, for example, the bankruptcy of the large carrier, American Airlines in 2002, has been linked closely to the drop in passenger numbers since the terrorist attack. The failure of tourist numbers to recover from the Foot and Mouth Disease outbreak in the autumn of 2001 in the United Kingdom was attributed at least in part to the relatively small number of US visitors compared to previous years coming to Britain in the autumn of 2001. The effect of events in the United States on tourism in the United Kingdom also indicates the global nature of this problem.

Although the terrorist attacks of 11 September 2001 have had effects on the tourism at a global scale, in the immediate aftermath of the attacks they were seen as having only indirect effects. However, in October 2002 this perspective changed radically when tourists became the major target of terrorists. On the Indonesian island of Bali, two night-clubs, containing mainly international tourists became the target of terrorists who were linked by the media to the groups that had perpetrated the attacks in the United States in September 2001. The nature and consequences of this direct terrorist attack on tourists is discussed in the following case study.

Case study

The Bali terrorist bombings of October 2002

October 12th's bombing of two night-clubs at Kuta Beach on the coast of the island of Bali, Indonesia, killed more than 180 people and was the worst terrorist attack in Indonesian history. By 18 October, 183 people were known to have died and more than 300 were injured. The largest group of dead and injured came from Australia, but British, Americans, New Zealanders, Germans and French were among the casualties, as well as local Indonesians.

In the immediate aftermath of the bombing no one claimed responsibility. But the apparent sophistication of the operation and the known existence of active groups of supporters of Osama bin Laden, led both the Indonesian authorities and President Bush to blame the terrorism on al-Qaida and its extremist allies.

This attack follows on from recent attacks on a French tanker and American soldiers in Yemen. One consequence of this action in Bali is that Indonesia will need to re-evaluate its relaxed policy towards terrorism. It is likely that the Indonesian people will, however, not be spared the long-term consequences of Saturday's attack or the failure of the government to deal effectively with terrorists. Approximately 1.5 million foreigners visited Bali in 2001, almost one third of the 5 million international visitors to Indonesia. Visitors to Bali contributed almost US$ 2 million to the Indonesian economy in 2001.

Indonesia is predominantly a Muslim country, but Bali is an island where the Hindu religion has been practised for several hundred years. The islands relaxed attitudes to sex and dress codes, as well as general expectations of tourist behaviour, compared to many other parts of Indonesia, has encouraged foreign tourists and particularly young Western backpackers to visit. It is probably the relatively unrestrained nature of life on an island surrounded by a country with generally stricter Islamic beliefs, coupled with the presence of large numbers of foreign visitors that has made Bali a suitable (and now it is recognised a too easy) target for militant Muslim terrorists.

As early as 2 days after the bombings, several tour operators from the United Kingdom, United States and Australia were flying clients out of the island. A large number of Western tourists in Bali were on round-the-world tickets and many of these were expected to be leaving earlier than expected. A senior spokesperson for the Association for British Travel Agents suggested that it would probably be a couple of years before the island recovered. He insisted that it would recover, arguing that it was unlikely tourist would be put off visiting Muslim countries. The Luxor Massacre in Egypt in 1997 was the worst terrorist attack on holiday-makers before the Bali outrage. Numbers here were severely depressed for 2 years but were back to pre-attack figures by 2000.

At the end of December 2002, a, somewhat confusing, picture of tourism in Bali post the attack was emerging. The UK-based *Guardian* newspaper showed photographs of empty beaches and suggested that tourists had abandoned the island, while the Australian newspaper, *The Sydney Morning Herald*, published a story that Qantas Airlines had reported almost full flights to Bali over the Christmas 2002 period.

(Based on reports in the following newspapers and their respective websites: *The Guardian*, *The Sydney Morning Herald*, *The Age* and the *Milwaukee Journal Sentinel*)

The Bali terrorist attack on tourists calls into question whether tourism will continue to expand in terms of visitor numbers, as well as spread relentlessly to all parts of the globe. Nevertheless, it is probably appropriate to assume that tourism numbers will continue to increase on a global scale, despite possible significant setbacks at specific locations, for the foreseeable future. Under such circumstances, if tourism reaches almost all parts of the earth, it will be vital that careful planning and management policies are adopted and applied. In the past, tourism planning and management has been viewed largely as the responsibility of government. In the future, it is likely that the private sector, in terms of representatives of the tourism industry will be more actively involved in planning and managing tourism. This may occur in the form of partnerships with sectors of government. Such partnerships are also likely to involve other interested parties including NGOs. It is a strong possibility that representatives of host communities will also be more involved in decision-making about future tourism developments in their immediate area.

The success of tourism planning and management in the early part of the twenty-first century in avoiding the worst excesses of uncontrolled tourism growth and in promoting more beneficial consequences of tourism, will depend not only on structures, organizations and individuals, but the political will that accepts that it is possible and desirable to plan and manage tourism.

Data in Chapter 1, indicated that one of the relatively unexploited areas for tourism, at the end of the twentieth century, was Africa. The final case study in the book considers the future of tourism in a new country in Southern Africa. This country, Namibia, which has significant tourist attractions, has only a fledgling tourism industry. The case study presents information on the obstacles to and opportunities for successfully planned, developed and managed tourism in Namibia.

Case study

Development of tourism in Namibia

Background

Namibia is an independent country located in Southwest Africa. It gained independence from South Africa in 1990, having once been a German colony. Hence, Namibia is a very new country. Prior to independence there was much political turbulence, but since there has been a high level of stability.

Tourist attractions

Namibia has many potential tourist attractions including an unusual landscape an abundance of wildlife, unique flora and diverse cultures. The landscape features of importance include the Namib Desert, which has the world's highest sand dunes, Fish Creek Canyon (the only deeper canyon is the Grand Canyon), and Etosha National Park where there is a large range of wildlife. There is also interesting heritage from the German colonial period, particularly in the capital Windhoek. The country has indigenous tribes, although there are only about 2 million people in total living there.

Tourism was the country's fourth major economic sector in the early 1990s, with about 300 000 visitors (approximately 60 per cent from South Africa and 11 per cent from Germany, reflecting the close traditional ties with these countries). The remaining visitors come from mainly Europe (United Kingdom, Italy, France) and North America. The growth in tourism was between 7 and 10 per cent per year in the mid-1990s.

As a new country, Namibia has a great opportunity to ensure its tourism development is cautious, well planned and managed. By the mid-1990s, as much as 15 per cent of the land had been designated as national park area. In 1992, the country created its first tourism master plan. This involved a 5-year strategy for the tourism industry. The plan contains statements on product development, organizational structure, the establishment of a tourism management information system, training and educating staff, marketing and financing. There is also a 'Green Plan' study, which is an attempt to control negative impacts of tourism. All tourism developers will need to conduct an Environmental Assessment Study. This study will be judged on how it contributes to sustainable development and minimizes damage to the environment.

A hotel school has been constructed near the capital Windhoek. Consultants from South Africa have been brought in to assist with the initial establishment of the school. Trainers come from a Namibian hotel chain, Namib-Sun. Short courses are planned (2–3 weeks) for front of house staff, reception staff, chefs and waiters. The school also plans to train managers. A Namibian Academy for Tourism and Hospitality has also been created and this offers training in tour guiding. This is just beginning to offer diploma and degree courses.

The tourism industry is fairly well organized in Namibia. There are associations for tour operators, hotels travel agencies and car rental companies. An organization, the Federation of Namibian Tourism

Association (FENATA) has been established to act as a link between public and private sector. The organization has representatives from the private sector and also government ministries. FENATA is used as a sounding board for new tourism developments in Namibia.

Unlike many other Southern African countries, Namibia's tourism infrastructure is relatively good. There is a well-maintained road system that reaches most parts of the country and other utilities such as electricity, water and telecommunications are generally dependable.

The accommodation sector is well organized and also well regulated. The South African 1–5 star system was used in the past, but a new system is currently being established which is better suited to Namibian conditions. There is a licensing system with over 4500 accommodation providers and approximately 10 500 beds. About two-thirds of the accommodation providers are privately owned. The government runs the other third most of which are situated in national parks. Accommodation varies from tented safari to air conditioned bungalows. However, there has been a shortage of up-market facilities and there are plans to upgrade existing accommodation as well as build new accommodation.

(Adapted from Echtner, C. (1999). Three African success stories. In *Tourism Development in Critical Environments* (T. Singh and S. Singh, eds), pp. 159–69. New York, Cognizant Communications.)

The case study suggests that Namibia has the potential to create a successful tourism industry. It also indicates that there is the likelihood of well-planned and managed tourism, in which environmental factors and socio-cultural aspects are well integrated. However, whether Namibia, like many other Developing countries, can develop tourism successfully may depend not just on factors internal to the tourism industry, but also on external aspects that are beyond its control.

Student activities

1 Why was Bali a particularly 'easy target' for a terrorist attack?

2 What factors both local and on a global scale would (a) deter potential visitors from going to Bali; (b) encourage visitor numbers to increase?

3 New York was a major target for the 11 September 2001 terrorist attacks and it is also a tourist attraction. Compare and contrast the ways in which New York and Bali responded to their respective terrorist attacks. What do you think is the long-term prognosis for tourism in each location?

4 Compare and contrast the tourism infrastructures of Namibia with those of a developed country/region with which you are familiar. Why are there differences?

5 What other factors (particularly external) than those presented in this case study are important for tourism development in Namibia?

6 Namibia is at a very early stage in its tourism development. Use tourism theories (particularly those of Butler and Doxey and also chaos theory) to prepare a number of different scenarios for tourism development in Namibia in the next 15–20 years.

7 Working, in groups of three or four, conduct a SWOT analysis of tourism in Namibia. SWOT stands for Strengths, Weaknesses, Opportunities and Threats. When preparing the SWOT analysis in your groups use the following headings:

Current location of tourism activity;
Current level of tourism development;
Nature of tourism infrastructure;

Number of tourists;
Types of tourism activity;
Resource implications – both human and natural;
Management strategies in relation to tourism.

Also consider the following (although you may know little at present):

Economic impacts of tourism;
Likely involvement of host population;
Changing attitudes of host population to tourism;
Environmental impacts of tourism;
Degree of each type of impact.

It is best to think of the SWOT activity in two parts:

(a) The strengths and weaknesses relate to the current situation (what exists at present).
(b) The opportunities and threats are related to the future. The work of applying tourism theories to Namibia in Question 3 will be useful here. Consider any other factors, such as political change, competition from elsewhere, economic change both locally and internationally and also environmental pressures.

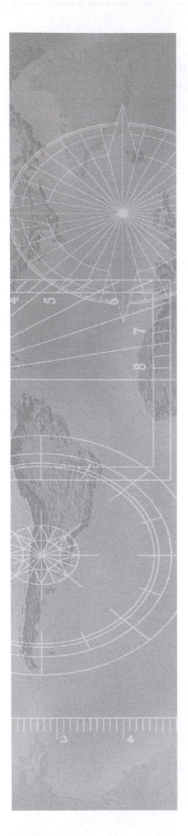

References

Agarwhal, S. (1997). The resort life cycle and seaside tourism. *Tourism Management* **18** (2), 65–73.

Ang, E. (1990). Upgrading the professionalism of tourist guides *Proceedings from the Travel Educators Forum*, PATA Conference Singapore, 11–14 July, PATA, Singapore, pp. 167–72.

Bartelmus, P. (1994). *Environment, Growth and Development: The Concepts and Strategies of Sustainability*. London, Routledge.

BBC (1991). *Ecotourism in Belize*. BBC London, Videotape.

Blamey, R. (1995). *The Nature of Ecotourism*. Occasional Paper 21, Canberra, Bureau of Tourism Research.

Boo, E. (1990). *Ecotourism: The Potential and Pitfalls*. Washington, WWF.

Bonzon-Liu, B. (1999). *An Accreditation Scheme for Ecotourism in New Zealand*. Masters Dissertation, Victoria University, Wellington, (unpublished).

Bramwell, B. and Lane, B. (2000). Introduction. In *Tourism Collaboration and Partnerships: Policy Practice and Sustainability* (B. Bramwell and B. Lane, eds), pp. 1–23. Clevedon, Channel View Publications.

Broad, G. (1996). Visitor profile and evaluation of informal education at Jersey Zoo – The Dodo. *The Journal of the Wildlife Preservation Trusts*, **32**, 166–92.

Burns, P. and Holden, A. (1995). *Tourism: A New Perspective*. London, Prentice Hall.

Burton, R. (1992). *Travel Geography*. London, Pitman.

Butler, R. (1980). The concept of a tourism area cycle of evolution. *Canadian Geographer*, **24**, 5–12.

Butler, R. W. (1991). Tourism, environment and sustainable development. *Environmental Conservation*, **18**, 201–9.

Butler, R. W. and Hall, C. M. (1998). Tourism and recreation in rural areas: myth and reality. In *Rural Tourism Management: Sustainable Options* (D. Hall and J. O'Hanlon, eds), pp. 97–108. Conference Proceedings, Ayr, Scottish Agricultural College.

Capra, F. (1982). *The Turning Point: Science, Society and the Rising Culture*. London, Flamingo.

Cater, E. (1994). Introduction. In *Ecotourism: A Sustainable Option*? (E. Cater and G. Lowman, eds). London, John Wiley and Sons.

Chadwick, G. (1971). *A Systems View of Planning*. Oxford, Pergamon.

Chadwick, R. (1987). Concepts, definitions, and measures used in travel and tourism research. In *Travel, Tourism and Hospitality Research: A Handbook for Managers and Researchers* (J. R. Brent Richie and C. Goeldner, eds). New York, Wiley.

Chavez, D. J. (1997). Mountain bike management: resource protection and social conflicts. *TRENDS*, **34**, 36–40.

Christaller, W. (1963). Some considerations of tourism locations in Europe: the peripheral regions–underdeveloped countries–recreation areas. *Papers of the Regional Science Association*, **12**, 168–78.

Clements, C., Schultz, J. and Lime, D. (1993). Recreation, tourism and the local residents: partnership or co-existence? *Journal of Park and Recreation Administration*, **11**, 78–91.

Coccossis, H. (1996). Tourism and sustainability: perspectives and implications. In *Sustainable Tourism? European Experiences* (G. K. Priestley, J. A. Edwards and H. Coccossis, eds), pp. 1–21. Wallingford, UK, CAB International.

Coccossis, H. and Parpairis, A. (1996). Tourism and carrying capacity in coastal areas: Mykonosd Greece, In *Sustainable Tourism? European Experiences* (G. K. Priestley, J. A. Edwards and H. Coccossis, eds), pp. 153–75. Wallingford, UK, CAB International.

Cohen, I. (1972). Towards a sociology of international tourism. *Social Research*, 39, 164–82.

Cooper, C., Fletcher, J., Gilbert, D. and Wanhill, S. (1998). *Tourism: Principles and Practice*. London, Longman.

Crompton, J. (1979). Motivations for pleasure vacations. *Annals of Tourism Research*, **6**, 408–24.

Crompton, J. and McKay, J. (1997). Motives of visitors attending festival events. *Annals of Tourism Research*, **24**, 425–39.

Cullingsworth, B. (1997). *Planning in the USA: Policies, Issues and Processes*. Routledge, London.

Cukier, J. and Wall, G. (1994). Tourism and employment perspectives from Bali. *Tourism Management*, **14**, 195–201.

Davison, R. (1996). The impacts of tourism. In *Tourism Destinations* (R. Davison and Maitland, eds), pp. 18–45. London, Hodder and Stoughton.

De Kadt, T. (1979). *Tourism: Passport to Development*? Oxford, Oxford University Press.

De Kadt, T. (1988). *Tourism: Passport to Development*? 2nd edn. Oxford, Oxford University Press.

Department of Tourism (1990). *Tourism Statistics 1988–9*. Department of Tourism, Kathmandu, Nepal.

Department of Tourism, Sport and Racing (1994). *Getting it Right: A Guide to Planning and Developing Sport and Recreation Facilities*. Brisbane, State of Queensland, Australia and Hillary Commission, New Zealand.

Dervis, D. and Harriot, V. (1996). Sustainable tourism development or the case of loving a place to death. In *Practising Responsible Tourism* (L. Harrison and W. Husbands, eds), pp. 422–44. New York, John Wiley & Sons.

Doorne, S. (2000). Caves, culture and crowds: carrying capacity meets consumer sovereignty. *Journal of Sustainable Tourism*, **8** (4), 34–42.

Doswell, R. (1997). *Tourism: How Effective Management Makes the Difference*. London, Butterworth-Heinemann.

Doxey. (1975). A causation theory of resident visitor irritants. In *The Sixth Annual Conference Proceedings of the Travel Research Association*, pp. 195–8.

Doyle, T. and McEachern, D. (1998). *Environment and Politics*. London, Routledge.

Drake. S. (1991). Local participation in ecotourism projects. In *Nature Tourism* (T. Whelan, ed.). Island Press, Washington.

Dunn-Ross, E. and Iso-Aloha, S. (1991). Sightseeing tourists' motivation and satisfaction. *Annals of Tourism Research*, **12**, 256–62.

Dye, T. (1992). *Understanding Public Policy*, 7th edn. Englewood Cliffs, Prentice Hall.

Dymond, S. J. (1997). Indicators of sustainable tourism in New Zealand: a local government perspective. *Journal of Sustainable Tourism*, **5**, 279–93.

Echtner, C. (1999). Three African success stories. In *Tourism Development in Critical Environments* (T. Singh and S. Singh, eds), pp. 159–69. New York, Cognizant Communications.

Elliot (1997). *Tourism Politics and Public Sector Management*. London, Routledge.

ETB (1991). *Tourism and the Environment: Maintaining the Balance*. London, English Tourism Board/Ministry of the Environment.

Faulkner, B. (2001). Towards a framework for tourism disaster management. *Tourism Management*, **22**, 135–47.

Faulkner, B. and Russell, R. (1997). Chaos and complexity in tourism: in search of a new perspective. *Pacific Tourism Review*, **1**, 93–102.

Fennell, D. (1999). *Ecotourism: An Introduction*. London, Routledge.

Fink, S. (1986). *Crisis Management*. New York, American Association of Management.

Forsyth, T. (1995). Business attitudes to sustainable tourism: self regulation in the UK outgoing tourism industry. *Journal of Sustainable Tourism*, **3** (4), 210–31.

Gilbert, J., Jones, G., Vitalis, T., Walker, R. and Gilbertson, D. (1995). *Introduction to Management in New Zealand*. Sydney, Harcourt Brace.

Getz, D. (1978). Tourism and population change: long term impacts of tourism in the Badenoch and Strathspey District of the Scottish Highlands. *Scottish Geographical Magazine*, **102**, 113–26.

Getz, D. (1994). Residents' attitudes to tourism. *Tourism Management*, **15**, 247–58.

Glyptis, S. (1994). *Countryside Recreation*. Harlow, Longman/ILAM.

Gningue, A. M. (1993). Integrated rural tourism lower Casamance. In *Beyond the Green Horizon: Discussion Paper on Sustainable Tourism* (S. Eber, ed.). Godalming, World Wide Fund for Nature/Tourism Concern.

Goodwin, H. (1996). In pursuit of ecotourism. *Biodiversity and Conservation*, **5**, 277–91.

Gow, L. J. A. (1995). Implementing sustainability: New Zealand's experience with its Resource Management Act. *Address to World Resources Institute/New Zealand Embassy Seminar*, Washington DC, 6 June 1995. Unpublished manuscript.

Gunn, C. A. (1988). *Tourism Planning*, 2nd edn. New York, Taylor and Francis.

Hall, C. M. (1992). Sex tourism in South East Asia. In *Tourism in the Developing World* (D. Harrison, ed.). Chichester, John Wiley and Sons.

Hall, C. M. (1995). *An Introduction to Tourism in Australia*, 2nd edn. Melbourne, Longman.

Hall, C. M. (2000a). *Tourism Planning*. London, Prentice Hall.

Hall, C. M. (2000b). Rethinking collaboration and partnership: a public policy perspective. In *Tourism Collaboration and Partnerships: Policy Practice and Sustainability* (B. Bramwell and B. Lane, eds), pp. 143–58. Clevedon, Channel View Publications.

Hall, C. M. and Jenkins, J. (1995). *Tourism and Public Policy*. London, Routledge.

Hall, C. M. and Kearsley, G. (2001). *Tourism in New Zealand: An Introduction*. Melbourne, Oxford University Press.

Hall, C. M. and Page, S. J. (1997). *Tourism in the Pacific*. London, International Thompson Business Publishing.

Hall, P. (1992). *Urban and Regional Planning*, 3rd edn. Harmondsworth, Penguin.

Hall, P. (1995). Towards a general urban theory. In *Cities in Competition: Productive and Sustianable Cities for the 21st Century* (J. Brotchie, M. Batty, E. Blakely, P. Hall and P. Newton, eds). Melbourne, Longman.

Hammitt, W. E. and Cole, D. N. (1998). *Wildland Recreation: Ecology and Management*, 2nd edn. New York, John Wiley & Sons, Inc.

Haralmbopolous, N. and Pizam, A. (1996). Perceived impacts of tourism: the case of Samos. *Annals of Tourism Research*, **23** (3), 503–26.

Harrill, R. and Potts, T. (2002). Social psychological theories of tourist motivation: exploration, debate and transition. *Tourism Analysis*, **7**, 105–14.

Harris, R. and Walshaw, A. (1995). In *Sustainable Tourism: An Australian Perspective* (R. Harris and N. Leiper, eds). Chatswood, Butterworth-Heinemann, Australia.

Hasse, J. C. and Milne, S. (1999). *Tourism and community development: stakeholder participation and GIS*. Paper presented at the *Tourism Policy and Planning Conference*, 12 September 1999. Oamaru, University of Otago, New Zealand.

Healey, P. (1997). *Collaborative Planning: Shaping Places in Fragmented Societies*. Basingstoke, Macmillan.

Hendricks, W. W. (1995). A resurgence in recreation conflict research: introduction to the special issue. *Leisure Sciences*, **17**, 157–8.

Hirschmann, A. (1976). Policy making and policy analysis in Latin America: a return journey. *Policy Sciences*, **6**, 385–402.

Holden, A. (2000). *Environment and Tourism*. London, Routledge.

Holden, A. and Ewen, M. (2002). Understanding the motivations of ecotourists. *International Journal of Tourism Research*, **4**, 435–46.

Horn, C. (1994). *Conflict in recreation: the case of mountain-bikers and trampers*. MA thesis, Lincoln University, Lincoln (Unpublished).

Howard, J. (1997). Towards best practice in interpretive guided activities. *Australian Parks and Recreation*, **Summer**, 1997–8.

Hunter, C. (1996). Sustainable tourism as an adaptive paradigm, *Annals of Tourism Research*, **24**, 850–67.

Hunter, C. and Green, H. (1995). *Tourism and the Environment: A Sustainable Relationship*? London, Routledge.

Innskeep, E. (1991). *Tourism Planning*. New York, Van Nostrand.

Iso-Aloha, S. (1980). *The Social-Psychology of Leisure and Recreation*. Iowa, Brown.

Jafari, J. (1981). Editor's page. *Annals of Tourism Research*, **8**.

Jafari, J. (1990). Editor's page. *Annals of Tourism Research*, **16**, 3.

Jenkins, J. (1991). Tourism development strategies. *Developing Tourism Destinations* (L. J. Lickorish, ed.), pp. 61–77. Harlow, Longman.

Jenkins, J. (1993). Tourism policy in rural New South Wales – policy and research. *Geojournal*, **29**, 281–90.

Jenkins, P. (1997). *Tourism Policy and Planning: Case Studies from the Caribbean*. New York, Cognizant Communications Corporation.

Jurowski, C. (1996). Tourism means more than money to the host community. *Parks and Recreation*, **31**, 110–18.

Knudson, D. M., Cable, T. T. and Beck, L. (1995). *Interpretation of Natural and Cultural Resources*. State College, Pennsylvania, Venture Publishing.

Kotler, P., Haider, D. and Rein, I. (1993). *Marketing Places: Attracting Investment, Industry and Tourism to Cities, States and Nations*. New York, Free Press.

Krippendorf, J. (1987). *The Holiday Makers*, London, Heinemann.

Lang, R. (1985). Planning for integrated development. Paper presented at *Conference on Integrated Development Beyond the City*, 14–16 June, Rural Tourism and Small Town Research and Studies Programme, Mount Allison University, Sackville, New Brunswick, Canada.

Lasswell, H. (1936). *Who gets What, When and How*. New York, McGraw Hill.

Leberman, S. I. and Mason, P. (1998). Mountain biking in the Manawatu: participants, perceptions and management issues. In *Rural Tourism Management: Sustainable Options, Conference Proceedings* (D. Hall and J. O'Hanlon, eds), pp. 309–21. Ayr, Scottish Agricultural College.

Leberman, S. I. and Mason, P. (2002). Planning for recreation and tourism at the local level. *Tourism Geographies*, **4**, 3–21.

Leiper, N. (1990). *The Tourism System*. Plamerston North, New Zealand Massey University Department of Management Systems.

Leiper, N. (1999). Ten myths about tourism. *Conference Proceedings 1999 CAUTHE National Research Conference*, Adelaide, pp. 1–11.

Lickorish, L. J. (1991). Roles of government and private sector. In *Developing Tourism Destinations* (L. J. Lickorish, ed.), pp. 121–146. Harlow, Longman.

Mabey, D. (1994). Youth leadership: commitment for what. In *Bold Ideas: Creative Approaches to the Challenge of Youth Programming* (S. York and D. Jordan, eds). Institute for Youth Leaders, University of Iowa.

MacAdam, P. (1999). Geographical information systems and their application within tourism. *Journal of Sustainable Tourism*, **7** (1), 62–74.

MacCannell, D. (1995). *The Tourist Papers*. London, Routledge.

McArthur, S. (1996). Interpretation in Australia: is it running on borrowed time? *Australian Parks and Recreation*, **Winter** 33–6.

McCabe, V., Poole, B., Weeks, P. and Leiper, N. (2000). *The Business and Management of Conventions*. Melbourne, John Wiley and Sons.

McCool, S. and Martin, S. (1994). Community attitudes towards tourism development. *Journal of Travel Research*, **32**, 29–34.

McKercher, B. (1993). Some fundamental truths about tourism: understanding tourism's social, and environmental impacts. *Journal of Sustainable Tourism*, **1**, 6–16.

Malloy, D. and Fennell, D. (1998). Ecotourism and ethics: moral development and organisational cultures. *Journal of Travel Research*, **36**, 47–56.

Mannell, R. and Kleber, D. (1997). *A Social Psychology of Leisure*. State College Pennsylvania, Venture Publishing.

Maslow, A. (1943). A theory of human motivation. *Psychological Review*, **50**, 7–23.

Maslow, A. (1954). *Motivation and Personality*. New York, Harper.

Mason, P. (1990). *Tourism: Environment and Development Perspectives*. Godalming, UK, World Wide Fund for Nature.

Mason, P. (1991). *Internal Report on the Annapurna Conservation Area Project*. Prepared for WWF UK, Godalming (unpublished).

Mason, P. (1992). The environmentally-friendly traveller. In *The Travellers Handbook* (M. Shales, ed.), pp. 32–6. London, Wexas.

Mason, P. (1995). *Tourism: Environment and Development Perspectives*. Godalming, UK, World Wide Fund for Nature.

Mason, P. (1997). Codes of conduct in the Arctic and sub-Arctic region. *Journal of Sustainable Tourism*, **5**, 151–65.

Mason, P. (1999). *Wellington Zoo: Visitor Survey and Keeper Evaluation. An Interim Report to the Zoo Management Committee*, Department of Management Systems, Massey University, New Zealand.

Mason, P. and Cheyne, J. (2000). Resident attitudes to tourism development. *Annals of Tourism Research*, **27** (2), 391–412.

Mason, P. and Leberman, S. I. (1998). *Mountain Biking in the Palmerston North Area: Participants, Preferences and Management Issues*. Report to the Recreation and Community Development Unit of the Palmerston North City Council, June. Department of Management Systems, Massey University, New Zealand.

Mason, P. and Leberman, S. (2000). Local planning for recreation and tourism: mountain biking in the Manawatu region of New Zealand. *Journal of Sustainable Tourism*, **8**, 84–97.

Mason, P., Johnston, M. and Twynam, D. (2000). The World Wide Fund for Nature Arctic Tourism Project. *Journal of Sustainable Tourism*, **8** (4), 305–23.

Mason, P. and Legg, S. (1999). Antarctic tourism: activities, impacts, management issues and a proposed research agenda. *Pacific Tourism Review*, **3**, 71–84.

Mason, P. and Mowforth, M. (1995). *Codes of Conduct in Tourism*, Research Paper No. 1, Department of Geographical Sciences, University of Plymouth.

Mason, P. and Mowforth, M. (1996). Codes of conduct in tourism. *Progress in Tourism and Hospitality Research*, **2**, 151–67.

Mason, P., Leberman, S. and Barnett, S. (2000b). Walkway users: an urban based case study from New Zealand. *Conference Proceedings: Tourism 2000: Time for Celebration?* (M. Robinson, P. Long, and B. Bramwell, eds), pp. 207–20.

Matthieson, A. and Wall, G. (1982). *Tourism: Economic, Social and Environmental Impacts*. London, Longman.

Middleton, V. (1994). *Marketing in Travel and Tourism*. London, Routledge.

Middleton, V. T. R. and Hawkins, R. (1998). *Sustainable Tourism: A Marketing Perspective*. London, Butterworth-Heinemann.

Moore, R. L. (1994). *Conflicts on Multiple-use Trails: Synthesis of the Literature and State of the Practice*. FHWA-PD-94–031. Raleigh, NC, North Carolina University.

Moscardo, G. (1996). Mindfull visitors: heritage and tourism. *Annals of Tourism Research*, **23**, 376–97.

Moscardo, G. (1997). Making mindful managers: evaluating methods for teaching problem solving skills for tourism management. *Journal of Tourism Studies*, **3**, 2–7.

Moscardo, G. (1999). *Making Visitors Mindful*. Champaign, IL, Sagamore.

Moscardo, G. and Pearce, P. (1986). Visitor centres and environmental interpretation. *Journal of Environmental Psychology*, **6**, 89–108.

Moscardo, G., Woods, B. and Pearce, P. (1997). Evaluating the effectiveness of pictorial symbols in reef visitor education. CRC Reef Research Centre Technical Report No. 15, Townsville, Australia.

Mowforth, M. (1992). *Ecotourism Terminology and Definitions*. Occasional Paper No. 1, University of Plymouth.

Mowforth, M. and Munt, I. (1998). *Toursim and Sustainability*. London, Routledge.

Moutinho, L. (2000). *Strategic Tourism Management*, Wallingford, CAB International.

Murphy, P. (1985). *Tourism: A Community Approach*. London, Methuen.

New Zealand Tourism Board (1992). *Residents Perception and Acceptance of Tourism in Selected New Zealand Communities*, Wellington, Ministry of Tourism.

New Zealand Tourism Board (1996). *Tourism in New Zealand: Facts and Figures*. Wellington, Ministry of Tourism.

New Zealand Tourism Board (1999). *Tourism in New Zealand: Facts and Figures*. Wellington, Ministry of Tourism.

New Zealand Tourism Board (2000). *Tourism in New Zealand: Facts and Figures*. Wellington, Ministry of Tourism.

O'Grady, R. (1980). *Third World Stopover*. Geneva, Risk Books, World Council of Churches.

Orams, M. (1994). Creating effective interpretation for managing interaction between tourists and wildlife. *The Australian Journal of Environmental Education*, **10**, 21–34.

Orams, M. (1995). Using interpretation to manage nature-based tourism. *Journal of Sustainable Tourism*, **4**, 81–94.

Page, S. J. and Thorn, K. J. (1997). Towards sustainable tourism planning in New Zealand: public sector planning responses. *Journal of Sustainable Tourism*, **5**, 59–77.

Parker, S. (2000). Collaboration on tourism Policy making: environmental and commercial sustainability on Bonaire, NA. In *Tourism Collaboration and Partnerships: Policy Practice and Sustainability* (B. Bramwell and B. Lane, eds), pp. 78–97. Clevedon, Channel View Publications.

Pearce, D. (1995). Tourism in the Pacific Region. *Progress in Tourism and Hospitality Research*, **1**, 1–9.

Pearce, D. G. (1989). *Tourist Development*. London, Longman.

Pearce, P. (1988). *The Ulysses Factor: Evaluating Visitors in Tourist Settings*, New York, Springer Verlag.

Pearce, P. (1993). Fundamentals of tourist motivations. In *Tourism Research: Critiques and Challenges* (D. Pearce and R. Butler, eds), pp. 113–34. London, Routledge.

Pearce, P., Moscardo, G., Miller, A. and Ross, G. (1998). *Tourism: Bridges across Continents*. Sydney, McGraw Hill.

Pearce, P., Moscardo, G. and Ross, G. (1996). *Tourism Community Relationships*. Oxford, Pergamon.

Pedersen, A. (1998). 'The Arctic Tourism Project' in *Arctic Bulletin*, 5 (Spring) 11–15, Oslo, WWF Arctic Programme.

Plog, S. (1973). Why destination areas rise and fall in popularity. *Cornell Hotel and Restaurant Administration Quarterly*, **12**, 13–16.

Pond, K. L. (1993). *The Professional Guide*. New York, Van Nostrand Reinhold.

Poon, A. (1993). *Tourism, Technology and Competitive Strategies*. Wallingford, CAB International.

Prentice, R. C. (1995). *Tourism as Experience. Tourists as Consumers. Insight and Enlightenment*. Inaugural Lecture Queen Margaret College, Edinburgh, p. 55.

Pretes, M. (1995). Post modern tourism: the Santa Claus industry. *Annals of Tourism Research*, **22** (1), 1–15.

Pretty, J. (1995). The many interpretations of participation, *Tourism in Focus*, **16**, 4–5.

Prosser, R. (1994). Social change and the growth of tourism. In *Ecotourism: A Sustainable Option?* (E. Cater and G. Lowman, eds), pp. 19–37. Chichester, John Wiley and Sons.

Prosser, R. (1998). Tourism. In *Encyclopaedia of Ethics*, vol. 4, pp. 373–401. Chicago, IL, Houghton Mifflin.

Ramthun, R. (1995). Factors in user group conflict between hikers and mountain bikers. *Leisure Sciences*, **17**, 159–70.

Raybould, M., Digance, J. and McCullough, C. (1999). Fire and festival: authenticity and visitor motivation at an Australian folk festival. *Pacific Tourism Review*, **3**, 201–12.

Richter, L. (1989). *The Politics of Tourism Asia*. Honolulu, University of Hawaii Press.

Ritchie, J. and Goeldner, C. (eds) (1994). *Travel, Tourism and Hospitality Research: A Handbook for Managers and Researchers*. New York, John Wiley and Sons.

Ritchie, J. and Zins, M. (1978). Culture as a determinant of the attractiveness of a tourist region. *Annals of Tourism Research*, **5**, 252–67.

Ryan, C. (1991). *Recreational Tourism*. London, Routledge.

Ryan, C. (1997). *The Tourist Experience*. London, Cassell.

Ryan, C. (1998). Visitor management in Kakadu National Park. In *Visitor Management at World Heritage Sites* (M. Shackley, ed.), pp. 178–92. London, Butterworth-Heinemann.

Seaton, A. and Bennet, M. (1996). *Marketing Tourism Products*. London, International Thomson Business Press.

Shackley, M. (ed.) (1998). *Visitor Management at World Heritage Sites*. London, Butterworth-Heinemann.

Simeon, R. (1976). Studying public policy. *Canadian Journal of Political Science*, **9**, 558–80.

Spink, J. (1994). *Leisure and the Environment*. Oxford, Butterworth-Heinemann.

Stewart, E. J., Hayward, B. M., Devlin, P. J. and Kirby, V. G. (1998). The place of interpretation: a new approach to the evaluation of interpretation. *Tourism Management*, **19**, 257–66.

Stonehouse, B. (1990). A traveller's code for Antarctic visitors. *Polar Record*, **26**, 56–8.

Stonehouse, B. (1996). *Briefing papers for Conference WWF Arctic Tourism Guidelines*, held at the Scott Polar Institute, University of Cambridge, August.

Swarbrooke, J. (1999). *Sustainable Tourism Management*. Wallingford, CABI Publications.

Theobold, A. (1994). *Global Tourism*. Wallingford, UK, CABI Publications.

Tilden, F. (1957). *Interpreting Our Heritage*. Chapel Hill, NC, University of North Carolina Press.

Tomlejnovic, R. and Faulkner, B. (2000). Tourism and world peace: a conundrum for the twenty-first century. In *Tourism in the Twenty First Century* (B. Faulkner, G. Moscardo, and E. Laws, eds). London, Continuum.

Tribe, J. (2000). 'The Philosophic Practitioner', *Annals of Tourism Research* **27** (3), 437–51.

Uhlik, K. S. (1995). Partnerships: step by step: a practical model of partnership formation. *Journal of Park and Recreation Administration*, **143**, 13–24.

UNEP (1995). *Environmental Codes of Conduct Technical Report* 29. Paris, United Nations Environment Programme.

Unry, J. (1990). The Tourist Gaze, London, Sage.

Valentine, P. (1992). Nature-based tourism. In *Special Interest Tourism* (B. Weiler and C. M. Hall, eds), pp. 105–28. London, Bellhaven.

Veal, A. J. (1994). *Leisure Policy and Planning*. Harlow, UK, Longman/ILAM.

Wall, G. (1997). Rethinking impacts of tourism. In *Tourism Development* (C. Cooper, B. Archer, and S. Wanhill, eds), pp. 1–10. Chichester, John Wiley and Sons.

Wallace, G. and Pierce, S. (1996). An evaluation of ecotourism in Amazonas, Brazil. *Annals of Tourism Research*, **23**, 843–7.

Watkins, R., Cocklin, C. and Laituru, M. (1997). The Use of Geographic Information Systems for resource Evaluation: A New Zealand Example. *Journal of Environmental Planning and Management*, **40**, 37–57.

Watson, A. E. (1995). An analysis of recent progress in recreation conflict research and perceptions of future challenges and opportunities. *Leisure Sciences*, **17**, 235–8.

Wearing, D. and Neil, J. (1999). *Ecotourism: Potential, Pitfalls and Possibilities*. London, Butterworth-Heinemann.

Wheeler, B. (1993). Sustaining the ego? *Journal of Sustainable Tourism*, **1**, 121–9.

Wildavsky, A. (1987). *Speaking Truth to Power: The Art and Craft of Public Policy Analysis*, 2nd edn. New Brunswick, Transaction.

Wilkinson, P. (1997). *Tourism Planning on Islands*. New York, Cognizant Communications.

Williams, S. (1998). *Tourism Geography*. London, Routledge.

Williams, D., Patterson, M., Roggenbuck, J. and Watson, A. (1992). Beyond the commodity metaphor: examining symbolic attachment to place. *Leisure Sciences*, **14**, 29–46.

Wood, D. and Gray, B. (1991). Towards a comprehensive theory of collaboration, *Journal of Applied Behavioural Sciences*, 414–32.

Wood, K. and House, S. (1991). *The Good Tourist*. London, Mandarin.

WTO (1991). *Yearbook of Statistics*. Madrid, World Tourism Organisation.

WTO (2002). *Yearbook of Tourism Statistics*, 52th edn. Madrid, World Tourism Organisation.

WTTRC (1995). *Database on Codes of Conduct for the Travel and Tourism Industry*. Oxford, World Travel and Tourism Council.

Ziffer, K. (1989). *Ecotourism: The Uneasy Alliance*, Working Paper No. 1. Washington, DC, Conservation International.

Index